PUBLIC ADMINISTRATION
AND DEMOCRACY

●

Essays in honor of
PAUL H. APPLEBY

Public Administration and Democracy

Essays in honor of
PAUL H. APPLEBY

•

ROSCOE C. MARTIN
editor

SYRACUSE UNIVERSITY PRESS

*Manufactured in the
United States of America*

Contents

IV. INTERNATIONAL PUBLIC ADMINISTRATION

V. SOME ENDURING CONCERNS

Author Identification

(in order of appearance)

ROSCOE C. MARTIN is Professor of Political Science at Syracuse University.

DWIGHT WALDO is Professor of Political Science at the University of California.

EMMETTE S. REDFORD is Professor of Government at The University of Texas.

JESSE BURKHEAD is Professor of Economics at Syracuse University.

BERTRAM M. GROSS is Professor of Political Science at Syracuse University.

FREDERICK C. MOSHER is Professor of Political Science at the University of California.

GUTHRIE S. BIRKHEAD is Professor of Political Science at Syracuse University.

JOHN M. GAUS is Emeritus Professor of Government at Harvard University.

ARTHUR W. MACMAHON is Emeritus Professor of Public Law and Government at Columbia University.

VICTOR A. THOMPSON is Professor of Political Science at Syracuse University.

LYNTON K. CALDWELL is Professor of Government at Indiana University.

DONALD C. STONE is Dean of the Graduate School of Public and International Affairs of the University of Pittsburgh.

HERBERT EMMERICH is Professor of Government and Foreign Affairs at the University of Virginia.

STEPHEN K. BAILEY is Dean of the Maxwell Graduate School of Citizenship and Public Affairs of Syracuse University.

ROWLAND EGGER is Professor of Politics and Public Affairs at Princeton University.

PUBLIC ADMINISTRATION
AND DEMOCRACY

•

Essays in honor of
PAUL H. APPLEBY

· 1 ·

Paul H. Appleby and His Administrative World

ROSCOE C. MARTIN

PAUL HENSON APPLEBY

Born September 13, 1891
Died October 21, 1963

NOT MUCH OF IMPORTANCE HAPPENED
TO THE DECEASED, SAVE TO HIM AND
HIS IMMEDIATE FAMILY, IN BETWEEN.

So might have read a self-epitaph written by Paul H. Appleby; for Appleby was not a man given to personal inflation. On the contrary, in a curious way he was wont to depreciate his efforts. So, approaching a colleague with a piece of writing, he was likely to request the favor of a critical review in these words: "Read this and tell me whether I've said anything." This was in no wise a false modesty, for Appleby was never sure just where (or whether) he fitted in. He was far removed from the stereotyped executive. His decisions, even his major decisions, emerged not in violent eruption but in a low, even key which betokened a certain diffidence.

For all his essential modesty, Paul Appleby enjoyed a career which for richness in quality and variety in scope has had few equals in American public life. Appleby was by schooling, preference, and experience a *public* man; he liked the word, and discoursed upon it frequently. One of his major philosophical contributions, indeed, lies in his elevation of the word and of the concepts which it connotes. Paul Appleby's public career spanned very nearly half a century. In conversations with friends toward the end of his life, Appleby himself recognized that this career had in fact embodied three separate sub-careers: that of newspaper man, that of public servant, and that of educator. To these three distinct and readily recognizable incarnations I have chosen to add a fourth: that of elder statesman.

1

THE CAREER

Paul Appleby would not wish us to spend much time in recitation of the facts of his career. To speak of career is to delve into the past, to indulge in an historical exercise. Appleby did not minimize the significance of history, particlarly history as interpretation, but he had little patience for personal history. It cannot be said with justice that he ran from the past, but it can be affirmed that he ran always, and to the very end, toward the future. He escaped almost entirely the anecdotage so generally visited upon the aging. Perhaps that was because he was largely spared the unhappy aspects of the aging process, in intellect at least. But the principal career signposts are relevant to this essay.

A passion for journalism ran deep and strong in Paul Appleby. It was manifested first when as a boy he acquired an old printing press and began publication of a juvenile paper. Shortly after graduation from Grinnell College he entered the field professionally as publisher of a weekly newspaper in Montana. This initial career phase carried him to other weeklies in Minnesota and Iowa between the years 1914 and 1920, at which time he was named editor of *Iowa Magazine*. In 1924 he became editorial writer on the *Des Moines Register and Tribune*, a position he left in 1928 to publish weekly newspapers in Virginia. His formal commitment to journalism ended five years later when he went to Washington. Appleby was proud of his career as a newspaperman; and while he refused to dwell on those days in later life, it gave him great pleasure to talk occasionally with friends about his experiences as a journalist. His mind was full of stories about newspapermen (particularly small-town ones) and their ways. This first career phase brought many friendships which he cherished to the end of his life.

With scarcely a backward glance Appleby left the newspaper field in 1933 to become Executive Assistant to Secretary of Agriculture Henry A. Wallace. Service here led to appointment as Under Secretary of Agriculture in 1940, a position which he left in 1944 to become Assistant Director of the Bureau of the Budget. His federal service terminated in 1947, though he returned briefly to the practice of administration as Director of the Budget of the State of New York from 1955 to 1957. His tenure in high administrative position, federal and state, therefore covered a period of 16 years. These years, particularly those spent in the Federal Government, were punctuated by a wide variety of high-level special assignments: as Chief of Food Missions to Great Britain (1941-42), as Chairman of the International

Wheat Council (1942-44), as Special Assistant to the Secretary of State (1943), as United States Delegate to the Hot Springs Food Conference (1943), and as United States Member of the Interim Commission on Food and Agriculture (1943-44), to name only the most exciting. It is noteworthy that, in the last two capacities named, Appleby played a key role in forging the Food and Agriculture Organization.

Appleby set high store by his years in the public service, returning to them often for conversation and more especially for illustration in his later years as teacher. His experience here afforded him unmatched opportunity for observation of the realities of government, opportunity which he was quick to seize upon and maximize both as administrator and, subsequently, as analyst of and commentator on public affairs. The government years provided Appleby with the raw material for the insights which became his hallmark in the field of public administration.

In 1947 Appleby left Washington to accept appointment as Dean of the Maxwell Graduate School of Citizenship and Public Affairs of Syracuse University. His service at Syracuse was interrupted by two foreign missions (presently to be noted), and was concluded in 1955 when he resigned to return to administrative work with the State of New York. It is perhaps a fair judgment that Appleby's leadership of the Maxwell School was more significant in intellectual than in administrative terms. Certainly it was during this period that he emerged as a teacher of note and as a writer of international renown. Public administration had long since become his adopted field, and from (about) 1945 on he devoted a large part of his time and energies to perceptive and incisive reexamination of that field. These were preeminently the Maxwell School years; they represented Paul Appleby at his intellectual best.

The fourth career, that of elder statesman, covered roughly the last ten years of Appleby's life. Since men do not achieve "elder" status by a particular dispensation at a given time, it of necessity overlapped with earlier careers. It began in 1952 when, while still at Syracuse, Dean Appleby was invited by the Ford Foundation, in behalf of the Prime Minister of India, to go to that country as consultant to its Government. The ensuing mission resulted in subsequent invitations which led to other trips in 1954, 1956, and 1960-61. The fruits of these consultations were extraordinary, primarily for Indian administration but also for the many Indian visitors who, in respect and tribute, later visited Appleby in his Washington home. His last appearance as elder statesman was in 1962 when, in response to an invitation suggested by a former student, he journeyed to Wayne State University to receive the honorary Doctor of Humanities degree. Already mortally ill, his acceptance address nevertheless ensured that neither the principal actor nor the occasion would be forgotten by the many friends who gathered to hear it.

This recitation of the bare facts of the Appleby career has already gone past the limits he would have set for decency, yet many will consider it inadequate. Omitted is mention of memberships on various governing boards, notably those of the National Institute of Public Affairs, the Public Administration Clearing House, and the Franklin D. Roosevelt Foundation. Omitted also is mention of membership in a number of professional organizations. Omitted finally is note of several honorary doctorates, for neglect of which Appleby's final rest will be the more serene. Here at least is enough to tell us in broad outline what the man did. It is pertinent to ask now, what kind of man was he?

THE MAN

All who knew Paul Appleby remember him with respect and many with affection, but each will have his own words to characterize the man. This is more apt to be true of close than of casual acquaintances, for Appleby was not a man to be categorized neatly with time. He was in truth a complex mind, one to be understood (and then only imperfectly) under conditions of long and intimate friendship. My own list includes five basic characteristics of mind and spirit.

First and foremost, under almost all conditions, Paul Appleby lived life as an intellectual adventure. In so far as it is given to a human being to be objective, Appleby was so; he saw things as he saw them, not as he wished he could have seen them. His intellectual honesty was sometimes painful, as any colleague who has asked his judgment on a manuscript will attest. At the same time, his integrity ran both ways; for if he could be mercilessly critical, he could also accept criticism with good grace. A professional conversation with Appleby was a growing and learning experience, thanks to his insistence on keeping the talk on an intellectual plane. Appleby much preferred to deal with concepts than with things, and this preference—and his ability to implement it—proved his greatest source of strength. His power to concentrate, to bore in on what seemed to him important at the moment and to shut out all distracting thoughts, made him the envy of his colleagues. His ability to observe a series of events and relate them to other events and other times and places—in short, to reason and to learn by analogy—made him a master of vicarious experience. Appleby's system of administration depended in large measure upon the primacy of thought.

Two subsidiary qualities flowed from Appleby's intellectual approach to life. It was his habit to ask not only what and why a particular thing was, but before that, *whether* it was. He accepted nothing on faith, least of all propositions long incorporated into the common law of tradition. A friend once characterized him as a "contrary" person, one who insisted on determining for himself the validity of a given conclusion. Easy assumptions were odious to him, and he took delight in destroying them. Regarding a proposed hypothesis his first question always was, "Does it square with observed fact?" Secondary questions followed: What purpose does it serve? How does it fit in? For Appleby was by preference and conduct a pragmatist. As an ethical man he was not above occasional moralizing, but he was much more concerned that a firm base for understanding be established by sound analysis.

Paul Appleby was in a very special way a simple man. T. V. Smith has spoken of two kinds of simplicity. First, there is the simplicity not only of the simple but of the simple-minded man, of one who lacks the curiosity, the sophistication, or the knowledge to think complexly. Second, there is the simplicity given to the man who has penetrated the gloom of the labyrinth and has emerged into the light on the other side: the simplicity beyond complexity. Appleby's simplicity was of the latter variety. He was indeed simple in the sense that he was artless, free of pretentiousness, and utterly honest. But in addition he understood the intricacies and the inconsistencies of public administration. He was able, through his deep understanding on the one hand and his ability to synthesize on the other, to introduce rationality where confusion had lately reigned. His system was not the simple one of building blocks; far beyond that, it was a complex system, made logical and understandable by reason. It was, harking back, an intellectualized system, but the process of intellectualization was firmly based on observation and experience. His capacity to seize the essence of a complex issue, to distill, to generalize was remarkable. In the language of his generation of public administrators, he was a generalist's generalist.

The Appleby philosophy was characterized by an intense commitment to humanism, for he was a champion of all mankind, a spokesman for man in the mass anywhere and everywhere. This of necessity made him, in the language of public affairs, a democrat—a badge he was proud to wear. His every work was aimed at the enlargement and improvement, and above all at the preservation, of democratic government. Some have seen in Paul Appleby a paradox, a man who, deeply concerned with the affairs of mankind, was sometimes forgetful of the individual men around him. Such critics are unmindful of his tendency to lose himself in philosophic contemplation—a tendency that sometimes verged on habit, particularly during his university career. Given a few more years on a campus, Appleby might have developed into a very model of the absent-minded professor. Called back from his reveries by a companion, he might excuse himself by confessing that he had got hold of an idea that seemed worth exploring and had set off in pursuit. Those who knew him well know that Appleby was no less a humanist in individual relations than he was in respect of mankind in the abstract.

Again, Paul Appleby was as sensitive a person as one is likely to meet: sensitive in observing and recording the phenomena of government which swirled about him, sensitive in his interpretations of events large and small, sensitive to situations requiring action, sensitive to the needs and aspirations, and to the interrelations as well, of those around him. This is not to belittle his decisiveness. It is to say simply that he was sensible of the need to take account of all known factors, and that his perception was such that he was able sensitively to identify and soundly to evaluate those factors. In one area Appleby's sensitivity largely deserted him; for having considered the available options and determined upon a course of action, he was almost completely oblivious of any criticism that might ensue. He was never to my knowledge guilty of exhuming the bones of past action to inquire whether he should or should not have done such-and-such a thing. This quality allowed him largely to ignore the bushwhacking of the McCarthy era, though himself a minor object of that witch hunt.

Last among the attributes I have chosen for mention is the Appleby sense of humor. If this is a minor quality in the makeup of most men, it was nevertheless important in the life of Paul Appleby. Observers standing before his portrait (which hangs in the Maxwell Hall Founder's Room at Syracuse University) have been heard to remark, "Why, that doesn't look like Dean Appleby!" In this view they may be more right than wrong, for the portraitist did not catch his subject in what most would consider his dominant public mood. In the portrait his mouth is drawn off-center in a wry, sidewise half-smile, as though the model had hold of a thought that he was not quite ready to communicate. Close friends knew this mien well; it signified that Appleby was about to make a humorous remark, or perhaps tell a story. Appleby was the victim of a fatal weakness for the pun, with which in turn he loved to victimize his friends. He was a consumer as well as a producer of good fellowship, and intimates remember well occasional evenings that were spent in the conversation reserved for good companions.

How may the mind and spirit of a Paul Appleby be summarized in a word? I have said that he was an intellectual who was at home in an intimate group, that he was possessed at once of a vast comprehension of detail and of an equal ability to generalize, that he was a humanist in a large sense while sometimes seemingly removed from the workaday world of his close associates, that he was highly sensitive as an individual yet virtually invulnerable to public criticism, that he had a well-developed sense of humor along with (I now add) moments of occasional and momentary moroseness. If the sketch makes Appleby seem a complex person then I have achieved my purpose, for he was complex in truth; but if it goes farther to suggest uncertainties regarding values, then I have overdrawn. His doubts were no more than were appropriate to a man who realized that all the facts relevant to a given decision are difficult to come by and are almost never at hand in time. His concern for humankind predisposed him toward inner doubt if not toward equivocation. But for all that he lived a rich and rewarding life which was dominated in extraordinary degree by high and consistent purpose. To what end?

The Legacy

Earlier I referred to Paul Appleby as a public man. His reputation in fact rests largely upon his work in the field of public administration, as practitioner, writer, teacher, and philosopher; and it seems reasonable to examine his legacy in those terms. We are, of course, too close to him as yet to venture anything approaching final judgment as to the value of his work. Some preliminary views may however be in order. I propose to examine briefly his contributions to the literature of public administration, to the profession itself, and to teaching in the field.

Appleby's writings were not voluminous; they comprise five books (four of which, interestingly enough, originated in lectures), two monographs, some thirty articles published in professional journals and symposia, and a number of book reviews. He was not given to wordiness, and none of his written pieces was long. Though he prided himself on his writing (sometimes mentioning to friends his newspaper background), he wrote in a tight, compact style which some felt made for heavy reading.

His first book, *Big Democracy* (1945), gave a portent of things to come; his second and third, *Policy and Administration* (1949) and *Morality and Administration* (1952), opened up new vistas on selected subjects which particularly interested him; his fourth, *Public Administration for a Welfare State* (1961), brought his philosophy of administration to bear on India; his last, *Citizens as Sovereigns* (1962), summarized his thinking on popular government. Meanwhile, the articles (which began to appear as early as 1942) elaborated various special phases of the Appleby "system." His books were widely reviewed, and anyone with the interest can learn how they were received by his contemporaries through perusal of the book review pages of the professional journals. For the record, a classified list of Appleby's writings is printed as an appendix to this book.

In a brief comment on the state of an area of knowledge or the practice of an art or profession at a given time, it is difficult to avoid overgeneralization. Public administration is no exception. Nevertheless certain broad observations may be ventured regarding that field as it was understood in 1940 and as it is known twenty-five years later. In the former year scientific management held sway. The literature was profoundly influenced by the writings of Frederick W. Taylor and his followers, who regarded administration as a science and sought guidance in universal laws. Administration was equated with management, as in the work of the President's Committee on Administrative Management of the late 1930's. There was much talk about what could be achieved through the practice of administration but comparatively little about the nature of the craft. Administration's search for identity, which had characterized the quarter-century just ending, had led its spokesmen to adopt positions and make claims for the emerging discipline that some were later to call extravagant. Many tributaries fed the growing stream called administration, but it is fair to say that to 1940 the dominant contributor was the scientific management movement.

The public administration of 1965, though readily recognizable as the descendant of that described above, is not to be taken as the same thing. For one thing, the *public* aspects of administration receive greater emphasis now than then; for another, the place of public administration in the governmental process commands more attention than before; for still another, the search for universal principles or laws has slackened in the face of recognized aberrations introduced by both human and environmental forces. Sociologists, cultural anthropologists, and social psychologists have asserted their interest in and have profoundly influenced thinking about the group enterprise called public administration. The administration-as-science school remains strong and the search for quantification continues, it may be with greater vigor; but something new has been added. The new element is found in the discovery that administration concerns people, and in the consequent impregnation of "pure" management with a powerful element of humanism. Significant too is the search for rationalization of administrative root and content in philosophical terms, a search that has quickened notably in recent years. In summary, it may be said that the public administration of 1965 has achieved, if not full maturity, at least an added measure of sophistication. Many minds and many voices contributed to the advancement of "the Science, Processes, and Art of Public Administration" during the years 1940-65. Among the most incisive and insistent of these were the mind and voice of Paul Appleby.

Appleby's contribution had to do largely with the philosophy of administration: with its elaboration on the one hand and its refinement on the other. Counters and counting did not concern him; he did not hold the computer business in scorn, but simply had no time for it. Appleby might have asked, of what avail is it to quantify while antecedent questions of fundamental significance and relevance remain unanswered? He set himself to the task of dealing with some of the underlying problems.

A theme which dominated Appleby's philosophy throughout his public life was announced in the first chapter of his first book, which was prophetically entitled "Government Is Different." Government is different from all other undertakings in almost every important particular, he argued, but especially in its "breadth of scope, impact, and consideration; public accountability; [and] political character." It is unique in the requirements it makes of its employees, in the public-interest attitude which dominates its officials, and in the special position occupied by public servants in the popular mind. Most of all, "Government is different because government is politics." This position, vigorously set forth in a chapter of less than ten pages, thenceforth placed its author in the front ranks of those who questioned the concept of administration as a monolithic phenomenon governed by universal laws. It was inevitable that Appleby should become a leading spokesman for the contrary view that public and private administration are divergent enterprises, differing in such essentials as purposes served, employee motivations, and relations with clienteles. Public administration is different because it concerns government, and government is different.

The last sentence almost attributed to Appleby the view that public administration *is* government. He would not have been offended at such attribution, for this is not far from his conception of administration. Deserting the traditional trichotomy, Appleby held that American government "lives by and operates through" eight distinct processes. These were, in the order of his listing, the presidential nominating process, the general nominating process, the electoral process, the legislative process, the judicial process, the party maintenance and operation process, the "agitational" process, and "the administrative or executive process, involving everything done by agencies other than the legislative and judicial ones." (The administrative process he placed last not because he believed it to be least in importance but because he wished to emphasize it.) In another connection, without intent to define, he remarked that "public administration is the conduct of programs that serve citizens and help make sense out of their activities." Conceived thus, administration is inseparable from the total process of government; indeed public administration in his view is nothing more (but also nothing less) than a way of looking at government. Appleby rejected the doctrine that administration can be separated either from government itself or from the total environment of public action and subjected to separate scrutiny. For him the study of public administration was the study of government; it consisted in affecting a special pair of lenses to permit emphasis on administration's role in the total business of government.

A strong thread of institutionalism ran through Paul Appleby's philosophy, as the second essay in this volume indicates. He had high respect for the hierarchy which orders the relations among public servants, and was thus in some sense an "organization man" long before William H. Whyte gave the term popular currency. For him big government organization and its personal embodiment big bureaucracy were inescapable companions of big society; and they were to be embraced and put to use rather than attacked as parasitic or otherwise evil. Administrative institutions had the virtue that they made possible the transaction of public business, which was in itself sufficient justification. Beyond that, however, they had certain inherent qualities not commonly appreciated. They had built-in balances, for example, which tended to correct any inclination toward excess. They possessed an inner drive toward organizational improvement which provided the best single guarantee against the "administrative lag" emphasized by others. They operated under a system of procedural rules identified by some as "red tape" but by Appleby as a necessary means for ensuring regularity and responsibility. Concerning red tape, Appleby observed in an unpublished fragment that "If all or most institutional red tape were actually cut through, the result would be irresponsibility and chaos. Cutting red tape as a general ideal, then, is nonsense. Improved systematic procedures are always and everywhere possible, but they will be produced by able bureaucrats, not by astrologers and casual onlookers."

Appleby's preoccupation with government led him direct to a companion and unashamed emphasis on politics. The latter he held to be inseparable from democratic government; and since his continuing concern was the preservation of democratic values, he was drawn inexorably to an examination of politics. Politics and administration he found to be reverse sides of the same coin, the two together called government. Eliminate politics (granting for a brief moment that could be done), Appleby maintained, and you eliminate democratic government. Moreover, you eliminate democratic administration at the same time, for politics is no more than administration (and administration no more than politics) seen through different eyes. Far from embracing the earlier concept of administration as a neutral activity, Appleby insisted that administration, whether as practice, as a subject for writing, or as an academic exercise, is chock full of politics. This is not only the way it is, but also the way it should be. It should be observed that the politics with which Appleby associated administration was the politics of policy negotiation and accommodation rather than that of raw partisanship, though that too had its place in his system of democratic responsibility.

Contemplation of the political role of the administrator, particularly the high-level administrator, and, equally to the point, of the administrative role of top political leaders, led Appleby to conclude that the heart of administration lay in the processes of negotiation and accommodation. In his view a basic task of the administrator was to consider the positions of all parties responsibly interested in a proceeding and, to the extent possible, to synthesize conflicting interests. This called for the qualities of a generalist rather than those of the specialist. It required "a sense of government," "commitment to the public interest," "capacity for abstraction," "ability to reason by analogy," all favorite phrases to be found sprinkled through Appleby's writings. It is scarcely necessary to say that his system made ample allowance for specialists and their work, which he considered essential, though he was more concerned with what went on toward the top of the organization. There, he maintained, the contribution of the technician attenuates, the generalist takes over, and administrator and politician become indistinguishable. The fusion favors the politician, who emerges as both political and administrative head of the organization; that is, at the very top, of the government.

If the instinct for humanism mentioned before ensured Appleby's early, vigorous, and lasting commitment to democracy, it also caused him to eye with suspicion the mechanistic view of public administration which prevailed widely when he came on the scene. He had a deep-seated distrust of scientific management, which seemed to him to obscure the essential element in administration. That element he conceived to be the human one. Appleby came early to the conclusion that administration is people: people purposefully engaged in the pursuit of a goal, people in association with peers and with higher-ups and lower-downs, people both beholding and being viewed by other people called the public. The prevailing doctrine condemned administration to a static role, he maintained, because it dwelled too much on form and structure and too little on the people who, in final analysis, *are* the organization. Appleby confided to friends that he was pushed into this position through confrontation with a dilemma, which he sought to resolve by characteristically pragmatic action. "I read the literature," he said, "then I looked around government to check the validity of what I had read. I discovered that what 'the books' were talking about and what went on in administrative offices often were two quite different things. I then asked myself: if 'the books' do not describe accurately what goes on in a government office, what *in fact* does go on? What is the true nature of public administration?"

Recognition of this dilemma led Appleby in the late 1940's to join with a small group of like-minded colleagues in sponsoring a series of case studies of public administration. These studies were not at the time dignified as "behavioral" analyses, but they were nonetheless behavioral in nature and intent. They emphasized the real as against the imagined conduct of public actors in a decisional situation. Anyone likely to have read this far will know that the case method, as elaborated and refined in recent years under the leadership of the Inter-University Case Program, has achieved wide acceptance as a means of studying (and teaching, and doing research about) public administration. Paul Appleby was one of the founders of the case method in public administration.

There are those who view strong administration as a threat to personal freedom. To Appleby the facts pointed to a contrary conclusion; to him a vigorous system of administration was the means by which democratic liberties are secured. The threat in modern times, he believed, lies rather in flaccid than in strong government. Big society is permanently with us, he reasoned; let us recognize the necessity of correspondingly big government, and let us shape it to our will. Further—and this thought is central to the Appleby system— let us devise safeguards that will ensure that the "administrative state" will be held democratically responsible. For Appleby responsibility posed no very serious problem, for he found many devices to prevent government's getting out of hand. One such device (a fact, rather) lay in the pluralism of American life. The doctrine of countervailing public influences found a vigorous champion in Paul Appleby. Another guarantor of responsible action resided for Appleby in the very complexity of government, which again ensures that there will be no sudden lurch toward an indefensible decision. The pluralism of government as well as that of society at large is a powerful deterrent to precipitate and unwarranted action.

At the center of Appleby's system of responsibility stood the American political system, in which he had unbounded confidence. "Wrong" decisions will be made from time to time, he granted, but they can be expected to be righted in due course through political adjustments. Some few decisions are dramatic and irreversible— Appleby cited a declaration of war as one such; but most, moving slowly along the road toward fruition, are incremental in character. In the process of taking form they are subjected to pressures for accommodation of a variety and strength quite beyond the comprehension of one not directly involved. These forces arise both within and outside the government. Appleby held such pressures to be of the essence of administrative decision-making; they are also of the essence of politics as he employed the term in an administrative context. His philosophy of course took account of the ultimate act in the political process, in which the voters turn out office-holders who have misread the times often enough and seriously enough. In its totality the political process constitutes the strongest single guarantee that American government will remain responsible, that administration will be the servant rather than the master of American democracy.

If Appleby's doctrines are generally accepted in 1965, consider whether they enjoyed equal acceptance in 1945. Pioneers grow old, and what was once novel doctrine at the frontier of a discipline presently becomes gospel truth and, in the fullness of time, tradition. Appleby's system of administration gained respectability years ago, and has now settled into a comfortable position as part of the lore. It is currently under attack (though not overtly) from a number of directions, but that is another story, one which need not concern us here.

As a professor at the Maxwell Graduate School, Paul Appleby taught graduate students of public administration for six years. He also gave lectures, both before coming to and after leaving Syracuse University, before student groups at a number of other universities. His contacts with students therefore, while not prolonged, were varied. They were also mutually rewarding and zestful, as I can testify from many conversations over the years both with Professor Appleby and with scores of his students.

In the early 1950's, Appleby developed at Syracuse a graduate course which was given the title "Public Administration and Democracy." The course permitted him to carry forward simultaneously inquiries into two parallel subjects which had interested him deeply for a matter of twenty years. The purport of the course was to reconcile sound public administration with the requirements of democratic government. His conviction as to the significance of this problem was such that he sought help in its exploration from many sources. Thus it happens that no fewer than five of the authors represented in these pages have come to Syracuse in times past to participate in the further development and conduct of the course.

Among other bequests, Paul Appleby left to his friends the challenge to write this book. It is not a matter of accident that the authors of these essays are, almost to a man, long-time colleagues and co-workers of the person memorialized; for he exercised a significant influence over both the content of the book and the selection of the individuals invited to write it. He even provided the title! In a real sense, then, this book stands as Paul Appleby's final tangible contribution to the science, processes, and art, but most of all to the philosophy, of public administration.

I. THE FIELD OF
PUBLIC ADMINISTRATION

•

· 2 ·

Reflections on Institutions and Their Ways*

PAUL H. APPLEBY

CIVILIZATION, BUREAUCRACY, AND GOVERNMENT

It seems undeniable that the advance of civilization depends more and more upon involvement in organizations of greater variety and, on the whole, of greater and greater complexity. Satisfactory living in the United States is no longer possible for anyone without this institutional involvement, even though in the backwaters of our society there are still a few thousand persons living on a self-sufficient basis.

Most people (many of whom are somehow confident that "bureaucracies" are bad) accept the necessity of dependence upon institutions thoughtlessly, and many establish close (but for the most part unverbalized) harmony with their organizational environment. For the vast majority there is little intellectual comprehension of the nature of their membership in it or of their benefits from it. Few have any ability to verbalize an understanding of even those institutions to which they are most deeply committed. Those who have attempted to examine and describe organizational phenomena, indeed, are usually persons rather less than normally immersed in them: their baptism, if they are believers at all, has been by sprinkling. For the most part, they have been skeptics. Or, changing the metaphor, they have viewed institutions telescopically, from a distance, or microscopically in attention to innumerable and endlessly variable small details—in both cases through the glass rather darkly.

Much of the orientation of those who have pursued the study of our institutions has derived from the writings or dialogues of ancient

* Paul Appleby left behind him some two hundred pages of unpublished manuscript. Somewhat more than half of this mass dealt with what he thought of as "The Public and Public Policy," which under other circumstances might have become the title of a book. Most of the remainder consisted of fragments clustering around his concepts of institutions. From the latter I have assembled this essay. Some rearranging has been necessary and some editing as well, but all the thoughts and almost all the words are those of Paul Appleby. R.C.M.

seers, whose references were to social materials not the same as ours. Other efforts, more modern and up-to-date, have been restricted by their limited resources to the study of small groups. Among them there has often been an assumption that a large organization is simply an assemblage of many small organizations, although some of the University of Michigan studies have been notable exceptions to this characterization.

George Horton Cooley in a book published in 1902 contrasted a view of General Grant's army from Missionary Ridge with a view of that army derived from an approach to each individual soldier. In a peculiar sense likely to mislead many who accept it, he was correct when he went on to make this remark: "A complete view of society would also be a complete view of all the individuals, and *vice versa.*" The "armies" and the individuals change in time and place, and in any event the limits of the perceptions of an observer require us all to make-do with much less than a complete view of society and all its members. But members of a highly advanced society are rather more likely to be enabled to advance still further if there is some effort to enlarge their understanding of the structures and workways of the institutions on whose utility and control advance is dependent. The present essay is a small attempt to bring to view some of the more obscure yet significant features of the principal organizational realities, especially pointed toward a view of government.

We all know that organizations have similarities and yet differ very greatly. They differ in time and place, according to structure, function, size, resources, membership, leadership, history, and environment. And, while berating "bureaucracy," we recognize at least dimly that organization of entities and energies is crucial to great attainment, and often the first essential for mere survival. We have seen the development of something like administrative leadership in subhuman life forms, in herds, schools, and flocks of animals. The "pecking order" is the sociologist-anthropologist term for this elementary phenomenon of organization.

Among humans, wherever establishment of order was associated with any marked cultural development, the system of status provided for a small levy upon the many for the sake of a privileged few. It was expected that some of these so taken care of would utilize energies freed from ordinary chores of subsistence for the exercise of general leadership or for new achievements. It was a slow and wasteful way, but the only one discovered, to make an early approach to higher civilization. Gradually, order thus established become associated with diversified and improved crafts, observation of the stars, and speculation about man and the universe. Before the dawn of recorded history large enterprises had been undertaken, with complex bureaucratic forms.

We know very little about the building of the Pyramids, the Sphinx, or the first portions of the 1400-mile-long Great Wall of China. They are marvels in considerable part because they seem, as organizational feats, much ahead of their time. They were almost certainly built by means of institutional oppression.

Some of the earliest and clearest written descriptions of hierarchical forms were of military organizations, notable among them the structure developed by Alexander. His syntagma (sixteen lines of sixteen men each) of 256 men was designed to permit flexible deployment and to utilize the available weapons effectively. The syntagma was a fourth of a chilarchia, which was in turn a fourth of a grand phalanx. A grand phalanx—with auxiliary troops which were rather crucial —constituted an army. With from six to eight armies so structured— making a total of from 30,000 to 40,000 men—he was able to defeat much larger forces and to conquer a large part of the known world. Yet we have persons today who have never really been convinced that an effective organization of 40,000 people is possible.

INSTITUTIONAL STRUCTURE

Within the syntagma, supervision was provided on a primary basis closely resembling the corporal's squad of today, and from level to level of an organizational pyramid the subordinate-to-superior ratio seems to have varied from four to six to eight. The syntagma was about the size of a modern army company, and the chilarchia about the size of the 1910 regiment. Later an improved structure of maniples, cohorts, and legions enabled the Roman Empire to survive for a considerable period after its leadership had distintegrated. Nonmilitary bureaucracy of the great Roman period developed alongside the military, providing the patterns that enabled the Catholic churches and the empires associated with them to have extended lives.

Early learnings about morale, converted slowly into appreciation of the importance of reciprocal relationships between leaders and followers, came when empires failed as their armies became dependent upon mercenaries and conquered subjects instead of patriotic and responsible citizens. As far back as Cyrus, too, there was realization that subject peoples resisted controls least when the controls were confined to the necessities of empire. The advancement of civilization is, in one essential aspect, a matter of improved organizational designs in varied efforts to pursue ever more numerous and ever more significant boons, including new means of personal development and self-expression.

Hierarchies facilitate a concert of the energies of large numbers of individuals. Within such organizations membership spontaneity adds importantly to both the quantity and quality of product. Hierarchies provide for the division of labor, stimulating specialized competence, which in turn is ever more dependent on a general organizing and directing competence. In a society where learning and technological achievement are pursued, this specializing division of labor multiplies itself, and thereby utilizes new knowledge and materials produced by specialization in a dynamic sequence. It is progressively capable of serving values newly disclosed or made realizable. This kind of division of labor may be thought of as basically lateral—distributed to the right and left among persons conceived of primarily as functional equals. It is characteristically accompanied by a division of labor which may be thought of as perpendicular since it differentiates responsibility for, and authority over, various specialized functions.

There are other graphic and intellectual views of the basic hierarchical relationship. Chester Barnard, while seeing no escape from the pyramidal conception, expressed a personal liking for the view that puts the chief executive of an organization at the center of a circle, with successive "levels" of personnel occupying successive concentric circles and with the "bottom" of the hierarchy constituting the outside circle. He mentioned in this connection the military layout in which the commanding general is located at about the center of an area at the rear of his fighting force. This, however, is more clearly a matter of physical than of status location, and is suggestive of innumerable problems in physical designs for facilitating communication.

Professor Floyd Allport, the social psychologist, developed another view in *Theories of Perception and the Concept of Structure*. He considered the incitation to an action and the responses to it as constituting a unity—graphically curved or circular. This happens to be harmonious with the democratic idea in that it permits one point or person to be located at the top of the hierarchy as the citizen sovereign at one moment or in one view, there inciting or directing action, and at the bottom of the hierarchy at another moment or in another view, there executing action or feeling the pressure of direction as a subordinate employee or as a citizen subject. The difference between the two situations depends graphically upon whether the particular point or person is at the top or the bottom of the turning wheel.

Professor Allport had no intention of straining graphics in this fashion, however, and his conception is relevant here chiefly because it lends itself better than any other yet offered to depicting multiple involvements. The primary circle to which attention is being given offers a series of points representing successive steps in registering need and achieving action: this circle may be transected by any number of other circles so as to bring into it tangential impulses and outlets; these circles may also be transected, and so on *ad infinitum*. This conception can be used to depict the way in which the social reality is enormously complicated by interacting organizations, resources, situations, personalities, facts, workways, and drives.

It would require a great deal of space to show in a graphic way the realistic complex of interactions working in and around the conventional pyramidal picture of a hierarchical organization. Yet use of the oversimplified pyramid is necessary because of past use of it and because it so clearly implies differences in responsibility.

The conventional pyramid is probably most important as depicting relatively ultimate authority and responsibility. In any large organization the person in high position assumes responsibility for what subordinates *have done* much more often than he assumes responsibility by modifying what they do. But his ability to require modification is one of the prime features of his responsibility. Much policy is inevitably made at subordinate levels, and other policy authenticated or enunciated at higher levels may have "bubbled up" more than it "seeped down." Because of such phenomena, and because of the dependence of high authority on subordinate assent, Harlan Cleveland is fond of emphasizing the reality of an "inverted pyramid." There is wisdom in this view. There is, however, great importance in the right, and the occasional exercise of the right, to reverse or modify subordinate action. There is also a function of rather constant *general* leadership, initiative, and supervision. Thus, the traditional pyramid also has validity.

The number of people who can be supervised or directly led by a single executive is one of the basic determinants of hierarchical structure. The single executive may extend his reach through personal assistants (sharing his responsibilities and having no other) when the undertakings are large and complicated. A particular person may be able to deal effectively with a few more subordinates, too, but the existence of a not-too-flexible span of control has never been challenged. That the strain on this span goes up in a geometrical progression with an arithmetical increase in numbers has been shown by Barnard and many others. Generally it may be said that when the work concerned is routine, repetitive, manual, or simply mechanized, the number of subordinates directly under a particular executive may be larger than when the work is novel, changing, controversial, or complicated.

The range in the number directly supervised may be said to be from two to perhaps thirty, though executives generally regard thirty as too large and two as too small a number. The actual number reporting is frequently larger—but sometimes smaller—than formal "job descriptions" and organization charts would indicate.

The span of control concept related primarily to direct supervision. A factor perhaps more determining of hierarchical structure in the large is the sense of need to hold down the number of levels between which communication must be carried on. Chester Barnard pointed out that in great and complex organizations the number of levels of communication is not appreciably greater than in smaller organizations. In most organizations of from 100 to 200 persons, he thought the number of levels would be from three to five, while in the Bell Telephone System, with over 300,000 working members, it was from eight to ten.

We can see quite easily how this would obtain if we merely oversimplify the matter by assuming a uniform subordinate-superior ratio of six to one. In each of eight hierarchical levels of such an organization the number of persons engaged would appear in this numerical pyramid:

$$1$$
$$6$$
$$3\ 6$$
$$2\ 1\ 6$$
$$1\ 2\ 9\ 6$$
$$7\ 7\ 7\ 6$$
$$4\ 6\ 6\ 5\ 6$$
$$2\ 7\ 9\ 9\ 3\ 6$$

This could represent the New Jersey Bell Telephone Company in the late 1930's. If there were only one level more, the total number of persons would be 1,679,616; with ten levels this pyramid would become an organization of more than ten million.

This set of figures provides an approach to an understanding of why the size of an organization may not pose as many difficulties as the tenderfoot may imagine. It also shows a way in which a bureaucracy may grow without much confusion, and be directed without an impossible strain on the top administrator, who might not be especially aware of any great difference in his duties or problems with the enlargement of his eight-level hierarchy to nine-level dimensions.

Actually, if the increase in size occurs slowly there is little shock and no overwhelming problem of adjustment in outlook and method for high-level executives. Some accommodation of growth would be made in connection with normal turnover of executive personnel without anyone considering organizational growth as a major factor in recognizably new administrative developments. New policy and new leadership would be thought by those involved to be more significant than change in the size of the organization.

The handling of patents is a simple illustration of the way growth has been accommodated in the executive branch of our government. Washington gave personal attention and his signature to patents in the first Administration, which were otherwise a special care of the Secretary of State. The function now rests with the Department of Commerce, but patents are issued there by the Bureau of Patents in a responsible and generally satisfactory way, usually without individual attention to particular patents by the Secretary, Under Secretary, Assistant Secretary, or even the Commissioner of Patents. Washington commanded nothing like the total specialized competence now to be found in the Patent Office; the patent business has ample general direction reinforced by public scrutiny and complaint; and the President has been freed to attend to new and more complicated problems.

TOP EXECUTIVES

The public usually regards principal officials of great industrial or commercial organizations as essentially specialists. Thus the president of Armour & Co. is thought of as a "packer," the head of Gimbel's as an expert in retail merchandising, and the top men in General Electric as wizards in electronics. Almost any subordinate employee in any such organization, however, tends to the belief that his company's highest executives are regrettably superficial, even ignorant. "If he only knew what I know!" or "If only he could see what I see on this job!" or "If he had had *my* experience . . ." are frequent thoughts. Both of these views have validity.

Increased complexity of the resources and tasks of ever-larger institutions is an outstanding expression of advancing civilization sparked by specialization of learning and function. The more generally responsible executives in these huge modern institutions are engaged with problems of new dimensions and content. In a sense, they are of necessity amateurs. Each promotion upward in the hierarchy confronts each such executive with new responsibilities for oversight and coordination of activities for which he could not have had a commensurate and directly relevant experience. Each promotion, therefore, in this sense enhances the amateurishness of any executive, relative to the whole operation.

It is at the same time true that each executive has much special competence in any given position that cannot be readily applied to a different set of responsibilities, or easily and quickly provided by a new appointee. Nevertheless continuous tenure for all employees and invariable "promotion from within" would be ruinous. An occasional judicious injection of some new, still more "amateurish" element into high place in the hierarchy makes for improved survival prospects for any institution.

For dynamism and for adjustability to changing society, some recruits will be much more effective than others; some executives brought from the outside will fit more quickly than others into the particular institutional "culture"; and some of the original executive team will prove out better than others when promoted to places of broader responsibility. To maximize these three favorable results is to achieve a very large part of what is meant by good administration. And the ability of those chosen for recruitment or promotion, like the ability of the executives who choose and deploy the persons so chosen, may tend on the whole to be rather less related to expertness in the particular company, technology, or commodity, than to an institutional and social skill in some measure peculiar to each one's functional field—banking, importing, retailing, manufacturing, and so on, and their specialized subdivisions.

In the 1920's and early 1930's, when the U.S. Department of Agriculture was said to be the largest research organization in the world, it was commonly observed that whenever a scientist was made a "bureau chief" he quit being a scientist. While abilities and equipment are never all of one kind, it surely is true that the higher any executive is in any hierarchy the more he is required to demonstrate institutional and social skill, and the less up-to-date and comprehensive will be his command of information, technologies, and other factors that are the more constant concern of his subordinates.

In an ascending order of generality or scope up the hierarchy it is the part of executives to give general direction, to maintain internal order, to see that proper systems are established and maintained, to use complaints to search out inadequate, inequitable or improper performance, to pass upon and stimulate development of new policy ideas, and to participate constantly in relating many kinds of actions, functions, and responsibilities to each other.

Barnard has said: "The higher the position in the line of authority, the more general the abilities required." Yet the usual tendency is for an executive to be the prisoner of his past, more limited preoccupations. His "13 years of experience" may be only one year of experience repeated 13 times. Getting out of prior experience what is significantly relevant to a position higher up or in a different functional situation is uncommon and extremely difficult, rather than something to be assumed because of present position or past experience.

Because institutions have vitality and momentum, high-ranking executives happily adjusted in an organization may not be notably competent. They may be passengers carried, perhaps unconsciously, by associates and by the organization as a whole. Further promotion may be unwarranted, and transfer to some entirely different field of action may be the height of unwisdom. No one's equipment can automatically include experience in jobs not held, and ability to lead persons in jobs the executive has not held is the prerequisite to successful promotion or transfer.

A distinct step-up in achievement in one job after another; success in markedly different types of jobs in different institutions; success in starting and heading an entirely new organization where there is no special advantage in patents, size of capital resources or the like; and success in crisis—these, in this ascending order, are convincing evidence of an executive's virtuosity. But all of these elements of proof are only rarely available. And for governmental top posts there are still more requirements.

For the immediate purpose it is perhaps sufficient to say that special capacity for promotion and transfer can be identified and cultivated, that the need for really top-flight administrative personnel increases rapidly, and that the need for high executives of political understanding and skill is the greatest of all personnel needs. These needs have increased disproportionately to growth in organizational size, because of heightened complexity and the quickened tempo of change in institutions and in society.

An executive is first of all action-disposed, but through institutional means, in an orderly and responsible way. He is not an agitator, even though he may campaign for and help achieve many innovations. He is not a commentator, not much addicted to verbal logic. Principally in the sense of authenticating or participating in a decision-making process, he is a leader and a decision-maker, but as a rule could not even satisfy himself with a recital of reasons supporting a decision he thoroughly believes in. Barnard, most philosophical of all executives thus far given to producing books, in an essay on "Mind in Everyday Affairs," says predominantly nonlogical processes are required of the politician, the statesman needs balanced mental processes but with emphasis on the intuitional, while for the major executive "logical reasoning processes are increasingly necessary, but are disadvantageous if not in subordination to highly developed intuitional processes." The politician statesman-executive needs a first-class mind of a sort which would cause this first-class rating to be questioned by many in other fields of work.

DELEGATION

Administration of large institutions is possible at all, of course, only through delegation. And in institutions there are problems that bear especially upon members whose status is quite subordinate, along with other problems which weigh most on top executives. Since most members of organizations are subordinate, the less familiar point of view is the one that highlights the top executives and the qualities and institutional equipment needed by those executives.

In one view, delegation complicates citizen or customer dealings with an institution. The citizen knows or may readily discover who the top executive is and where he is located, but may feel that he would not know how to reach the appropriate subordinate. Actually, use of subordinates is easy and normal. The local forest ranger, the nearby social security people, the post office staff, local or nearby internal revenue officials are so much a part of the landscape that we often fail to recognize them as responsible members of great bureaucracies carrying on delegated functions. Further, whenever a citizen writes to any governmental office his letter gets responsible hierarchical treatment—much more attention, in fact, than could possibly be given it without a system of delegation.

Sophisticated citizens prefer generally to deal with subordinates for the sake of prompt decisions on matters a higher-ranking official could not decide without first getting subordinate advice. Speaker Rainey of Illinois in the early 1930's was a brilliant example. He came once to call upon a new Secretary of Agriculture without bringing any business; he also came to see me once without directing attention to anything in particular. But we heard of him often as he prosecuted matters of interest to constituents in the various bureaus.

A small instance of the use of subordinates to simplify work is provided by the way in which I often dealt with Senators or Cabinet members through their secretaries or other personal aides. (I did not invent the method, which was and is in common use.) Instead of waiting until I could speak to the superior officer I would tell an aide in his office my story. This was more convenient for all concerned, and the understanding shown of the aide's problem tended to slant him favorably toward my request. This is often half or more of the battle. A cooperative and understanding attitude will go a long way, while "pulling rank" or demanding high-level attention will only irritate. It may also tend to suggest desire for some improper favor.

Delegation is facilitated by the fact that communication from subordinates upward is easier and quicker than communication from the top downward. That is to say, communication upward in a hierarchy is easier and quicker *in terms of the needs of higher officials* than is the corresponding communication downward *in terms of the needs of the subordinates.* This dictum is related to the fact that the upper positions have broad scope while in the lower positions responsibilities are much more uniformly and clearly particular. The broad includes the narrow, but the narrow does not include the broad. In a small way, the distinction is similar to the one between a philosopher and a craftsman.

To give general instructions is one thing, to act in a particular case is something else. Even to get a proper understanding of a general instruction in terms of its meaning in a particular situation requires initially a kind of intellectual translation and then formulation of a sufficiently conforming action. Many times I have seen conscientious and intelligent subordinates badly misinterpret executive instructions. I have known and rather closely observed some quite incompetent executives in high posts, but their inadequacies did not seem to me especially based on failure to understand subordinate reports.

There is need for occasional level-skipping on the part of subordinates in communicating upward, and this need should be recognized and provided for. An aggrieved employee should have means of appeal without dealing with every person in the hierarchical line above him, and should be protected from reprisals for having gone over the heads of higher officers. The reporting of irregularities out of channels requires similar protective arrangements. But for daily business as a whole the process of upward communication calls for a step-by-step procedure for the sake of upholding responsibilities *and for translation of the material into terms quickly meaningful at the next level.* The tendency of each subordinate is to report matters in terms of his own situation. The need at each hierarchical level is to facilitate understanding at the next adjoining level—and that is usually the maximum justifiable strain on capacities.

In any case, in large institutions the need for communication both up and down is very great. Such communication is quite difficult and it cannot possibly be adequate in a conventionally simple pyramid.

This is to say that a President cannot be a competent chief executive by dealing only through department heads, and a department head cannot manage his agency well merely by his personal dealings with bureau heads. While criticisms growing out of rivalries between bureaus, field inspection trips, citizen complaints, and congressional complaints and inquiries will provide top executives much useful perspective, these all together are insufficient. To round out the picture there is need for staff aides and special staff units whose only reason for being is to serve the central executive authority.

The departmental personnel office will develop a systematic method for handling the personnel in each bureau, and will insist on the maintenance of acceptable standards and practices. The departmental budget and finance office will not only exercise financial controls but will add to the top executive's equipment a systematic view of bureau performances and attitudes. Departmental information offices, a solicitor's or counsel's office superior to any bureau attorneys, and other such coordinating entities are similarly of great importance to the delegating department head. In addition, personal assistants to top executives are more essential at most important executive levels than past practice has fully recognized. And of course the needs served by such functionaries are peculiarly acute at the level of the Presidency.

At all levels, the choice of personal aides should be made by the executive to whom they are subordinate, with a veto power alone vesting in *his* superior. This dictum applies to such officials as Under Secretaries and Assistant Secretaries as well as "assistants to the Secretary" and similar aides to Under Secretaries and Assistant Secretaries. The objective is a collegial group, free from internal rivalries, congenial, and capable of easy intercommunication.

With every precaution it is extremely difficult to bring together an effective team. I know enough about the situation as far back as the Wilson administration to assert that only in the State Department, and there only for periods in the Truman and Kennedy administrations, has there been any consistent success in maintaining a smooth, congenial, and effective top team which made much use of Under Secretaries and Assistant Secretaries. (The Defense Department under Secretary McNamara is probably another exception, but as this is written the time period needed for appraisal has not yet elapsed.) To the layman it is probably startling to hear that Under Secretaries and Assistant Secretaries are usually not very importantly occupied. A satisfactory and systematic way to select and utilize those who are theoretical deputies can hardly be said to have been discovered; the usual situation is one of mutual frustration for all concerned.

The so-called "career" Assistant Secretary for Administration is something of a special case, first developed in the 1940's. Experience with it has been rather disappointing, and in my observation the somewhat similar "permanent secretary" provision for departments in Canada, Britain, India, and other Commonwealth nations, while more congenial to conditions there than it would be to our more volatile society, is less than ideal. It works as well as it does because practice makes for more political and personal control than the theory would seem to make possible. Lord Woolton when Minister of Food in Great Britain told me of his way of circumventing the permanent secretary he inherited from a predecessor who had been fired, and attributed his own survival in the Cabinet to this circumvention. For U.S. departments I think it is clear that department heads must be free to pick, from registers of eligibles, and by transfer to displace at will those who hold these positions. Perhaps some Foundation will find it possible to develop suitable registers for each incoming administration for an experimental decade or two.

To round out a general discussion of delegation two further aspects of it need exploration. One raises for all members of a hierarchy the simple but fundamental question: "To be a satisfactory delegate, what should I decide on my own (or delegate to *my* subordinates), and what should I tell my boss?" The answer is that there is no formula, because bosses and problems are infinite in their variations. It follows, and there may be some guidance in this, that one should tell one's boss a little (but very little) more than he seems to want or need to know, so that both he and you may be sure that he is amply informed. One should be especially sure to tell him everything that may reflect adversely on the reporter so that he will not be surprised when he hears it from someone else. Tell him promptly about anything that may be expected to meet with criticism, or anything that is beginning to arouse unexpected criticism, without minimizing the resistance. If criticism is less in vigor or duration than you had given him to expect, he will gain confidence in your reliability and judgment.

One should of course avoid simply dumping trouble into the superior's lap. The subordinate's prime role in these matters is, and should be stated as, one of providing information: "We are doing such-and-such; this is novel, and there is likely to be a good deal of criticism for the next few months. It represents an improvement in our practice, however, and by the end of six months we think you'll hear no more about it, except perhaps an occasional word of surprised approval. In any case, I think we're on top of the situation; we'll let you know if we need help."

In a somewhat different situation, the subordinate might describe a problem and indicate that search for a solution had resolved itself into two possibilities. These are identified for the executive's information with a statement of preference, and perhaps the remark that "unless you think differently, that's what we'll do." The subordinate in such ways lives up to his responsibility and at the same time keeps the superior in a position to live up to his greater responsibilities.

The question put in terms of what and how to delegate similarly can be answered only in practice. To find out what subordinates can handle through the resources available to them, to help increase their capacities, and to support and guide them: these are the obligations—and the opportunities—of the delegator. The executive should delegate as much as possible so that occasional intervention or reversal will emerge as merely one aspect of a general attitude of support. Good administration is based on mutual respect for interdependent responsibilities.

Delegation is not abdication and it is never final, either in the choice of a delegate or in acceptance of what that delegate does. It is, on the contrary, tentative, with the higher executive remaining in a position to intervene to modify or remake decisions, and to end a particular delegation. No executive in an institution of any size can do everything, but responsibility requires that every executive reserve the power to change almost any decision taken by a subordinate.

DECISION-MAKING

The individual person is a complex of drives and concerns. In the process of becoming a well-adjusted or "integrated" person and in managing his life he achieves a degree of balance among divergent inclinations. Over a period of time conventions and experience come to point to judgments for which the earlier rationalizations have disappeared from consciousness. When a number of inconsistent drives are involved in a single problem, judgment may be clear without his knowing just what factor was decisive.

Concerning institutional action, it is often asserted that "policy decisions are made; then they are expressed in action." Lindblom puts forth an opposite view:[1] that policy is made concurrently with execution. He declares also that many decisions avoid decision (as in our constitutional position against an established church), that many issues are never decided, and that many decisions express agreement on

---

[1] Charles E. Lindblom, "The Science of Muddling Through," *Public Administration Review*, Vol. XIX, No. 2 (Spring 1959), pp. 79-88.

action in spite of disagreement in principle. Mediation often provides examples illustrating this last point: employers and employees may agree on a particular wage settlement without accepting any of the arguments made by the opponent. Similarly, one bureau chief may accept less than he thinks is due him and his program when, confronted with a competing bureau chief, he recognizes practical limits to what his superiors may concede.

Public administration—using the term in its broadest sense as meaning all policy-making and execution in the governmental field—is in one instance ascertainment of whether settlement of an issue is necessary. The various slavery compromises in the period before the Civil War were decisions to avoid a fundamental decision. In another instance, administration may be directed to the actual settlement of an issue. The Civil War finally settled the issue of secession. Settlement thus appears as the sometimes tragic fruit of a failure to avoid crisis, which is an important function of administration. In many cases administration achieves balance between conflicting social drives, maintaining a general, *moving* balance between major interests within a changing society. Successive small adjustments may reflect and effect great change in the course of time, and so avoid the shock of drastic change.

Some decisions may be largely choices of tools or work methods, but all are expressions of preference of some kind, reflecting some evaluation of alternative data, ways of doing a particular thing, and what thing to do. Judgment requires perspective, involving comparisons, relationships, discriminations. Choices are not between the sensible and the absurd; they involve weighing—in most important cases in terms not translatable into figures—different but positive values represented in terms of persons, functions, facts, ideas, hopes, and interests.

Institutional judgment is such an evaluation arrived at by members of an organization under the peculiar discipline of that entity. It is a multiple judgment. In contrast with a vocal solo (itself a composite product of composer, singer, and accompanist), it has the character of some particular symphony played by a particular orchestra for a particular audience.

An executive decision not accepted by his subordinate organization is ineffective, as well as damaging to the executive. A governmental decision affecting the public but not in fact acceptable to most of the citizens will not stand, and a leadership that enunciates such a decision suffers. The search of public policy-makers is first of all, and quite properly, for decisions that will be acceptable. This pursuit is difficult enough, in view of the enormous range of differentiated interests in a country as large and diversified as the United States. Before testing a decision for acceptability, it must be known to be technically and administratively feasible, and publicly defensible in terms felt sufficient in view of the educational efforts and prestige the backing of responsible leaders will provide.

Acceptable decisions are easier to arrive at than consensus judgments, and they may be clearly preferable, Even a majority agreement on an established church, for example, might tear the country apart, while citizens of all faiths accept rather happily the absence of a national commitment to any particular religion or denomination. The acceptable decision may also embody more foresight than consensus would reflect. Similarly, it may reflect more of imagination, be more inventive and perceptive. In contrast, consensus would be mediocrity-prone.

It is largely the function of leadership to identify and effectuate acceptable governmental decisions. To identify and develop the area of the acceptable is in some part a responsibility of citizen—as distinguished from official—leadership. Those who occupy the manifold positions of leadership in our almost innumerable social groupings have great responsibilities in this matter. They are presumably more readily educable than the rank and file, and should be especially able to interpret public policy problems to their special followings. They are in some ways dependent upon official leadership for important raw materials capable of being processed for wide utilization; nevertheless a fundamental responsibility lies with them. But a major shortage is in the absence of a sense of truly public responsibility on the part of private organizations. Very rarely do private groups do more in their association with government than solicit favors for themselves and oppose favors for competitors. At the same time, too few official leaders engage enough in popular education; they tend too much to operate as receiving stations, too little as sending stations.

The result is that the processes of decision-making in the field of public policy are bumpier and inflict more bruises than an ideal procedure would. Policy develops in jerks, after need for it has become overwhelming. Political debate tends, therefore, to proclaim crisis as actually present when it is still some distance away, and to insist that crisis is not in prospect when in reality it is coming around the corner. Politicians thus discredit their own serious intentions of keeping the society in dynamic order by juggling a brokerage function of supreme importance.

Yet the process is thoroughly, if not elegantly, democratic. This is particularly so at the national level, where more varieties of citizen interests, ideas, activities, and aspirations are taken account of than at any other level of our government. Our citizens exhibit greater variety—in interests, in membership in private organizations, in ethnic origins—than the citizens of any other nation. These things our political and public-institutional processes reflect.

Given more truly popular representational patterns, more uniform access to actual suffrage, more actual two-party jurisdictions, and abandonment of the seniority system in Congress and several rules changes there, our basic arrangements would be richer and more satisfying. But even now the quality of government here is as high as it is anywhere, and much higher than it ever was anywhere in bygone times. And our government at the national level has very special competence and a highly democratic character.

The national government is more representative than the nation's founders could have anticipated. The Congress, of course, is the branch traditionally thought of as representative. Because one-party jurisdictions roughly offset each other nationally, the Congress is more representative than most of the state legislatures. Personnel of the executive branch, drawn from and located in all parts of the nation, have some sectionally representative character, but are more important as representatives of national functions, professions, and interests, and of the broader and deeper character of modern knowledge.

There are formal and informal interchanges between executive and legislative personnel, between all of these and citizens, between officers in any one agency and those employed in all others having related concerns and responsibilities; between field offices, district offices, regional offices, and Washington headquarters; between bureaus, between sections of bureaus, between divisions and sections, between bureaus and divisions, between bureaus and departmental offices. These interchanges are vital paths by which facts, ideas, opinions, drives, interests, functions, laws, instructions, conventions, and workways clash, fertilize, illuminate, placate, compromise, and otherwise contribute to the emergence of acceptable decisions.

Most of the basic activities of the government constitute programs through each of which substantial elements of the citizenry feel themselves desirably served. The functional specialization which prevails causes employees to be representative of varied and manifold citizen interests as well as of a profession or a body of knowledge. Thus, the governmental institution is an arena in which many interests and ideas of popular significance compete for recognition, for shares of available resources, and for general influence on policy.

To an extent, policy is produced somewhat mechanically from the interaction of competing, divergent or convergent, and complementary functions. Some of the functions and drives cancel or modify each other because of competition for scarce resources; others reinforce each other because of various kinds of interrelatedness. Beyond the bounds of the automatic or mechanical adjustment, however, are other processes of review, clearance, and administrative appeal.

REVIEW AND CLEARANCE

The budget-making process is an outstanding example of review. Contrary to common belief, dollars are always scarce in the government in relation to the public needs. Government budgetary requests on the whole are reviewed more searchingly at more different points of responsiblity and more times than any other important budgets anywhere. The pattern is not invariable, of course: there are differences in emphases, in conditions, in competence, and in functions which need to be recognized. In the crisis of war, victory is more important than marginal dollars; and the function of national defense consequently, even in time of peace, is not characteristically controlled by managerial and economical standards. Even in the defense organizations, however, zealously supported objects of expenditure are so competitive with each other that there is a widespread sense of deprivation which cannot be easily disregarded.

Political officers hate more than anything else to share responsibility for imposing new taxes on citizens, and want more than anything else to provide services important—and, if possible, pleasing—to the public. Balancing of these negative and positive concerns is at the heart of policy-making, although other values enter into the balance-seeking. In developing the budget, the effort at each level in the hierarchy is to submit a request that cannot be denied even in the face of the toughest competition. Section heads compete with each other, division heads with each other, bureau heads with each other. Departmental budget and finance offices manage and take advantage of this competition. The department head is anxious to have a budget request that will stand up before the critical and searching review he can anticipate at the Budget Bureau and by the members and staffs of the congressional appropriations committees. Anyone who in his newness tries to outsmart the two final levels of review by padding his request as a bargaining or insurance device is likely to find himself with a smaller appropriation than if he had submitted a tighter, less vulnerable budget.

Clearance differs from review in that it involves lateral action across hierarchical lines to eliminate competition, lay incipient misunderstanding, or invite cooperation. The Department of Agriculture in handling exports of farm surpluses or providing technical assistance to an underdeveloped country is conducting affairs of collateral concern to the Department of State, hence may think it wise to inform subordinate State personnel acquainted with that kind of business and to secure an opinion of probable State Department reaction. The opinion may be that there would be no objection. In that event the action by Agriculture will go forward, and if higher-ups in the State Department are unhappy after the fact the blame will fall chiefly on their own subordinate. This being true, a subordinate's assurance usually will not be given if he has even a shadow of doubt about it; in the latter case he may submit the problem for consideration at higher levels within his own department before taking a position.

Clearance in this fashion testifies to cooperativeness and avoids much more elaborate formal communication up one entire hierarchy, across to another, downward there then upward, across to the originating department, thence downward to the point where the particular action is proposed to be taken. Most of the Alice-in-Wonderland pictures of governmental procedures one sees in the public prints are pictures of this more formal—but in fact *less* intricate—process which is very rarely pursued but which, as a reserve mechanism, protects all responsibilities concerned.

Review and clearance are combined in such a process as that employed by the Budget Bureau in handling legislative proposals made by executive agencies, bills already introduced and ready for committee consideration, and measures passed by Congress and submitted for Presidential action. In these cases all agencies conceivably interested are asked for their opinions.

While clearance secures coordination in the usual case, it may also be a means of effecting positive cooperation. The snow survey by which farmers are given forecasts of the quantity of water to be available the following season for irrigation purposes initially provided an important new service at a net cost of less than a hundred dollars by spontaneous partnership between personnel in five or six bureaus of the Departments of Interior and Agriculture. Such cooperation is more normal between employees of the two departments than their much-publicized controversies. But the critical cross-scrutiny also contributes information that is useful to executives.

A constant, penetrating influence and a reserve resource of great importance to institutional performance is the administrative appeals process illustrated by the interchanges between the Budget Bureau and the program agencies. In the normal course, the lowliest examiner for the Budget Bureau, in inquiring into operations, expresses opinions to program agency executives in various subordinate levels. These opinions are listened to carefully, since they are uttered by an official serving in a staff office of the President. When such an opinion is not objectionable, it will be accepted. If it is felt that program values would be adversely affected, the departmental official will report to his superior, who may discuss it with the examiner's superior, or report it to the next ranking official above him in the department. Interchange between the department and the Budget Bureau may take place at each higher level of responsibility and may result finally in a conversation between the department head and the President—usually with the Budget Director there too. *The operating responsibility for the final decision rests with the official who decided not to pursue the matter further.* So far as the public, the press, and the Congress are concerned, responsibility rests always with the President and his department head. The Budget Bureau has no power except as it is upheld by the President, and its responsiblity is only to him. The responsibility is to inform him and to argue with him, as well as to carry out his instructions.

What has just been said of the Budget Bureau as a special staff office of the President is true also of the executive agencies of government generally, for this is the way in which all delegated responsibilities are exercised. Subordinates always act subject to appeal "over their heads." Even in the case of action by the so-called independent offices and agencies, the public may carry an appeal or protest to the President and the Congress, which can change the law that establishes a degree of independence. Actually, citizen appeals to higher levels of responsibility occasion a very considerable part of the daily business of government, and contribute importantly to the refinement of decision-making.

All of the complicated intragovernmental interaction of persons, units, and activities is related, of course, to a continuous interaction between the government and citizens. Governmental actions are in part responses to actual citizen reactions to actions already taken by government, and in part shaped by anticipations of future citizen reactions. Tens of millions of letters are addressed annually by citizens to officials in Washington and in thousands of field offices. Tens of millions of conversations, face-to-face and by telephone, add to this interchange. Additionally a governmental eye and ear are cocked attentively to printed and spoken discussions of governmental activities. All of this has point chiefly because of popular elections, past and future.

Much of the dealing between government and citizens occurs in the conduct of programs. The mail carrier, the forest ranger, the park ranger, the state trooper, the public school teacher or state university faculty member, the traffic officer, the weather forecaster—these are familiar examples of public servants who deal with citizens frequently, provide valued services, and gauge citizen attitudes. Behind them are persons developing statistics, records, and forms that result in formulations of significant information or in the issuance of social security checks or other benefits and payments. Interactions within the government inevitably reflect these dealings with citizens, bringing together the representative fruits of a very great many public exposures. Intragovernmental interchanges also facilitate the pursuit of technical soundness, operating effectiveness, and planning.

The result of all this is a kind of institutional wisdom important to all concerned. It is frustrating to a degree, and especially for the novice, to find it necessary to defer to so many interlocking responsibilities and to have to utilize so many different facilities. But on sober thought it is also reassuring, constantly reminding the participant in institutional business that he can assert his view so as to enrich the process of decision-making. The truly responsible person is similarly reassured by daily evidence that institutional decisions made last week, or last year, or ten years ago, can nearly always be modified without too much damage having been done. Certainly no one person, no matter how wise, could make so many decisions as well as they can be made through utilization of great institutional resources.

· 3 ·

Public Administration and Culture

DWIGHT WALDO

My subject has three sources. One is some central interests of Paul Appleby. Turning again to his writings for inspiration and guidance, it strikes me that his central concern might be put in such an expression as "the Good Life in a democratic society," and that his special interests bore upon the way that government in general and administration in particular relate thereto. The second source—in part but another manner of putting the first—arises from the orientation given by the title of this book and the circumstance that my remarks concern the "field" of public administration. The third source is some thoughts of mine that concern "culture," and that seem to me to relate to Appleby's concerns and the field of public administration. Whether the relationship I think I perceive is only personal and psychological or has some logical validity and empirical importance the sequel will signify.

The culture of which I speak is of course the social sciences' culture, not the humanities' culture. By culture I mean first of all and usually the totality of distinctive ideas, symbols, patterned behavior, and artifacts of a human group; their way of life as a whole, but as consisting of parts that have something of a separate existence and also interact.[1] I shall use the term loosely, hoping that this essay does not come to the attention of some anthropologist who has staked his professional life on a particular, precise definition.

I appreciate the important scientific problems that are involved in the differing conceptualizations, and the serious questions posed by applying to complex contemporary societies a concept and perspective developed with primary reference to the simpler societies that have been the anthropologist's prime interest. I shall try to avoid taking

[1] The conceptual-definitional difficulties are indicated by the opening language for the Culture entry (by Clyde Kluckhohn) in *A Dictionary of the Social Sciences* (New York: Free Press of Glencoe, 1964): "It is difficult to settle upon a single definition of this complex and extremely important term." Six meanings are distinguished.

sides in the various quarrels, but inevitably I shall be taking a position on some matters; and on the more important of these the position is appropriately set forth now. I assume that the concept of culture is a respectable scientific instrument and that it is proper and useful to apply the concept in analysis of complex contemporary societies, recognizing however that our use in the latter cases especially is imprecise and characteristically takes us only to the insight and hypothesis stage of social science. My position on the relation of whole and parts is a middle-of-the-road, commonsensical one. I believe it is useful for some purposes to speak of "French," "Western," "peasant," or "Hindu" culture, while fully admitting the difficulties that arise when one attempts to specify with any precision the defining boundaries of what he is talking about. I believe it is useful to think of cultures as wholes in some ways and for some purposes, though recognizing that in an interacting Great Society these wholes are but convenient frames for observation and analysis and not independent, closed systems. I believe it is useful to think in terms of subcultures, that is, to conceptualize a culture as consisting of parts that have some measure of autonomy and are meaningful units for observation and analysis in trying to understand the total. I believe that the parts, the subcultures, interact with and affect both each other and the whole—and it is indeed this which gives meaning to the notion of a whole consisting of parts—but that it is not necessary to assume that any and every change in a part is reflected in the other parts or in the whole.

As this list of "believes" will suggest, it is difficult to keep the anthropologist's cultural approach to the social world distinct from the sociologist's approach through social structure and even structural functionalism. This in fact appears to be a real problem for the "pros" in this area of social science. My own conclusion is that the large perspectives of anthropology and sociology are (1) alternative (according to taste or purpose), (2) complementary, and (3) competitive. For present purposes it is not necessary to grind and sort more finely. One matter, however, deserves comment. I have elected to speak in terms of culture, and hence I shall tend to speak of the component parts of a culture as subcultures; for example, and especially, administrative subculture.[2] The anthropologist may well be uncomfort-

---

[2] To give the reader a basing-point for calculating the extent to which my use of the concept of subculture is legitimate, I quote the definition (by M. M. Gordon) given in *A Dictionary of the Social Sciences*: ". . . a subdivision of a national culture, composed of a combination of factorable social situations such as class status, ethnic background, regional and rural or urban residence, and religious affiliation,

able at my use of the term, and the sociologist of the opinion that what I am referring to should be designated by the language of structural functionalism. This is not a matter for concern as long as the meaning is clear.

Let me now pose questions of the type that seem pertinent. What sense does it make to speak of an administrative culture, or sub-culture? Presuming this makes enough sense to make further inquiry worthwhile, what in general and/or in this specific American instance are the relationships between this administrative culture and the larger cultural entity(ies)? (In "systems" idiom, what are the inputs and outputs?) Is it fruitful to think of a *public* administration subculture? If so, what are its characteristics and what are its relationships with the larger cultural environment, including the other subcultures in the environment? In particular, what are its relationships with the political, economic, and educational subcultures? Can there be identified a necessary or generic function for the administrative subculture(s) in a modern culture? Assuming the affirmative, how much diversity in cultural style or mode is nevertheless possible, in the subculture(s) and in their relationships with the larger cultural environment? In general or in a specific instance (as our own) what is the present empirical function of the administrative subculture(s) in perpetuating and improving the larger cultural entity(ies)? In this vein what is theoretically possible and morally desirable? Would it be useful to think *explicitly* in terms of improving and perpetuating our culture through the agency of the administrative subculture?

Such questions are listed to suggest the range of fruitful inquiry, not to provide the agenda for a modest essay. In what follows it must suffice to indicate some of the dimensions of and possible approaches to the exploration of two or three basic questions.

On the Idea of an Administrative Culture

One need not debate the question whether an administrative culture is possible. *We now live in one.* A letter dropped in a mailbox in Portland is delivered to a specified address in Chattanooga. A purchase made in Hong Kong is paid for (via credit card and billing through Chicago) by a check cleared through an international banking network. Ninety people unknown to each other gather at an airport at a prearranged time but with no consultation among themselves, and

---

but *forming in their combination a functioning unity which has an integrated impact on the participating individual.*" (Italics in original.) The word "national" may be legitimately omitted, and with this amendment the definition fits fairly well what I have in mind when I speak of the public administration subculture.

six hours later arrive at a common destination twenty-five hundred miles away. Income earned in New York is taxed directly by two governments, and the tax money (after "homogenization") goes for the support of governmental activities mostly far removed from the daily concerns of the taxpayer. The mortgage payments on my house are made through a bank to an insurance company that "bought the paper" (as I was informed); the "money" I never see, as my employer deposits my monthly salary—marks on a piece of paper—directly in my bank, and if and when some insurance policy-holder or stock-owner receives some of this money, it will be represented by other marks on a piece of paper.

Is this not all remarkable, truly a wonder? Why would an anthropologist choose to study the attachment of Dobuans to the yam, rites of passage in an Indian village, or the fertility cults of ancient Mesopotamia, when his own culture is plainly so strange and wonderful?

It *is* strange and wonderful. The culture suggested by my examples is very recent in human experience and with the scale and depth suggested still limited to a minor fraction of humankind. But what warrants our designating it administrative? To be sure, there are many other legitimate and useful ways of designating it, of trying to catch in a word, frame in a concept, the significant and distinctive features of our contemporary culture. Focusing on those close to our own perspective and purpose, one could characterize this culture by such terms as industrial, or urban, or scientific-technological; many such factors intimately relate to its "administered" quality.

Still closer are two words and concepts: bureaucratic and organizational. These are useful, highly relevant terms, worthy of examination here. But first, my reasons for choosing *administrative* culture. These reasons concern my purpose, my emphasis; the associations and connotations of the three terms. *Bureaucratic,* despite its neutralization in social science, inevitably comes trailing some of the pejorative associations of the term. More, it has a certain rigidity which I should like to avoid. Its virtue is its defect: the very fact that Max Weber gave it a firm meaning and a foundation in history, economics, and sociology means that it has these meanings and associations. And I should like a looser term, which admits more phenomena and permits a transcendence, so to speak, to a possible postbureaucratic stage of development. With regard to *organization,* this is a bit too broad, too simply descriptive, too static. I should like to center attention on the larger, more formal organizations; and by the term "administrative" suggest emphasis upon the science and art of operating organizations.

To say something about bureaucracy and about organizations, however, is to speak to the subject of our administrative culture.

I shall not stop to explain what Weber meant by the term bureaucracy, but rather assume that a reader of these essays understands the meaning and associations he gave it. Now our culture on a comparative scale is a highly bureaucratized culture. In general, in our history the presuppositions and causes that Weber catalogued have existed and operated. Our perceptions and attitudes have been affected by a "rational" theology, by the growth of a subtle and sophisticated law and complex legal institutions, by the elaboration of a pecuniary economy, by the spirit and ethic of Protestantism, by the rise of modern science. We live under the jurisdiction of a State controlling a large land mass; we have experienced the leveling of social differences of democracy and the almost complete disintegration of medieval social attitudes and institutions that were unbureaucratic.

In result (or for whatever reasons) we live in a society that, comparatively, has many and large bureaucracies. To be sure, no single bureaucracy is, by the ideal-typical specifications, completely bureaucratic, and many of our bureaucracies are only loosely so. On the other hand, it should be noted that in the now two generations since Weber wrote much has been learned about how to be bureaucratic effectively. There has been a tremendous increase of knowledge bearing on administration and available to an administrator. In Imperial Germany administration was a combination of social structure, legal tradition, empirical lore, and personal experience. The idea of administration (or management) as a distinct function or profession had hardly been born; and the idea of a science of administration as it is often or even typically conceived today, is in Weber at best inchoate.

Turning to organization, it is commonplace that we are experiencing an Organizational Revolution and that the typical middle-class male is an Organization Man. There is (to my knowledge) a disconcerting scarcity of hard data on these matters, but the assertions and assumptions run like this: The number of organizations constantly increases in proportion to the number of people, and organizations wax in their "organizationness," tending to become larger, to control more affairs, and to control more effectively what they control. The lives of people tend to be affected and dominated more and more by organizations of a bewildering variety with respect to purposes, size, and technique. Formal or bureaucratic organizations tend to grow at the expense both of older, more "natural" social organization and of individuality and privacy. Organizations tend not only to provide the work and the work environment of most people, but to provide the instruments and ambiance of recreation and leisure; indeed for the whole of life, from organizationally certified birth in a hospital run by an organization to organizationally certified death and burial in a cemetery run by another organization.

This is all familiar enough, and I rehearse it only to explicate and emphasize my thesis that we can sensibly think in terms of living in an administrative culture. If this is a sensible, realistic perspective, then what can we see or see better about administration and its role and relations by reversing the anthropologist's glass and examining ourselves? Perhaps nothing not noted before and said in another idiom. But no two idioms say quite the same thing. To me there comes what I think is a new and valuable type of knowledge about the configuration of the whole and the interrelation of the parts. To take as thesis and perspective that we live in an administrative culture, to accept this as our condition, gives us clarity in seeing why this is true, how it is true, and what the peculiarities, potentialities, and limitations of that condition are.

As to the why and the how, there is altogether a vast amount of data in the literature of history, sociology, psychology—in the social sciences generally—bearing on the subject, but it is not put into a single frame. The most penetrating and useful conceptualization by a wide margin is Weber's conceptualization of bureaucracy, and this is perhaps the necessary starting point, if only for a thesis against which to pose antitheses. There would now be general agreement that Weber's conceptualization was erroneous and inadequate in many respects; that Weber for all of his world-ranging scholarship was too much an Imperial German, whose views were shaped if not warped by the social structure, philosophies of history, and so forth, of his milieu. We need a new analysis and synthesis which takes cognizance of another half-century of history, of the developments of "administrative science," of the developments in the social sciences generally—a view with less rigidity and determinism, one refreshed by the development of comparativeness and one that assesses the implications of moral-ideological choices rather than assuming that administration (bureaucracy) is a neutral instrument that serves them all equally. In short we badly need a major synthetic work with a title such as *The Administrative Culture*.

These reflections are in part inspired and given relevance by the plea of an anthropologist (Wayne Untereiner, in an unpublished paper) that we stop thinking piecemeal, that we seize this sorry non-scheme of things entire and think boldly in terms of the cultural design and development of contemporary society. This is acceptable, given proper definition and qualification. I assume—as does the anthropologist—wide participation in the process of designing and a high value given to individuality and freedom in the objectives sought. In the spirit and to the end of the proposal, I suggest that to think effectively about cultural design and development we need to recognize the central importance of administration. I present some thoughts that seem illustrative of what might be implied.

It has long seemed to me that our approach to administration is far too much "producer oriented," far too little "consumer oriented." I mean by this that we expend a great deal of effort studying and teaching how a relatively small number of us can administer effectively, with the implicit assumption that most of us will be the "material" that is effectively administered. Now I do not wish to express an unrealistic, sentimental equalitarianism; I accept the necessity for a considerable amount of authority, hierarchy and even coercion, for as far into the human future as I can imagine. But if we value not only efficiency and productivity, but also seek to increase human equality and the values of participation, do we give these the attention they deserve in and relating to the administrative process? If we live in an administrative culture, and also seek equalitarian values, should we not teach everyone how to administer and also in some senses how not to be administered?

Let me come at the matter another way. Harlan Cleveland has written that it is erroneous and dangerous to think of the increasing number and size of organizations as only and necessarily a threat to our freedoms, that in many ways organizations preserve and create freedoms.[3] He emphasizes the desirability of learning to live in and among organizations, and emphasizes the increased freedoms of those especially who move up the hierarchy and really master this man-made environment—hence the desirability of learning administrative skills. With this argument I agree. But I should like to see it carried further: "democratized," so to speak. Let us be sure that everyone knows that we live in an organizational society, that we have an administrative culture; and let us be sure that everyone understands what this implies. Let us be sure that it is ability, and decisions made on the basis of taste and inclination, that determine function and role in organizations, not accidents of education and training. In the game that is being played, let us be sure that everyone knows at least the basic rules. Everyone can then play to the extent that his skill and inclination dictate.

[3] "Dinosaurs and Personal Freedom," *Saturday Review* Vol. XLII, No. 9 (February 28, 1959), pp. 12-14.

Moving in this direction will not, of course, solve all our problems. In fact, it is obvious that some new ones would be created. If everyone learns the present rules of the game, then the game will change in more or less unpredictable ways. On the other hand, I am confident that the concept advanced relates to important problems: it relates, for example, to the phenomenon of estrangement, of alienation in mass society. If our culture is importantly an administrative culture, and so few participate in it with real understanding, of course many are alienated. To be sure, many of the alienated think they know well what manner of thing this administrative culture is; and precisely because they think they know are in rebellion. I can only say of this that in my opinion few of them really understand it as it is, much less have caught a vision of what it might become.

A few thoughts may be ventured on the measures that would be necessary or effective in carrying through the general program proposed. Certainly formal pedagogy would be involved, and at every level from the nursery to the postdoctoral levels. This formal instruction would take as its objective or orientation not teaching how to administer, but how to participate in an administrative culture. Learning of three types would be involved: (1) knowledge, (2) attitudes and (3) abilities (skills, etc.).[4] But more than formal pedagogy, at least as carried on in formal educational settings, clearly is implied. Many of the measures that would be involved are suggested by the somewhat broader concepts of acculturation, socialization, and resocialization.

Let me note specifically that I do not have in mind what is sometimes implied in or imputed to the phrase "a planned society," much less the creation of a completely ordered society of the ants. I would hope that we could achieve greater mastery of some of the forces that degrade and destroy human life, and indeed threaten to bring the human experiment to an end. Presumably a conscious program of "cultural design and development" would help achieve more order, stability, and safety in those areas where present evidence would indicate the desirability of such a program. On the other hand, to think purposefully in terms of an administrative culture is to think and plan intelligently regarding the preservation of large areas of freedom and spontaneity, to allow for the differences in human gifts and tastes (even for much "withdrawal" by those who so elect). Indeed, unless we do so these risk being destroyed or ignored. The

---

[4] My terminology here follows the schema in *Factors in Effective Administration*, by C. E. Summer, Jr. (New York: Graduate School of Business, Columbia University, 1956). The essential point is that more than just the cognitive is involved.

ever more rapid ascent of the physical-human technology available to organizations and administrators indicates that the only alternative to the human use of human beings is the inhuman use of human beings.

On the Idea of an Administrative Subculture

Let us now consider whether it is sensible, realistic, and useful to think in terms of an administrative subculture, or subcultures, in our society. Having just argued that we live in an administrative culture, can it now be argued that within that culture is an administrative subculture, or subcultures?

There is in fact no important or essential contradiction; rather, what seems a contradiction is explicable in terms of perspective or emphasis, the density of the phenomena, and time and consciousness. The first suggests simply a closer examination of a part of the whole. The concept of density signifies that the phenomenon under consideration, though significant enough throughout the whole to give it a distinctive quality, may be found in concentrated form in certain parts. Time and consciousness is a matter of emphasis and awareness. The argument that we do now live in an administrative culture became an argument that we should become conscious of that fact and act on its implications in the future. In treating of the administrative subculture I shall be speaking to very present realities—whatever the future.

Historically, there was a long period of preparation for the emergence in the modern West of bureaucratic subcultures: these subcultures emerged slowly, but with greater mass, with increasing concentration of bureaucratic characteristics, and with increasing tempo as the modern centuries, and then the more recent decades, passed. These bureaucratic subcultures peaked in the Church; in the apparatus of the rising nation-state, particularly in and about its armies, its administration of justice, its collection of taxes, and its systems of mercantilism; and in the service of (more or less) private economic enterprise, especially as this grew in scope and impersonality through the devices of the joint-stock company and the protean corporation. I use the term *bureaucratic* culture because in analyzing and describing developments up to late in the nineteenth century I think this conceptualization is by all odds the most useful. Though outmoded in some respects, the Weberian perspective retains an enormous relevance and fertility. For example, many sophisticated conceptualizations are now available to us for making sense of and dealing with the data of comparative administration; but who, as he contemplates the present difficulties in trying to establish an effective administrative apparatus more or less bureaucratic in form in many areas of the world, can deny the tremendous relevance of the historical-cultural conditioning factors, the "presuppositions and causes" that Weber delineated?

But even as Weber wrote, important events were taking place that made his conceptualization of bureaucracy less and less relevant to certain parts of the world. These parts are designated in general by the term, the West. Perhaps this decreasing relevance is true for various reasons for a broader spectrum, but in what follows I speak about Western Europe and most specifically about the United States.

Above I referred to the nature of German bureaucracy as of the time Weber wrote and the incorporation of what he perceived into his ideal-type bureaucracy. He spoke of "office management," of the importance of "the files" and of "general rules" for the guidance of action (and in the background was the monumental structure of German administrative law). However, there is at best but the germ of a concept that has since become very widely held and is of the highest significance: the idea that administration is or can become a science, that administration (or management) is a distinct social function, a profession perhaps. This is what I refer to as the arrival of self-consciousness; it is speaking prose knowing it is prose and paying attention to prose style. This is an event of such historic importance that I have elsewhere designated it a "mutation in human culture." I have no doubt that this change in perspective was an event of the greatest significance for the human experience, already altering the course of history and of the highest relevance for future history.

Accompanying the birth and development of the notion that administration is a thing-in-itself (whether science, art, profession, or some combination) has been a swelling stream, fed always by more tributaries, of new knowledge and devices relating to administration, contributing to its complexity and effectiveness. Indeed, so many things are involved and their interrelations are so complex that it is difficult to designate them in short compass. The past two or three generations have been great ones in human history for the development of the social sciences and the behavioral sciences. Some would say that for the first time we have achieved, or at least approached, genuine social science. In any event, the development of data and concepts concerning individual and group behavior has been remarkable. This new information has been widely diffused; and is more or less known and available to and used by administrators or (what is not the same thing but also of great import) in administration. How management science, or management sciences, would be defined and described depends on the describer and his purpose; but permit me for the present to regard management science(s) as that part of the social and behavioral sciences most relevant to the concerns of the administrator: an inner core, so to speak.

Accompanying this development on the social and behavioral side has of course been an explosion of knowledge in physical science and technology. Of particular moment is the development of machines and techniques for facilitating communication; and for storing and manipulating data in such mass and with such speed that the mind boggles in trying to understand what is now possible, let alone what is confidently anticipated.

It is enough to note these developments. Who has not heard of the scientific revolution of our day, and who in public administration has not been urged to consider what the computer revolution means for him and his organization? What seems less well understood is the close interrelation of the developments on the social side and the physical side. My own view is that the dichotomy suggested by these two terms is seriously misleading. We are ill-served by too great and too continuous attention to the question whether the social sciences are, or may become, "real" sciences, on the model of the advanced physical sciences. Whatever the conclusions, in ideas or in events, of that argument, it diverts our attention from the extremely important fact that if we think in terms of social science technology—that is, accept a looser, pragmatic definition of social science—then the achievements are immense. This is demonstrated in the fact that we have achieved and do operate (however imperfectly) an economic-social-political entity without any near parallel in human history in terms of magnitude and complexity.

Nor are the achievements in physical science and technology and the achievements in social science and technology separable. The essence of the matter is that the two sets of achievements are closely interacting, in important respects, but are different aspects of the same phenomenon: a thrust forward in human knowledge in which the social and the physical mutually support and stimulate each other. A judgment that our social science is primitive whereas our physical science is highly advanced rests upon arbitrary definition resting in turn upon a cultural bias.[5]

[5] This view is developed in my essay on "Reversing the Glass," in *Perspectives on Administration* (University, Alabama: University of Alabama Press, 1956). While some of this now seems rather primitive to me, I would not now retract but rather would push the argument further.

My view of our administrative subculture is that it represents the peaking in our total culture or society of the developments I have been indicating, beginning with the historical-cultural preparation for the rise of bureaucratic organizations in the West and including now the emergence of administrative self-consciousness and an unprecedented outpouring of knowledge relating to administration. Our administrative subculture, in terms of its members, consists of those whose knowledge, attitudes, skills, and authority place them in the center of these long-range and now contemporary developments. It consists of practicing administrators, researchers, teachers, and many others who are more or less knowledgeable and who participate in it more or less by virtue of location or function.

The image of a mountain range comes to mind. A massif has been thrust upward; totally it is our administrative culture, and its peaks are the administrative subculture. The risks of distortion of sense are obvious, but the metaphor has one very pertinent advantage. It enables us to conceive of the administrative subculture as collectively the peaks, but also as consisting of various peaks of differing height, location, composition, and even aesthetic qualities. That is, we can think both of an administrative culture and of *various* administrative subcultures, and these with varying location, eminence, function, and so forth.

It is useful for some purposes to think not only of major administrative subcultures but to perceive them as consisting in turn of sub-subcultures, and to carry this analysis into components as far as may serve understanding and utility. This can be done even within a single organization if it is of any size.[6] It is a common fact of life that Budget has a style of life different from that of Division X, that Sales' view of the world is different from Production's view, and so forth.

But the chief usefulness of the concept of administrative subculture would seem to lie in another direction. It lies in the fresh insights gained and enlightening perspectives afforded when one thinks of the relation of the administrative subculture as a whole to the culture as a whole, or to the other major subcultures; or when one

[6] There come to mind the very interesting, and scientifically highly relevant, distinctions found by Alvin W. Gouldner between "mine" and "surface" cultures (as I am calling them) in the gypsum company he studied. *Patterns of Industrial Bureaucracy* (Glencoe, Ill.: The Free Press, 1954). The discipline and the idiom were those of sociology, but the research approach closely resembled that of an anthropological field study of an exotic tribe.

takes major parts of the subculture and similarly considers their relationships.

In this examination of part(s)-in-whole there is nothing that in a formal sense cannot be done in another idiom, such as that of systems theory or structural functionalism; or for that matter, in the simple language of parts and whole. My position is that each of the idioms has distinctive advantages, and that the cultural idiom, bearing as it does the rich suggestiveness of generations of anthropological observation and speculation, may afford us *apercus*—even hypotheses that can be "researched"—we would otherwise miss. For we, too, are a native tribe, however extraordinary our technology, however complex our social structure, however remarkable our mores.

As one approach it might be asked: What are the basic values of American culture and what is the relationship of the administrative subculture to these values? This is a tangled skein, and to pursue the subject with any depth would require a book-length effort. But a few thoughts may be hazarded.

Certainly there is much evidence to indicate a relatively high commitment to the values of both equality and freedom, however complex each is in itself and however much more complex matters become when one seems to negate the other either in logic or in the world. Another value commitment of which there is abundant evidence is materialism, using the word not as a condemnation but descriptively to indicate attachment to a "high standard of living," manifested centrally by abundance of economic goods. Still another on which there would be much agreement is efficiency, the matter of getting things done quickly and with a minimum expenditure of human labor. Taking just these four, what is the relation of the administrative subculture to them?

A moment's reflection will indicate to anyone well acquainted with the literature of public administration that he has arrived in familiar territory by a perhaps unfamiliar route. Certainly the history of public administration in the United States has posed aspects of this question again and again, and in the literature of the public administration movement (beginning, say, with Wilson's famous essay in 1887) the questions involved are argued with more or less explicitness. Is administration to be conceived as instrument, to be measured only in terms of its efficiency? If so, in terms of what values and how exactly is this efficiency to be mesured? If decisions about values outside of administration are or should be made *in* administration, then by whom, by what warrant, and in what fashion? If we are committed to the values of equality and freedom in our culture does this mean that we should not only try to realize them through administration as an instrument but within administration as a large and increasingly important subculture? If so, how can we reconcile equality and freedom with the hierarchy and authority that are presumably so central in that subculture? And what, if we take the matter seriously, happens to efficiency? All this is familiar enough: familiar not just in public administration, but in the other parts of the administrative subculture, though perhaps presented and conceptualized in different fashion.

It is to be expected that such issues will be posed (though often concealed in other issues) more often and more insistently with the passage of time. This follows from three factors, one a fact of the past, another a widespread phenomenon of the present, the third an inevitable tendency of the future. The fact of the past is that administration has been conceived instrumentally, neutrally. The widespread phenomenon of the present is that this instrumental interpretation is being widely challenged; that is, questions such as I pose are being asked, discussed, and decided throughout a wide spectrum of contemporary administration. The inevitable tendency of the future is that the administrative subculture will continue to grow in size and importance.[7] As it embraces, or at least affects, more and more of life, it will embrace more and more of values, and more and more decisions on values. I return here to the phrase and proposal of the anthropologist: cultural design and development. Inevitably, as the questions are put and answered, we shall be doing just this. It can be done with more skill and wisdom if we are conscious of what we are doing— always presuming that we have some control of our destiny.

Let us turn briefly now to another theme: the relationship between the administrative subculture and the literary subculture. This may be approached best, perhaps, by reference to Sir Charles P. Snow's widely discussed book of 1959, *The Two Cultures and the Scientific Revolution.* Sir Charles' concern was the disadvantages and dangers

[7] "Inevitable" is both dogmatic and doubtful in human affairs. Two factors that may affect and even reverse trends that are now prominent may be noted. (1) We simply do not know, at this point, the long-range effect of the "computer revolution" on the organizational-administrative world of the future. To the extent that our problem becomes consuming what can be produced rather than producing what we need, will this "loosen" the grasp and reduce the number of organizations? (2) It is at least theoretically possible for us to decide to "deorganize" our culture, decide that we prefer more "nonorganization values" and act accordingly. Here I am thinking of returning to a more primitive state. Below I suggest the possibility of achieving deorganization, if we wish it, by the paradoxical route of greater complexity better understood and controlled.

arising from a growing breach between the older humanist culture and the newer scientific-technological culture. As is Sir Charles, I am concerned with a breach between two cultures, and there are certainly similarities (but also some differences) in the breaches and in the perils observed.

By literary subculture I mean, in terms of persons, those who write and read "serious" literature, and in terms of ideas, attitudes, and skills, those of such people. While my reference is primarily to such persons and their attributes, I mean to refer secondarily to a larger subculture (or related subcultures) to which *littérateurs* more or less belong and of which they can for present purposes be taken as representative and symbol. I refer to those suggested by the terms artist and humanist.

For many years I have made something of a hobby of reading novels set in organizations or in some fashion treating themes of organization and administration. While I began with the presumption one could by this entertaining route learn much about our professional concerns, I became increasingly impressed with the fact that the man of letters (more broadly, artist and humanist) characteristically is ignorant of and/or hostile toward the administrative subculture. The terms estrangement and alienation are relevant to the phenomenon to which I refer, at least if we regard our culture as a whole as having a dominant organizational-administrative tone. This estrangement or alienation is an obvious fact of the contemporary world, but one which does not appear to be widely appreciated for all that.

A discussion of what is involved and implied is the subject of another essay, but a few observations may be offered in the present connection. The estrangement between the administrative and the literary subcultures is a matter of prime importance, whatever one's values and whatever his hopes for the future. The fact that it *exists* is relevant to all values and all hopes. There are, of course, various hypotheses of and arguments among the anthropologists that bear on the subject. I refer to such matters as whether a culture must in some sense be integrated, a whole; the relationship between changes in ideas or symbols and changes in things; how change in a subculture affects change in other subcultures. The hypotheses bearing on such matters strike me as useful in thinking about all relationships between the administrative subculture and the whole and the other parts. They sensitize to trends and problems, they help pose relevant questions, they put us onto the search for facts and force us to examine our values. But—it must be confessed—they stop far short of giving us answers.

It is unrealistic to hope that the contemporary culture of any large country can be integrated in the sense and fashion this can be true of an isolated traditional society, and most of us would regard it as undesirable even if it could be achieved. On the other hand, there would be considerable agreement that deep division, estrangement, and hostility between subcultures is dangerous and presents serious problems. Perhaps the optimum situation is enough divergence to generate creative tension but not so much as to produce chaos or destructive hostility.

The present breach between the administrative and the literary subcultures needs attention in these terms, for there is too little creative tension, too much bootless or destructive hostility. The man of letters strikes me as often ignorant and confused. He is hostile or unhappy, and he strikes out against the administrative culture or subculture that seems to him to create, or represent, the shabby, nasty, dangerous world he sees. But his knowledge of the real world (as it is judged by the social scientist or the man of affairs) is so shallow and partial his reactions are often but childish temper fits. What he really wants, it would seem, is an unreal world which has all the essentials of modernity (a well-stocked deep-freeze in his country home in Connecticut or the Big Sur) without the irritations of bureaucracy and the rat-race of contemporary affairs.

On the other hand, who among us does not find bureaucracy irritating and does not wish the rat-race were less of a race (and had fewer rats in it, of course)? Is it possible that we have not listened as attentively and sympathetically as we should to what the man of letters has been saying—and because we have not listened, have encouraged him to be ever more shrilly hostile, ignorant, and alienated? Does not the *littérateur* have at least an important part of the truth about our administrative culture? One might hope for more knowledge, sensitivity, and sympathy on both sides, more complementary action toward clarified and not too disparate goals. In any event, the fact that the man of letters is estranged from our subculture is an important fact, if only because the writer has readers. To be oblivious of this is to invite unreality and irrationality into our calculations, to risk that our judgments will be futile or dangerous.

ON THE IDEA OF A PUBLIC ADMINISTRATION SUBCULTURE

If we attempt to view public administration as a subculture, what distinguishes it? This is a question that must embarrass us because we are so ill-prepared to answer it. It is not universally taken to be a pertinent and important question. But for my part, I regard well-buttressed ideas affirming the position that public administration is a distinctive subculture as highly desirable, indeed essential if public administration is to continue long as a defining and orienting term.[8]

The reasons why we are ill-prepared to speak to the "publicness" of public administration are several. Public administration as a self-conscious point of view was born with the assertion (by Wilson and others) that there is an important and growing aspect of government submerged in and neglected by historic political science; it was sheltered in its early years by the politics-administration dichotomy, by the notion that policy execution is or can be made a science, and for that reason deserves setting aside for special treatment. Though thus sheltered from political science, techniques and ideas from other areas, especially from scientific management and later and more generally from business administration, were welcomed if presumed to contribute to the chosen instrumentalist role.

For now nearly a generation, the politics-administration dichotomy has been in disrepute; it is widely, if not in fact universally, acknowledged that much policy is made in or by public administration, and indeed there is an acute and sophisticated literature bearing on the subject. However, the momentum of instrumentalism has been great enough to carry us in many sectors up to the present. What is more important, the instrumentalist outlook and mood has been reinforced or replaced by new factors. Some of these may be regarded as products of scientific management, now vanished as a distinctive movement under this name, but carrying forward in manifold ways under many names. Some are products of the mood and movement known as behavioralism. One important factor relates to and springs from both. This is the belief that all organizations are essentially alike in their "organizationness," and that hence the really important scientific task is to search for the basic laws governing all organizational behavior.

The point of these observations is not that the efficiency of instruments is irrelevant or that the pursuit of a general theory of organization is meaningless, but that much in our history has operated to take our attention off the adjective "public" and to focus it intently upon the noun "administration." Thus, ironically, what began as a strategic stance to gain autonomy threatens now to make us in an important sense irrelevant and obsolete. For if "public" is only a formal legal

[8] The point of view developed in this section has recently been expressed also in an essay written for the twenty-fifth anniversary number of *Public Administration Review* (March 1965). In some respects, the viewpoint here expressed is more fully developed in that essay, *"The Administrative State Revisited,"* particularly with respect to political science and business administration.

category and is descriptively, operationally, scientifically, and philosophically meaningless, then schools and curricula of public administration may well flourish because government will continue to grow as a big industry, but they will be but pragmatic adjustments to a market and lacking a defining, orienting disciplinary core.

I propose a serious effort to give meaning to our adjective *public*. Our starting point should be the affirmation with which Paul Appleby began his first book: "Government is different," taken as an hypothesis to be tested. Without abandoning the search for "commonalities" and while continuing to recognize the continuities within the culture which as a whole may be regarded as an administrative culture, we need now to seek for and become knowledgeable about the differentiating features of *public* administration.

On the one hand, I do not know how it is possible to have much experience with government and business enterprises without concluding that these are different in very important respects, not simply in superficials.[9] On the other hand, I presume that the differences range along a scale, or scales, not only with no sharp discontinuity, but perhaps with some bunching at the mean: that, say, the Department of State and a furniture manufacturing enterprise display great and important differences, but that the TVA and a large utility empire do indeed have much in common.

There is need for a program of inquiry in depth and breadth into the significance of "publicness," a program including both empirical research and theoretical-philosophical analysis, and embracing public administration in all senses. Our ignorance of some things we should know something about is startling. In *Politics, Economics and Welfare,* Robert Dahl and Charles Lindblom did do some suggestive "scaling" along the lines indicated in the preceding paragraph, but to my knowledge no one has tried to extend and refine this beginning. Most important, there has been no empirical research to guide and give content to such an attempt. It would be of general scientific value to have more data and hypotheses bearing on such matters as these: What, in terms of social, economic, and educational factors, and especially in terms of personality and value orientation, differentiates members of public organizations from members of private organizations? (As indicated above, "public" and "private" are only gross categories, and much attention indeed would have to be given to the relevance and significance of comparisons.) What, when closely ex-

---

[9] One interesting exercise in this connection is to examine the very different interpretation of the case method as applied in public administration and business administration.

amined in terms of actual operations, is the weight and significance of the old distinction of profit orientation? What differences exist in the decision-making processes in the level at which, the manner in which, and the values in terms of which, decisions are made? What, if anything, distinguishes the two spheres in their implementation (or negation) of the dominant values of the culture? What values? Through what mechanisms? It is my judgment that questions such as these are as important as any matters to which we could be addressing ourselves at this time.

In trying to assess our position and potential as public administration subculture, it will be useful to consider carefully what has been set forth in two (often closely related) sectors of recent political science. One is the proposal to think (research, act) in terms of *political* culture(s). This is a stance to which my own in this essay is roughly comparable. Undertanding for political science as a whole, and especially for the "political" part thereof, is advanced by taking the anthropological (or anthropological-sociological) perspective, that light is thus thrown upon institutions and the smaller units of conceptualization and analysis—the role, for example—by viewing them in their environing and conditioning contexts of political culture. The other is the proposal to think of political systems as *systems*, that is, to import or employ more or less of the language and concepts of general systems theory, conceiving of political systems as having boundaries, inputs and outputs. With this approach what I propose in this essay has formal similarities: cultures can be (and are) conceived more or less as systems, and subcultures thus can be conceived more or less as the subsystems on the nature and interrelations of which systems analysis concentrates.

We would be negligent not to scrutinize carefully the theory and data set forth in connection with these two developments in political science for what light they may shed upon an attempt to view public administration as a subculture, and indeed upon the enterprise of public administration even if the cultural approach be thought to be wrongheaded and unrewarding. However, it is necessary to guard against an undue and untrue subordination of the "administrative" in both cases, a possibility arising from the understandable interests and values with which their proponents begin. An analysis which places political culture first will have a built-in bias similar to that which, in a purely formal sense at least, characterizes this essay, which invites especial attention to our administrative culture. In the case of those conceptualizations of the political system that have come to my attention, there is a disposition to identify administration too simply and wholly with the output side of the analysis, in a manner reminiscent of our politics-administration past. In fact, one cannot regard these "models," no matter their fashionableness and sophistication, without being uncomfortably reminded of our outworn simplicities. Albeit, we can learn something from both approaches.

ON PUBLIC ADMINISTRATION IN AN ADMINISTRATIVE CULTURE

As indicated above, this essay owes a certain debt to Paul Appleby. It reflects his concern that academic public administration has a fractured nature, possessing many parts but no whole that is readily recognized and agreed upon. Sharing his concern, I have tried to imagine what might give the teaching and practice of public administration a unity, coherence, and emphasis[10] it now lacks: in the commonsense meaning of the term, a philosophy. This led me to some thoughts combining administration and the cultural perspective. I do not imagine, of course, that this is the only approach to the achievement of clearer focus, and it may not prove to be the best: systems theory, for example, needs close attention in this connection. But let me conclude by trying to draw some of the threads together, to make what has been said or suggested as relevant as possible to our central disciplinary or professional concern with definition.

Part of our difficulty may stem from definitions of public administration that are too narrow. The classic statement is, of course, that public administration is the management of men and materials in the service of the State. There have been many variations on the theme, but the theme has remained essentially the same. Ironically, we have long since taken doctrinal positions (embracing or at least asserting the pervasiveness and importance of policy and politics) that are far from our neutral, instrumentalist beginnings, but we have not "redefined" public administration to make it consonant with what the new doctrinal positions assert. We need to think less in terms of what public administration *is* in a system of government, more in terms of what it *does* in and for our culture (or society, country, etc., in other idioms and conceptualizations). Our public administration subculture has an important guiding as well as instrumental role in a total administrative culture, and an important advance in understanding is made in recognizing that it does and then seeking to understand what is implied and entailed.

The disadvantages of taking the total frame of culture and the heroic notion of "cultural design and development" for disciplinary-

---

[10] To invoke the trinity beloved of my English composition teacher.

professional orientation may lie in their breadth and sweep. The danger is that in seeking a broader context in which to site ourselves we may select one so broad we wander about unable to site ourselves in it. It may be argued, however, that in an administrative culture there is nothing that is not somehow relevant to the concerns of public administration, given what democratic governments are now asked to do, not what they may be asked to do in the future. Surely it must be acknowledged that a formal virtue of the orientation to culture is that nothing is thereby excluded on grounds of irrelevancy.

What "purchase" on problems might be gained by thinking culturally, using this phrase as a shorthand designation for what is said and implied above? I am bold to believe that thinking culturally gives us considerable help with troublesome problems of educational philosophy and the more immediate problems of curriculum construction. To emphasize what was said above, everyone should study administration; for if ours is an administrative culture, then everyone in a democratic society should be acculturated, should have equal opportunity to learn the rules of the game. In a conclusion to an essay the details of pedagogy—at what levels, using what teaching methods, and so forth—can conveniently be put aside. But the guiding line is this: The point and aim of this universal teaching of administration is not how to administer (though some will later be learning advanced techniques) but the why and what of administration. We need quite new instructional materials putting flesh onto—and breathing life into—the frame sketched above.

Thinking culturally should help us bridge some of the chasms, repair some of the schisms, between parts of the curriculum and between philosophies of education now divided and often hostile: between theory and practice, between specialist and generalist, between the humanities, the social sciences, and the biophysical sciences. In this connection two things come to mind. One is Sir Eric Ashby's excellent *Technology and the Academics: An Essay on Universities and the Scientific Revolution.*[11] In this Sir Eric develops the thesis that technology can be "humanized"; indeed, that it must be if we are to survive in an age which demands more and more specialization while needing more and more of what humanism has historically supplied. "Specialist studies," he argues, must become the "vehicle for a liberal education"; technology must "become the cement between science and humanism."[12] I add my own view: (1) All technologists should

---

[11] London: Macmillan Co., 1958.
[12] "What is needed is nothing less than a revision of the idea of a liberal educa-

learn about their—our—administrative culture, and (2) the administrator (public or other) is a special kind of technologist whose knowledge, attitudes, and skills must be made appropriate to his special role.

The other matter to which my thoughts run is the "crisis" to which Victor Thompson and Robert Presthus have recently addressed themselves: the conflict in our administrative culture between knowledge and authority, between the information necessary for decision-making and the formal location of the right to make decisions. I judge this to be closely related to Sir Eric's problem, for the three of them seem to be speaking of the same matter from somewhat different approaches. It is my view that more knowledge and differently structured and presented knowledge, which has become the common property of all parties to these divisions and dichotomies, is relevant to them: that more commonality in the "definition of the situation," more widely known and shared information, attitudes and skills relating to an enterprise recognized as shared, has relevance to the solution of problems.

The starting point and guiding impulse for this essay were certain central and recurring concerns of Paul Appleby: the role and function of public administration in a society committed to democracy, the implications of the plain, important fact that much policy is made in and by public administration; the problems involved in insuring that administrators are representative and responsive—these and others in addition to his concern for a unifying "something" in education for administrative careers. Thinking culturally does not of course give me ready solutions to such problems. It does put them into a common perspective, shed new light on them, suggest approaches to answers not before thought of.

My plea that we view our culture as an administrative culture is not to be construed as a plea for an *administered* culture, the complete bureaucratization of life, the erection of the complete and final anthill. On the contrary, I share with many with whom I otherwise seriously differ a grave concern for the enormous "disutilities" of our administrative culture, in terms of dehumanization, alienation, and so forth; in fact, I think we are already into a period of crisis, which will

tion. . . . The technologist is up to his neck in human problems whether he likes it or not. . . . The social consequences of his work are therefore an integral part of his profession. . . . The habit of apprehending a technology in all its completeness: this is the essence of technological humanism, and this is what we should expect education in higher technology to achieve. . . . A student who cannot weave his technology into the fabric of a society cannot claim even to be a good technologist." Quotations from pp. 81-82.

compel serious reassessment of some of our social processes and institutional arrangements. But too often, it seems to me, the reaction (right, left or center) is essentially ludditist: high in emotion and low in social knowledge and skill, ignorant and confused, dishonest and misleading in suggesting that in some simple fashion we can have our cake and eat it, that we can return to the "simple life" but retain the high standard of living which is the product of present scientific-technological-administrative skills.

In my view, the way forward is forward. I propose that we accept the fact that we have an administrative culture and use that culture to get as much as possible of the goods of life. To me it is not contradictory to urge that we use our administrative culture to make that culture more humane and less costly in important human values now ruthlessly attacked or shamefully wasted. In fact, an administrative culture is one eminently adapted to remaking culture. We may well decide we want, and find ways to achieve, much less organizationness, less bureaucracy, than we now have; but I see no way to achieve this end (as against a condition of chaos)[13] but by the route of greater administrative knowledge, skill, and participation (in the senses indicated above) in the administrative culture.

---

[13] I am reminded of Appleby's position that power, authority, and functions cannot be *de*centralized until they have first been centralized and that otherwise what one is talking about is some condition of feudalism, confusion, or chaos.

· 4 ·

Business as Government

EMMETTE S. REDFORD

Paul Appleby announced in his first book his belief that "the dissimilarity between government and all other forms of social action is
greater than any dissimilarity among those other forms themselves."
Government was "different." The key to the difference was the "government attitude"—the sense of "public responsibility" which derived
from government existing for "the function of promoting and protecting the public interest." "The governmental function and attitude"
differentiated government in three ways: "the breadth of scope, impact and consideration"; "public accountability"—"the way in which
it is subject to public scrutiny and public outcry"; "political character"—"Government is different because government is politics."[1] He
added later, in *Policy and Administration,* that "an official, an action,
a function or an agency of government is viewed as 'more political' or
'less political' according to degree of involvement in the various processes characteristic of government, degree of subjection to popular
control through elected officials and representatives, and degree of
exposure to citizens." "More political" connoted "democratic virtue
and responsibility," for it meant controls "by and on behalf of the
whole public."[2]

Since Appleby wrote these things, other observers of the contemporary scene have commented on the governmental character of
business. Norton Long, for example, has told us that "organizations are
governments" and that organizations infused with values to preserve
"are in effect embryonic polities."[3] I am lured, therefore, by my topic
to an exercise in comparative politics and administration. In what sense

[1] Paul H. Appleby, *Big Democracy* (New York: Alfred A. Knopf, 1945), pp. 1-
10.

[2] *Policy and Administration* (University, Alabama: University of Alabama Press,
1949), pp. 26-27.

[3] Norton E. Long, "The Administrative Organization as a Political System," in
Sidney Mailick and Edward H. Van Ness, *Concepts and Issues in Administrative
Behavior* (Englewood Cliffs, N. J.: Prentice-Hall, 1962), pp. 110, 120.

is business government? And is business government similar to public government?

GOVERNMENTAL QUALITIES OF BUSINESS

On the plane of management the similarity between business and government, particularly large business and large government, is apparent. Whether one looks at accounting, personnel management, supply management, or organizational arrangements, he will see much similarity in methods and problems. Commentators have often referred to this as use of business methods in government. Although this kind of reference sometimes contains some nonsense—that good methods are best described as business methods and that good governmental methods cannot be different from good business methods, it is nevertheless true that government has found lessons for its practice from business experience. It is also true that when government undertakes a banking or commercial function (lending money, selling electric power, etc.), it takes on some attributes of business. I am not interested here in these well-trodden fields of discussion, but in the converse and neglected question: How does business take on the quality of government?

There are three ways business reflects functions and operations characteristic of government. All of these have been recognized in the literature of law, economics, and political science; hence, all that is new in this portion of the discussion is presentation of the correlative effects of three social trends.

The first is where business organizations have become agencies of administration for government. There comes to mind promptly the Defense Department contract, the channeling of 90 per cent of the Atomic Energy Commission's funds to private companies, and the flow of money for research and development to business corporations, as well as to educational institutions and specially created organizations like RAND and the Aerospace Corporation. Don Price has asked us to think of this as cooperative government-business federalism comparable to federal-state federalism.[4] It is again federalism on the administrative level, with money as the link that unites the partners. It is, like federal-state relations, a system of delegation of functions with reserved controls. Either system of federalism can be, it may be added, more than a system of administrative delegation. In federal-state cooperation the federal government may be facilitating programs already in operation at the state level, as for example, in

4 Don K. Price, "The Scientific Establishment," *Proceedings of the American Philosophical Society*, Vol. 106 (June 1962), pp. 235-45.

education. Similarly, in government-business federalism government may be assuming a partnership in execution of business purpose, as when the Atomic Energy Commission assists in nuclear power development for industrial use and private sale. Nevertheless, the dominant characteristic of the cooperative federalism embodied in the public-private contract is not the coopting of government for business purpose but the coopting of business to serve as administrative agent of government.

It may be suggested that public administration through private contractors is old and familiar—characteristic of government when street paving and utility construction were among government's largest functions. There are, however, differences in magnitude and in characteristics between the old and the new. A very large segment of the national economy is now bound to government in an agency relationship. And the features of the new—cost-plus as a formula of payment, joint planning of development projects, frequent replanning and revision of production or research plans, security checks of employees, government aid on privately initiated projects, bookkeeping and reporting requirements—create a more complex and hand-in-glove relationship than characterized the city-specifications, contract-letting, checking-for-conformity-with-specifications sequence of street and utility construction.

The consequences of this agency position for business are enormous. Much of American business is dependent upon a single customer. Although particular companies may seek to diminish the effects of this dependence by diversification and by balance between public and private markets, the level of economic operations, the well-being of large segments of the economy, and the profit or loss position of many companies is materially determined by scale, timing, and choices of government projects. Moreover, business as administrator becomes subject in new ways to administrative regulation by the state. In part, this is the normal regulation by contractor of contractee. A network of requirements on performance of the contract develops. Some of these are boilerplate, others are variable with the contract but determined in it, others are adjustable in the course of performance. In part, however, the regulation embodies purposes of the state extraneous to the purpose of the contract. Labor provisions, buy-American requirements, security clearance of employees, and ethical standards (e.g., against contingency fees or against gratuities in the form of entertainment or gifts) may be incorporated into the contract.[5] Although

[5] See Arthur S. Miller, "Administration by Contract: A New Concern for the

the social purposes of government with respect to such matters as minimum wages and nondiscrimination in employment are now being imposed on business generally, the contracts often contain additional requirements, or special sanctions for requirements imposed on business generally.

The broader consequence is that old ideas about business cease to be descriptive of realities. The nature of business risk changes from dependence on an open market to chance of contracts with government. Profit becomes, not a reward for risk in the market, but a fee for administrative service in the public interest. Bargaining with government and subjection to its controls take the place of the arbitrament of the market on matters of production and price; the arrangements for business become administered arrangements. Business corporations under contract become arms of government, supplying quasi-public executives for the performance of public functions. The great public need for their availability and for their efficient and responsible performance of public functions affects them with a public interest. The basic premise of business philosophy—that business is private—must yield to a new concept of the quasi-public character of that business which is agent of government.

Beyond these effects upon the quality of business itself are sociopolitical consequences of great significance. Because government needs large-scale enterprise for nuclear, missile, and other projects, and because it is easier for government to deal with one than with many companies, contracts go usually to the large firms. This effect can be only moderately checked by laws and administrative directives in favor of grants to small companies. In turn, the big corporation gains power over the small ones through subcontracting. Hence, not only is business incorporated into government, but business is further centralized.

In addition, the contract system produces a merger of concentrated business power and concentrated government power. It was this merger of power which led President Eisenhower to warn in his last State of the Union message of the dangers of an industrial-military complex. Some observers will see in the unity of interest between business and government a disappearance of the balances between public and private power which have existed in the past. They will see a danger of the undermining of the assumption that society is protected by the coexistence of competing public and private systems. Others

Administrative Lawyer," *New York University Law Review*, Vol. 36 (May, 1961), pp. 957-90, for these and other features of the contract system.

will note dangers in the politics of contract. They will see a revival of the threat to the independence of government which was presented by contractor strength in city politics. Politics and administration will not here be separated, for new corporate bureaucracies and subgroups, and community-associated interests, will travel the avenue of politics to obtain administrative grants of contracts. For business there is an increased thrust into politics, for government an increased need on the one hand of insulating itself against particularistic politics of those seeking favor and on the other of obtaining the broad support from community (i.e., national) politics which will prevent its becoming subservient to those upon whom it depends for administration of its policies.

The coopting of business into government is reflected in other developments. Some of these are now quite old and traditional. The Federal Reserve System, with its commingling of public and private, and the farm credit system, with mutualized but government-sponsored and supervised institutions, are now a half-century with us. More recently, the achievement of public purposes through private instruments is seen in an elaborate set of insurance and banking institutions for home construction. Administration of agricultural programs through farmer committees is accepted. Comsat is a private corporation with profit in view but with controls in the President and the Federal Communications Commission to ensure that it serves as a public agent. These illustrations suggest the substantial scope of private participation in administration of public programs.

These developments, too, call for revisions in thought patterns. We have traditionally thought of two separate but interacting universes of human endeavor—private and public. But the fact is that if one looks at almost any function performed for people in our society—education, housing, banking, for example—he will see a mixture of public and private initiative, and complementary performances by public and private institutions in what can adequately be described only as a system of mixed public-private enterprise. There are constraints which force private organizations to work within a public framework and which sometimes produce a real coopting of the private organizations into a system of public administration.

While operating as administrative agent of government, business reflects the quality of government in a second way. Business—the corporate system—is now itself a system of power. Imperfect competition, oligopoly, market power, administered prices, cost-plus inflation are concepts which register the breakdown of the assumptions of automatic control by market forces and the parallel recognition that business is a system of power. The power is limited by countervailing powers in labor, business, and government, but it is nevertheless immense. It is aggregated in "concentrates," as Adolf Berle has stated it;[6] in addition, the concentrates are frequently interlocked, and they all share the attitudes and interests and contribute to the influence of the corporate community.

The corporate power is revealed in many ways. On the supply side it is revealed in the ability of corporations to retain savings and determine the rate of investment, and their ability to determine the rate of use of facilities and to achieve a profit margin on unused facilities; on the demand side by the ability, with "Madison Avenue" techniques, to influence consumer choice and to determine the socially accepted rate of obsolescence. It is revealed in the pattern-setting price movement of industry leaders and the pattern-setting wage bargain between industry and labor leaders. It is amplified by the distributive effects of price movements in some key industries, such as steel.

There has now arisen, also, the idea of the metrocorporation—the corporation whose purposes are multiple, extending beyond the making of profit to the maintenance of a welfare system for its members, support for education and culture, and concern for political affairs. The metrocorporation adds a second feature to business as a system of power. In addition to controlling the market for profit the business system is a distributor of social income and a guardian of the political health of the nation. It shares the functions of the state, indeed may rival it as a welfare institution, and aims toward a "desired" balance between public and private services.

There is conflicting opinion about the metrocorporation. Some—for example, Hayek—say that the corporation should stick with its function of making profit for its owners and stay out of the welfare field.[7] Some others are fearful of corporate influence on education or on politics. But the metrocorporation, condemned by some, is defended by others, and more significant, it is already with us. The corporations are welfare as well as profit institutions.

Whether the corporation performs traditional or new roles, the large ones are centers of power. The economy is managed by men, as well as influenced by the market; the economic system can best

6 Adolf A. Berle, Jr., *The 20th Century Capitalist Revolution* (New York: Harcourt, Brace, 1954), p. 26.

7 See Friedrich A. Hayek, "The Corporation in a Democratic Society," in Melvin Anshen and George Leland Bach, *Management and Corporations, 1985* (New York, Toronto, and London: McGraw-Hill, 1960), pp. 99-117.

be described as a system of power relationships. It is a political (i.e., power) system as well as an economic system. It matters not that the structure allows for some conflict and competition, and is not monolithic; these too are qualities of other pluralistic systems of government, and an overall view of the pluralism of power in the economy and in government indicates the probability of a larger amount of concentration and unity in the former than in the latter. I conclude that to the extent that the market can be managed by business leadership, it is inappropriate to talk of business in private or purely economic terms. It becomes a system of power, takes on a quasi-public character, and must in the course of time face the same issues of public responsiveness that began to be faced four hundred years ago in the modern state. The size, pervasiveness, and public character of the corporation make its responsibility, that is, its political responsiveness, a matter of public concern.

While, however, the economy is internally politicized by the substitution of managerial power for the impersonal controls of the market, it is further politicized in the decision-making process. While substantively a system of power it is also procedurally political, and this is the third way in which business is government.[8] Business organizations are operating coalitions of groups of people—stockholders, bondholders, executives, white-collar bureaucracies, blue-collar laborers. The objectives of these several groups are often in conflict. Moreover, the business organization operates within a matrix of associated and conflicting organizations to which it must adjust or from which it will expect adjustment. The decision-making process in such a setting of cooperation and conflict is not merely one of rational calculation of response to market factors; it is, in addition, a process of adjustment of group interests.

These things are reflected in the position of the corporate executive. He was, according to traditional organization theory, in a command position, and according to traditional economic theory, in a position to make decisions toward the single objective of maximizing profits. In fact, as an administrator he is a broker compromising—and hence yielding to—groups within his firm, and as an entrepreneur he reconciles the goal of profit maximization with the objectives of groups within the organization. He is more broker than commander or economist. He is, however, agent as well as broker. As presumed head of the enterprise he must bargain with a conflicting labor power, in

---

[8] The discussion on this point parallels that in my *American Government and the Economy* (New York: Macmillan, 1965), pp. 28-30.

one sense within, in another sense outside the firm. He must represent the enterprise in a multitude of bargaining relations with independent or semi-independent bankers, suppliers, affiliates, even with governments which award contracts, or regulate prices, or move in other ways.

The organization executive—either corporate or union—acts, therefore, in two capacities: as agent for groups and as broker among groups. His conduct is determined by a context of men and organizations perhaps more than by that of a market. His role can be described in words drawn from the realm of government and politics—representation and bargaining, compromise, and command. Kenneth E. Boulding has noted this change from economic entrepreneur to organization man:

> One can almost describe the history of the present era as a continuous encroachment of politics on economics. We mean here by "politics" the conscious organization and planning through the instruments of authority and subordination, private and public; by "economics" the conscious and automatic coordination of human activity through the market and the price-profit mechanism.[9]

Boulding, however, overstates the role of "authority and subordination," in contrast to representation and bargaining which he emphasizes elsewhere in the same discussion. The significant point is that administration and politics in business follow sociopolitical processes similar to those in government.

RESPONSIBILITY OF BUSINESS AND OF PUBLIC GOVERNMENT

Although business is an administrative agent of government, is itself a system of power, and operates by political processes, is it for all that like government? I think that to answer this question we must turn, as Appleby did, to questions of responsibility.

We can begin by reference to the organic law of two bureaucratic systems—the administrative law and the corporate law, terms used comprehensively to include, respectively, all the law which controls public agencies and all the law which regulates corporate action. Administrative law is the law controlling the departments and their bureaus, commissions (or boards), and government corporations (or authorities). It is built in constitutions, statutes, judicial decisions,

⁹ Kenneth E. Boulding, *The Organizational Revolution* (New York: Harper, 1953), p. 49.

and the common law (i.e., common practice) of agencies. It is most highly developed for functions which are called quasi-legislative and quasi-judicial, but also establishes standards and limitations for other types of function. When business becomes administrative agent of government and supplies a fourth instrument of administration (alternative to bureaus, commissions, and corporations) it is directed and confined to a certain extent by the administrative law. The administrative law is embodied in contract terms and conditions and in rules and standards applicable to the contractual relationship, and the new problems created by this relationship are now receiving increased attention from students of administrative law.

Business in general, however, operates under the corporate law, called by one author "the public law of American capitalism."[10] This law is less directive than administrative law, the latter defining purposes and methods which administrative organizations must pursue. It is, first, enabling, for the corporation gets its existence and its authorization to do business from the state, and may—if in a regulated business—have to return frequently for extension or redefinition of authorizations. It is, second, restrictive, and the restrictive law today extends diversely to such matters as fiduciary relationships, security issues and transactions, restraint of trade, health and safety regulations, product standards, advertising and marketing practices, and many other matters. Since corporate law is essentially enabling and restrictive, rather than directive, it may leave more discretion to economic than to public bureaucracies. And in this country the substance of corporate law has left much to private decision: except for foods and drugs, product standards are generally undefined by law; with exceptions, price is determined by private decision; and law leaves more to be determined by collective bargaining than in most countries. These and other areas of "liberty" for the corporate and union executives are outside the corporate law and within the area of discretion. Where, then, we are subject to a government of men rather than to a government of law, or to effective market controls, how does business responsibility compare with public responsibility?

Adolf Berle has said that the legal controls over self-perpetuating corporate oligarchies are so limited that "the only real control which guides or limits their economic or social action is the real, though undefined and tacit, philosophy of the men who compose them." He concludes that "the corporation, almost against its will, has been

[10] Eugene V. Rostow, *Planning for Freedom: The Public Law of American Capitalism* (New York and London: Yale University Press, 1959).

72   EMMETTE S. REDFORD

compelled to assume in appreciable part the role of conscience-carrier of twentieth-century American society."[11] David Lilienthal believes the conscience is good. There is, he says, "a new kind of 'top boss' of large business undertakings. He is a man with a strong and practical sense of responsibility to the public, and an awareness of the ethics of present-day competition."[12] Yet Michael Reagan quotes industrial leaders' statements that the standard of judgment in corporate decisions will be institutional survival and good health of the corporation.[13] This is a different kind of motivation from either profit-making or social benefit; although it may allow some measure of consideration of public benefit, it is basically a new standard of enlightened corporate self-interest. Under this standard, the claim for corporate conscience is in effect a claim that what is good for the corporation is good for the United States. However, judgments on what is good for the corporation will be made by men who, because of the organizational positions they occupy, are under constraints from and may have opportunities to promote certain specialized intracorporational interests, such as those of the stockholder and the executives.

What men hold the power and thus become the conscience-bearers of the corporation? They are men who theoretically are responsible to stockholders. But corporate brochures now often boast that all members of the board of directors are officers of the corporation (the apex of the corporate bureaucracy), and the stockholder control over these officers elevated into directors is virtually nonexistent. Paul Harbrecht has called this a "paraproprietal society"—that is, one that has passed from "a property system to a power system."[14]

Some restoration of stockholder control over investment could be restored by bold changes in public policies, for example, heavy taxation of undistributed profits and prevention of postponement of profits by requirement of straight-line depreciation in federal income tax reg-

---

[11] Berle, op. cit., pp. 180, 182.
[12] David E. Lilienthal, Big Business: A New Era (New York: Harper, 1952), p. 27.
[13] Michael D. Reagan, The Managed Society (New York: Oxford University Press, 1963), Chap. 7. See also on corporate conscience Ben W. Lewis, "Economics by Admonition," The American Economic Review, Vol. 49 (May 1959), pp. 384-98.
[14] See Paul P. Harbrecht, Pension Funds and Economic Power (New York: Century Fund, 1959). And also Adolf A. Berle, Power without Property: A New Development in American Political Economy (New York: Harcourt, Brace, 1959), and the Berle-Harbrecht pamphlet, The Paraproprietal Society (New York: Twentieth Century Fund, 1959).

ulations. Yet even if these were deemed wise public policies, they are unlikely to appeal to stockholders. Moreover, mere return of corporate investment policy to the investment markets would not create stockholder control over the full scope of corporate policy. Any effort to solve the problem of corporate responsibility by stockholder control of corporate bureaucracy would almost certainly be proven impractical. It would, in addition, be a quite undemocratic solution to the problem of corporate power.

This means that the issue of corporate conscience is one of conscience of corporate management. The conscience of this group is more complex than is recognized in most discussions of the topic. Chester Barnard—whose executive experience in business makes him a credible commentator—has shown that the corporate manager is affected by "numerous systems or codes or attitudes of morality" created within organizations.[15] His loyalties and responsibilities are of various types. There is personal responsibility—that is, the character of the individual, including his "avoidance of criminal acts, gross and public immoralities and in particular stealing and lying; a willingness to recognize the interests of others to the extent of ordinary courtesy; and, finally, a willingness to discharge commitments, that is, to perform duties accepted, to honor promises." There are representative or official responsibility (that is, on behalf of others), organizational loyalties (to "an entity—an organization"); technical and technological responsibility (that is, to high standards of performance, particularly of technical work); legal responsibility (that is, to statutes, court decisions, and regulatory rules); and other types of responsibility.

One thing is missing from Barnard's statement of the businessman's responsibility. A loyalty not listed is one to the public interest. The question presented is not whether this should be a loyalty of the corporate manager in his corporate decisions, but whether it can be. Can corporate management take on community goals and thereby legitimize its position? The community goals which are significant are, of course, macroeconomic goals, such as economic growth, economic stability, and shared welfare. One question is whether the corporation staff will include experts whose function is to focus attention on such purposes and the means of converting them into specific courses of action. The main question, however, is whether corporate managers,

---

[15] Chester I. Barnard, "Elementary Conditions of Business Morals," *California Management Review*, Vol. 1 (Fall 1958), pp. 1-13.

although they may share the goals, are constrained by the organizational positions they occupy to place such objectives above other interests represented in the group structure of the corporation.

Although conscience, or enlightened self-interest, may have moved us far from the robber baron period of corporate and individual aggrandizement, many commentators regard both as slender bulwarks for responsibility for possessors of market power and allocators of social income. Economists either regard public conscience as pollution of purpose of corporate organizations (diverting them from efficient pursuit of profit) or deny that it can prevail over private ends in such organizations. Historians know that the accountability of public officeholders came not by the benevolence of feudal chieftains or national monarchs but by the constitutionalization of power. Paul Appleby, student of morality,[16] knew that values men serve are the crucial element in responsibility, but he also knew that these values are not born in men or the result of good spirit only, but are created by the organizational positions they occupy. Sociologists describe this by reference to the roles men play because of their positions. It is from such perspectives, I think, that dependence upon conscience has yielded to discussion of a corporate constitution.[17]

The idea of a corporate constitution is a fruitful one and need not be as vague as it is in the current discussions of it. Political scientists know that it takes many components—of which the documentary constitution is only one—to form an operating constitution. They talk of judicial interpretations of the document, basic statutory elaborations of structure and policy, and custom and party practice as parts of the operating constitution. Or they describe the political constitution in terms of the formal and informal sharing of power among institutions and groups. The components of a comparable corporate constitution are discernible. Corporate law, internal bureaucratization of corporations, countervailing powers, bilateralism in labor determinations, governmental policy decisions, and investor and customer reactions are components comparable, to a quite considerable degree, to documentary constitutions, specialization of functions, checks and balances, and public opinion in the public constitution.

A function of a constitution is to allocate power. The evolving corporate constitution, like our still-evolving public constitution, distributes powers among different decisional (brokerage) and agency

---

[16] Paul H. Appleby, *Morality and Administration in Democratic Government* (Baton Rouge: Louisiana State University Press, 1952).

[17] See the imaginative treatment in Richard Eells, *The Government of Corporations* (New York: Free Press of Glencoe, 1962).

centers. Power is divided among corporate executives, labor representatives, and public authorities, and within corporations among components of corporate management and control. To the extent that this
is true, analysis of the corporate system as one concentrating power
in corporate managers is faulty. Not only the old system of thought
based upon the assumption of automatic controls by impersonal
market forces, but the new system of thought based upon a concentration of power in corporate managers, must yield to a concept of a
corporate constitution producing shared powers.

Nevertheless, the sharing of powers under the corporate constitution does leave a heavy concentration in a limited number of power
centers. Decision-making power in the American economy is highly
concentrated on labor matters in business-labor negotiating centers,
and on investment, product, production, and price in business centers.
The problem of the corporate constitution, perhaps ultimately the
Achilles heel of the claim of corporate independence, is the non-
representativeness of the decision-makers. Power is placed in officials
*who are not representative of all the interests to be served by their
decisions.* These officials—business and labor—make public decisions,
that is, decisions affecting interests of men generally, and yet their
organizational positions make them agents of particular interests.
Hence, the problem of the corporate constitution is a problem of
representative government. Hence also, the present state of the corporate constitution leaves us with the same question as does the claim
for corporate conscience: can we expect men who are coerced by
their organizational positions into roles representative of some interests
to nevertheless represent all interests?

The unrepresentative nature of the decisional authority under the
corporate constitution is further emphasized by the allocation of power
to managers of separate corporations, or of these acting jointly with
labor representatives. Thus a decision on wage increases, made in
negotiations for the automobile industry, may become a pattern for
increases in other industries, or a decision on price in the steel industry
may set off a chain reaction in industry generally. This would be
comparable to delegation in the public system of authority to state
legislatures, or state bureaus, commissions, or departments to determine issues for the nation: such delegations do sometimes exist (for
example, in state regulation of insurance), but politics will retrieve
them if they are exercised with sweeping or controversial results.
"What is good for General Motors" may be good for the nation, but
it could hardly be expected that decisions by General Motors would
be dominated by that consideration.

It is now possible to return to the question of comparable responsibility in business and in public government. Business responsibility accrues from the various codes of morality developed in corporate organizations, from sharing of popular values—including macroeconomic goals—by corporate managers, from the multiple restraints of the corporate constitution, and from the necessity of making the correct decisions in terms of corporate survival and the health of the corporate enterprise. But business responsibility is still different from public responsibility, for reasons stated by Paul Appleby.

First, the function of government, if not unique in nature, is unique in scope. Even if private organizations were democratized, government would still have a differentiated function: "the great task of relating them [private organizations] to each other and to them as a whole in terms of values different from their separate ones would still remain."[18] Government is still the only all-inclusive structure within society—the only structure which has the power to resolve the conflicts which erupt from the substructure of interests and organizations, and to set standards for the society as a whole. In a pluralistic society this is a reserve function, exercised when the arrangements for brokerage of interests within and among groups and their organizations seem to be inadequate. Stated differently, when market forces and the political processes operating within corporate and other structures and between such structures do not produce solutions satisfactory to the dominant political forces in society, the function of government is called into play. In our day government is becoming better equipped for its function through the existence of the Council of Economic Advisers and other staff agencies whose role is to push for recognition of macroeconomic goals. The distinctiveness of government is, as Appleby said, "the breadth of scope, impact and consideration." It is, in short, the ultimate instrument for relating and synthesizing the values of men in solutions for which a claim of accord with the "public interest" can be made.

The difference between business and government rests less, however, in the formal position and power of the latter than in its representativeness, for the effective assertion of power by government must rest ultimately upon the validity of the claim that government is more representative of the nation than anything else is. We are speaking here of government as a whole, not of bureaus or commissions, for it should be recognized that the function resting in corporate managers is top policy-making and hence must be compared with top policymaking in government.

18 *Morality and Administration in Democratic Government,* p. 115.

The second distinction Appleby saw in the position of government was simply that it was more representative than other structures. The values to be represented by government were *"public* values" (Appleby's italics). Public values were attained only through a political process. By "political" Appleby did not mean any of the things heretofore associated with business as government. "Political" is not merely exercise of power, either as agent of government or of power independently possessed; it is not merely political processes—exercise of agency, brokerage, or even leadership functions. It is something representative and democratic in character. For Appleby, it was a product of the total governmental process: "Nothing is so representative of the public as the product of the totality of our political processes." But basically it was popular control: "subjection to popular control through elected officials and representatives, and degree of exposure to citizens."[19]

Appleby recognized that business could, to a degree, take on even this quality of government. He saw "private organizations becoming steadily 'more political'—more concerned with various popular values, more considerate and less arbitrary."[20] This may be regarded as recognition of the claims of corporate conscience, or, contrariwise, as recognition of the multiple restraints of the corporate constitution on corporate management. The latter would mean that the concern for "popular values" was the result of the totality of the influences impinging upon economic behavior, including corporate conscience, roles of agents of groups, and public law and policy. It would not mean, however, that corporate management, or corporate management and union management, could claim the same involvement in a "political process" that characterizes government in a democratic political constitution serving a pluralistic society.

Appleby also was conscious of the fact that the public morality he attributed to government was not always reflected in its practice. The most serious threat, in his view, was that government would not be sufficiently "political." He noted such dangers as overrepresentation of small publics in bureaus, of imbalances in pressures upon government, even of government's "preemption by special-interest publics," and observed that "the power of the government may be too slight in support of the majority public." He knew the dangers of limited exposure of government, and the limitations upon the voter.[21] In

---

[19] *Ibid.,* pp. 2, 173; *Policy and Administration,* p. 26.

[20] *Morality and Administration in Democratic Government,* p. 205.

[21] *Ibid.,* pp. 209, 155, 207; see also Paul H. Appleby, *Citizens as Sovereigns* (Syracuse: Syracuse University Press, 1962), particularly Chap. 6.

other words, the partial representation of interests which we have described as characteristic of the role position of corporate managers might exist also in government's administrative and supreme policy-making structures.

It is relevant to remark, because of implications of this discussion, that in addition to the potential loss of the presumed representativeness of government, there are other hazards in public decision-making for the economy. It may not be sufficiently rational, that is, efficient in the realization of shared values and brokerage of group values. Decision-making can be efficient only it it is based upon correct analysis of the consequences of decisions, and government may not have the expertness or proper organization for analysis, or may be prevented by special pressures from following its dictates. Moreover, it will be efficient only if government can discover and apply means of efficient intervention in the economy—means which are adapted to ends and do not produce unacceptable or undesired side effects. For these reasons, in spite of government's greater representativeness, men may prefer, as Appleby did, a society in which there is an appropriate "moving balance" between public and private action.[22]

There are many in our society who have less faith than Appleby did in the attainability of the "public interest" through democratic political institutions, and there are others who are more concerned than he was with imperfections in the existing political constitution. Yet I think his basic points have validity and fix the limitations upon the concept of "business as government." Expressing, I believe, the same point of view as Appleby, I conclude that business can never be government, nor be like government *in the most significant sense* because neither the traditional corporation, seeking profits, nor the metrocorporation, seeking a social role, nor corporate management, serving as agent for some interests and broker among others, can have the breadth of view ("public interest" perspective) required of government, and because corporate management will not be as representative of and responsive to the total interests served ("democracy") as government under the American political constitution can claim to be.

CONSEQUENCES OF THE COEXISTENCE OF BUSINESS AND PUBLIC GOVERNMENT

The consequences of the coexistence of business and public power and of the differences between the two are great. Paul Appleby thought of the public interest as arising out of public needs. There

---

[22] *Morality and Administration in Democratic Government*, p. 12.

will be a consciousness of public needs to be met in the operations of corporations. The fact that corporations cannot claim the same breadth of perspective and public representativeness as the President and Congress will lead to continued interventions by the latter to satisfy public needs as these are viewed in the political structure. Where business is government's agent, in a measure supplying alternative bureaucracies to public ones, then an expanded administrative law will define public needs (or interests) and seek their realization. For business generally there are two lines of development. One is the expansion and refinement of the corporate law—a process that goes on continuously, as in new statutes, rules of the Securities and Exchange Commission, decisions of the courts on antitrust.

Berle, recognizing that corporate conscience is not enough, concluded: "It may be said of the corporation as old Bracton said of the Crown: 'There is no king where the will and not the law prevails.' "[23] But law will not go the whole route. "Will"—discretion—will remain. The second line of development is discretionary public policy. The Federal Reserve Board and the many other regulatory agencies now possess discretionary powers over corporations. President Theodore Roosevelt assumed power in a coal strike in 1902 and forty-five years later Congress authorized and regularized Presidential interventions when interruptions or threats of interruptions of commerce by labor disputes threatened the public interest. President Kennedy assumed power in face of an announced steel price increase in 1962 and thus showed the nation that the unilateral corporate power over price might, like the bilateral corporate-labor power over worker benefits under the Taft-Hartley Act, be subject some day to regularized policy interventions by government. Public policy interventions on price and worker benefits are now large, and a big issue of the future is whether, or by what methods, the influence of government in these matters will be further extended.

One way to summarize this first consequence is to say that a chief, perhaps *the* chief, element in the corporate constitution will be public law and public policy. Berle's corporate conscience, Galbraith's countervailing powers, Lilienthal's "new competition," will not by themselves ensure responsibility in the economic system and, though they may limit, they cannot prevent the intervention of public law and public policy when large public needs are felt.

The purposes and modes of this intervention can be expected to be quite different from much of the intervention in the past. Prevention of

[23] *The 20th Century Capitalist Revolution,* p. 188.

abuses, although necessary, and specific regulation of price and production, although having a place, will be less significant than the macroeconomic policies designed to ensure employment, economic growth, and income for all the varied interests in the economy. The modes of intervention may be expected to be adjusted to the mixed character of the economy. They will probably expand in various ways the public-private federalism which has developed. Two of the possible lines of development will illustrate the point. The mediatory efforts of government in labor relations and the government's desire to affect policy in key decisions may lead to more positive efforts to influence without controlling decisions *at the bargaining table*—a possibility which has been suggested by some experts. Second, the enlisting of business advice—even the institutionalization of this advice through business councils, advisory committees, or whatever they may be called—may be expanded, and the possibility of this has also been suggested. Such cooperative arrangements will not mean that government will not itself have organizations for independent study and policy planning. Their suggestion does indicate that in a mixed public-private economy the independent action of each party may be limited by the evolution of cooperative techniques through which government's influence may be felt at the point of decision and business's influence felt upon the development of public policy.

This reference to the limitations on the independence of each party leads to further comments on the consequences of the coexistence of private and public power. The second consequence is that the power of business must ultimately be public power. It must exist by public favor or by public nonintervention. Business, therefore, must battle for control of government. The corporation will inevitably engage in politics, and where it cannot do so directly, it will do so through its agents. The development of market power in the corporation is a prelude to the threat of public power, and with this threat business becomes, not merely an internal system of power, but a more active participant in public power politics. Every increase in private power enlarges the possibility of public intervention and therefore the scope of politics. If private power is the child and heir of the corporate revolution, public power and public politics are its residuary legatees.

The third consequence is that the power of government, although often independently large, is limited by business power. This is the larger meaning of the political-economic federalism. It is not merely an administrative federalism—though this exists; it is not even at root a political phenomenon only; it is a social phenomenon—one which is inherent in the dualism of two coexisting power systems. Where one power seeks to limit the other, as does government the corporate, the control potential is limited by the necessity for accommodation between the two. The regulatory commission as an organ of administration is itself a compromise between the two power systems—a regulatory instrument acceptable to the regulated. In their operation regulatory agencies often have powers of approval or disapproval (enabling powers) which are dependent upon private initiative for their exercise.[24] Even when government agencies have initiative for rule-making and orders, with compulsory authority, they ultimately find a *modus vivendi* with established private organizations. Reform tends to expire and stability is found in functional subsystems, in each of which there is a triangle of agencies, congressional committees, and clienteles only infrequently disturbed by outside forces. Beyond all this, the system of government intervention must allow the reconciliation of the political purpose, representing felt public needs, and the economic purpose, which is the efficient production and distribution of goods. Government must, while it controls private power, avoid impairment of private incentive.

This does not mean that any particular balance of economic and public power is foreordained or permanent. Economic power has accommodated itself in the past to larger exercises of public power. The fourth consequence of the coexistence of the rival and complementary systems of power is that the balances between the two will always be on society's agenda of problems. The balances between the two will be partially determined by decisions within the corporate system. The hope that nonrepresentative private decision-makers will act as though they were representative, that is, will act in response to public values, will be tested. The balances will also be affected by the demonstrated or presumed utility of the techniques of standing law, publicly announced policy, and cooperative public-private arrangements as means of attaining public values. But basically the balances will be determined by public politics. Business will struggle by politics to keep government out of business, or to restrict or control government when it intervenes. But business alone will not be the determining factor. Other interests will push for recognition. Rival interests, often strengthened by representation in organizational structures, will vie for legal protection and promotion. Government must seek consensus, compromise, or choice among these. It alone is in a position

---

[24] For fuller discussion of the necessity of private initiative in systems of regulation see my "The Significance of Belief Patterns in Economic Regulation," *The Western Political Quarterly,* Vol. 14 (September 1961), pp. 13-25.

to do this for society. This is the highest of all social functions and, if done with sufficient measure of rationality and of responsiveness to all interests, is among man's greatest achievements. This is government, politics in the largest sense; this is a function business cannot perform, because it does not have the public representiveness required for responsiveness to all interests concerned. Because of this difference between government and business the balances between the two will be determined in the political struggle. Perhaps, therefore, the most vital issue for society is the adequacy of its public constitution. Can it operate representatively, that is, responsively to a pluralistic society? Can it also operate rationally, that is, efficiently toward attainment of shared purposes?

II. THE PROCESSES OF PUBLIC ADMINISTRATION

•

· 5 ·

The Budget and Democratic Government*

JESSE BURKHEAD

The growth in the size and complexity of the public sector in both developed and underdeveloped countries is undoubtedly one of the most important of recent political and economic changes. It is a phenomenon that has slowly altered the structures of economic systems and, of course, the distribution of economic power within these systems.

There are no signs of abatement. In the underdeveloped countries private entrepreneurship is often lacking and nationalized enterprise expands to take its place. Central governments not only assume responsibility for traditional governmental programs and for social welfare, but also for resource planning and allocation, all in the interests of economic growth. In the developed countries the public sector continues to increase, relatively and absolutely, in response to the forces of urbanization, with the increased specialization and inter-dependence that accompanies and contributes to an increase in urban economic activity. The public sector also grows because some public activities complement private, as with highways, and because there is at least some income elasticity in the demand for public goods. A portion of increases in income will be directed toward more affluent levels of community services.

The inevitable increase in the size of the public sector is not, of course, accomplished without the greatest of frictions in almost every country. This country, in particular, is marked by heated controversies over the level and scope of government programs. In some sense this is not surprising, since resources devoted to public purposes cannot be devoted to private purposes and the control of resources is a most contentious matter in any society. In addition, our system of fiscal federalism imparts some further elements of contention over the level

* I am indebted to my colleagues Jerry Miner and Douglas Price for their helpful comments on an earlier draft of this manuscript.

of government that shall control public resources—shall government be "close to the people" or shall "the superior resources of the federal government" be devoted to what were once regarded as wholly state and local functions?

Unfortunately, much of the contemporary controversy in this country has an aura of unreality. Federal government expenditures, defense and nondefense combined, have not increased as a proportion of gross national product in the past ten years. In this country the increases in governmental activity have come at the state and local levels, where expenditures increased 23 per cent in relation to GNP between 1955 and 1962. Moreover, those antagonistic to the growth of government seem often to be unaware that an increasing portion of expenditures at all levels in such areas as health, education, and research and development add substantially to the productivity of the private sector.

The growth of the public sector has a great many consequences. For one thing, it gives rise to theorizing, particularly on the part of economists and political scientists, about the processes by which decisions are or ought to be made concerning the size and composition of public programs. Academics undertake research projects on public decision-making. Practitioners become more conscious of the bases on which their decisions are made. Ancient and honorable concepts, such as the "public interest," are reexamined. Organization theory comes to the forefront as an effort to conceptualize complex arrangements. And all of this becomes more difficult as the traditional lines between "public" and "private" break down.

The involvement of colleges and universities in public affairs, the increased use of government contracts to private agencies rather than the conduct of "in-house" activities, the intertwining of government with business firms in research and development, and communications and information systems—these and other developments suggest that "public" vs. "private" is an increasingly fuzzy dichotomy. Nonetheless, the distinction must be preserved for many analytical and operational purposes. However vague the line of demarcation, there are still important differences between the "public sector" and the "private sector."

The growth of government has had the further consequence of placing considerable strain on traditional management processes. New technologies intended to provide greater efficiency have become the major obsession of the traditional organization and management specialist in government. Personnel problems and morale become acute in the frenzied competition among government, industry, and the universities for the highly skilled and competent. New systems of financial management must be introduced to cope with increased size and complexity. And, of course, the traditional responsibilities of budget officers grow and change, and new budget techniques must be devised.

Twenty years ago, when these developments were under way after World War II, Paul Appleby did not view the increased size and complexity of government with any considerable alarm. In fact his first major work, *Big Democracy,* took quite the contrary view. For Appleby the task of government must remain very much the same, regardless of changes in size and complexity. This task is to assure that government continue to be responsive and responsible. The budget function is important for this purpose, but is only one of the processes of government intended to assure such responsiveness and responsibility.

Recent attempts to theorize about the nature of public decision-making, on the part of both economists and political scientists, has its counterpart in recent experience in budgetary practice. Not surprisingly, the conceptual difficulties in the theory are matched by operational problems encountered by the practitioners. These developments will be examined in turn.

FISCAL THEORY

For almost two hundred years economic theorists have devoted considerable attention to resource allocation decisions in private markets. Out of these efforts has come a vast body of literature and a widely accepted theory that is thought to be reasonably useful in understanding and evaluating private market behavior.

In this framework the starting point is the preference of households (consumers) for goods and services. The distribution of income is assumed to be given at any moment in time. Business firms, with knowledge of their production possibilities and the costs of factors of production, will seek to maximize their profit positions. In so doing their decisions about price and output will maximize consumer satisfactions. There are many difficulties in the application of this (oversimplified) model to the market conditions of the real world. Knowledge may be imperfect; the mobility of factors may be limited; the distribution of income among households may not be ideal. Nevertheless, and with all its difficulties, the traditional theory of private markets has been useful in evaluating private behavior.

A theory of choice for the public sector, to provide an explanation of and guidelines for the selection of the levels and composition of government output, is of much more recent origin. Although some efforts were made by economists at the end of the last century, usually in terms of marginal utility economics, it was not until very recently that a complete attempt at elaboration was undertaken. Paul A. Samuelson made major contributions to this effort; a more complete framework appeared in 1959 with the publication of *The Theory of Public Finance* by Richard A. Musgrave.[1]

Musgrave proposes that the public sector be viewed as comprised of three branches or "budgets." The first he terms the allocations branch, which embraces decisions about the provision of government goods and services for such purposes as national defense, highways, public health, education, and the like. The second branch embraces decisions about economic stabilization, with the utilization of taxes and expenditures to control the total volume of economic activity. The third is the distribution branch, where decisions are made about the size and composition of income among households, and among groups and regions.

Decisions in the stabilization and distribution branches are social decisions, made collectively to reflect community consensus about the appropriate level of economic activity and about the distribution of societal rewards. But decisions in the allocations branch are (or should be) nonnormative efficiency judgments. They do (or should) reflect the underlying preference patterns of the citizenry for public goods, and their choices between public and private goods. Consumers cannot be expected to reveal directly their preferences for public goods, since individual taxpayers, regardless of who pays for the public good, cannot be excluded from the enjoyment of the collectively provided service. Since price tags cannot be attached to specific units of general government goods and services, it becomes the task of the political process to ascertain the underlying preference patterns of the citizenry and to translate these into decisions about the size and scope of government programs. Voting solutions will not yield determinate results since voters may favor either a low budget or a high budget but not one in between. Political decision-makers must attempt to ascertain the incidence of benefits of government programs. With decisions in hand on the distribution of income and the proper level of stabilization, taxes for the allocations branch should be imposed on a benefit basis; this will approximate a market solution. In the allocations branch the prices of commonly provided public goods will differ among taxpayers in accordance with their subjective evaluations of

[1] New York: McGraw-Hill.

benefits. This is in contrast to private markets where prices are identical for all buyers.

This approach to the public sector provides a kind of general field theory that unites the public and the private sector. For both private markets and government programs, the consumer is sovereign. An "efficient" solution is one that maximizes consumer welfare with respect to both private and public goods. Musgrave specifically rejects any social determination for the allocations branch as authoritarian and undemocratic.

The three-branch approach is a substantial contribution to clarity in thinking about the economic responsibilities of government and hence about budget determination. There *are* important conceptual differences in programs for the provision of goods and services, for stabilization, and for income distribution. In so far as possible these considerations ought to be separated in decisions about the budget. And, of course, any effort to provide a general theory of the public and private sectors ought to be applauded; this approach has, at minimum, provoked systematic thinking about the economic characteristics of public and private activity. For example, one refreshing conclusion emerges from the consumer choice approach. It is that there are no arbitrary limits to the size of the public sector vis-à-vis the private. If consumers prefer more public goods and fewer private goods, an efficient solution requires that their demands be satisfied. There is no *economic* reason for restricting the public sector to 20 per cent, 25 per cent, or any other arbitrary proportion of the total.

Unfortunately, there are difficulties with this framework. Indeed, it would be rather surprising to discover that a market efficiency solution could be applied with clarity and ease to the public sector at a time when there appears to be a cumulative drift away from a generally effective private market system.[2]

One of the most serious difficulties with the economic choice approach to the allocations branch is the inadequate attention paid to externalities or spillovers—the third party or neighborhood effects that are so characteristic of all government transactions.

In private markets there are, of course, spillovers as well. The housewife's purchases of food from the grocer are of particular concern to the housewife and her family and to the grocer (and his

---

[2] See, for example, Ewald T. Grether, "Consistency in Public Economic Policy with respect to Private Unregulated Industries," *American Economic Review*, Vol. LIII, No. 2 (May 1964), pp. 26-37.

suppliers). But the community at large, in an imprecise kind of way, derives some benefit from the fact that the housewife's family is well fed and nourished. Indeed, it is difficult to find any economic transaction that does not carry with it some volume, however small, of third party benefits.

In the private sector it is customary to think that the proportion of external benefits to internal benefits is relatively small, and that external benefits do not affect preferences for specific commodities. But in the public sector the situation would appear to be reversed. Activities come to be "affected with a public interest," to use the old public utility phrase, as the proportion of external benefits is large in relation to the internal benefits, and as these are taken into account in demands for public goods. The immediate beneficiaries of a youth recreation program may be the children themselves, and the benefits may be roughly measurable in terms of their improved health and welfare. But externalities may be widespread. Taxpayers may benefit from reduced expenditures for police protection and public health. Employers and stockholders may benefit at some time in the future as their employees are more productive. And so it goes.

In fact, a case can be made for the proposition that activities come to be public in character simply because the proportion of externalities is high and these externalities are widely diffused. One economist has suggested that this condition—the remoteness of benefits from government programs—tends to hold down the size of the government budget below its true optimum; budgets are "incorrect" because of a lack of information about external benefits.[3]

If this is the case it follows that there is no way to attain an efficiency solution for the allocations branch. The citizenry cannot be expected to support government programs whose benefits are not perceptible. Even if citizens were to vote directly on budgets for the allocations branch in an effort to express their preferences, optimal solutions would not obtain.[4]

A further difficulty arises in the allocations branch because government programs are not always directed to the benefit of consumers. Producer groups benefit as well, sometimes from the end product, sometimes because they participate in public programs as suppliers. A forty-foot channel is constructed on the Delaware River and the major

---

[3] Anthony Downs, "Why the Government Budget is Too Small in a Democracy," *World Politics,* Vol. XII, No. 4 (July 1960), pp. 541-63.

[4] The conceptual difficulties with voting solutions were first explored by Kenneth S. Arrow in *Social Choice and Individual Values* (New York: John Wiley & Sons, 1951), and are discussed in Musgrave, *op. cit.,* pp. 116-35.

beneficiary is a single steel producer; the company's stockholders may benefit, but a consumer benefit is most elusive. The producers of cement and road construction machinery are important supporters of highway programs because of their expected profits from contracts with government agencies, not because of their interest as consumers in the use of the highway. Comparable situations exist in the private sector where motivations may run in terms of power, prestige, and possession and not in terms of the maximization of consumer satisfaction. Unfortunately, in these circumstances there is no simple conceptual framework by which these varieties of demands for public or private goods can be aggregated into a preference schedule that reflects the wishes of consumers.

In addition to the foregoing difficulties with the allocations branch there is a series of operational problems. In the policy-making arena the branches are not, of course, independent one of another. Distributional considerations are not examined separately from allocations decisions. On the contrary, goods and services expenditures directly affect the distribution of private incomes as between the rich and the poor—public health, public housing and recreation, for example— and the distribution of incomes among regions, as with resource development projects. Executives and legislatures may make reasonably direct and clear-cut decisions about the distribution of income as tax measures are proposed, modified, and adopted, but the expenditure side of the budget has its effect on income distribution in a nonexplicit fashion. The consequences are there, but they are seldom specified.[5]

Stabilization considerations are similarly intertwined with allocations and distributive concerns. If incomes are to be increased in the interests of moving to a higher level of economic activity for the economy as a whole, there will be some persons and groups whose incomes are increased more than others; stabilization programs are not neutral with respect to the distribution of income. Some of the distributional consequences may be intended; others may be largely unintended.

Rational choice solutions for the allocations branch also require a unitary budget, that is, all decisions about government goods and services expenditures must be brought together as a comprehensive decision-making process. This, of course, is very far from attainment in any government. In this country the federal government budget

[5] Musgrave attempts to deal with this problem as a special case within the allocations branch in terms of "merit wants." However, almost all public goods and services have "merit" or income distribution effects.

does not comprehend the growing volume of activity in the trust funds, and state and local budgets are fragmented almost unbelievably by special funds and earmarked revenues. Moreover, the very nature of a federal system means that unified budgetary consideration is basically unattainable. With the exception of international affairs, there is no government program which is not in some way or other conducted by at least two levels of government. The economists' ideal of a comprehensive allocations branch budget that reflects consumer choices between public and private goods is clearly beyond realization in practice.

Most of the conceptual and operational difficulties in the economic theory of the allocations branch lie in the starting point—the consumer approach to public resource allocation. The best framework for analysis may not be a unified theory but one of two economies—a market economy where consumer preferences may be used as a starting point for analysis—and a budget economy where consumer preferences as such play little part.[6] Social welfare functions and social preferences are very elusive concepts and economists' efforts to impart some reality to them have not been successful. But it may be that, vague and fuzzy as these constructs are, they come closer to describing real-world conditions of budgetary decision-making than the conceptually neater approach through consumer preferences.

THE ROLE OF MEASUREMENT

The world of budgetary theory and practice is divided in two. There are those who feel that budget decisions should be governed by a maximum of calculations and marginal comparisons of costs and outcomes, and there are those who feel that budget decisions are or should be governed by considerations of strategy and bargaining. In the first group there are none who feel that value judgments are or should be eliminated from the budgetary process but major emphasis, it is contended, must be placed on the quantification of the costs and benefits of government programs. Only in this way can value judgments be made explicit. In the second group there are none who contend that measurements are useless, and it is generally argued that wherever possible measurement techniques should be extended. But the essential rationality of budgeting, it is urged, is and must continue to be a political rationality, expressive of the conflicting values of interest groups, legislators, and administrators.

6 See Gerhard Colm's elaboration of this viewpoint in *Essays in Public Finance and Fiscal Policy* (New York: Oxford University Press, 1955), pp. 258-86. Musgrave discusses and rejects this approach; *op. cit.*, pp. 86-89.

Generally speaking, most economists, whether academic or budget practitioners, are in the first group. Economists by nature are quantifiers and for the last ten or fifteen years have demonstrated a lively interest in extending the limits of measurement in public decision-making. As a rule, most political scientists, public administrators, and budget practitioners are nonquantifiers, or at least continually express doubts about the value of efforts to measure government costs and output.

The most forceful protagonists of the nonquantified view of budget decision-making are Charles E. Lindblom, an economist, and hence an exception to the foregoing generalization, and Aaron Wildavsky, a political scientist.[7] Lindblom's thesis in brief is that in budget decisions (and in most other public policy areas) a rational means-ends calculus is not possible, and indeed its pursuit would be unrealistic. The synoptic (means-ends) ideal calls for a sharp separation of values and goals from the techniques of implementation. But in the real world it is beyond human ability to consider the complete range of policies and means alternatives that are available. Means and ends are continuously intermingled, as are long-range values and short-range choices. The processes of partisan mutual adjustment require that there be agreement on means, but not on ends. An economic efficiency rationality is not possible; decisions on public policy are always made at the margin; a comprehensive budget policy is unattainable. Disjointed incrementalism best describes the technique of decision-making both with respect to the budget and with respect to other matters of public policy. Lindblom is not opposed to comprehensive or synoptic analysis, such as the measurement of budget costs and benefits where it is possible, but he is convinced that the area where such techniques are appropriate is not large, and may not be expanding.

Wildavsky is concerned to emphasize that government budgets are not solely devices for resource allocation, as economists would have

[7] Lindblom's major contributions are contained in "The Science of Muddling Through," *Public Administration Review,* Vol. XIX, No. 2 (Spring 1959); "Decision-Making in Taxation and Expenditures," in National Bureau of Economic Research, *Public Finances: Needs, Sources, and Utilization* (Princeton: Princeton University Press, 1961), pp. 295-329; with David Braybrooke, *A Strategy of Decision* (New York: Free Press of Glencoe, 1963). The *Public Administration Review,* Vol. XXIV, No. 3 (September 1964) has an interesting symposium on Lindblom's system (pp. 153-65). Wildavsky's views are set forth in "Political Implications of Budgetary Reform," *Public Administration Review,* Vol. XXI, No. 4 (Autumn 1961), pp. 183-90 and in *The Politics of the Budgetary Process* (Boston: Little, Brown, 1964).

it. A budget is, or may be "an expectation, an aspiration, a strategy, a communications network, or a precedent."[8] Budgeting is always incremental, never a total review of resource allocation. The decision process in the federal government is dominated by the strategies employed and the conflicts that arise among the participants: clientele groups, agencies, departments, the Bureau of the Budget, the President, congressional subcommittees and their parent committees. The conflicts give rise to definable strategies that require such things as the cultivation (on the part of an agency) of an active clientele, the development of confidence among other government officials, and skill in following tactics that exploit temporary opportunities. Budget strategies differ in accordance with whether the agency is attempting to hold the line on its existing program, expand the existing program, or add a new program. Budgeting is fragmented; it is repetitive—not every problem has to be resolved this year; and it is sequential—each problem is dealt with in turn, in partial isolation from all other budgetary problems. The reasonably stable roles that are played by major participants makes the process manageable. Comprehensive budgeting, complete budget calculations, and formal coordination by a single person or agency are unfeasible, undesirable, or both.

Wildavsky argues that there is a high degree of coordination in the process, but that it is informal coordination in anticipation of what others are likely to do. A very wide range of interests are thus considered. Paul Appleby once expressed something like this point of view as follows:

> The budget is not made merely by technical processes; it is made on a field where mighty forces contend over it. It is not made in a public arena, but the public is somehow well represented. This is one of the most mystifying of government phenomena.[9]

There would appear to be no reconciling Musgrave's fiscal theory of public sector choices with the pragmatic and descriptive system of Lindblom and Wildavsky. This is not a difference between "theory" and "practice," but a difference between the starting points of analysis. In the Musgrave view the citizen must be viewed as an individual consumer of government services. To Lindblom and Wildavsky the citizen must be viewed as a part of a social decision process.

[8] *The Politics of the Budgetary Process,* pp. 3-4.
[9] "The Influence of the Political Order," *American Political Science Review,* Vol. XLII, No. 2 (April 1948), p. 281.

The Progress of Practitioners

Since the end of World War II there has been a large number of efforts to reform and strengthen the practice of budgeting in governments at all levels in the United States. A great many of these have come under the rubric of what is customarily described as performance or program budgeting. The federal government has engaged in such efforts in the name of cost-type budgets. A number of states and a very large number of municipal governments have reformed their budget classifications in the name of "performance."[10]

In its ideal form performance budgeting costs out the end products of government activity—the goods and services that are produced. It thus permits comparisons over time of the relationships between inputs and outputs and facilitates budget decisions in terms of agency accomplishment and efficiency. Performance budgeting thus (ideally) provides much of the information necessary for arriving at an optimum budget for separate programs in the allocations branch. But even in its ideal form it does not provide information for making comparisons among programs.

No thorough survey of experiences with performance budgeting has been undertaken, so that appraisals of the varied and sometimes conflicting results are most difficult. The greatest benefits would appear to lie at the agency management level, where this approach encourages attention to new ways of looking at programs, with emphasis on accomplishment and technological efficiency in securing that accomplishment. Performance budgeting is probably less useful at departmental, central budget office, or executive review levels, where choices among programs depend more on social, political, and economic judgments as to the "worth" of a program. Performance budgeting has not been generally popular with legislators, who find it easier to "control" the administration by attention to the traditional framework of obligations and the details of personnel and other objects of expenditure.

The challenge of the performance approach lies in the difficulties encountered in the measurement of government output—difficulties that are inherent in the conceptual scheme of economists who write about fiscal theory and also in the day-to-day work of the agency budget officer who is trying to measure end products with precision.

---

[10] For an excellent review of this and other recent developments at the state level see the report on a survey of 14 state budget administrations by Arlene Theuer Shadoan, "Developments in State Budget Administration," *Public Administration Review*, Vol. XXIII, No. 4 (December 1963), pp. 227-31.

The same range of problems is encountered, naturally enough, in efforts to measure productivity in government.[11] It is easy enough to measure the things that government buys; it is generally possible to measure the activities of government, although ingenuity is occasionally required here; it is perennially difficult to measure government output except for repetitive discrete products such as postal service. But in spite of the perhaps insuperable difficulties in some areas of government output, measurement efforts will continue and they will be useful, sometimes more for their by-products than for their direct results. In an increasingly quantified society it is hardly to be expected that the public sector shall remain isolated from measurement efforts.

The recent sweeping changes in programming and budgeting in the U.S. Department of Defense are illustrative of both the possibilities and limitations in budget quantification.[12] Since 1961 the defense budget has been organized in terms of nine basic programs: (1) strategic retaliatory forces, (2) continental air and missile defense forces, (3) general purpose forces, (4) airlift and sealift forces, (5) reserve and guard forces, (6) research and development, (7) general support, (8) civil defense, and (9) military assistance. Each program is subdivided into program elements, such as a specific missile or aircraft type. The program elements are costed in terms of research and development, initial investment, and annual operating expenses with five-year projections of each element. Costs are continually studied in relation to effectiveness for each weapons system. The result is an attempt to unify military planning and budgeting, with the linkage between the two established in terms of the program elements. The program structure, however, is used primarily for internal Department of Defense

[11] See John W. Kendrick, "Exploring Productivity Measurement in Government," *Public Administration Review*, Vol. XXIII, No. 2 (June 1963), pp. 59-66; U.S. Bureau of the Budget, *Measuring Productivity of Federal Government Organizations* (Washington: Government Printing Office, 1964).

[12] Much of this development is associated with the work of Charles J. Hitch, Assistant Secretary of Defense. The economic theory underlying the DOD budget system is set forth in *The Economics of Defense in the Nuclear Age*, with Roland N. McKean (Cambridge: Harvard University Press, 1960). See also "Management of the Defense Dollar," *The Federal Accountant*, Vol. XI, No. 4 (June 1962), pp. 33-44; David Novick, "Costing Tomorrow's Weapons System," *Quarterly Review of Economics and Business*, Vol. 3, No. 1 (Spring 1963), pp. 33-40; Alain C. Enthoven, "Economic Analysis in the Department of Defense," *American Economic Review*, Vol. LIII, No. 2 (May 1964), pp. 413-23. Hitch has described the system in testimony before a Subcommittee of the Committee on Government Operations, House of Representatives, *Systems Development and Management*, Part 2, 87th Cong., 2nd Sess., 1962, pp. 513-47.

purposes. The budget presentation to the Congress is in traditional categories centering on procurement and personnel.

The DOD budget system appears to have enjoyed the same kinds of general advantages that are characteristic of other, more modest efforts at performance budgeting. Marginal costs and marginal effectiveness are under continuous review; alternative defense systems are continuously scrutinized; the relationship between investment and operational costs is specified.

But, as Assistant Secretary Hitch has made clear on a number of occasions, program budgeting for the Department of Defense does not resolve the value judgments about the appropriate level of defense expenditures. It has certainly centralized decision-making authority in the hands of the Secretary of Defense, as against the separate services, to permit better-informed judgments. It may provide some insight on whether as a nation we are "better defended" this year than last, although this is doubtful. But program budgeting cannot yield a computerized answer to the question: should we spend another $5 billion on defense?

In one of the few detailed studies available of budget decision processes—an examination of the defense budget for fiscal 1950—Schilling observed:

> The defense budget, while susceptible to rational analysis, remains a matter of political resolution. Choices of this order can be made in only one place: the political arena. There the relative importance of values can be decided by the relative power brought to bear on their behalf. There the distribution of power can decide matters that the distribution of fact and insight cannot.[13]

Paul Appleby once put the point succinctly: "There are few problems for which there are single right answers simply and clearly revealed by technical analysis."[14]

THE BUDGET AND THE GENERAL INTEREST

The efforts of economists in recent years to construct a general theory of public finance with resource allocation principles to guide both the public and the private sector have been stimulating and

[13] Warren R. Schilling, Paul Y. Hammond, Glenn H. Snyder, *Strategy, Politics, and Defense Budgets* (New York: Columbia University Press, 1962), p. 15.
[14] Paul Appleby, "The Budget Division," *Public Administration Review*, Vol. XVII, No. 3 (Summer 1957), p. 156.

provocative, but they fall short of providing operational guides to budget decisions. The efforts of budget practitioners to measure government performance have been useful and have certainly tended to improve the efficiency of some government operations, but they cannot be applied in important areas and in any event do not assure that proper choices will be made among programs or with respect to program levels. Nevertheless, the efforts of both the fiscal theorists and the performance budget practitioners have been very much worthwhile. Fiscal theory has provided a systematic way of looking at the economic functions of government; performance budgeting has integrated costs and outcomes in some decision processes.

The difficult problem that remains for performance budgeting is the determination of its area of applicability. We may be able to "muddle through" a great many decisions without attempting to measure costs and outcomes, but there is no assurance that incremental decisions will provide for the effective use of public resources just because they are incremental. A great many urban transportation systems which were constructed incrementally stand today as magnificent monuments to inefficient resource allocation. Even if one is persuaded that Lindblom and Wildavsky have done an excellent job of describing the reality of public decision processes, it should still be possible to add some economic calculations here and there that will help to guide the next incremental decision. Moreover, efforts to quantify will change the terms of trade on which decisions that are essentially political will be made. Measurement efforts no matter how imperfect will, at minimum, discipline and structure political decision processes.

There is no reason for an all-or-nothing attitude toward decisions systems, or for an all-or-nothing attitude toward performance measurements. It is not necessary to make a general choice between incrementalism and a rational means-ends calculus. Some governmental programs permit one and some permit the other. A multiplicity of approaches is possible. One would hope that the operations of the Post Office Department, for example, would be subject to the continuous application of operations research techniques.

Larger questions about the size and scope of government programs and the relative division of resources between the public and the private sector are now and will probably remain unanswered, either by fiscal theory or by the work of the practitioners. At one time, perhaps as recently as ten years ago, it was possible to discuss these questions in terms of "the public interest" or "the public welfare," but these notions have been so strongly attacked that they no longer seem to contain any systematic content.[15] We have also discovered that the "public interest state" can have some seriously adverse effects on the civil liberties of individuals.[16]

What we have left are some old-fashioned notions about the importance of a budget organization that, hopefully, provides a center of executive responsibility so that elected officials may ultimately be held responsible. We must rely on a budget procedure that is in the process of continued improvement with respect to the flow of information and the interrelatedness of programs.

Budgeting is and must remain a political process. If it is to be a democratic process those who are vitally affected must have an opportunity to be heard. The costs and benefits of government programs thus come to be reflected in the expressed feelings of persons and interest groups in terms of the intensity of demand for public programs and sensitivity to their costs.

There are some grounds for moderate optimism with respect to the ability of budget procedures to handle the larger issues. As society becomes increasingly urbanized, interdependent, and complex the volume of externalities for both public and private activity increases. Persons and groups affected by such external effects press their claims as budget decisions are made. The growing volume of externalities would appear to be the principal causal factor in the growth of the public (nondefense) sector. As long as political processes remain open to influence by affected persons and groups, and as long as concentrations of market power can be held reasonably in check, we should be able to assure an increasing measure of procedural due process in budgetary decisions. But there is no way by which we can determine whether we have achieved an economically efficient optimum between the public and the private sector.

15 See, for example, Glendon A. Schubert, Jr., " 'The Public Interest' in Administrative Decision-Making: Theorem, Theosophy, or Theory," *American Political Science Review*, Vol. LI, No. 2 (June 1957), pp. 346-68; Frank J. Sorauf, "The Public Interest Reconsidered," *Journal of Politics*, Vol. 19, No. 4 (November 1957), pp. 616-39.
16 See Charles A. Reich, "The New Property," *Yale Law Journal*, Vol. 73, No. 5 (April 1964), pp. 733-87.

• 6 •

The Managers of National Economic Change

BERTRAM M. GROSS

In the modern world every nation-state is committed to some degree of responsibility for the guidance (or management) of national economic change. In the great majority of nations—whether developed or developing, noncommunist or communist—this responsibility is formally expressed in one or another form of "national economic planning." In both the United States and West Germany, the only major countries where national economic planning is usually disavowed, the central government is nonetheless held responsible for achieving various objectives through the promotion and coordination of a vast amount of activity by both governmental and nongovernmental organizations.

No matter how interpreted, this responsibility has presented an unprecedented challenge to the managerial and policy-making capacities of national government leaders. Managing a national economy, even when the goals are limited, is infinitely more complex than managing a giant government department or a huge international corporation. The hierarchically subordinate units are scattered through complex bureaucracies with well-developed capacities for resisting central coordination. The planning, activation, and evaluation of new policies and programs is enormously difficult. This difficulty is rendered greater by the substantive intricacies of economic affairs at the national level. It is magnified by the abundance of inaccurate, misleading, or irrelevant information clogging the channels of government communication. It is compounded by the opposition, apathy, or independent activity of well-organized groups and unorganized masses outside the central government. Indeed, the opportunities for detailed, central direction of an economy are so limited that the term "guidance" may seem more appropriate at the national level—particularly for those to whom "management," in the old-fashioned quasi-authoritarian sense, suggests rigorous central control.

To meet the unprecedented challenge of this responsibility for

101

national guidance, many new institutions of central government have come into being. Some of these are outgrowths of old-time, long-standing departments, ministries, or bureaus; some are new organizations. These new institutions are of increasing importance to the functioning of modern government. They are an important part of the environment of all large-scale organizations, private or public. To get his own job done, the manager of any such organization must always take them into account. For a nation as a whole, they are the institutional basis of any national efforts to promote such objectives as economic development or growth, full employment, regional balance, stability, or social justice.

A truly rational approach to economic policy requires some genuine understanding of this institutional basis for the managing of national economic change. Only by identifying the multiplicity of functions these institutions are called upon to perform is it possible to take effective steps toward building or strengthening them. Only by appreciating the complexity of the linkages among them (and between them and the broader social structure) is it possible to avoid thinking of them as self-operating mechanisms and to understand the vital role of leadership strategy geared to the exigencies of unique situations.

In this essay, without dealing with leadership strategy, I shall attempt a preliminary contribution to the understanding of these institutions by: (1) stating the case for "unique models," rather than "ideal types," in analyzing the central institutions of national economic guidance (or "central guidance clusters"), (2) identifying major roles played by the many actors in central guidance clusters, (3) discussing the role permutations among Central Planning Organs (CPO's), and (4) presenting certain hypotheses concerning the dynamics of central guidance clusters and CPO's.

In covering these points, I shall be carrying on the spirit of discussions and correspondence with Paul Appleby from early 1961, when I worked with him in India, to the time of his death. Appleby was vigorously committed to the idea that modern government must take the initiative in encouraging economic growth and development. Part of his devotion to India was based upon the depth of commitment to democratic national planning by India's top leaders. But Appleby was equally vigorous in condemning oversimplified approaches to the coordination of government programs and equally devoted to the development of public administration concepts capable of grappling with the vast complexities of "real life" government. Many of his ideas—often sent to me in long, personally-typed letters—also entered into various chapters of my *The Managing of Organizations.*[1] In drawing upon some of these chapters, I indeed find difficulty at times in knowing whether I am quoting myself or him.

In dealing with the managing of national economic change, I am fully aware of the fact that I am entering an area as yet barely touched by modern management theory. The *de facto* experts on national economic planning have for the most part been economic technicians with strong personal interests in the creation of agencies for technical economic analysis and little background in broader governmental operations or in the study of national leadership or organizational behavior. The few "administrative experts" called upon to advise on national planning have usually been narrow specialists preoccupied with administrative techniques and old-fashioned "organization chart notions." Moreover, the most modern management theories—no matter how sophisticated with respect to single organizations—cannot be automatically transferred to the Big Society without very considerable adaptation and reformulation. Finally, much more empirical research is needed on the actual behavior of central guidance clusters. The observations in this essay are based largely upon preliminary, impressionistic surveys in Britain, France, West Germany, India, Israel, Italy, Mexico, Morocco, the Netherlands, Tanzania, Tunisia, the U.S., the U.S.S.R., and Venezuela.[2] They are merely the prelude toward more definitive depth studies on the building of national planning institutions.[3]

CENTRAL GUIDANCE CLUSTERS: UNIQUE MODELS

Traditional comparative government describes differences among governments through distinctions between democracy and dictatorship, between parliamentary and presidential systems, and among

[1] Bertram M. Gross, *The Managing of Organizations*, 2 vols. (New York: Free Press of Glencoe, 1964).

[2] Preliminary studies of these countries have been prepared as part of the cross-cultural study of national planning under the sponsorship of the Maxwell School. These studies are soon to be published by Syracuse University Press as a series. The National Planning series will include studies of national planning in Tanganyika, Tunisia and Morocco, Mexico, Venezuela, Israel, the Soviet Union, the Netherlands, Italy, Great Britain, West Germany, and the United States.

[3] An intensive study of the processes of building central planning institutions in developing nations has been initiated by the author as part of the research program of the Inter-University Research Program in Institution Building. This program, supported by the Ford Foundation, is a cooperative endeavor by Indiana University, Michigan State University, the University of Pittsburgh, and Syracuse University.

various electoral and political party systems. The more modern students of comparative government distinguish between different types of bureaucrats, elites, interest group structures, and communication systems; their work points toward a richer understanding of social systems as a whole. Both groups have gone far in setting up "ideal types" to help illuminate national differences. Neither has paid much attention to the managerial, administrative, or guidance functions of government.

In focusing directly upon the central guidance institutions of national government, it is more helpful to start by identifying certain general sets of roles that are common to all national governments. As indicated in the accompanying chart, these may be referred to as (1) general leadership roles, (2) financial management roles, (3) critical problem roles, (4) special staff roles, and (5) general staff roles.

At first glance this set of roles may seem to be an "ideal type," a model which—in the tradition of Max Weber—attempts to describe all central guidance institutions in general. But an ideal type, in my judgment, is always too remote from the actual, the desirable, or the attainable. It is of little use in explaining the operations of government in any country. It is a dangerous guide to institution-builders. Only a unique model is capable of dealing with the special combination of conditions peculiar to any given country. The role set herein described, therefore, is presented not as an ideal type but as a framework to help planners and scholars construct *unique models* of what *is* or *should be* in their individual countries.

Any specific role, of course, is played by specific actors. Some of these are small, self-contained units—such as the small groups of people in the personal office of a Prime Minister or President (and, of course, including the Prime Minister or President himself). Some are the top units of large organizations that, in addition to their central management roles, also carry on major activities throughout a nation—such as tax collection or foreign currency control. Some are the most conspicuous parts of the formal machinery of central government. Others may be the key leaders of political parties, banking institutions, or national federations representing producers and employees. Most organizations play various roles. Many of the key actors wear many hats.

In different governments each of these roles tends to be developed in a somewhat different manner. The detailed roles are distributed among the various components of the central cluster in many ways. This role distribution cannot be understood merely by looking at

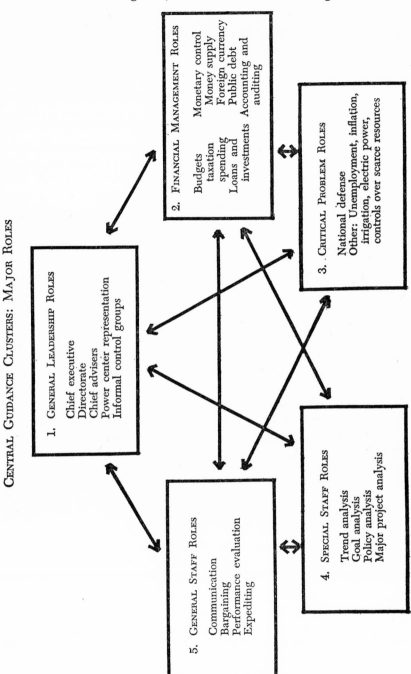

CENTRAL GUIDANCE CLUSTERS: MAJOR ROLES

1. GENERAL LEADERSHIP ROLES

Chief executive
Directorate
Chief advisers
Power center representation
Informal control groups

2. FINANCIAL MANAGEMENT ROLES

Monetary control
Money supply
Foreign currency
Public debt
Accounting and
    auditing
Budgets
taxation
spending
Loans and
    investments

3. CRITICAL PROBLEM ROLES

National defense
Other: Unemployment, inflation,
    irrigation, electric power,
    controls over scarce resources

4. SPECIAL STAFF ROLES

Trend analysis
Goal analysis
Policy analysis
Major project analysis

5. GENERAL STAFF ROLES

Communication
Bargaining
Performance evaluation
Expediting

the names of agencies; the external label never reveals the contents of the package. Nor is it enough to know that the central institutions operate within a certain constitutional framework, are linked with a certain kind of political party system or exercise a certain degree— high or low—of control over the economy. With any particular type of constitutional and party structure and degree of control over the economy there are tremendous variations in the structure and performance of central guidance institutions. These can be illuminated only by building unique models showing the actual or desired role permutations in specific countries.

CENTRAL GUIDANCE ROLES

"Roles" may be defined as the kinds of activity in which people or groups are expected to engage and which serve as criteria for judging their performance. Since governmental activities are extremely complex, any single role classification can merely scratch the surface. When applied in any specific country, therefore, the following role classification would need to be subdivided much further and crisscrossed by other role concepts.

1. *General leadership roles*

The general leadership roles are those dealing with the manning of key posts in government, the mediation or integration of the major disputes in a society, and the formulation—or at least legitimation—of general national policies. These are all political roles in the highest sense of the term "politics." At the same time, many of them require from their incumbents a considerable amount of skill and knowledge on economic matters—since many appointments, disputes, and policies involve economic problems and programs.

    a. *Chief Executives.* The role of chief executive rarely leaves an incumbent much time to give sustained attention to economic guidance. Sometimes his major role in economic guidance is merely to support others in the central guidance cluster, protect them from attack, and help popularize their ideas. Sometimes his own political career is associated with a major new departure in economic policy— as with Khrushchev's proposals for greater emphasis on the chemical industry as opposed to steel, Johnson's "war against poverty," and Nyerere's "villagization" program. Yet even those chief executives who spend most of their time on nation-building, foreign affairs, and national defense may be, indeed, helping build the framework for national economic change. This has certainly been the case with Nehru, de Gaulle, and Ben-Gurion.

The chief executive, it must be pointed out, is never a strictly one-man show. "The President is many men" is an apt way of referring to the large number of people making up the Presidency in the United States. A Prime Minister is also many men. The office of both usually includes a personal secretariat of a general nature and, increasingly, a set of specialized staff services. Although any such office usually operates behind a screen of anonymity and secrecy, it often includes one or more persons or units serving the chief executive on issues of national economic guidance. Their services may range from the drafting of major speeches and state documents to help in reconciling major disputes among top officials.

b. *Directorates.* Almost every chief executive operates in close association with a collegial directorate such as a cabinet, council of ministers, executive council, or party praesidium. In some cases, as in the United States, its main function is to advise the chief executive. In other cases, as in India and the Netherlands, it is the place where decisions on economic policies are formally made. In most cases, as with the boards of directors of large corporations, special committees are developed to deal with particular problems—such as the National Security Council in the United States and the Committee of Economic Ministers in Israel. These committees and their staffs—even when dealing with matters of defense and foreign policy—often play a major role in formulating and implementing major economic programs. Sometimes, as in Pakistan, a cabinet committee is given the formal responsibility for implementing the economic plan. Sometimes, a cabinet committee may be supposed to formulate plans—either with its own staff, a group of people assigned to it from various ministries, or a specialized plan formulation unit under its jurisdiction. In the U.S.S.R. the central directorate is not the relatively weak Council of Ministers but rather the praesidium of the Communist party—and the Chief Executive is more the party's general secretary than the premier.

c. *Personal advisers.* Entirely apart from specialized planning units, there are usually many economic planning advisers scattered through the central guidance cluster. The chief executive and the key members of the directorate will each have an array of both formal and informal economic advisers—some within the government service, some in strategic posts in the legislature or political parties. Sometimes an economist whose formal role is the head of a business enterprise, labor union, or university, or an agency performing professional research services, will build an informal role for himself as a personal adviser to the Chief Executive. This has happened with a few of the various chairmen of the Council of Economic Advisers in the United States.

d. *Power center representation.* The implementation of plans for significant economic change invariably involves building a "support base" among powerful groups in a country. This action requirement has often led to three kinds of representative groups: (1) general councils composed of national representatives of major interest groups (such as the Economic and Social Council in France and the Social-Economic Council in the Netherlands), (2) sectoral or cross-sectoral representative groups, usually with government participation (as in both France and India), and (3) groups that bring together centers of governmental power (the High Planning Council in France), states with central government (India's National Development Council), or state enterprises with regular ministries.

The actual roles played by these groups are often extremely hard to determine. Sometimes, they are little more than an empty facade, relics of old and abandoned ideologies of syndicalism or the corporate state. Often, as with the French Economic and Social Council, their major role is to legitimate plans made elsewhere. Many of the French working committees comprise coalitions of business interests and government officials with power not only to formulate plans but to carry them out as well. India's National Development Council seems to be concerned mainly with the continuous tug-of-war concerning the distribution of the central government's development funds among the states.

e. *Informal control groups.* No classification of formal roles can ever establish a neat set of pigeonholes into which all roles will fall. Nor can a set of formal roles always provide the special kind of interpersonal relations often sought when major controversies are faced.

There is good reason to believe, therefore, that informal control groups (sometimes called "kitchen cabinets") often handle the hottest issues at the very center of government. Thus the final touches upon a new economic plan or a new departure in economic policy will often be made by a group comprising, let us say, the chief executive, a favorite advisor, a close minister or two, a political leader, and—perhaps—a trusted civil servant. The composition of these groups will often vary from issue to issue. At times, the chief executive will not himself be a member. Sometimes control groups of very substantial significance come into being through regular after-hour meetings of like-thinking government officials at the civil service and professional level. Sometimes, nongovernment leaders, apart from the provision of personal advice on selected matters, will play a major role in a continuing control group. In Barnard's phrase, "the things that are seen are moved by the things unseen."[4] Out of the hidden recesses comes the power that shapes the ends of men.

2. Financial management roles

One of the continuing problems of formal organization is whether specialized central planning units should be subordinate to or independent of the central agencies of financial management. The case for subordination rests upon the tremendous influence of the top officials of government dealing with budgets and other financial matters. The case against it rests upon the negativistic, restrictive, conservative, or antichange attitudes that often seem to stem from the exercise of central financial functions. Any serious judgment concerning the comparative advantages and disadvantages of each alternative could be made only in terms of the specific conditions and the specific objectives sought in a given country.

In general terms, however, without differentiation among countries, and without reference to the details of organizational structure, there is no doubt that the central financial institutions *always* play a tremendous role in the formulation and implementation of national economic plans. This role is rooted in the tremendous significance of money as a claim against resources, in the political as well as the economic significance of budgetary, monetary, and lending decisions, and in the administrative significance of accounting and auditing operations. It is strengthened by the fact that financial agencies are often the oldest and most redoubtable of government bureaucracies, with an influential network of local offices scattered across a country. Where these agencies are not well-developed, there is an institutional gap that cannot be filled.

a. *Budgets.* The two major roles here are in the field of (1) tax policy and revenue collection, and (2) the budgeting of expenditures. Each has a great influence upon economic activity. The budget as a whole is a major instrument of economic planning and plan implementation. Yet while the budget may provide intellectual coordination between taxation and expenditure programs, the two roles are so highly developed that a separate bureaucracy usually deals with each. The fact that they usually sit together under the hierarchic umbrella of a Minister of Finance (instead of being formally divided as in the case of the U.S. Department of the Treasury and Bureau of the Budget) rarely minimizes their stubborn sense of independence.

---

[4] Chester Barnard, *The Functions of the Executive* (Cambridge: Harvard University Press, 1938), p. 284.

b. *Monetary control.* Here we find the roles played by (1) central banks in controlling the volume of legal currency and influencing interest rates and credit policy, (2) the agencies handling foreign currency control and foreign currency budgets (sometimes central banks) in countries troubled by deficits in the current balance of international payments, and (3) those handling government borrowing, and the accrued public debt, both internal and external. In this area considerable attention is often given to the old dichotomous question as to whether the central bank should be independent of or subordinate to the treasury. Increasingly, as it becomes clear that the answer is usually "a little of both," this dichotomy is replaced by the trichotomy of fiscal and monetary policy: treasury (or finance ministry), central bank, and specialized planning unit. Here also, the real question is not which one runs—or should run—the show, but rather how they work—and how they should work—together.

c. *Loans and investments.* The multiplicity of financial management institutions is usually added to by the central government's creation or promotion of specialized lending and/or investing corporations. Usually referred to as development corporations, these institutions promote economic expansion in special sectors (industry, small business, agriculture, export trade, etc.) or in "underdeveloped" regions. Frequently, as in Mexico, there are many such corporations, with some much more powerful than regular ministries and some intimately involved in the operation of major enterprises.

d. *Accounting and auditing.* In the accounting and auditing operations of central governments, the negativism and conservatism of financial institutions usually reach their most extreme point. The traditional role of these institutions is usually to prevent malfeasance, the use of government funds for nonauthorized purposes, or deviation from financial rules. This function often takes precedence over the more modern role concept of attacking inefficiency. It is often discharged through record-keeping and double-checking procedures so time-consuming as to become a major cause of inefficiency and so complicated as to facilitate manipulation by corrupt officials. Thus one of the most difficult problems in the managing of economic change—and one which is persistently dodged—is how to renovate a government's accounting and auditing institutions.

3. Critical problem roles

From time to time in almost every country critical problems arise whose handling has a wide impact throughout the economy. The heads of the agencies handling these problems are usually thrust—or, more typically, thrust themselves—into the central guidance cluster.

a. *National defense.* The most typical critical problems of this type relate to national defense. Full-scale war has, in the past, brought on a controlled war economy, with the military always playing a major role in the control process, even if only through the formulation of military requirements and the direction of procurement. Even in the case of a competitive arms race, new roles and new agencies are invariably created to deal with critical problems of technology, production, planning and logistics. Thus in the United States the National Security Council, in dealing with defense and foreign policy problems, has at times played a major role in shifting the pattern of federal expenditures.[5]

b. *Other.* In addition to defense and foreign policy crises, there are many other sources of critical problem roles. In a period of depression, new roles will be created to deal with unemployment and public works. Until these roles become accepted and understood, the officials handling them—as in the case of the early New Deal in the United States—will be at the center of national affairs. As the roles become routinized or as the problem itself abates, they will fade into the periphery. This same phenomenon takes place in many industrially underdeveloped countries with respect to the top officials handling critical programs of water supply (irrigation and flood control) in arid countries, electricity generation, land distribution, cooperative organizations, or the creation of a new industrial complex. Typical examples are the High Dam in Egypt, the Gezira scheme in the Sudan, villagization in Tanzania and the Guayana regional program in Venezuela. When there are critical shortages of basic resources, a central role in economic guidance may be played by any control agency with the task of juggling priorities for, or increasing the supply of, the scarce resource.

4. *Special staff roles*

Modern government has seen a vast proliferation of specialized staff functions. These develop, and must develop, in connection with any specific economic program and every major government organization with economic functions. Specialized staff is also needed in the central guidance cluster to help coordinate these many programs and indicate where special promotional efforts may be needed. Thus far, most of this staff work has developed in terms of economic research

[5] A helpful review of the work of the National Security Council is provided by Stanley L. Falk, "The National Security Council Under Truman, Eisenhower and Kennedy," *Political Science Quarterly* (Sept. 1964), pp. 403-34.

by professional or would-be professional economists. As economists themselves become increasingly aware of the limitations in handling the cultural, psychological, political, and administrative aspects of economic problems, it is likely that there will be a slow trend toward more staff research roles by sociologists, anthropologists, political scientists, social psychologists, management analysts, and operations researchers.

a. *Trend analysis.* One of the most important staff roles is the interpretation of nationwide data on past economic developments, current trends, and future probabilities. This role usually involves the use of national economic accounting. The actual collection of basic data is usually handled or coordinated by others. This process is in many countries unbelievably defective, with many margins of error ranging beyond 30 to 50 per cent. The economists and statisticians in the central guidance clusters, while usually promoting vigorously the collection of more accurate and meaningful data, tend to publicly exaggerate the accuracy and significance of the data they use.[6]

b. *Goal analysis.* Another special staff role relates to the formulation and adjustment of macroeconomic goal analysis. Here economic specialists prepare projections of future output and income, consumption, investment, the balance of payments, prices, and employment. The term projection is often used ambiguously to refer to (1) a probability statement divorced from any new government action, (2) a probability statement based upon some considered change in government policies, and/or (3) a proposed goal toward which government policies should be adapted. Input-output calculations are often used to help achieve consistency within a multiple set of goals.

c. *Policy analysis.* This involves active participation in the formulation of major policies or programs designed to help attain macroeconomic goals. It often crisscrosses with financial management roles, but may go far beyond financial aspects and enter the substantive considerations in agriculture, education, scientific development, and other sectoral or cross-sectoral programs. This approach supplements and deepens the strictly budgetary review of new policies usually undertaken by financial management institutions.

d. *Major project analysis.* The central economic specialists are

---

[6] The errors and inaccuracies on governmental economic calculations are analyzed with impressive skill by Oskar Morgenstern in *The Accuracy of Economic Observations,* rev. ed. (Princeton: Princeton University Press, 1963). Morgenstern gives many examples of this tendency and hammers the point home by stressing the failure of government statistical agencies to publish estimates concerning the margins of error in their data (*op. cit.,* pp. 304-05).

at times called upon to deal with major projects with important national implications. Sometimes the regular agencies of government simply do not have the trained manpower needed to initiate or review a needed project. Sometimes the review process leads to controversies that can be settled only after professional analysis at the highest levels of government. Under such circumstances engineers, scientists, and program specialists are usually needed to work together with the economic analysts.

5. General staff roles

From the viewpoint of sectoral ministries and economic programs, the central economists are sometimes viewed as a "general" economic staff.[7] From the viewpoint of the general guidance of an economy, however, they provide specialized staff services. In this sense the term "general" is more applicable to those whose roles involve the coordination of many types of specialists.

a. *Communication.* A vital general staff role is the promotion of multidirectional communication among vital centers of power and among the key actors in a central guidance cluster. This is a major role of the "planners" or "planning generalists" in the French *Commissariat du Plan.* The economic analysts, instead of belonging to the Commissariat, sit in a special division of the National Institute of Statistics (INSEE), where they enjoy protection against political interference. Their macroeconomic projections and evaluations are brought before the sectoral and cross-sectoral committees representing business, labor, government ministries, and independent specialists. The planning generalists serve as an intermediary among these many committees, between the committees and the economists, between both of these groups, on the one hand, and the Minister of Finance and the Economic Council, on the other.

b. *Bargaining.* As communication links, the French general planning staff promotes a fluid process of negotiation, compromise, and integration among these various groups. It also seems to enter the process as behind-the-scenes bargainer in its own right. A similar role—together with policy analysis—was played briefly by the Council of Economic Advisers when, at the outbreak of the Korean War, it moved quickly to take the leadership in formulating needed adjustments in the federal government's economic policies.

---

[7] This concept has been used in Bertram M. Gross and John P. Lewis, "The President's Economic Staff during the Truman Administration," *American Political Science Review* (March 1964), pp. 114-30.

c. *Performance evaluation.* In a vague way the analysis of current economic trends gives some "feedback" on the presumed results or by-products of certain economic programs. More specific evaluation activities, however, must be geared to individual programs. In France, the general planners probably undertake such evaluation on a highly selective basis only, and mainly in connection with nationalized industries or private applications for major government aid. In India many highly centralized evaluation functions have been undertaken by the Planning Commission, but with questionable communication links to those capable of taking remedial action.

d. *Expediting.* The role of the expediter is to go beyond evaluation and get improved action on vital matters. This is sometimes referred to colloquially as "knocking heads together" or "twisting arms." It also includes the formulation of detailed moves that might be taken by chief executives, directorate members, and their advisers. These functions are at times informally undertaken by people whose official duties are limited to specialized research. Sometimes they are officially undertaken by special inquiry commissions which get so preoccupied with evaluation that they never get around to exerting any positive effect upon action.

THE SPECIAL ROLES OF A CENTRAL PLANNING ORGAN (CPO)

It should be perfectly clear from the previous discussion that *no single agency could ever handle all the many roles involved in the guidance of national economic change.* They are too numerous, specialized, and different to be embodied in any single organization. Any effort to incorporate them all in a single organization would inevitably lead to such a large amount of subdivision as to convert the boundaries of the total organization into a formal façade. The subdivisions would become *de facto* separate organizations. The central guidance of national economic change requires not merely some single agency with certain planning functions but *a complex and flexible network or system of central government institutions embedded in a broader system of relations with the society as a whole.* This is what is meant by "central guidance cluster."

Yet economists have traditionally discussed national planning in terms of the decisions made by a "central planning board"[8] or "ministry of planning."[9] Political leaders have habitually used the

[8] Oscar Lange, "On the Economic Theory of Socialism," in Benjamin Lippincott, ed., *On the Economic Theory of Socialism* (Manchester: University of Manchester Press, 1938).

[9] Abba P. Lerner, *The Economics of Control* (New York: Macmillan, 1944).

creation or reorganization of some conspicuous central planning unit as a way of inaugurating or dramatizing new economic programs. Many studies made for international bodies have given concentrated attention to the national "planning or programming unit"[10] or "central planning organ."[11] In one of these recent studies, the able French economist, François Perroux, points out that "a general trend to entrust the preparation of planning to a single central organ can be observed. From the moment a government takes the political decision to plan development, i.e., to act on the economic structures by defining economic objectives and the methods of achieving them, this overall conception involves a central, specialized, and permanent administrative structure."[12] Thus, one of the first questions asked by the leaders of new nations has been how to set up a central organ for planning. Similar questions are asked by the leaders of developed nations upon contemplating any major increase in the economic responsibilities of central government. In practice, these questions have been answered by the creation of many scores of central planning organs. Although these organs may be referred to as commissions, councils, boards, inspectorates, offices, bureaus, departments, or ministries, most of them carry the word "planning" in their titles. In countries with a much weaker commitment to the economic responsibilities of central government, these agencies bear such titles as National Economic Development Council (Britain), Expert Council for Opinions on Economic Development (West Germany), and Council of Economic Advisers (United States). No matter what their title, these agencies usually become prominent symbols of the national planning process or of specific plans. This role is emphasized by their issuing public documents analyzing economic trends and potentials or setting forth policies or plans for future improvement.

1. *The limitations of specialized planning agencies*

Modern administrative theory has clearly recognized that in single organizations, whether public or private, the administrative processes of planning, activating (or in older technology "directing"), and evaluating are interwoven at all hierarchical levels. In particular, all the

---

[10] Gruseppino Treves, *Government Organization for Economic Development* (Brussels: International Institute of Administrative Sciences, 1963).

[11] François Perroux and Michel Debeauvais, *Administrative Aspects of Planning in Developing Countries,* prepared for United Nations Meeting of Experts on Administrative Aspects of National Development Planning, June 1964, Paris. Mimeo.

[12] *Ibid.,* p. 4.

higher organs of management play vital roles in planning—that is, in developing commitments to desired future situations and sequences of action. Thus Simon, Smithburg, and Thompson long ago pointed out that "when we establish special organizational units that are designated as 'planning units,' these specialized parts of the organization will account for only a very small part of the planning." These units will often concentrate upon research services to be used by more active planners in other units or upon long-range problems divorced from the current decisions that determine future developments. In reviewing the activities of municipal and state planning agencies, Simon, Smithburg, and Thompson arrive at two interesting conclusions: (1) "almost any government agency that is entrusted with a goal and with very few and ineffective means for achieving that goal is likely to be called a 'planning' agency"; and (2) in any democratic structure specialized long-range planning units must always remain the most vulnerable units in the administrative organizations."[13]

At the level of a nation also the specialized planning units account for only a very small part of the national economic planning that actually takes place. They tend to concentrate upon certain research functions involving the analysis of general economic trends and the formulation of proposals to be decided upon by others. But the CPO's are not—and could not be—the only source of high-level proposals. Nor are they even the coordinators of national economic policy and programs. In fact, their specific functions are extremely varied and it is impossible to determine what these functions really are—or should be—without seeing them as an integral part of the complex network of *many* organs at the center of national government.

The widespread tendency to overconcentrate upon the CPO as the instrument of economic change has had many results. It has strengthened the position of economists and econometricians by gaining them some degree of access to the inner sancta of national policy-makers. It has resulted in greater recognition of the need for economic research and analysis. It has provided national leaders with planning units of considerable symbolic, ceremonial, and (as attested to by their vulnerability to frequent reorganization) sacrificial value. It has promoted a widespread working acceptance of the planning-execution dichotomy, as the CPO's frequently formulate proposals for what is deemed economically desirable in bland abstraction from the hard realities of political and social strategy. It has distracted attention from the larger tasks of institutional innovation. Indeed, it has seriously distorted any

[13] Herbert Simon, Donald W. Smithburg, and Victor A. Thompson, *Public Administration* (New York: Knopf, 1950), pp. 445-47.

serious efforts to understand the varying functions of the CPO's themselves. It is as though the early inventors of the airplane had concentrated their attention upon the design of wings without thinking seriously about such matters as engines, propellers, and fuel. After all, birds have wings, so flying machines must have them also. If this doctrine had been followed, the airplane designers would have indeed considered the relation between the wings and the rest of the airplane —just as the present-day CPO-designers try to consider the relationship between the CPO and other agencies. But they would have missed looking at the airplane as a whole—and the best we could have obtained would have been some good gliders capable of sophisticated adjustment to wind currents. In the same sense the ability of many CPO's to adjust to political currents is no substitute for machinery capable of providing genuine guidance of major economic change.

2. Role Permutations

The best way to disabuse one's self of the idea that a CPO can be omnipotent or omniscient on economic matters is to examine the actual functions of such agencies. More important, such an examination provides an ideal starting point for looking at a central guidance cluster as a whole and getting into broader problems of institutional, innovation and improvement.

An examination of actual CPO functions, however, is not an easy task. The boundaries of a CPO are often far from clear, since it may operate through committees with representatives *from* other organizations and may send CPO representatives to participate *in* other organizations. These boundaries are further blurred by multiple roles. Some CPO members wear many hats, and one cannot always tell which hats have a CPO insignia. Any CPO plays a multiplicity of different roles that are distributed in unpredictable ways among its various members. These roles receive different degrees of emphasis and indeed undergo fundamental changes with shifts in economic and political situations, in the structure of the central guidance cluster as a whole and in the CPO's own personnel and leadership style. Finally, some of the most important CPO functions are often shrouded in secrecy or at least by a smokescreen of "officialese."

An illustrative—and to some degree, speculative—comparison of the varying roles of CPO's in different countries is suggested by the table "Central Planning Organs: Major Roles." The information consists of judgments based upon sketchy published materials, personal visits to a number of these countries (Britain, France, India, the Netherlands, Tanzania) and intensive personal experience in CPO's in two

CENTRAL PLANNING ORGANS: MAJOR ROLES

CPO	General Leadership	Financial Management	Critical Problems	Special Staff	General Staff
Britain:					
National Economic Development Council	X			XX	
France:					
Commissariat du Plan	XX	X		X	XXX
India:					
Planning Commission	X	X		XXX	X
Israel:					
Economic Planning Authority	X			XX	
Netherlands:					
Central Planning Bureau				XX	
Tanzania:					
Ministry of Planning and Development	X			XX	
U.S.A.:					
Council of Economic Advisers	X	X		XX	
U.S.S.R.:					
GOSPLAN			X	XXXX	X
Venezuela:					
CORDIPLAN	XX			XX	XX

Key: X — occasional handling of some role in this role set
XX — regular handling of a few roles in this role set
XXX — intensive, sustained handling of many roles in this role set
XXXX — intensive, sustained handling of almost all roles in this role set
The XXX and XXXX notations do not imply any CPO monopoly of such roles. Even in areas of CPO concentration, other agencies may play significant roles.

(the U.S.A. and Israel). These judgments relate to the situation at the end of 1964. In a few cases reference is made to earlier periods. No attempt is made to predict future role patterns. Ceremonial, symbolic, and scapegoat roles—important though they may be—are ignored. Finally, no indication is given of the extent to which the specified roles are played by other agencies. Even in an area where a CPO plays many roles in an intensive and sustained fashion, other agencies may play more significant roles.

CPO's often start out with restricted roles in the preparation of official national plans or general economic policy documents. These may be linked with somewhat different roles in helping bring together representatives of important power centers—either heads of major government agencies or key "influentials" outside of government. Later they may go in one of two directions—toward the intensification of special staff work through advanced econometric analysis or toward general staff work as communication links, bargainers, evaluators, or expediters. Progress in either direction is usually enhanced if one or two CPO people win positions as informal personal advisors to chief executives and other high directorate members. Movement in both directions may be facilitated by "contracting out" econometric work to quasi-autonomous research institutions.

THE DYNAMICS OF CENTRAL GUIDANCE CLUSTERS

The previous two sections clearly suggest that in all societies—no matter what the social and political system or what the level of industrial development—the CPO's themselves are invariably small cogs in the machinery of national economic guidance.

Accordingly, any serious understanding of the institutional base of guided economic change requires the comparative analysis of central guidance clusters as a whole. To do this it will be necessary to observe the varying role permutations not only of CPO's but also of the many other actors—formal agencies, informal groups and key individuals—playing the various roles involved in general leadership, financial management, the handling of critical problems, and special and general staff work. It will be necessary to view every central guidance cluster as a subsystem of a broader social system and to analyze its linkages with other elements in the society. It will be necessary to study not only the structure of the subsystem but its performance under varying circumstances and the presumed connections between its performance and the various changes in economic and social performance that actually take place.

On the basis of preliminary surveys already conducted, it is possible to present four general observations on the dynamics of central guidance clusters. These may well serve as "springboard hypotheses" in intensive studies of the institutions of central economic guidance.

1. Their inner conflicts

The first observation is that *cooperative action among the actors in a central guidance cluster invariably emerges as an outcome of sustained and hectic conflict.* The formal hierarchic authority of chief executives or directorates is never enough to establish a "smoothly working machine."

A number of classic central guidance conflicts are well known—particularly those existing among the bureaucratic chieftains in charge, respectively, of the budget (usually in the Treasury or Ministry of Finance), the central bank, and central economic analysis. Indeed, the first two customarily establish their own economic staffs to compete with—or even displace—the "central" economic staff. Any newly established CPO, particularly one concentrating upon special staff research roles, customarily faces a prolonged battle for a place in the sun, if not a veritable struggle for survival. Where critical problems are created by shortages of goods or manpower, inevitable conflicts are created between those in charge of each and among them and the partisans of fiscal policy. The intensity and bewildering variety of these conflicts has been well portrayed in the histories of World War II economic planning in Britain[14] and the United States.[15] In the U.S.S.R. the high degree of central management has brought forth an unprecedented proliferation of competing bureaucracies. Even under Stalin, as Fainsod has pointed out, "Behind the monolithic facade of Stalinist totalitarianism, the plural pressures of professional bureaucratic interests found expression."[16] Since Stalin, there has been much more room for free play among these divergent and often sharply conflicting pressures.

Interwoven with the competition among bureaucratic interests one may also find informal role differentiation adding to the tensions. Thus there are invariably sharp tensions between

[14] Ely Devons, *Planning in Practice* (Cambridge: Cambridge University Press, 1950).

[15] U.S. Bureau of the Budget. *The United States at War* (Washington, D.C.: Government Printing Office, 1946).

[16] *How Russia is Ruled*, rev. ed. (Cambridge: Harvard University Press, 1963), pp. 578-79.

the Doctrinaires	and	the Pragmatists
the Risk Takers	and	the Risk Avoiders
the "Go Fast" Advocates	and	the "Go Slow" Warners
the Austerity Advocates	and	the Consumption Promoters
the Market Manipulators	and	the Market Replacers
the Rule Enforcers	and	the Rule Breakers
the Grandstand Players	and	the Behind-the-Scenes Operators
the Doers	and	the Thinkers or Technicians
the Authoritarians	and	the Compromisers and Integrators
the Career Oriented	and	the Task Oriented
the Empire Builders	and	the Consolidators
the Old Timers	and	the Newcomers
the Yes Men who support the whims of political leaders	and	the No Men who will try to "educate" the political leaders.

These roles are not listed for the purpose of suggesting that some are helpful and others harmful. The point, rather, is that they complement each other. While they tend to appear at the upper levels of any complex organization, they are particularly significant in the upper regions of government where vast power is mobilized and exercised. They bring to the fore the complementary considerations needed to make the use of power somewhat more rational and tolerable.

The complementarity, however, does not come into being through the simple interplay of logic or the meshing of carefully coordinated gears. It emerges, rather, from the heat and bitterness of clashing objectives and clashing personalities. In democratic societies, some of these internal conflicts become publicly aired from time to time—particularly when a dramatic resignation or reorganization takes place. In totalitarian societies much less information is available. When purges take place, top planning officials may suddenly disappear— with no explanation of what has happened to them. In both situations, however, detailed knowledge of the ebb and flow in inner power conflicts is a *sine qua non* of effective operations (if not survival) by the key executives and bureaucrats in the central planning cluster. Under such circumstances they are not likely to share this knowledge (except many years later in calm retrospect) with academic researchers.

2. *Their relations with "the people"*

The second observation is that *the tensions within a central guidance cluster always reflect, in part, the group conflicts and value conflicts in the society as a whole.*

A central guidance cluster, indeed, must be viewed as a specialized subsystem within the social system of a nation. It is part of the broader system whose structure and performance it tries to change. It is heavily influenced by the other subsystems. Indeed, the most effective actors within the central guidance cluster are those who have mobilized power through a network of alliances with important organizations and individuals outside the central guidance cluster.

The importance of these links with other parts of the social system can be illustrated by noting the "in the middle" rather than "on the top" position of the would-be managers of national economic change. An oversimplified representation of this relationship is presented in the following chart.

THE MANAGERS IN THE MIDDLE

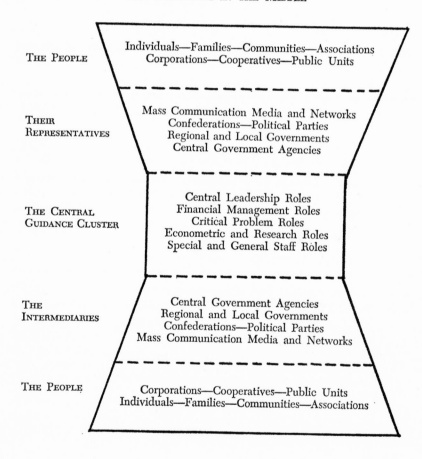

THE PEOPLE

Individuals—Families—Communities—Associations
Corporations—Cooperatives—Public Units

THEIR REPRESENTATIVES

Mass Communication Media and Networks
Confederations—Political Parties
Regional and Local Governments
Central Government Agencies

THE CENTRAL GUIDANCE CLUSTER

Central Leadership Roles
Financial Management Roles
Critical Problem Roles
Econometric and Research Roles
Special and General Staff Roles

THE INTERMEDIARIES

Central Government Agencies
Regional and Local Governments
Confederations—Political Parties
Mass Communication Media and Networks

THE PEOPLE

Corporations—Cooperatives—Public Units
Individuals—Families—Communities—Associations

At the bottom of the double pyramid we find "the people." These are not only individuals but the various overlapping groups into which people come together and through which they undertake the bulk of economic activities in any society. In some societies, of course, much greater activity is undertaken in families and communities; in others, much more by corporations and public units. In any society, however, the people are always engaged in a bewildering variety of economic activities. These activities include a very considerable amount of planning and attempts at implementation. Some of this planning is routinized and entrenched—as with family and household planning in predominantly agricultural societies. Some of it may be oriented toward dramatic changes—as in organizations engaged in technological innovation. Some of it—as with large corporations undertaking long-range investments—may be extremely sophisticated. Much of it may involve plans for competition or conflict with other groups. All of it will tend to resist externally imposed plans.

When governments engage in national planning, the objective is always to influence the behavior of this large array of individuals and collectivities. Thus national planning may be regarded as a process in which national governments, using many intermediaries, try to participate in or influence the plans of the people.[17] From this point of view the people and their groups belong at the *bottom* of the pyramid.

Yet in another sense the same people are always at the *top* of the pyramid also. They are the formal source of ultimate authority in any society. Obviously, this ultimate authority is much more meaningful in democratic systems, much less meaningful in authoritarian and dictatorial systems. But in any system the people also participate—even though indirectly and ineffectively—in the plans of the national government.

The most formal variety of participation is through the elected representatives of the people in the central government and in regional and local governments. The most numerous representatives are those who serve in legislative assemblies. Although there is a widespread tendency for legislatures to decline in significance, their roles in national economic planning may nevertheless include some or even all of the following: (1) ratifying the broad outlines of policy, whether

[17] For this idea I am indebted to the stimulus provided by S. S. Khera's comment in connection with Indian planning that "it is not so much the people participating in the [government's] programme; rather it is a people's programme in which the functionaries of government participate in different ways." *District Administration in India* (New York: Asia Publishing House, 1964), p. 195.

at national, state or local level, (2) serving as an arena for bargaining and mutual adjustment of competing interests to be served by plans, (3) serving as an arena for voicing of complaints concerning action or inaction under plans, (4) vetoing specific programs or program provisions, and (5) providing an instrument of popular education and communication concerning plan objectives and methods.

Elected executives (even where election is indirect) may be even more influential. They may serve as (1) representatives of all the people in an area (even where election is indirect), (2) leaders of legislative assemblies, (3) the key figures in central guidance clusters or in regional and local government, and (4) personal symbols and popularizers of national planning objectives.

Outside the formal government structure, but often closely allied with it, are the various national and state federations representing organized groups of producers, workers, and others. Some of these are confederations covering all sectors—as with national chambers of commerce and national federations of labor. Some are national groups limited to specific sectors. Each may be broken down into regional or local subsystems. These groups are often colloquially referred to as "interest" or "pressure" groups (a terminology reflecting the quaint idea that government agencies have no special interests or do not use pressure methods).

One attitude toward these groups is that they are obstacles to national planning. This is based upon formalistic ideas of the governmental process, exaggerated self-images of government planners, or wariness against one-sided pressures. Another attitude is that they are basic instruments of national planning. This is based upon an acceptance of the realities of power, the desire to organize a widespread coalition of interests, or a willingness to become associated with an exclusive set of organizations.

In some systems major groups of this type are made a formal part of the government structure. As already indicated, the leaders of some of these associations may be members of an informal control group in the central guidance cluster.

Leaders of political parties may also participate in the informal control groups of central guidance clusters. But the major roles of political parties—no matter what the party system—are intermediate; they serve as (1) a unifying element among national government agencies and national associations, (2) a unifying element between national, state, and local governments, and (3) a general instrument of communication throughout the population, particularly with respect to the broad objectives of national plans. These three roles in the national planning process are based upon party activities in placing personnel in particular positions—through both appointments and elections. In many developing nations they are the most essential factors in national integration—often in the form of parties of "entrenched dominance" (as in India and Israel) or single-party systems (as in Tanzania and Mexico).

3. Their relations with "the intermediaries"

The third observation is that *while a central guidance cluster cannot influence the plans of the people without strong intermediaries, strong intermediaries will usually resist coordination by the central guidance cluster.*

As already shown by the double pyramid chart, the managers of national economic change are themselves subject to considerable management—both formal and informal—by the same organizations that serve as their instruments for influencing the plans of the people. Beyond this, the multitudinous ministries or departments of central and state governments and the central agencies of local governments have tremendous potentialities for developing special interests and considerable power of their own. Where these potentialities are underdeveloped they can do little to influence "the people." When they are more fully developed, they are powerful enough to bargain with the central managers on the substance of national policies and programs. Often, they may lose out in so far as the letter of national plans are concerned but may have their own way at the stage of actual implementation.

It should be pointed out in this connection that simplistic hierarchic coordination is rarely feasible throughout this bureaucratic labyrinth. Even among the agencies of central government (including, of course, the "quasi-independent commissions" and public enterprises), multiple hierarchy is more frequent than the simplistic subordination of the classic "unity of command" model. Every significant agency is subordinated to many masters, control agencies or coordinators. Each one has its own lines of communication to key points in the central guidance cluster. Since the chief executive can "coordinate the coordinators" only at occasional times of crisis, lateral and polyarchical relations of mutual accommodation become decisive.

At the lower levels, polyarchy multiplies. Distance and detail breed independence and surges toward greater autonomy. Constitutional federalism, to be sure, provides a formal underpinning for this dispersion of power. But it does no more than ratify, and at times exacerbate, centrifugal tendencies that are inherent in the social structure itself and in the dynamics of extremely large-scale organization. Constitutional shifts of formal authority from states and localities to central governments would have little effect upon the organizational federalism which seems to be the only way of building a national web of influence.

4. Planning as structured competition

The final observation is that *national economic planning*—in the sense of developing purposefulness or guiding significant economic change—*is a form of structured competition or institutionalized social conflict.*

The institutions of market competition have, indeed, often been sharply contrasted with the institutions of planned economic change. The strong point in this distinction is the contrast between situations in which governments rely upon markets to govern economic events and those in which governments themselves assume certain responsibilities for influencing economic behavior. The distinction is particularly valid when people are sophisticated enough to distinguish between many kinds of markets (instead of assuming some stereotyped "perfect" market) and recognize the government's contribution to the existence and operation of any market.

Yet this old distinction between market competition and national planning breaks down at three points. First of all, national economic planning in its most extreme form can never replace markets. Even under the Stalinist Five-Year Plans, consumer goods were distributed through controlled markets. Government enterprises obtained labor in controlled labor markets. Uncontrolled markets grew up throughout government-operated industry in the form of quasi-legal but officially tolerated varieties of *blat* (personal influence) and *tolkach* (expediters).[18]

Second, to be effective, the managers of economic change must use—or even expand—market institutions. In most communist nations the planners have already learned that price systems and market manipulation are indispensable instruments of effective planning. In the industrially underdeveloped nations, one of the major objectives of the planners, no matter how socialistically oriented they may be, is to contract the demonetized nonmarket areas of peasant agriculture

[18] Joseph Berliner, *Factory and Manager in the USSR* (Cambridge: Harvard University Press, 1957); and Peter Wiles, *op. cit.*

and promote the wider exchange of goods and services in large-scale markets. In the industrially developed democracies the planners are invariably involved in various efforts to broaden market mechanisms and utilize them more effectively. This often involves cooperative relations with major private enterprisers in the formulating of growth goals for private as well as public investment. Thus national planning becomes a way of promoting, not doing away with, market competition.

Finally, and no less significant, the very process of national planning itself is a structured form of competition. In the very behavior of the central planners and managers themselves, we find a competitive struggle that resembles in many ways the competition that takes place in the marketplace. In bitterness and intensity this struggle is probably far more intense than that presumed to exist in "perfect" markets. The comparison with "real" economic markets, namely the markets of "imperfect" competition, is even more meaningful. As in imperfect markets, the distribution of power tends to be uneven. The flow of information is defective. New entries are extremely difficult. Exits usually take the form of merger or reorganization. The results are not statistically determinable in advance.

From this point of view, it is not enough to banish the myths of central omnipotence and omniscience from our view of CPO's. We must get rid of such illusions even within the broader area of central guidance institutions as a whole. No "master plan" can get away from the power struggles and social conflicts of the "political market" and the "bureaucratic market." These new markets may, indeed, serve to guide and humanize what happens in economic markets. But they offer no simple and easy solutions to man's difficulties in satisfying divergent human interests. For better or worse, they point toward larger and more complicated problems of governance. Markets are institutions of relatively unorganized complexity and considerable uncertainty. The organs of central economic guidance are institutions of highly organized complexity and still greater uncertainties concerning future patterns of action and interaction.

• 7 •

Some Notes on Reorganizations in Public Agencies

FREDERICK C. MOSHER

Students of public administration as well as the majority of our educated citizenry have long associated and even identified the word *reform* in the administrative realm with *reorganization*. There is ample etymological justification for such an association. *Reform* has literal origins in the giving of new or different form to something; and, in treating organizational matters, new form signifies new organizational structure. *Reform* has a strong normative connotation: as a noun, it signifies "change for the better"; as a verb, "to change from bad to good." *Reorganization,* though somewhat more restricted and precise in its definition, has come to acquire nearly the same meaning in American culture, both in its descriptive and in its normative senses. For a good many decades, American students—and probably the citizenry in general—have relied upon reorganization as a principal tool as well as symbol of administrative improvement, i.e., of reform. At least since the advocacy of the strong-mayor system before the turn of the century, municipal reform has been nearly synonymous with improvement in administrative structure—the commission plan, the council-manager plan, and, more recently in large cities, the mayor-administrator plan. A parallel emphasis has occurred in the states and the national government during the last half-century, beginning with the report of the Taft Commission in 1912 and 1913 and including in its sweep the wave of state reorganizations begun during the ensuing decades and renewed after World War II, as well as the studies of the Brownlow Committee and the two Hoover Commissions. The proposals of most of these groups emphasized the realignment of powers among agencies and officials and the rearrangement of functions and activities. Most of these studies aimed to promote "economy and efficiency" and were so justified; indeed, one or the other, or both, of these words found their way into the names of many of these commissions.

129

Faith in reorganization as an important instrument of administrative improvement is exhibited at governmental levels well below these sweeping jurisdiction-wide surveys—in individual departments and agencies, divisions, sections, field offices. Efforts to reorganize at these levels are less generally known to the public, but they are a common event in the official lives of most bureaucrats and, over the long pull, they may well have more impact than those more widely heralded. It is probable that such internal efforts to reorganize occur most frequently in new agencies whose programs, procedures, and personnel are still in flux, like the Office of Economic Opportunity; in agencies whose programs are controversial and vulnerable, like that whose current name is the Agency for International Development; and in those operating in a situation of high pressure and rapid change, such, for example, as the military departments during wartime and Cold War time, or the National Aeronautics and Space Administration. Overt efforts at reorganization seem to have been less frequent among those older agencies which are more or less protected from political exposure and from rapid changes in demands, in environment, and in technology. But even among these they do occur. In fact, reorganization in one or another agency and of one kind or another is a common though sporadic phenomenon in governments at all levels.

It is somewhat surprising that there has been so little dispassionate and objective analysis of public reorganizations. Many practitioners and many students of public administration have taken part in studies and in decisions intended to bring about reorganization. But rather few have looked back systematically at their experience and the experience of others in order to relate their efforts to the context in which they were working and to assess the effects of their efforts in the ongoing process of administrative development.

More specifically, there has been rather little objective treatment of three aspects of reorganization: (1) the underlying reasons and occasion for it in the changing context within which an agency or a group of agencies operates; (2) the process whereby it is carried out (or fails); (3) the appraisal of its actual effects on the operations of the agencies concerned. Although students of administration have contributed a great deal of thought and imagination to the bringing about of reorganization, they have devoted little scholarly attention to the totality of the process or to the later assessment of effects. Most of our work has been normative and prescriptive—a description of what is, followed by a prescription of what should be. It is typically represented by the familiar "before" and "after" charts—two still pictures lacking in the dimension of motion, of the dynamic process whereby the "after" supersedes the "before."

Yet the study of reorganization processes has a particular value for students of organization in general. As anyone who has survived a reorganization process—and this includes most of us—well knows, major organizational change or just the threat of change can be a traumatic experience in the career of an agency and in the lives of many of its members. It brings to the surface the aspirations, the anxieties, the conflicts, the motivations which are in more normal times submerged or sublimated—not easily recognized by observers of day-to-day administrative operations. From it we may be able to note and analyze attitudes and responses that are only faintly detectable during more normal times.

The paragraphs that follow contain some tentative observations and hypotheses which are directed principally to the first two questions above (the reasons for and the process of reorganization). They are based upon three principal sources of information. First are the previous writings in this field, admittedly few and thin although there are prominent exceptions. Second are my own observations and experiences with reorganizations in government. Third and perhaps most important are my interpretations of a series of about one dozen case studies of governmental reorganizations which were carried on under the auspices of the Research Committee of the Inter-University Case Program and the Institute of Governmental Studies of the University of California, Berkeley. These cases were focused upon efforts, succesful and unsuccessful, to reorganize governmental agencies at national, state, and municipal levels of government. Although their primary intent was to test the empirical validity of the hypothesis of participation as an effective instrument in bringing about success in organizational change, they shed much light upon the reorganization process in general.[1]

INCREMENTAL CHANGE AND EPISODIC CHANGE

Organization itself is an essentially static concept implying regularized behaviors, rules and roles, activities and relationships. It relies heavily upon predictability of actions and responses; and it implies a considerable degree of continuity and stability through time. It is interesting to note that even those organizations whose business it

---

[1] The agencies which these cases concerned include: (1) *national government*—the Agricultural Research Service, the Public Health Service, a defense research and development laboratory and the Children's Bureau; (2) *state governments*—Division of Architecture, Department of Employment, Fish and Game Department, Highway Patrol, Personnel Board, and a psychiatric clinic; (3) *city government*—health department, City Clerk, and certain other departments. The cases, together with an analytical commentary by this author, will be published by Bobbs-Merrill.

is to bring about change in the matters with which they deal and in the world around them are often, if not usually, internally stable and appear resistant to internal change. Thus a university, a good part of whose mission is the enlargement of knowledge, the improvement of research method, and the transmission of new knowledge and method to students, may be among the most conservative of institutions so far as its internal policies, rules, and relationships are concerned. The same is often true of research laboratories, of psychiatric clinics, and of government budget offices. Change is their business, but within themselves is a remarkable stability.

Yet it is a commonplace of most observers of governmental organizations in the United States—and of observers of private organizations as well—that change occurs over time within organizations, sometimes very dramatically. Its pace and dimensions vary enormously among different agencies and within the same agencies at different times. The expectability of organizational change has come to be nearly a hallmark of our society, sharply distinguishing it from many of the so-called primitive societies in which a significant institutional change was—and in some places still is—a threat to the social structure and to the survival of the culture.

Paul Appleby, in one of the earliest and still one of the most insightful essays on the subject, distinguished between two types of organizational change.[2] These he labeled, respectively, *constant* change and *episodic* change. The first, which is herein referred to as *incremental* change, has to do with the daily and weekly modifications in organizations, the continuing adjustments, none of which are conceived as "reorganizations" although many are consciously and purposefully planned and carried out. They include, for example, the shift of recruitment standards, the reclassification of a position, the promotion of an incumbent, the expansion or contraction of a budget, the addition of a new activity, the opening of a field office. More important and more subtle than these official and structural modifications are the changes in the members of the organization and in their relationships—their attitudes toward their jobs and toward organizational purpose, their developing skills, habits, and work ways, the routinization and modification of procedures, and others. Finally, there are changes arising from outside the organization, from the dynamics of the social context in which it works which are the sources of changing policies, changing emphasis in programs, changing clientele relationships, and many others.

2 "The Significance of the Hoover Commission Report," *The Yale Review*, Vol. 39, No. 1 (September 1949), pp. 2-22.

Over the course of years, such incremental modifications in the workings of an organization can be and perhaps usually are enormous, even though no one of them would qualify as a "reorganization" in the usual sense. Like members of a growing family, the members of the organizations themselves are perhaps least likely to notice such changes and their impact as they happen, but an observant visitor or consultant who comes back after two or three or five years is often struck by the transformation that has occurred in his absence. Such alterations over a period of time are as significant as any which consciously planned reorganizations might bring about, but some elements in every organization are more resistant to incremental change than others, leading over the years to internal maladjustments between the elements which have responded rapidly and easily to dynamic forces and those which have not. Among the latter may be included work habits, attitudes, particularly of older personnel toward their agency and their jobs, long-established routines, and venerable traditions. Thus, paradoxically, it is the cumulation of small changes which periodically creates the requirement for comprehensive and systematic efforts.

Among government agencies in particular the difficulty of modifying the legal basis for programs and procedures in constitutions, statutes, charters, and regulations is often a major source of organizational lag. In other words, what Appleby has referred to as *episodic* reorganization may be best understood as a requisite periodic process to bring absolescent elements in the organization up to date. In fact it may be postulated that every organization should undergo such an episodic reorganization as a matter of course every few years, its frequency dependent upon the nature and severity of such lags. It is this kind of episodic change, herein referred to simply as *reorganization,* to which we address ourselves. As distinguished from incremental change, it is characteristically planned, intended, and to some degree comprehensive. It is viewed by its participants not as an adjustment but in fact as a reorganization.

UNDERLYING REASONS FOR REORGANIZATION

Examination of the reorganization cases referred to earlier suggests that this kind of partial obsolescence was an underlying reason for reorganization in almost every instance. They arose from a failure or partial failure of the organization to respond to the dynamics of new times in one or more of six different dimensions. The first of these was simply *growth*—growth in size, growth in workload, growth in scope, etc. There has been an unfortunate absence of research on the effects of growth upon organizational structure, especially in government agencies.[3] It is a matter of common observation that large organizations are structured differently than small ones, even when their objectives and functions are exactly the same. For example, a growing organization, initially organized on a functional basis, must at some point move to a unitary structure (on the basis of clientele or geography or materials dealt with) because of the multiplying difficulties of communication and coordination and the congestion of procedures as among different related functions. Growth must certainly be a major underlying reason for decentralization and regionalization of both decision-making and operations. It may be noted also that the reverse process, contraction, can usually be expected to have the opposite effect upon structure.

A second source of obsolescence is the failure to respond adequately to *shifting problems and needs* in the area of activity in which the agency is operating. Public programs in the international field and in social and economic fields at home are replete with examples of this. In the field of public health the emergence of environmental health problems and of chronic disease are gradually surpassing in importance the more traditional emphasis upon sanitation and communicable disease. The mushrooming growth of metropolitan areas is having tremendous impact on virtually all domestic programs of government and indirectly upon their organization structures. The transformation of our foreign policy and the international programs to carry it out since World War II has been virtually total, and the repeated efforts to reorganize our foreign policy agencies are basically a structural response to rapidly changing demands.

A third source of obsolescence, usually related to the second, is *changes in the role of government* itself, both in the field of activity in which an individual agency operates and in the larger arena of governmental activities that are related to that field. Such changes in turn are a reflection of governmental response to the dynamics of the social and economic context within which governments operate. Thus, the growing responsibilities of cities in the fields of transportation (airports, freeways), of physical development (housing, urban renewal, open spaces), and of social development (the poverty pro-

[3] One of the relatively few examples was the study, reported by Mason Haire, of the structure consequence of growth in four private businesses. ("Biological Models and Empirical Histories of the Growth of Organization," in Mason Haire, editor, *Modern Organization Theory* (New York: John Wiley & Sons, 1959.) See also the study, described by Bernard P. Indik, on "The Relationship Between Organization Size and Supervision Ratios" *Administrative Science Quarterly*, Vol. IX, No. 3 (December 1964), pp. 301-12.

gram, civil rights) have almost everywhere created organizational maladjustments, giving rise to needs for reorganization. The explosions of the responsibilities of the national government in the past three decades have given rise to even more striking organizational obsolescence in almost every field—economic programs, social and welfare programs, military programs, natural resource development, science, research, and education. Our national response to new problems and new programs has, at least since the beginning of the New Deal, been typically opportunistic. New agencies are set up for each new problem area—the alphabet agencies of the New Deal, the hodge-podge of war agencies, more recently the Peace Corps and the poverty program's Office of Economic Opportunity. Later, when the emergency has subsided, or at least the new programs have matured from the stage of newness to one of "normalcy," we undertake the arduous business of integrating them with older ones where logic might have dictated their location in the first place.

The history of federal bureaus, many of which long antedate the great depression, illustrates another kind of obsolescence: that arising from the *changing shape and character of the administrative structure in general*—and outside of the internal functioning of the individual bureaus themselves. Some were initially established as independent units, at least partially because there appeared at the time no appropriate department in which to house them. Others were located in departments which, at the time, were clearly the most appropriate places for them. But over the course of decades, the accepted missions and scope of the departments changed and the berths became increasingly awkward to the point, in a few instances, of absurdity. Good examples of this phenomenon are provided by the older bureaus which were brought together under the canopy of the Federal Security Agency, later the Department of Health, Education, and Welfare:

Bureau	Department of Origin	Date of Origin
Public Health	Treasury	1798
Office of Education	Interior	1867[4]
Food and Drug Administration	Agriculture	1907[5]
Children's Bureau	Labor	1912[6]

[4] The Office of Education was originally established in 1867 and became part of the Department of the Interior in 1869.

[5] Carried on under various titles from 1907 to 1930 when it received its current title.

[6] Originally in the Department of Commerce and Labor, the Bureau moved to the newly separated Department of Labor in 1913.

The original location of each of these bureaus was entirely proper and logical in terms of the then current roles and structures of the then federal departments.

A fourth source of organizational obsolescence, actual or potential, is the *development of new technology, new kinds of equipment*, and *new knowledge* which are applicable in the performance of agency activities. The introduction of automated equipment and automatic data processing is best known in this category today. Very often, the decision to install new equipment of this sort occasions a simultaneous major reorganization; or sometimes, after halting efforts at incremental adjustments, a major reorganization follows. The effects of automation appear to be in some ways opposite and counteracting to the effects of growth cited above. By mechanizing routine decisions, automation changes the kinds of decisions that must be made by human minds as well as the kinds of processes that must be carried on by human hands. The role of top and middle management, and the introduction of management specialists and programmers, so alter ongoing individual functions and relationships that a major reorganization becomes almost inevitable.

A fifth source of organizational obsolescence is the *changing qualifications of personnel* in the fields of operation in which an agency works. This arises principally from changes in the educational system and its reflection of new and enlarging knowledge in different fields that are relevant to an agency's responsibilities. These changes in education may themselves be a response to changing problems and needs (second item above) of government agencies and may be initiated or stimulated by the agencies themselves. There is evidence that a good many of the professional schools in the United States were developed in response to such emerging governmental needs. Two of the best examples are the fields of forestry and agricultural sciences, but more recently we may cite social welfare, foreign area specialization, nuclear physics, and many specialized fields devoted to health research. In several of the cases of reorganizations cited earlier an underlying motivation was to enhance the qualifications, the stature, and the prestige of some of the professional personnel—biologists and wild life experts for fish and game wardens, psychiatrists in the field of mental health, public health officers, and others.

Finally, organizational obsolescence may arise from *actions taken by higher echelons* of a department or government or by higher levels of government. These may take the form of basic policy and program changes or of reorganizations, initiated and sometimes enforced from above, which make the current structure obsolescent in terms of the total organizational context. Thus, a basic change in structure at the headquarters of an agency may have the effect, directly or indirectly, of forcing a complementary reorganization in its field offices. Likewise, higher levels of government, through new and changed grant-in-aid programs, have brought about fundamental organizational changes in the recipient jurisdictions, sometimes making a reorganization a condition of receiving the grant. Reorganizations thus encouraged or imposed from above have had, over the years, enormous impact upon the structures of states, counties, cities, and districts in such fields as highways, welfare, public health, and education.

GOALS OF REORGANIZATION

In the foregoing section I have suggested that "episodic" reorganizations are a response to organizational obsolescence which has not been met by incremental adjustments; and I have cited six sources of such obsolescence which appear to be frequent. Reorganizations, however, may not be perceived in the general and impersonal terms indicated above by those who sponsor them. Nor are they usually perceived primarily as efforts to achieve greater economy and efficiency in the narrow and traditional senses of those terms. It would appear that the majority of reorganization efforts stem from the initiative of the top management of individual agencies—departments and bureaus and major divisions. The reorganization objectives of these officials may for convenience be classified in four major categories.[7]

First and most frequent are goals related to the *changing of operating policies and programs,* and frequently the expansion of the scope and extent of programs. In some instances, the goal is to implement or to make feasible a shift in program emphasis already decided upon; in others, its aim is to shift the loci of power in such a way as to facilitate desired program changes later. In either case the basic goals have to do with the broad directions and extensiveness of the substantive operations of the agency.

A second category of goals is directed toward the *improvement of administrative effectiveness* in the carrying out of existing agency

---

[7] I distinguish organizational (or reorganizational) goals from individual motivations, although the latter of course condition and provide part of the base for the former. Herbert A. Simon has recently written: "By *goals* we shall mean value premises that can serve as inputs to decisions. By *motives* we mean the causes, whatever they are, that lead individuals to select some goals rather than others as premises for their decisions." "On the Concept of Organizational Goal," *Administrative Science Quarterly,* Vol. IX. No. 1 (June 1964), p. 3.

responsibilities. In a good many instances, the improvement of administration is seen as a corollary or a secondary objective to accompany changes in program. And in very few cases is the improvement of administration omitted from the stated goals of an aspiring reorganizer. The administrative objectives may themselves be classified in five main categories: (1) increased control at the top and thus presumably better-coordinated operations, (2) decentralization of decision-making and operations, (3) increase in productivity and/or improved quality (efficiency), (4) reduction of costs in carrying on going programs (economy), and (5) the application of administrative principles.

It is interesting that among the cases referred to earlier the goal of economy was dominant only once, and then in connection with the installation of automated equipment. And efficiency, as defined above, also occurred only once as a dominant objective. "Administrative principles," though usually advanced in terms of economy and efficiency, appear to carry some independent force of their own: only seldom could any clear-cut relationship be established between organizational performance and principles such as clear-cut lines of authority and responsibility, symmetry and propriety of the organization chart, and limited spans of control. It was not a dominant goal in any case, though it was a secondary aim and provided justification in many of them.

A third type of goal for reorganization has to do more or less specifically with *personnel*, their qualifications, their welfare, their job satisfaction, their advancement, and in a few instances the removal or alleviation of individual personnel problems. As has already been indicated, reorganization is often seen as a device whereby qualifications and the performance of personnel can be upgraded. The realignment of activities and responsibilities is sometimes helpful in this regard and, in instances where there is some type of position classification system, it is virtually essential. In some reorganizations a major objective is the elimination of sources of employee unrest and unhappiness or, more positively, the enhancement of opportunities for advancement of individuals and groups and the enlargement of jobs. In fact some reorganizations are a direct response to employee demands of this kind. While comprehensive reorganizations to eliminate individual personnel problems are seldom so acknowledged, it appears that many are used in part for this purpose.

Finally, reorganizations are sometimes undertaken in response to, or in anticipation of, *criticism or threat* from the outside—whether another agency of the administration, the legislature, or pressure interests. Our studies suggest that such stimuli are fairly frequent provocations for organizational surveys, sometimes initiated and conducted from outside the agency itself, sometimes carried on from within to forestall outside action. They may explain the high frequency of reorganization efforts in agencies like AID whose programs are constantly under criticism. Such reorganization efforts are essentially protective or defensive in nature.

The Setting of Agency Reorganizations

A reorganization is by definition a change or a set of changes in a going system of relationships established and internalized over a period of time. That is, the organization which is to be changed has a history. It is here hypothesized that every such complex organization includes among its members individuals and groups whose ambitions, aspirations, and views of organizational purpose are in some degree at variance with one another. There are within each such organization, at least in latent form, *tensions* in the relationships among its different members.[8] There are also frequently links between such internal tensions and the groups and individuals outside the organization who are concerned with its activities—in the executive branch, in the legislature, among clientele and other pressure groups. Some of these external tensions often parallel and support some of the internal ones. That is, there are individuals and groups outside, whose views and influence can be expected to coincide with those of some organizational members and who can exercise their influence in appropriate directions when the occasion arises.

In the other direction, outsiders may call upon allies within the organization to gain bureaucratic support. Intraorganizational tensions within many agencies are a kind of mirror of continuing tensions of competing groups within the government and in the society as a whole. Among some of the embattled agencies which have little articulate external support and are laboring under a barrage of external criticism the tension may exist between organized external groups and the agency as a whole. Such a situation may contribute to the drawing together of the agency internally and the consequent reduction in the virulence of the internal tensions which might otherwise be expected. In the absence of issues or crises, tensions of these kinds may normally be considered to be latent and inactive. They

---

[8] A tension is here understood as a quality of a relationship among people or among identifiable groups of people centering around one or more issues on which there is underlying and continuing disagreement.

rise to the surface when a particular problem or action out of the ordinary run of things activates them. A reorganization or a threat to reorganize is usually such an event in so far as it promises or proposes a shift in power over agency purpose and over the relative status and advancement opportunities of different individual groups. In fact reorganization may be a particularly useful time to study an organization for this very reason; it permits an examination of the underside of the iceberg.

The study of a number of reorganization efforts reveals certain common and expectable types of tensions, even in organizations having vastly different purposes and activities. Thus complex public organizations typically include two or more different professional groups vying with each other for influence, recognition, and status. This situation differs from that discussed in much of the literature on private business where stress is laid upon the tension between management and worker on the one hand or between management and professionals on the other. In many or most public agencies management itself at the very top is normally a professional group in a functional field such as public health, psychiatry, forestry, and military. This top professional group seems usually to be the one whose field of specialism is historically identifiable with the overall function of the agency. But there are always other professions or subprofessions also engaged in agency work—administrative support officers such as budget, supply, personnel, legal officers, and usually operating personnel in related professional fields such as engineers, nurses, librarians, etc. Almost every reorganizational proposal involves or at least suggests a shift in the going power and status situations as among these different professional groups.

Another expectable kind of tension usually closely related to the first arises from different views as to organizational purposes and the relative emphasis to be given in the agency program to different kinds of problems. As indicated earlier, shifting emphases on purpose are perhaps the principal goals of reorganization as seen by their initiators.

A third common type of tension is that between higher and lower echelons of an agency: the pull of the higher level to maintain or enhance control and power over the lower *versus* the pull of the lower echelon for a greater degree of autonomy and self-control. This centrifugal-centripetal tension occurs both within the agency and perhaps at every level thereof, and between the agency as a whole and outside groups such as the chief executive, his staff agencies such as the budget bureau, and the legislature. It is closely related and sometimes identical with another type of tension: that between individuals and groups seeking to maintain or preferably enlarge programs and those seeking to restrain or contract programs.

Finally there is the kind of tension frequently found within agencies between those favoring the established and secure ways of doing things and those desirous of innovation and change. This is the well-known conflict between the old and the new, the conservative and the liberal. It is likely to be found among different groups of personnel: the senior *versus* the junior, the old *versus* the young, the high seniority *versus* the low seniority.

There are clearly a number of other kinds of tensions found in different kinds of organizations, such as tensions between management and labor, tensions between members of elite career services and others not so favored, tensions between political officers and career officers, tensions arising out of educational attainment, social and religious groups, sex and race differences, and personality clashes. But the ones listed above appear to be more or less generic and predictable in almost every organization and for the purposes of this discussion to be fundamental elements in the situations in which reorganizations are attempted. In our study of individual reorganization cases we found that almost every reorganization attempt had a considerable background in the agency's recent history. In most cases there had been one or more earlier efforts to reorganize and most of these earlier attempts were only partly successful or were truly unsuccessful. The themes of the subsequent reorganizations were usually fundamentally similar to the earlier ones and the kinds of continuing tensions revealed were also similar.

THE REORGANIZATION PROCESS

Reorganizations which are undertaken by and within individual agencies for the most part follow a fairly standard sequence of steps: (1) a spark, (2) a study leading to the development of a plan, (3) consideration, negotiation, and decision, (4) a study or studies on how to put the plan into effect, and (5) implementation. The sequence is not pursued religiously in every instance. Where the basic decision (step 3) is negative, the last two steps, of course, do not occur. Sometimes the initial planning includes a fairly detailed plan for implementation and the fourth step is omitted. And in a few instances there is no study at all where prior information is considered to be adequate for the decision. Each of these steps is discussed briefly in the succeeding paragraphs.

The Spark

Most organizations in the normal course of events operate in what may be considered to be a condition of dynamic equilibrium. That is, those individuals and groups who desire a major change in one direction are balanced against those desiring no change or desiring a change in the other direction. Or the desirability of the change, even when the bulk of persons concerned would favor it, is more than overbalanced by the upset and the dangers implicit in a major reorganization. One may therefore ask why in such a situation is reorganization undertaken? What is it that upsets the equilibrium of continuity and stability? The answer seems to be some particular event or combination of events which temporarily unhinges the equilibrium and makes possible the serious consideration of basic organizational change. This I have labeled a "spark." The spark need not be directly related to the organization's inner structure. And it appears from our review of reorganization cases that the spark is more often than not ignited from outside the agency itself; that is, although the main problems and the main tensions encountered in reorganization may be internal, their ignition is usually consequent upon some external event beyond the control of the agency or any of its members.[9] Our cases suggest that the most frequent kind of spark is a change in leadership at the very top of an agency. This may be the consequence of an election of a new chief executive or it may result from the retirement or resignation of the agency's head. In any case, it appears that a successor for at least a temporary period following his appointment has a freer hand, a "honeymoon period," for the consideration of organization changes. In fact, in many instances he is expected by both his superiors and his subordinates to bring about such changes, and in a few instances his own appointment is conditioned on the understanding that he will reorganize.

A second kind of spark is a significant change in the agency's budget by the legislature or by the executive budget agency.

A third is a criticism or a threat to the agency or to a major part of it from the outside—the chief executive or his staff, a legislative committee, or outside pressure groups. A major mistake or calamitous event in agency operations may give rise to outside criticism which in turn ignites a spark for reorganization.

---

[9] As a well-known example of this phenomenon on a very broad scale one might cite the reexamination and reorganization of school systems all over the United States which was begun immediately after the Russians launched Sputnik.

Illustrative of the reorganization sparks in the case studies were the following: (1) replacement, on the retirement of an agency head, by his erstwhile deputy, (2) appointment of a new agency head from outside following the election of a new governor, (3) refusal by central budget agency to consider a proposed budgetary increase until a major reorganization study had been made, (4) protest by an organized clientele group against a proposed increase in fees, conveyed to a legislative committee which thereupon ordered a study, (5) proposal by a chief executive's staff unit that a particular division be transferred from one department to another, and (6) suggestion by leaders of a legislative committee that they would require by law that an agency set up a new bureau to handle certain kinds of activities. Most interesting for our purposes is that, whereas the situation, the problems, and the tensions which reorganizations confronted were largely internal and had existed and been recognized for some time, the ignition of efforts to do something about them in almost every instance came from some event outside the agency in question.

Reorganization Studies

The initial gestation of thinking and negotiation as to whether a reorganization attempt should be undertaken and the scope of studies leading to such projected reorganization is usually carried on by the top agency executive and a small coterie of officials and advisers close to him. Where he feels it advisable to obtain informal approval in advance from above and outside the agency—its superior executive, the budget bureau, the personnel office, the appropriate legislative committee—representatives of these groups are consulted. At this stage, however, the discussions are typically a closely guarded secret within a small, narrowly circumscribed number of officers. The decisions made at this stage—as to the "givens" and the constraints within which the study is to be made, the methods to be pursued, the problems on which the study is to focus, and perhaps most of all who will make the study—are crucial. For they to a substantial extent determine the kinds of recommendations which will be forthcoming and the degree to which such recommendations will prove to be feasible of accomplishment. In fact, it is probable that most skilled administrators can predict in advance the general nature of recommendations that will emanate from a study on the basis of the way it is set up.

Thus a study may be purely exploratory with no prior instructions as to directions and focus; it may be specifically directed to the solution of particular problems, itemized in some detail; or it may fall at some point on the continuum between these extremes. It may be limited to the consideration of possible actions which appear to be politically and administratively feasible to the boss; it may be initiated with instructions to seek the best possible answers without any regard to their practicability;[10] or it may fall somewhere on the continuum between these two extremes. With regard to scope, it may be sweeping, covering all aspects of an agency operation; it may focus only on certain elements of structure, policy, and procedure; or it may be comprehensive with the exception of certain areas of operation which are declared "off limits." Finally it may be directed to the determination of the goals and objectives for the organization to pursue in the future, or it may be limited to the problems of implementing goals that are already decided. In all of these dimensions, the initiatory decision of the authority who sets the study under way to a substantial extent predetermines the nature of the study and the report which it will produce.

Just as important is the prior determination of what individuals or groups will participate in the study and in what ways. Accompanying this question and often of major significance are the prior determinations as to whom the report will be addressed to; in what form and with what specificity it will be prepared; how much time will be permitted for the study; and at what stages and to whom the copies of the written report, if any, will be made available.

It is useful to consider different kinds of study groups as falling on a continuum between those completely outside the organization concerned and presumably outside its direct control and influence on the one hand, and those completely inside the organization and immediately subject to the control and influence of the top line officials. At the extreme outside end of the continuum might appear a commission of private citizens established under authority of a legislative body or the chief executive, or a legislative investigating commission, or a mixed Hoover-type commission. At the extreme inside end of the continuum might be a study conducted by the principal executive himself without any assistance. In between would lie a variety of arrangements such as the use of private consultants, outside staff agencies, inside staff agencies, and line personnel. A hypothetical pattern of possible arrangements for organization studies is shown below.

10 Such an instruction is said to have accompanied President Johnson's "marching orders" to his various task forces during the fall of 1964.

OUTSIDE-INSIDE CONTINUUM OF REORGANIZATION STUDY GROUPS
IN ROUGH ORDER OF RELATIONSHIP TO AGENCY STUDIED

Outside

private citizen group, established and reporting to superior executive and/or legislature

legislative committee or group responsible to it

mixed or "Hoover Commission" group

private consultant, engaged by and reporting to legislative body or to chief executive or his staff

private consultant, engaged outside of agency by superior and reporting to him

government staff agency without agency invitation and reporting above or outside agency

Intermediate

private consultant working with agency officials on agency invitation and reporting to agency head

outside staff agency, working with agency officials on agency invitation and reporting to agency head

Inside

agency staff personnel, reporting to agency head

agency line officers, temporarily relieved of operating responsibilities, with or without assistance of staff personnel

agency line officers, working part-time on reorganization problems concerning their particular line responsibilities

agency head, with or without assistance of his immediate aides

The observation of a number of cases of reorganization study groups suggests certain hypotheses with regard to the expectable consequences of their location on the "outside-inside" continuum. Those relatively far toward the outside extreme are likely to (1) take longer and cost more, (2) be more comprehensive, (3) be more objective in considering agency program and welfare, (4) lay more emphasis on structural arrangements and administrative principles and less emphasis on substantive, program considerations, and personnel, (5) result in longer and more elaborate reports, (6) be more extreme and radical in recommendations, (7) require an "inside" follow-up study to consider problems of practicability and implementation, and (8) be more imitative of other like organizations in the same field of activities.

Studies conducted by groups or individuals near the "inside" end of the continuum are likely to (1) be less elaborate and less expensive, (2) result in shorter and more focused reports (sometimes they are not even written), (3) pay more attention to the problems of political and administrative feasibility, (4) give more emphasis to implementation and to the probable impact of organizational changes upon the welfare of personnel, (5) pay more attention to substantive policies and program and less to administrative principles, (6) be more focused on specific and known problems rather than covering the universe, and (7) be easier and quicker to implement.

There is of course a wide variation arising from special circumstances with respect to different types of studies, but these generalizations would appear to have validity. It should be noted however that studies conducted by outside groups, presumed to be immune from the influence or bias of the officials and personnel of the agency concerned, often have certain distinctive characteristics. Where a study is initiated primarily in response to external criticism, the presumed objectivity of a completely outside survey group has obvious advantages, at least from the standpoint of those who initiated it. Likewise, when an administrator is reasonably assured that the study group's basic recommendations will accord with his own objectives and when his aim is to gain the support of power centers beyond the limits of his agency (such as the chief executive or the legislature or pressure groups) the aura of objectivity provided by a reputable outside survey group may greatly strengthen his hand in his search for external support. In such situations the purely inside study might be useless or even negative in its impact. Not infrequently, in fact, outside surveys are sought for the primary purpose of providing an administrator objective and professional support to do what he wanted to do in the first place.

There seems to be an almost infinite variety of methods and style in the conduct of organization surveys, more than can be fruitfully described here. Suffice it to point out that the methods employed have a very substantial impact in at least two major ways: first, in the accuracy, validity, and wisdom of findings and recommendations; and second, in the acceptability and persuasiveness of the recommendations, which in turn depend partly on the relevance and the invulnerability of the findings.

The Reaching of Decision

Normally, following the receipt of a survey report there is a considerable period of discussion, negotiation, and consideration before a decision is made. This gestation is likely to be more prolonged if the report and its recommendations were prepared in secret and if they were prepared by a relatively outside group. It is not unknown, however, for individual recommendations to be discussed and put into effect during the course of the survey itself, especially when the study is conducted by an inside group.

Final decisions are typically made by the principal executive in the agency, usually with the advice of his immediate aides and subordinates and often following discussions and clearance with superior officers, superior staff agencies, and legislative representatives. At this stage of deliberation, the question of political and administrative feasibility appears to be at least as important as that of desirability. And like the initiatory decision discussed above, discussions at this stage, as well as the study report itself, seem usually to be held on a confidential basis within a limited circle of top officials. In the cases of sweeping recommended changes the decision is seldom totally affirmative. Some recommendations are usually turned down, modified, or delayed. Particularly sensitive questions may provide the occasion for further and more intensive study and the establishment of new and more specialized study groups.

Implementation

The reaching of a basic decision to reorganize is only the beginning of a long and arduous series of tasks. These may include: the drafting of legislation, new regulations, instructions, and manuals, and a variety of other directives; the revision of budgets and personnel classifications; reassignments of personnel; and, perhaps most important and most difficult of all, the education and training of personnel as well as of outsiders as to the new ways of doing things and the reasons for doing them differently. When the initial study has given little attention to the requisite steps for implementation—as outside studies usually do—the preparation for implementation gives rise to a new planning process which is more or less formalized and is typically conducted on an inside basis under the immediate direction of line officials.[11] The planning for implementation must comprehend in great and specific detail the duties and relationships of individual positions, the reactions and capabilities of individual people, the locations of equipment, furnishings, supplies, and people, and a host of other matters. It is therefore ordinarily more arduous and time-taking than the initial study. In fact, the total process of implementation, including its

[11] Although consulting firms as well as staff offices sometimes conduct implementation studies.

planning and replanning, is a matter of months and sometimes years. It often settles into the ongoing process which was referred to earlier as incremental change.

The machinery established for planning implementation and for the implementation itself—they are sometimes inseparable—is often elaborate, involving a variety of committees and subcommittees, task forces, staff meetings, special study groups, trial or demonstration runs, etc. At these stages more than any other does a reorganization give rise to employee participation in planning and in action. Indeed, some participation is almost by definition inevitable since ultimately the individuals whose routines and behaviors are to be changed must participate in bringing about the changes. But the nature and style of the participation, the degree to which ideas and suggestions are invited, accepted, and considered, vary a great deal. The cases suggest that a substantial degree of participation in the planning and carrying out of the implementing steps is generally conducive to willing and even enthusiastic employee acceptance of a reorganization. But, of course, from the standpoint of top management, extensive participation at this stage, as at any other, has its dangers. It provides disaffected individuals and groups, of whom there normally are some, the opportunity to plant road-blocks and sometimes to nullify the intent of proposed organizational changes.

In fact, the process of giving effect to the plan is the "cutting edge" of a reorganization, an aspect too often overlooked in organizational study. It provides the test of the plan—its wisdom, its practicality, its acceptability—a test of the administrators who are seeking change, and a test of the employees themselves. It is here that substance and intent may give way to form and title; that unanticipated costs of change appear and may be purposively magnified by dissidents; that the goals of change may be misinterpreted both within and outside the agency, sometimes with damaging—even disastrous—results to the agency's program.

THE EFFECTIVENESS OF REORGANIZATION: A CONCLUDING NOTE

The assessment of the success of reorganization efforts is a hazardous business in most, but not quite all, cases. Results are seldom objectively measurable—in terms of either the values achieved or the costs entailed. And the comparison of what happened as a consequence of the effort and what would have happened had it not been made is at best hypothetical. It would seem, at first glance, that one could easily identify the total failures—reorganization studies which were made and abandoned in the files. In fact, it would appear that uch "failures," complete or substantial, are more frequent than "successes." But such a verdict is often itself doubtful, even where the recommendations are at the time ignored or repudiated. I once conducted a study of a large division and presented my recommendations in some detail to its chief. He thanked me for the suggestions, said he didn't agree with them, and filed them away. Several months later he was replaced, and his successor almost immediately unburied the proposal and put almost all of it into effect. A more frequent consequence of an unsuccessful reorganization effort is that it provides a precedent and guidelines for future reorganization studies and for incremental changes carried on during the months and years which follow it. This is probably a common result of many of the sweeping outside studies of organization when the administrator deems it unwise to proceed at once. Often he will use the study as a road map for subsequent piece-by-piece changes in law, in budget, in personnel, in assignment, etc. Under such circumstances, it would be inaccurate to attribute total failure to the study, even though its immediate effects were nil.

Another kind of difficulty in assessing the success of efforts to reorganize arises from the cost side of the equation. All such efforts entail some costs, but only a part of the costs are measurable. An organizational survey alone may itself be accurately costed, particularly if it is contracted out to a consulting firm—at five, or fifty, or one hundred thousand dollars. This fee will of course not include the incidental costs of staff time and other charges incident to the study, most of which are not susceptible of specific valuation. Potentially more significant are the hidden costs of putting proposed changes into effect in terms of work, of retraining, of morale, of time from regular duties, of separations and new hiring, etc. Such costs are hardly measurable and seldom even estimated. In fairness, one should observe that there are often values in reorganization of the same kind —increased motivation of personnel, better morale, new and better qualified people—which are equally difficult to quantify.

Perhaps the greatest difficulty in appraising the success of reorganization efforts is the fuzziness and the controversiality of the criteria, the yardsticks, against which to measure. Earlier paragraphs of this discussion should have made clear that reorganization is seldom an end in itself. Rather it is a means to the accomplishment of other ends such as change in policy and program, or greater operating efficiency, or the increasing satisfactions of personnel, or the quieting of outside criticism. One may accept the goals of the initiators and sponsors of reorganization, who are usually the heads of the agencies themselves, as the criteria against which to judge—as was done in connection with the cases referred to earlier. Or one may substitute his own criteria, his own view of the public interest in the functional area of the agency studied. The former seems the wiser course in the assessment of reorganizational efforts, in so far as the goals may be reliably determined. The public interest, however reasonable and specific it may be to each of us individually, is a vague, even mystical guide for an entire polity. Judgments on the merit of reorganizations which have to do with policy and program—and these apparently include the majority of them—can hardly escape the underlying difficulty of the "policy sciences," as some have dubbed them, the problem of social values in a democratic society. Who is to determine what is good and what is bad?

This is not to be construed, however, as an argument against systematic organizational review and assessment. The acceleration of change in our society and in the world makes ever more necessary rapid change in our government. As has been suggested in earlier paragraphs, incremental adjustments can seldom keep pace with these dynamic demands on every front. It is likely that planned reorganizations—"episodic" changes, as Paul Appleby labeled them—will occur with increasing frequency in the future. Perhaps they will be put on a regular, expected, and scheduled basis. Such an arrangement might at the same time increase their prospects of effectiveness and diminish their costs.

· 8 ·

The Changing Intergovernmental System

GUTHRIE S. BIRKHEAD

Paul Appleby liked to play debunker, in the style of the small-town newspaper editor. He was in this frame of mind when he wrote that federalism is not one of the "essentials of popular government."[1] Dean Appleby deduced this from his general reading of American history and from his first-hand observation of government operations at the national, state, and local levels. By saying it, however, he joined hands with a goodly company of political scientists. He might have cited James Madison: "As far as the sovereignty of the States cannot be reconciled to the happiness of the people, the voice of every good citizen must be, Let the former be sacrificed to the latter."[2] I suspect Appleby also knew he had support for his opinion in the writings of Tocqueville, Bryce, and many twentieth century scholars. Professor Arthur Macmahon, for example, has referred to federalism in the United States and elsewhere as an "expedient."[3]

It is difficult to see the need to alter this judgment as applied to the broader concept of intergovernmental relations. Classical usage of the term federalism ordinarily covered the relations between a central government and its major component parts. Discussion in the recent American literature, however, has increasingly revolved about intergovernmental relations as a whole, including contacts with and among local governments of all types and horizontal relationships among governments at all levels. "Cooperative federalism" is, for example, a term that is commonly used to refer to the same set of phenomena as "intergovernmental relations." In this paper, "federalism" and "intergovernmental relations" will be used almost interchangeably.

This essay begins with the hypothesis that federalism is not a cardinal national issue. The changing relations among various parts of the intergovernmental system is nevertheless a lively area for con-

[1] *Citizens as Sovereigns* (Syracuse: Syracuse University Press, 1962), p. 49.
[2] *Federalist 45* (New York: Modern Library, 1937), p. 299.
[3] *Federalism Mature and Emergent* (Garden City: Doubleday, 1955), p. 3.

tinuing study, in the first place because "federalism" is a favorite piece of camouflage. Paul Appleby knew this well, and he deplored the "confining application of the 'federal' idea, States Rights, and other such theoretical formulations as a way of opposing the popular will on particular issues."[4] It is unfortunate that even today most of the talk on behalf of state and local governments still springs from a desperate desire to salvage vested interests, preserve racial segregation, or resurrect a curious brand of latter-day chauvinism. Senator Barry Goldwater's candidacy made such ambitions appear more popular than in fact they were, although his defeat has not eradicated the slogans.

A second reason for serious continuing examination of American intergovernmental relations is less emotion-ridden: that system is the principal vehicle for carrying on domestic governmental business, and it is constantly changing. It is, indeed, an intricate, nearly infinite series of relationships among national, state, and local governments and officials. In a sense the system is an equilibrium moving through time, and a change in one part will produce effects elsewhere. This balance among diverse governments, groups, and individual actions and attitudes has endured because it has continually been patched, reshaped, and augmented to fit the increasingly complex problems of the United States.

Federalism has of course been different at different times in our history, in terms of Supreme Court decisions, political party strength, programmatic relationships, finances, and other measures. In this century the system has been undergoing continual alteration. In this paper a few prominent features of the federal landscape today will be reconnoitered. First, the gross dimensions of intergovernmental relationships in finances and in scale generally will be described. Second, there will be a look at what appears to be the developing role of the state governments. What might the states do that would make them worth preserving? Finally, international affairs and American federalism are more closely related today than ever before, if not in our minds then certainly in the minds of our friendly and not-so-friendly critics abroad. To what extent may we recommend that the newer nations seek to emulate our federal experience?

INCREASING COSTS

Governments today generally have more powers and employees, do more, spend more than ever before. All parts of the federal system have participated in this expansion. Comparison of some aggregate

[4] *Op. cit.,* p. 52.

finances may indicate broad directions. In this century (1902-62) gross public expenditures have increased from 7.7 per cent of gross national product to 31.7 per cent of GNP. Local direct expenditures during that time went from 4.4 to 7.9 per cent of GNP; state direct expenditures from 0.6 to 3.8 per cent; and national direct expenditures from 2.6 to 16 per cent. On a per capita basis in 1962 national expenditures were about 21 times the 1902 level, state expenditures also about 21 times that of 1902, but local only about five times. Another way of seeing the change is to note that the national share of total direct expenditures for *domestic* purposes during the same period has grown from 17 to 27 per cent and the state share from 10 to 24 per cent, while the local share has dropped from 73 to 49 per cent.[5]

By all odds the biggest changes in these finances came about in the 1930's. The magnitude of all expenditures shot up, and the three "levels" assumed approximately their present relative positions. Since the 1930's both states and localities have slightly increased their shares of domestic expenditures. And the dimension of intergovernmental aid may be added to these figures. Both state and federal aid have grown in absolute terms since the depression years, but they have grown at about the same rate. In 1962 the states received 22.8 per cent of their general revenues from Washington, but they paid out 33.9 per cent of their general expenditures to localities. Local expenditures have grown in proportion to the growth in aid from higher governments. Grant receipts as a proportion of local expenditures amounted to 26.4 per cent in 1962, as compared with 27.5 per cent in 1935, the peak depression year.[6]

Thus gross expenditure data indicate a surprising amount of stability in the finances of the federal "equilibrium." State governments have grown the most during this century, although of course much of their money has passed directly to localities. Most of the growth of all levels was associated with the depression years. Finally, both state and local governments seem to be strong at present and in little danger, absolutely or relatively, of having their financial bases wither away. Property taxes have continued to produce more and more income for local governments, somewhat to the consternation of long-standing critics.[7] State revenues also have continued to grow with

[5] Frederick C. Mosher and Orville F. Poland, *The Costs of American Governments* (New York: Dodd, Mead, 1964), Chap. III and Table 4.

[6] *Ibid.*, pp. 54-57. This book contains many more useful and insightful comparisons.

[7] See Jesse Burkhead, *State and Local Taxes for Public Education* (Syracuse: Syracuse University Press, 1963).

the population and the economy. It has been the state sales and income taxes that have permitted expansion of state activities and of
state subventions to local governments in several states (not, of course,
to denigrate the contribution of federal grants). It might be argued
that federal aid to states, state aid to localities, and local revenues
from local sources have all expanded at more or less the same rate
because they have kept up with the national economy. Whether or
not that is the case, there has been little relative change in the financial
position of the component governments of our federal system since
World War II.

The newest major departure from tradition in the financial patterns is that of the direct federal-local aid for housing, urban renewal,
airports, and a few other programs. In 1962, $782 million went to
local governments directly from Washington through these channels.
This sum was slightly over 10 per cent of total national intergovernmental expenditure in that year, $7,735 million.[8]

INCREASING SCALE

It has long been acknowledged that performance of almost every
function of government is shared by two or more levels of the federal
system. The cases of draft boards, National Guard, or infraction of
traffic ordinances are trite substantiations of the point. But large-scale
and direct involvement of subnational governments has come about
in recent years mainly through the big new programs. Annually it
seems the number of such programs depending on intergovernmental
relations is augmented. In 1964 Congress in one law—the Economic
Opportunity Act—created about nine new enterprises which will
feature active participation by state or local governments or their
instrumentalities.[9] Rare indeed is the state legislative session that does
not create a new educational endeavor or alter an old one. The resulting mosaic of money, people, and agencies is confusing not only
to the outsider but also to the insider. The scale of transactions—
letters, reports, interviews, trips, conferences, consultations, plans, and
payments—is indeed vast. This is the stuff of our public administration.

In this welter the search for a way of organizing these linkages—
of integrating programs on an areal basis below the national level—
has been revived. And one has an uneasy feeling of déja vu. This
aspiration to integrate haunted the National Resources Planning Board

[8] U.S. Bureau of the Census, Census of Governments, 1962, Vol. IV, No. 4,
Compendium of Government Finances (Washington, 1964), Table 1.
[9] P.L. 88-452, 88th Congress, August 20, 1964; 78 Stat. 508.

in the 1930's—a much simpler era for federalism. The Board and its successors examined river basins as well as many other uni- and multi-functional concepts with reference to improving national field as well as intergovernmental program administration. The U.S. Bureau of the Budget has toyed with the problem also, for example in its old regional offices. Interior and HEW among other federal departments have long tried to draw program efforts together in the field. All the familiar study commissions looked at, were appalled by, and recommended remedies for the syndrome of related but uncoordinated activities.

It is sobering to realize how little of the thinking of those days rubbed off on the busy officials who were the creators of, among several examples that might be chosen, the battery of urban development undertakings. One might almost say that it has fallen to the lot of the local chief executive or urban renewal chief to pick and choose, to make an Appleby "mesh" for his locality from among over forty available federal programs and here and there a state program or two.[10] The local man has always received excellent help from HHFA and other field officials, and the workable program with all its faults has been a help also. In effect, however, the invitation went out from Washington for individuals with entrepreneurial bent to invade this market place and carry out the integration in the locality. The idea has worked well in a number of medium-sized local governments. This is perhaps as great a testimony to the men who performed the local brokerage function as it is testimony to the program.

The entrepreneurs have had greater difficulty in the big metropolitan areas. Recently it has been officially noted that integration of urban development programs at a level above the municipal corporation, the metropolitan level, is becoming an urgent need. The Advisory Commission on Intergovernmental Relations, in its unobtrusive way, has grappled with the issue for four years. In a 1961 report[11] ACIR called for the national government to give financial and technical assistance to metropolitan planning agencies and to vest certain review functions in connection with grants-in-aid from Washington in such

[10] U.S. Senate, 88th Cong., 2d Sess., Committee on Government Operations, "Impact of Federal Urban Development Programs on Local Government Organization and Planning." A Report by the Advisory Commission on Intergovernmental Relations, May 30, 1964, p. 2.

[11] U.S. Senate, 87th Cong., 1st Sess., Committee on Government Operations, "Governmental Structure, Organization, and Planning in Metropolitan Areas." A Report by the Advisory Commission on Intergovernmental Relations, July, 1961, pp. 43 ff.

agencies. Its research activities, with their resultant findings and recommendations, have combined to make ACIR the best official thing
that has happened to intergovernmental relations in years. For a
second example, in 1964 ACIR recommended six governmental integration measures to the Senate Committee on Government Operations.
It was intended thereby to begin "reorienting Federal programs to
facilitate and encourage cohesive organization and effective planning
processes in State and local governments receiving Federal urban development aid, and . . . coordinating urban development policy within
the Federal Government." In brief, ACIR asked Congress and executive agencies to favor general-purpose governments above special-
purpose governments in making grants, to encourage joint action and
to "require and promote" effective planning by and among such
governments. They asked the states to pass enabling laws for such
joint enterprises. With six dissents, they agreed to encourage the
states in this field by channeling grants to them when states take positive action to join in financing and to some extent managing the programs.[12] Thus ACIR seems to see a place for integrative activity at the
local level (mainly through planning) *and* at the state level.

Congress meanwhile has actually legislated a little assistance to
metropolitan planning efforts, first of all in the grants authorized by
Section 701 of the Housing Act of 1954. Most recently, in the Urban
Mass Transportation Act of 1964, Congress made financial assistance
conditional upon preparation at the local level of what is called a
"unified or officially coordinated urban transportation system as part
of the comprehensively planned development of the urban area."[13] This
comprehensive planning would be the general equivalent of the workable program for a single government, and the intent of the framers is
to promote a measure of interlocal integration as well as planning. If
large grants-in-aid become available in the next few years to meet
urban transit planning and expansion costs, this program may bear
fruit.

Planning is such a slender reed that it needs to lean upon the
lustier, better financed functions such as transit. For planning almost
always lacks a close tie-in with the decision-making centers of government. Further, planning integration of the foregoing type may increase
in the immediate future, for horizontal relationships among governments are now multiplying in other fields. Functional consolidation
through interlocal contracts and joint enterprises is proliferating in

[12] See below, pp. 160-61.
[13] P.L. 88-365, 88th Congress, Secs. 3c, 4a, and 5.

many states; intergovernmental conferences are slowly increasing; and even interstate cooperation on a variety of urban problems is growing. Indeed, functional consolidation of these and other types is perhaps the principal structural expedient today keeping the states and localities in relatively good health. ACIR is correct that there are too many single-purpose governments by any common-sense measure, nonetheless *ad hoc* units often have a vigor and produce results that put general governments to shame.

WITHERING?

The vigor reflected in the financial aggregates quoted a few paragraphs back also negates the view that states or localities are withering away. In financial terms, the federal structure is stronger than ever, mainly but not solely because the upper levels have aided the lower ones. And a considerable diversity is of course concealed in the totals. New York's tax picture varies from that of New Jersey. State-local relations are of a somewhat different type in North Carolina than in Missouri.

The "withering" metaphor may be applied to some of the old units of local government—towns, villages, municipal corporations.[14] It certainly is not an apt way to speak of any other developments at state or local levels, in the wake of the population and economic growth the United States continues to experience. When Congress has lowered taxes and when there is serious discussion of per capita grants to the states, it should cause no surprise that economic growth has also kept state and local income sources lucrative.

Analysis of metropolitan growth and problems is plentiful and systematic today. The states, however, are not often considered; so let us look at them for a moment. They perform important if rather colorless functions: election administration, records-keeping, licensing, law enforcement. Law-making is the states' most pervasive function and is indeed the major way in which formal standards are set for the society: civil and criminal codes, regulation of man's relationship to man and to organizations. State common and statutory laws are greater in bulk and substantive coverage than are national laws or

---

[14] For example, Professor York Willbern, *The Withering Away of the City* (University, Alabama: University of Alabama Press, 1964). He is referring of course to the increasing importance of activities which cover areas larger than the old municipal corporations, but also more than that. On page 134, Willbern says that "the city as a definable, corporate community of friends and neighbors with common interests which can be furthered by integrated, unified political processes" is withering away.

local ordinances (at least, they would probably be found so if there were ways of making the measurements). To list these traditional functions is to reflect on their impact on the individual person. One comes face-to-face with the state government in the courts, in paying income or sales taxes, in buying an auto license, or observing an unemployment insurance deduction. If not boredom, then perhaps anger is the emotion most often associated with state government.

The states are, however, gaining shares in managing some newer governmental functions. There is a respectable list of newer, rather exciting and interesting state activities in water use, recreation, higher education, scientific research, and promotion of industrial development. One well-known instance is that of California which (of course, with national and local help) is well along with realization of a statewide water plan entailing huge capital outlays and employment of up-to-date engineering techniques. Four Eastern states since 1962 have been working with the national government for the same purposes in the Delaware River basin and adjacent areas.

Another example of functional strength is provided by the states' role in higher education. As student numbers and the costs of education and research have risen, at least some of the states have struggled manfully with their university systems. Aid from Washington has been crucial, but the state portion of the work has been tangible and very worthwhile. Or take automobile safety, another kind of policy area, but also one in which the state role has not been insignificant. It was action by two states that persuaded manufacturers to put seat belts in all automobiles.

Such examples illustrate only that there is a little life left in the old states, however, and do not demonstrate that they are models of financial, program, or institutional strength. For both state and local governmental institutions and procedures are still being criticized roundly by taxpayers' associations, bureaus of research, and a few academicians. The yardsticks of economy, efficiency, and "democracy" are still in use around the nation. This is no longer so true in the universities, where the generation of political scientists and economists who gave full time to indicting constitutions, organization, taxation, confusing laws, and so on is seemingly in eclipse. The conditions they identified as needing reform have not been eradicated by Little Hoover Commissions, constitutional conventions, or waves of reform sentiment. That the old concern, the enchantment with gadgetry that so many political scientists used to have in connection with state and local "problems," was not effective probably means two things. It may mean that political scientists were not very influential, and that little of the feeling that reform was a high priority matter lingered long in the minds either of the electorate or of many opinion leaders. Today the most scholarly attitude seems to be that state and local problems, if they exist at all, can best be surmounted through dependence on some kind of political market place.

One suspects that both the market-place watchers and the old-style gadgeteers were delighted, however, with the breakthrough on state legislative representation in 1962-64. No doubt, malapportionment of legislatures was the most basic dilemma confronted by the states until 1962. In the decision of Reynolds v. Sims[15] the Supreme Court has produced what looks to be the biggest revolution in federalism since the 17th Amendment or perhaps even since the Civil War. The Court simply directed that representation in both houses of every state legislature be based on population.

Now the lower federal courts are at work directing development of specific means for implementing the decision in Reynolds v. Sims. One sure result will appear in the legislative bodies: urban and suburban-based minority delegations will be transformed into majority parties in many states.[16] They are then bound to fumble and stumble while looking for program direction, for legislative leadership will develop more slowly. More often than in the recent past these majorities in both houses will be of the governor's party, and thus they may depend more upon his leadership. If, as supporters of reapportionment hope, the long-term result is also to make legislatures more representative of widespread popular opinions, then state governments will be stronger for the change. Reputationally, they will be stronger anyway.[17]

STRONGER STATES?

The prospective reapportionment then gives basis for hope that the states may become more viable political entities. When and if that happens, more will be said about the theoretic advantages of strengthening state governments otherwise. In theory the very size of the states is a point in their favor. Wide boundaries endow them with greater human and material resources, with larger populations and

[15] 12 L. Ed. 2d 506.

[16] The Johnson landslide of 1964 was so heavy that it transformed one long-standing minority into a majority without reapportionment: New York's Democratic legislative delegation.

[17] Reapportionment of state legislatures is causing repercussions in local governments. There will be some reapportioning and redistricting of county and city councils, by analogy. This is coming about through state court decision, new laws passed by reapportioned legislatures, and by local charter amendment.

more diversity of interests. Among existing subnational governments the states have recourse to the most lucrative tax bases. They are also in the best position geographically to speak or act on metropolitan or regional matters when, as frequently happens, one state embraces an entire urban complex or two states may find interstate cooperation possible.

This is of course a point of theory, hard to demonstrate in operational terms. State politics is not as well understood as it might be. What is known of state performance, however, in struggles with railroads, contractors, oil producers, insurance companies, organized crime, or citizens' councils, does not lead to great confidence in their capacities. Nor does it lead to desire to give the states more to do. On the other hand, it could be that the new apportionment will alter old political power distributions and provide opportunity for the states to become more potent in developing consensus through debate.

The states could become more viable politically if their new legislative majorities and minorities would reflect the kind of diversity in economic and social interests that the broad boundaries of most states comprehend. Paul Ylvisaker has stressed the "central importance of diversity of interests and debate as instruments of liberty and welfare."[18] In 1964, many local governments—one-industry cities, a variety of suburbs, governmental units in one-party areas, even larger cities where little tradition of interparty competition exists—could not survive this test. General local units of governments for our spreading cities are appearing only at the rate of two or three per decade (Miami, Nashville). Meanwhile, there are the states, in theory not a bad choice for doing a lot of things that are not being done today, for encompassing diversity and providing a forum for debate.

It has already been mentioned that the Advisory Commission on Intergovernmental Relations in 1964 moved "to encourage a more meaningful and effective role for the States in urban affairs." ACIR recommended

> that the States assume their proper responsibilities for assisting and facilitating urban development; to this end it is recommended that Federal grants-in-aid to local governments for urban development be channeled through the States in cases where a State (a) provides appropriate administrative machinery to carry out

[18] "Some Criteria for a 'Proper' Areal Division of Government Power," Chap. 2 in Arthur Maass, ed., *Area and Power* (New York: Free Press of Glencoe, 1959), p. 37. Ylvisaker is speaking of criteria for dividing governmental powers among general governments. He values debate above efficiency or participation.

relevant responsibilities, and (b) provides significant financial contributions, and when appropriate, technical assistance to the local governments concerned.[19]

Eleven programs related to urban development already are administered through the state governments, but ACIR wants more "definite contributions to program objectives by the States." This clearly means that more state appropriations for urban development would be welcomed by ACIR, although it is not so evident that they would welcome state contributions on matters of policy.

Indeed it may not be practicable to think of the states as becoming heavily involved in public policy-making in any of the new programs being initiated in Washington. Administrative structure as well as policies are quite fragmented in the national government, and to bring them into a coordinated package at the state capital is today patently impossible. Even, however, if national organization and policies could miraculously be improved, what is the legerdemain by which a governor or state party can make a logical whole out of old state activities and new intergovernmental programs? It seems that in no state has the strong-governor concept been effectuated sufficiently to make possible a useful and meaningful unity of state programs. In New York, where the governor for years has had high prestige as well as much of the formal authority adjudged necessary by reform polemicists, key functions like social welfare and education still remain screened from his leadership by the constitution. His relations with the majority (normally his own party) in the legislature have rarely been peaceful. Who else in state government might inject policy judgments into the new intergovernmental programs? Would advisory councils be better suited, in view of the functional orientation and background so often vital to understanding the new and complicated programs?

Any fledgling chance to strengthen the states was probably set back by the favorable reception given in a number of state legislatures (but also by wider publics) to the three constitutional amendments proposed by the Council of State Governments in December, 1962. The amendments would have erected a new way for state legislatures to amend the federal Constitution without any real check by Congress or convention. They would also have taken state legislative apportionment beyond federal control or judicial jurisdiction, and would have set up a court of state chief justices to review certain

[19] "Impact of Federal Urban Development Programs on Local Government Organization and Planning," p. 30.

kinds of judgments of the United States Supreme Court. The proposals were "so bad they defy adequate critical description or characterization. . . . More than anything else they are a reaction against decisions of the Supreme Court involving protection of human rights."[20] The reputation or standing of the Council of State Governments may of course recover from this ridiculous blunder. The episode has reminded us, however, that state governments and especially legislatures can do rather absurd things. Some people will go so far as to wonder whether reapportionment can really overcome this variety of parochialism.

The state cause is being retarded in a more serious respect by state and local law enforcement officials and courts in the South, as Burke Marshall has recently indicated:

> Those who say that civil rights issues cut into the fabric of federalism are correct. They cut most deeply where police power is involved, for the police as well as for those in conflict with the police. There would be vast problems in any attempts at federal control of the administration of justice, even through the moderate method of federal court injunctions. Yet vast problems have been created already by police indifference to Negro rights in the South, and they will grow if the trend is not turned. The loss of faith in law—the usefulness of federal law and the fairness of local law—is gaining very rapidly among Negro and white civil rights workers. The consequences in the future cannot be foreseen.[21]

For more than a century the framework for our discussion of the American racial situation has been set by the federal system. To the extent that that circumstance has retarded the elimination of segregation it has been most unfortunate. By stronger federal laws, stronger federal law enforcement, and maybe even by state legislative reapportionment, racial problems may be dragged from behind the skirts of the states. That change will not eliminate racialism, but it will improve the debate. Meanwhile, the states will have suffered another blow to any proposed strengthening of their policy-making role.

Scarcely anyone outside the far right is thinking seriously of augmenting the policy-making role of the states. What about an alternative future for them, that they may slowly be growing into centers primarily of administration? Such a model could be projected as a

20 Jefferson B. Fordham, "To Foster Disunity," LII National Civic Review (September 1963), p. 418.
21 Federalism and Civil Rights (New York: Columbia University Press, 1964), p. 81.

logical consequence of the increasing scale and size of intergovernmental programs. The business generated in state administration by those new programs has already dwarfed the traditional state functions. The trend continues and could ultimately make the states into record-keepers, communications centers, post offices, indeed, for national programs with nationally prescribed standards. In such a model, questions about "balancing" all programs in the state budget or about major policy decisions by well-apportioned legislatures would arise secondarily if at all. Most emphasis would be placed on reconciling local variations and peculiarities with standards or criteria laid down by Congress and central departments. The model could provide opportunity for a state to provide extra money for a function adjudged worthy of special effort, as they are able to do in some grant programs today. It was, indeed, some such model that the majority on ACIR had in mind in making the recommendations for more active state participation in urban development work, cited above.

It seems likely, however, that political parties would not stand still for the open and deliberate deemphasis of the policy-making role of the states. Mutual strength derives from the close association of states and local governments with the parties.

> The basic political fact of federalism is that it creates separate, self-sustaining centers of power, privilege, and profit which may be sought and defended as desirable in themselves, as means of leverage upon elements in the political structure above and below, and as bases from which individuals may move to places of greater influence and prestige in and out of government.[22]

Professor William H. Riker claims that "this decentralized party system is the main protector of the integrity of states in our federalism."[23] On the other hand, parties have always had greater organizational resources at the local level than at the state level. In both cases parties are accompanied and bolstered by, but are never identical with, galaxies of private firms and interest groups. These would not wish a radical change in the states either.

It is easy to make too much of party influence in state affairs. Furthermore, if party power in local government is suffering from population growth, the slowdown in immigration, the dwindling of bosses,

---

[22] David B. Truman, in Arthur W. Macmahon (ed.), *op. cit.*, p. 123. It should also be said that Paul Appleby understood this kind of explanation of party power and its relation to the federal system. He was also an outspoken critic and foe of the nonpartisan idea.

[23] *Federalism* (Boston: Little, Brown, 1964), p. 101.

the spreading of urban areas beyond the central city, why are not state-based parties stronger today? Perversely, they are not. The answer to the question is straightforward if not simple: state parties are weak for many of the same reasons that state governments are less than perfect. If old-fashioned constitutions (with their provisions for too many elective officials and powerless governors) have retarded parties, so also have some of the favorite reforms of a generation ago: for example, the direct primary. It is too bad that men who are willing and able to contend with the anomalous bundle of policy and program problems vested in the states do not spring automatically from the political process. Even when a strong state leader appears, he often devotes his main energy to working with national issues or vying for national office.

IMPACT OF WORLD AFFAIRS

A concrete interaction between foreign affairs and federalism is easy to demonstrate and interesting to speculate about, but it is difficult to decide what to do about that interaction. In times of international crisis, pressures from outside any country with a federal form of government can lead to strengthening the central government. That has occurred in every war the United States has had, and it also has been observed in other federations.[24] At least in the case of the United States, however, it would be hard to prove that component governments have suffered any corresponding permanent diminution in their fiscal powers or their personnel, or in their standing otherwise. Today's continuing international crises may be profoundly different from previous ones, especially since such quick military reaction is now possible. The problem is such as to raise the question whether continuing the diffusion of governmental power as it now exists in the federal system is wise. Leaving management of race relations largely with the states has to an extent injured our national image in other lands—e.g., when a photograph of a policeman kicking a sit-in demonstrator appears in foreign newspapers. Other examples also illustrate the point: handling of foreign ships in U.S. harbors, state or city trade representatives abroad, and so on.

In the total conduct of foreign affairs these relationships are of course minor. It is just as reasonable to speculate that sheer preoccupation by Washington with foreign affairs could eventually result in more and more reliance on state and local governments to handle domestic affairs. But it is growing increasingly difficult to say what is

---

[24] K. C. Wheare, *Federal Government*, 2nd ed. (London: Oxford University Press, 1964), pp. 252-55. See also Riker, *op. cit.*, p. 12.

purely domestic.

One prediction about federalism's victimization by international pressures, however, is safe enough. It is that those pressures will *indirectly* serve to keep states and local governments strong. In 1964 it appears the national government will continue to evolve policies to keep the economy growing, to keep defenses up. The ongoing expansion of the economy will then be reflected in increasing personnel, budgets, and shared functions for state and local governments. That is the way it has been for years, and that is the way it probably will continue to be, barring outright war.

Only a disastrous war or the most foolish of domestic policies—as in Mississippi today?—could conceivably lead to any drastic change in the system of intergovernmental relationships. Reapportionment of state legislatures—the most dramatic development in years—looks more like the start of a rejuvenation of states than like a threat to them. The question of getting along without federalism is academic, for there is little chance we shall have a choice on that subject in this century. Too many social, economic, and partisan interests are vested in its maintenance.

Federalism has served well the complex, shifting needs of the nation. In 1965 national, state, and local governments are fiscally strong. The big programs originating in Washington have been a major source of strength for all levels, but state and local income from traditional sources also continues to hold up well.

Governor Nelson Rockefeller sees our federalism as more than an expedient device. He expresses the kind of conservative, emotional attachment to it that many other Americans doubtless feel:

> The historic application of the federal idea—reconciling unity and diversity—is probably the supreme American contribution to the struggle of all self-governing peoples to build political structures strong enough to assure freedom and order in their lives.[25]

One really hesitates, however, to rank federalism so high among American "contributions." Especially should we go slowly when recommending the use of federalism *a l'américaine* to people in new nations. As Americans assist the developing countries, it would be an elementary error to think that this structural device or any other will serve abroad the same purposes it has served or is serving in the United States. At the same time statesmen and scholars there do have feder-

[25] *The Future of Federalism* (Cambridge: Harvard University Press, 1962), p. 27.

alism as a live alternative while they are shaping their governing institutions.

Today American federalism is the great, groaning apparatus for carrying on domestic governmental business. Another country might not find this an adequate excuse for adopting a federal constitution. Federalism also in some lesser but undisclosed measure serves to keep pluralism alive in the United States. The two functions are worth serving in this country.

III. PUBLIC ADMINISTRATION
AND PEOPLE

•

• 9 •

The Citizen as Administrator

JOHN M. GAUS

Once in a blue moon a rich and challenging book is reviewed by a person worthy of the opportunity. Such was the happy fate of Paul Appleby's *Policy and Administration*,[1] based upon his lectures at the University of Alabama. It was reviewed by Professor Arthur W. Macmahon of Columbia University, in the *Public Administration Review*. The strategy of the reviewer related Appleby's most fundamental ideas of government to a focal point. He sought their implication for the structures and processes placing politicians, administrators, and citizens in "reasoned social relations which, with no pedantry or limiting legalism, is nobly called constitutional government." And in his concluding sentences he says to Appleby that his book is "a summons, even in its silences. We are greatly in your debt."[2]

We are still greatly in debt to Paul Appleby. We dare not think of why he is silent now. We of his generation may repay something of our debt to him by seeking to understand him. And we may repay something by helping a new generation of students to become acquainted with him even if we are not able to convey the feelings we experienced with him as a friend and colleague which affect our interpretation. Even his "silences," like the dark spots in a nebula, are a "summons."

The mingling—and at points separation—of his experience in journalism, public service at home and abroad, study, teaching, meditation, and silence confronts one whose purpose it is to interpret and appraise Paul Appleby's views concerning "the citizen as administrator." Three of his books have indices: none of these indices includes the word "citizen," although it is in a chapter title. One index includes

[1] Paul H. Appleby, *Policy and Administration* (University, Alabama: University of Alabama Press, 1949).

[2] Arthur W. Macmahon, "Policy and Administration," *Public Administration Review*, Vol. IX, No. 4 (Autumn 1949), pp. 278-82. The passages quoted are at p. 282.

the word "administrator" twice and relevantly: "administrator and the politician," and "administrator as a 'rare bird' "!

Democratic Aspirations

Did Paul Appleby express some thoughts about "the citizen as administrator"? There is enough ambiguity in the phrase to make explorations somewhat hazardous. Presumably all or most administrators are citizens of the states in which they practice their calling. Perhaps the "citizens" of our title should be viewed as laymen, not regularly employed in public service other than as voters, but "brought in" administration for some special task. I could not recall, from earlier study of his writings and use of them in my classes, any discussions in them of this. And so I reread his books with this cross-secting search for Appleby on "the citizen as administrator" as my central inquiry. I began to wonder whether the citizen as administrator dwelt and labored at all within his range of thoughts on "public administration and democracy." And then, almost at the end of my searching, I came upon a passage in that one of his books which had challenged me least and puzzled me most—*Morality and Administration in Democratic Government.* I had found a direct reference, albeit within question-inviting quotation marks, to something which I might claim as the topic assigned to me now. His phrase " 'citizen participation' in the operating business of government" is close enough to "the citizen as administrator" for me to feel warranted in starting down the trail indicated by this blaze. So I will place this phrase in its context—a paragraph hinting at his personal experience and his reflections upon it. He had been describing briefly our federal system of government as one of checks and balances; home rule at the local level; a three-level system of government; the multiplication of jurisdictions and special authorities; on two levels the separation of powers and bicameral legislatures; executive government based often on a long ballot; "state rights" a symbol of virtue, "centralization" a symbol of evil. And he continues:

> Democratic aspiration within this very loose structure has reached variously toward many co-operative arrangements which divide and cloud responsibility. It has propelled us also toward means for "citizen participation" in the operating business of goverment without much uniformity or clarity of pattern, and without very critical concern for the feasibility or fairness of many arrangements. Often by such means special privileges are conferred without achieving the really representative and responsible per-

formance intended. Private benevolent activities come into association with the newer public welfare functions provide one example of a degree of private control of public activities without public responsibility. Private—very private and self-perpetuating—organizational development into a pattern similar to the three-level governmental pattern as a kind of private federalism has added complications to the complicated intergovernmental relations of health, hospital and welfare activities. A special kind of citizen representational function thus has become recognized with real power but extremely fuzzy responsibility and inadequate representational character. Within the field of strictly intergovernmental relations there has been revealed by the studies of Professors Anderson and Weidner a distinctly professional interaction with its own professional sovereignty confusing to governmental responsibilities.[3]

Is not Appleby here warning us against the "citizen participation" whether in "the operating business of government" or when performing "a special kind of citizen representational function"? A decade later, in giving his last advice to his friends in India in his fourth visit there as well as warnings and lessons from some aspects of our experience in the U.S.A. through lectures at the Indian School of Public Administration, he touches upon the areal aspect of the dangers of "fuzziness" and the need for "feasibility." "Enlisting citizen participation in community development" is increasingly unrelated to "the pursuit of a more expanded democracy." In his lecture entitled "Some Thoughts on Decentralized Democracy," he concludes:

> The advance of civilization will complicate the nongovernmental activities of citizens, so as to require more and more time and attention as well as more and more specialized competence. The same thing will be happening to governmental affairs, even those carried on at the grassroots. Citizens as citizens will become less qualified for these governmental tasks as they become more qualified for other tasks. This point I merely repeat in order to lead to a final question: What, then, can be said positively about citizen activity on behalf of democratic government, an activity that will not become obsolete?
>
> I think the participation in public affairs important to citizens and peculiar to democracy is participation in *politics*. [italics in original] . . .

[3] Paul H. Appleby, *Morality and Administration in Democratic Government* (Baton Rouge: Louisiana State University Press, 1952), p. 202.

Politics in a democracy is peculiarly qualified to uphold the mass interest—the general interest. For this function it is not relevant whether some members of the public do or do not carry on some of the operating work of government as a quasi-private kind of matter. The thing that is important is that the public appraises and chooses governments and parties-in-power. As party members they also have to do with choosing party leaders. . . .

All government is politics: the resolving or balancing of conflicting interests, functions and ideas in pursuit of a more *general* interest. Democratic government is widely popular politics, systematically bulwarked to provide orderly transitions and *to keep future choices open.*[4] [italics in original]

My journey was, for the moment, ending. In the search for the Paul Appleby conception of the citizen in administration, I had been brought back by his familiar emphasis on the bigness and complexity and supreme and comprehensive place of government; of the hierarchy of levels with continuous movement of policy-making up, down, sideways; of the consequent necessity for centralization before decentralization should be permitted if a democratic society is to be protected from the greed and ignorance of the partial and limited minds and groups seeking public advantages without payment or responsibility; and of a morality of and for administration deriving from the duty of serving the larger and wider public ends and needs as against the private and parochial ones.

I need not emphasize that these views challenged the "folklore" and "prevailing wisdom" of his time, and complemented the conclusions of, for example, V. O. Key, Jr., and Roscoe Martin. Martin, in his *Grass Roots*, struck at the sentimental and uncritical view of local, especially rural, units of government as Tocquevillian combinations of the Greek city-state and the Colonial New England town in their equipment of knowledge required to solve their problems and wisdom with which to use it; but he also called for areas of government "appropriate to the issue to be resolved," a point on which Appleby did not write.[5] Key, in his classic and prophetic "Politics and Administration," published in 1942 in the tribute volume to C. E. Merriam

---

[4] Paul H. Appleby, "Some Thoughts on Decentralized Democracy," reprinted from the *Indian Journal of Public Administration,* Vol. VIII, No. 4, pp. 443-55. The quotations are from the reprint, pp. 12-13.

[5] Roscoe C. Martin, *Grass Roots* (University, Alabama: University of Alabama Press, 1957), p. 81.

(*The Future of Government in the United States*) noted the dangers to the nation in the alliance of bureau, experts, professions, and economic groups of a given field of activity and the necessity for strengthening the central political controls. In these central political controls "the discerning audacity of lay direction of the expert" is of prime importance. And "at the risk of appearing to commit heresy against the cult of adoration of administration," he noted "some of the characteristics of hierarchical behavior . . . that operate to handicap administrative agencies in policy formation especially under conditions of governmental monitoring of the economic system." But he notes also that "it could be argued that one of the great functions of bureaucratic institutions is as a conservator of the values of a culture. In the purposes, procedures, ceremonies, outlook, and habits of the bureaucracy are formalized the traditional cultural values. Where the rub comes is when social purpose abruptly changes or becomes unclear or divided."[6]

CATASTROPHIC CHANGE AND THREATS TO COHERENT POLICY

In 1933, "the rub came" at many points in the operating human machinery of government in the United States. This was true in the agency which Appleby entered at the very top point of policy-making and of comprehensive view—the Office of the Secretary. "If the change in social purpose is sufficiently gradual," (to return to Key's diagnosis again) "friction between the hierarchical inertia and social purpose may not be serious, but seldom is a bureaucracy agile enough to adapt itself to rapid change of social purpose without many accelerated retirements and judicious transfers from key positions as well as considerable 'political' dilution." It is the good fortune of students of American Government that they had an observer in Paul Appleby at so strategic a point when a "rapid change of social purpose" seemed to be emerging.

There were signs of this change even before the First World War in agricultural policy. At the close of that war, basic changes in international and national technology and economy were affecting agriculture and getting reflected politically in legislation, administration, and the formation of the Farm Bloc. The policy of the Hoover Administration for further positive intervention through a Farm Board and the effort to finance carry-over surpluses was found to be in-

[6] V. O. Key, Jr., "Politics and Administration," Chap. VIII, *The Future of Government in the United States*, Essays in Honor of Charles E. Merriam, Leonard D. White, ed. (Chicago, Illinois: University of Chicago Press, 1942), pp. 150, 160-61.

adequate for better adjusting production, carried on in a vast number of farm units, to available markets. This issue contributed to the F. D. Roosevelt victory in 1932, and the new political leadership included for the U.S. Department of Agriculture Henry A. Wallace; and he appointed, as his first assistant in the Office of the Secretary, Paul Appleby. His experience in that post provided him with first-hand acquaintance with happenings at the point where policy and administration intermingle more complexedly than at any other point in the process of government, and where more can be seen and heard about high policy-making than anywhere else by a person with some "higher" education, relevant experience, and intelligence—plus. That "plus," with Appleby, included a recognition of the importance of thinking about what he was observing; of reading about other experience and ideas relevant to his observations; and of ultimately recording and publishing resultant thoughts about their application to the problems of government. At this spot of strategic and tactical importance, we students of government had a kind of intellectual surrogate to record and what is more to speculate about problems of government on which he has reported to us.

As to the detailed application of the thoughts quoted here earlier concerning " 'citizen participation' in the operating business of government," the published writings are not revealing. But the silences, with the generalizations, do reveal much that is important to understanding some changes and innovations in politics and political science in our country in the past fifty years. I refer to ideas (and practices) relating to "centralization" and "decentralization" of policy and administration whether by area or by function. With both there have been associated ideas (and practices) of "citizen participation" through local units or through economic and other associations not formally a part of the government. In our country the use of citizens elected to part-time participation in decentralized or original local units of government has been employed. It was as a part of the New Deal program of the United States Department of Agriculture that some of the most significant experience with such practices accumulated through the years.

Both the functional and areal aspects of the effort to retain what was generally viewed as a traditional, indigenous, and democratic American system were present in the problems of organizing the administration of the new national programs in agricultural policy. Historically the Department itself had directly administered regulatory powers and had also cooperated in some regulatory work with state market regulatory agencies. It administered directly through its own agency, the Forest Service, the lands set aside from the public domain or purchased for the National Forests. The Department had developed research programs but cooperated with the land grant institutions on some research. Extension-education work was largely assigned to the state land grant institutions with the establishment of the "cooperative" extension service program fifty years ago; national funds were given to the state land grant institutions for extension education reaching down to county or other local units through their "farm bureaus." State federations of representatives of these had formed, and a federation of state federations in turn had become the American Farm Bureau Federation. This sought to cooperate with the land grant institutions to strengthen the programs and increase the resources, whether from national, state, or local governments, of the extension organizations.

Should the depression-inspired new powers of the national department that followed the collapse of the Farm Board program be administered directly by the Department, or through the state extension organizations? Should the soil conservation programs, operated by various agencies (and thus involving rivalries) on national lands, be assigned to state agencies—e.g., state extension services—where they applied to private lands, over which some held the national government had no constitutional powers—since the states possessed such powers? Or should the Department press upon the states legislation which would provide for soil conservation districts, which might be given zoning and other powers over privately owned land, to be exercised "democratically" by owners and occupiers?

The shift of social policy reflected in the elections of 1932 and the early days of the new administration brought moves toward further public intervention in the adjustment of agricultural production "within the fences of the farm" to markets outside affected by national and international forces. Participation by farmer-elected county and local community committees in applying the statutory and administrative order provisions of the program to the individual was urged and adopted. This would continue some of what was thought to be the traditional freedom of the farmer in the management of the farm.

The problem with soil conservation programs was somewhat different. The Agricultural Adjustment Administration program may be said to have "bought" consent to crop-restricting practices. The soil-conserving practices might require joint adoption of land regulations for a small watershed, the consultative services of the service experts in the field, or the use of heavy equipment that could be afforded only by cooperation among many farmers. Hence a new local unit of government having power to contract with the national government, and to undertake local programs of equipment financing and supply, and even, possibly, to enact regulation of soil practices affecting neighbors, was urged upon state legislatures. There are now over 2,800 such districts. Their powers, like those of the Soil Conservation Service, now include water programs of the upstream type, and their elected Boards of Supervisors have created a National Association which serves to do for its membership and its administrative and economic and political allies what the American Farm Bureau does for its.

Meanwhile the problem of getting some integrated and balanced land use and policy through top administrative policy preparation is exacerbated. A number of political scientists have studied these problems of agricultural policy both within and without the fences and the myriad of associations and the public agencies. The alliances and rivalries between public agencies, commodity growers, processors and distributors, general and special farmer societies, legislative committee and subcommittee members, have been recorded and appraised. The conclusions of Key, quoted earlier, on the divisive and dispersive influences of "some of the characteristics of hierarchical behavior" are amply supported by these more special studies. The zeal of the expert and the greed of the wheeler-dealer, the return to the Dust Bowl, the little pork barrels of the little streams trying to keep up with the big ones of the larger systems—irrigation, river navigation, flood control on river bottoms designed by nature for floods—all are there. And out of these pieces, how fit patterns that would help, and not hinder, the sponsoring national party of a national administration in some total policy victory?

When Appleby stated that "I think the participation in public affairs important to citizens and peculiar to democracy is participation in *politics*," he was warning his Indian friends from his daily experience as first assistant in the Office of the Secretary of Agriculture in a period of social change. The Department affected the oldest of our industries. Its public policies were interwoven into all three levels of government, required the services of countless types of career professional-scientific specialists and general administrators, and were affected by a myriad of special-interest associations, as well as by the hopes and aspirations of millions of rural and village families and urban processors and distributors. The resultant Department, legally the comprehensive, encircling, and directive instrument, contained powerful old and new substantive line agencies and auxiliary services. It dealt with the proud and powerful major Agriculture Committees of the House and Senate and the relevant subcommittees of their respective committees on appropriations. What a laboratory-library-conference room it provided for a man of such intellectual curiosity and speculative mind as Appleby possessed! And the anarchy he observed in the scene before him led to the effort to find some alternate way than devolution and deconcentration and decentralization to a democratic government that would govern. He began to set down his principles in *Big Democracy,* based upon the Department in which he had been challenged to "make a mesh out of things."

His treatment of these questions in that book challenged widely held views. Some years after its appearance, passages relevant to the present discussion were attacked by Mr. Roger Fleming, Secretary-Treasurer of the American Farm Bureau Federation, at its meeting in Seattle on December 9, 1952.

I doubt whether any of us fully realise the implications of the thinking behind the decision to utilize a system of federally controlled "straight line" agencies to administer farm programs rather than a decentralized system based upon the grant-in-aid principle of government administration—a system of federal-state cooperation most meaningfully symbolized to farmers by the Land Grant College system.

For many years I have interested myself personally in trying to discover the basis for the decision made about 1934-35 to federalize farm program administration. I should like to report briefly on my findings.

In 1942 I heard several of a series of lectures given on the campus of Iowa State College by Paul Appleby. . . . The content of these lectures shocked me. . . .

In 1950 I discovered that he had published these lectures in book form. . . . It is entitled "Big Democracy." It is frankly a defense of "big government." . . .

One of the most shocking things in Mr. Appleby's book is the fact that nowhere does he give any recognition whatsoever to the constructive role performed by free institutions, such as the Farm Bureau, in the development of sound public policy. . . .

We have been in the midst of a battle to determine whether the philosophy of "centralization," as symbolized by the quotations I read from Appleby's book, or whether the philosophy of "decentralization" as provided for in the Constitution of the United States, is to prevail. This issue isn't settled! It is certain to be a live one in 1953.[7]

[7] Roger Fleming, "Annual Report of Roger Fleming, Secretary-Treasurer, American Farm Bureau Federation," December 9, 1952, Seattle, Washington (mimeographed), pp. 7, 8, 10.

It is still unsettled in 1965, and will continue to be, from the nature of the practical problem of adjusting instruments and policies of public housekeeping to countercoerce the coercions of physical and social change in the universe. In the Post-World War I and Depression setting of the United States in the 1930's, an expansion of the use of government on every level took place, and more dramatically in the national government because of the constitutional distribution of powers (finance and commerce, for example) that were required to meet the problems of nationwide catastrophe. Whether these powers should or constitutionally or economically could be exercised on a grant-in-aid basis was and is a necessary issue for analysis and debate. Appleby challenged some prevailing folklore views of our federal system and of the location of democracy primarily in the local community or interest association.

Free Political Enterprise

Adequately to appraise Appleby's apparent dismissal of "the citizen as administrator" in the sense popular among many, we should note what was his positive view of the citizen in government. "Government is different from all other professions because it is broader than anything else in the field of action. Purely speculative thought may range a wider field, yet even this may be doubted for government must be concerned with intellectual and emotional outreachings too. Government is different because it needs to take account of all the desires, needs, actions, thoughts and sentiments of 140,000,000 [1945] people. Government is different because government is politics."[8] And in the chapter which follows, he describes the range of functions and organizations in the United States Department of Agriculture to illustrate his point. This approach to government as a functional supplement to the actions of citizens and associations is the clue to his thoughts about the relations of citizens to and in the processes of their government in a democracy.

It seems plain that both within government and outside of government, and probably for the same reasons, the trend is toward bigness. Responsible citizens, including those who like bigness least, have therefore the duty of helping to give it form and content. . . .

"Inevitably we shall strive to deal with these demons of size and complexity by exercising our powers of simplification. For simplification enables us to organize our affairs and reduce them

[8] Paul H. Appleby, *Big Democracy* (New York: Knopf, 1945), pp. 9-10.

to manageable proportions. . . . On what terms and by what technique can we develop the unity our complexity demands and do it in a way that will harmonize with our history of freedom and our ideals of individual worth?"[9]

Note that Appleby assigns here a task of solving the problems of size and complexity "by exercising our powers of simplification." Yet it is "citizens" who by the multiplicity of their purposes and interests and organizations—what Appleby termed "Free Political Enterprise" —create within, around, and without government the conflicts, duplications, and complexities which have to be given some reconciliation —or else disaster.

Henry Adams, studying the emergence of these characteristics of American life in the decade at the end of the Civil War, noted:

> The Civil War had made a new system in fact; the country would have to reorganize the machinery in practice and theory. . . . The world cared little for decency. What it wanted, it did not know; probably a system that would work, and men who could work it; but it found neither. . . . The political dilemma was as clear in 1870 as it was likely to be in 1970. The system of 1789 had broken down. . . .
>
> Yet the sum of political life was, or should have been, the attainment of a working political system. Society needed to reach it. If moral standards broke down, and machinery stopped working, new morals and machinery of some sort had to be invented.[10]

Appleby was, like Adams, a close witness of our government in a period of national stress, not of readjustment to a Civil War (although still affected by its unfinished business and moving in the long rollers of the aftermath of that vast storm) but to the First World War, the Great Depression, then participation in a Second World War and its aftermath. He was as a participant in constant first-hand touch with the divisiveness of structure, process, and pressures characteristic of the making of policy. The rapid adoption of new policies and the speeded-up evolution of old ones in the United States Department of Agriculture from 1933 on raised difficult problems of adjustment across bureau lines and created the task of obtaining "an organization product." But how balance the inertia and resistance of the substantive bureau and its affiliations with professional organiza-

[9] *Ibid.*, p. 27.
[10] Henry Adams, *The Education of Henry Adams, An Autobiography*, Sentry Edition (Boston: Houghton Mifflin, 1961), pp. 249, 280, 281.

tions and standards, commodity groups and congressional committees? By calling decisions up to a "higher level."

But there is not only the divisiveness of the substantive groupings. There are the constitutional statutory and administrative divisions and distributions of power and responsibility between and among national, state, and local units of government for many functions. How to make a mesh out of things became, naturally, a major object of a member of the inner policy circle of a great department, and the subject of his writings as he entered upon a more formally educational career.

Big Democracy was Appleby's first effort to report to the citizen upon this complexity. "The book," he states in the preface, "consists much less in what I have seen and experienced than in what I have come to think as a result."[11] And so his points are made broadly, to educate the citizen in what he considered the elementary truths that were necessary to win his participation, rather than the "shibboleths," "debates," "snapshots," or "microscopic examinations" of "procedures, mechanics and operational detail." "The organized government comprehends in some way, it impinges upon and is affected by, practically everything that exists or moves in our society."[12] And government is "the single greatest resource of the American people." From this dominating and central position flow his views of organization and procedure whereby "an organization product" can be achieved. "It is out of extensive interactions of bureaucracies, political administrators, political leaders and citizens that there is distilled a pragmatic learning, a wisdom applicable to nation-wide activities appropriate and acceptable to the society."[13] The distilling process proceeds from level to level up the hierarchy; and the consequence, in a federal system, is that "nothing can be decentralized properly which has not first been centralized. The basic essential is national controllability,"[14] if the national and public interest is to be protected from the divisive forces of particular interests.

The citizen participations in these processes of "interactions" is exercised, he argues, in part by delegates such as courts, legislative bodies, executive officials, in part through parties and pressure groups, as well as through the vote and the threat of the vote. "Citizens vote, then, by adding their names and energies to membership rolls. They vote by swelling, or failing to swell, the circulations of particular

[11] Paul H. Appleby, *Big Democracy* (New York: Knopf, 1945), p. v.
[12] *Ibid*, p. vi, viii.
[13] Paul H. Appleby, *Public Administration for a Welfare State* (New Delhi: Asia Publishing House, 1961), p. 44.
[14] *Big Democracy*, p. 104.

newspapers or periodicals. They vote by contributing to the popularity of particular radio or newspaper commentators. They vote by writing 'letters to the editor.' They vote much more potently than they know when they write or talk to members of legislative bodies and to administrative officials. They vote as they express themselves in labor unions, farm organizations, business and professional bodies. They vote in every contribution they make to the climate of opinion in a thoroughly political society. They vote more effectively still as they organize to exert influence. They vote effectively in proportion to the persistence of their efforts, for persistence is an index to intensity of feeling."[15]

But I wonder if we are "a thoroughly political society" or one in which the private and private-group concerns and outlook are so permeating and deep-rooted that a public policy and attitude (in the meaning used by John Dewey) is largely eclipsed or undiscovered?

I have referred to Henry Adams' account of the frustrations in the government in the period immediately following the Civil War, when so many problems confronted the nation. It was not until the latter years of the McKinley Administration that he found "a system that would work." And so, thirty years later, as the new emergent American society of electrical power and trusts and city growth and immigration and the Spanish War and financial panic gave him fresh data, he detected a new "system" that seemed to "work" and with a supporting morality, of which McKinley was a symbol. "Mr. McKinley brought to the problem of American government a solution which lay very far outside of Henry Adams' education, but which seemed to be at least practical and American. He undertook to pool interests in a general trust into which every interest should be taken, more or less at its own valuation, and whose mass should, under his management, create efficiency. He achieved very remarkable results. How much they cost was another matter; if the public is ever driven to its last resources and the usual remedies of chaos, the result will probably cost more."[16]

Entering upon his strategic post in 1933, Appleby was witnessing, perhaps, some of the milder applications of the public's "last resources and the usual remedies of chaos." Some people decided that an

---

[15] Paul H. Appleby, *Policy and Administration* (University, Alabama: University of Alabama Press, 1949), p. 168. For a further and final statement of his theme of the dominance of citizens in a democratic political system, enriched with many observations based on his experience, see his last book, *Citizens as Sovereigns* (Syracuse, New York: Syracuse University Press, 1962).

[16] *The Education of Henry Adams,* pp. 373-74.

alternative system might cost less than the bankruptcies, foreclosures, and lay-offs that were already catastrophic. And the remedy in the 1930's, that perhaps is reflected in Appleby's system for Big Democracy, certainly has some likeness to Adams' conception of President McKinley's "solution" by a pooling of "interests in a general trust into which every interest should be taken." We even "had to do something for silver," which despite Mr. Bryan had lost out nearly forty years before.

A POLITICAL, ADMINISTRATIVE, AND CITIZEN ENTERPRISE

Are we really sufficiently "a thoroughly political society" to guarantee the complete utilization of whatever the citizen has to contribute to government, through the electoral and party strategic points of policy-making only? Even with Appleby's emphasis on this as the place in the long "continuum" (I agree with Macmahon it should be qualified by some differentiations or what I have called "strategic points of policy making") he does have his citizen "voting" by writing or talking not only to legislators but to administrative officials as well. And there is still left, at the end of the line of official policy formulation and interpretation in administering the resultant statute —there still is left a discretionary choice to the individual official when he applies the law to the given concrete individual or group at whom it was directed.

But this is not all. Much legislation must be completed by the citizen-client consumer. His consent has still to be won—even his active participation, and not only in the great mass of measures of a permissive, service-offering type (results of research, fruitful use of public libraries or parks or health information and facilities, and the like) but even with the compulsory programs of the armed services, and the maintenance of public safety and welfare. And still more! A citizen may by virtue of some kind of experience and knowledge have some contribution to make to the policy left to officials well down the line of the government process—and, with relevant treatment by those officials, well up the line also. The policy-administration "differentiated continuum" is two-way if the Appleby objectives are to be realized.

Now what are the possible citizen-administrator contributions to the ultimate points in the administrative sector left to the discretion of the bureaucracy and citizen-client in the process of government? They are of at least three types: vocational, regional, and personal. The best are a mingling of the three.

Of the first, I think of the fruitful ideas and practice of John R.

Commons and those whom he directly influenced in one of the high periods of creative colleagueship of politician, expert, and administrator. This was in the years in which he was Professor of Economics in the University of Wisconsin, adviser to Governor Robert Marion LaFollette of Wisconsin, a member of its Industrial Commission, and adviser to the City Council of Milwaukee. He has recorded that the State Civil Service Law he drafted was his most useful contribution, as it was a basis of all other development. It was from him and the members of his graduate seminar at the University as well as colleagues in the State and municipal government that the ideas of policy formulation aided by the research of scholars, the preparation of experts, and the recruitment of participants in employments affected by a public interest were encouraged. On the "vocational" side, there evolved the placing of employers and employees with technicians in the spelling out of what a "reasonable" application of general objectives of safety in industrial processes called for in the statute might be.

And how could a newly elected city council, confronted with responsibility for a business larger and more complex, generally, than any other enterprise within the area, be aided to establish some set of priorities against the urgent pressures for special favors, apportion the available tax and human resources, and appraise the results attained by their decisions in the total plan authorized in and through their budget process? Here again the citizen-politician of the council would from sheer necessity need the sense of the less participant lay citizen. He might thus grow into a kind of regional knowledge. We witness today its need beyond the ward, beyond the city, even beyond—as in air and water pollution—the metropolitan to the rurban and watershed region.

And the personal contribution, beyond or supplementing the vocational and regional? What I grope for is given concreteness by the phrase employed by Irving Dilliard in his tribute to a great living American. His article is entitled "Grenville Clark—Public Citizen."[17] Such men as he and many American men and women are citizens so creative and responsive beyond the ordinary public duties of voting and obedience to law that they become a most important part of the administrative points of policy-making as part-time members of the structure and personnel at those points. They are "public" citizens. And from this group recruits are sometimes drawn into complete

---

[17] Irving Dilliard, "Grenville Clark: Public Citizen," *The American Scholar,* Vol. 33, No. 1 (Winter 1963-64), pp. 97-104.

participation in the political level, which as Appleby emphasized is the most important because most comprehensive.

But I would supplement V. O. Key's skepticism at the "cult of administration" by a similar warning as to the "cult of politics" which is perhaps a current phase of political science. To discover the greediness and corruption and conflicts of interest and power struggles of agencies that are the substance of administrative sociology contributes usefully both to the science and practice of government. But sometimes it reminds me of the Dutch discovering Holland, and should remind us all, let us say, of Hobbes with a seventeenth-century state of nature so nasty, brutish, and (hopefully) short that the Strong Man was desirable. Madison, too, and the Fathers of the American eighteenth century had no illusion, but they fashioned a government for the substantial and urgent tasks they saw confronting the country. Adams, we have seen, sought a nineteenth-century "system that would work."

We struggle in the twentieth century with the same basic problem of providing an adequate instrument of public housekeeping with the prevention of its abuse by the weaknesses of human beings. In our own country the task of achieving some understanding for government policy-making is not easy. We are a subcontinent of varied regions and ethnic groups, undergoing a shifting of population proportions by space and age. We must achieve working unity at both political and administrative levels. The contribution which Paul Appleby made to the study of our problems was to emphasize the importance of government, and within the government the importance of protecting national policy from the disruptive alliances of special interests. He was a critic of sloppy, sentimental, and unexamined use of terms—and of unexamined loyalties and institutions. And if we lament that we are not left in his published writings more discussion of how the New Men and Women are to be developed who can be more equal to the tasks of politics and administration, we can be grateful that he turned to their education as the logical completion of his career.

· 10 ·

Responsibility and Representativeness
in Advisory Relations

ARTHUR W. MACMAHON

Lyman Bryson, noting how little was known as late as midcentury about "the techniques and difficulties of trying to put knowledge at the service of power," truly said that their right relation is "one of the key problems of our age."[1] Among difficulties that are almost dilemmas is the question of the ways and degrees in which provision for advice may be structured. Paul Appleby soundly spoke against any arrangement that gave a monopoly of access to public bodies.[2] This view was part of his belief in a comprehensive political process. It is indeed the essence of freedom that the prime sources of policy should remain unstructured, diverse, open for the invention and subtle gathering of ideas. The veteran head of the British cotton board, a trade group, remarked that "the valuable functions of developing ideas about possible new policies are performed by academic economists in their books and articles and by other writings in the weekly journals and reviews."[3] He also testified to the crucially intermediate role of the political process in laying the basis for advice in the later stages of implementation. Alluding to his experience in consulting about tariff matters under a European common market, he recalled: "It struck me very forcibly then how little can be prepared by investigation and consultation before the moment when the broad decision of policy has been firmly taken." It is a telling point, quite in Appleby's mood, although it may seem to belittle the preparatory role of advisory bodies. Their important subsequent roles involve not only the execution of policies in matters where the government commands or directly serves but also the projection of publicly stated goals for voluntary acceptance and mutual adjustment.

[1] Lyman Bryson, "Notes on a Theory of Advice," *Political Science Quarterly,* Vol. 66 (September 1951), pp. 321-39 at 339. Reprinted in R. K. Merton and others, *Reader in Bureaucracy* (Glencoe, Ill.: The Free Press, 1952), pp. 202-16.
[2] Paul H. Appleby, *Big Democracy* (New York: Knopf, 1945), p. 35.
[3] Sir Raymond Streat, "Government Consultation with Industry," *Public Administration,* Vol. 37 (1959), pp. 1-8.

An unstructured situation in advisory relations may be fragmentary and unbalanced, at odds with the ideal of open access. Growing attention on this score was notably shown in the movement that led to a presidential order in 1962 on advisory committees in the national government. The movement itself was a phase of the concern that has attended the intimacy and interdependence of public and private affairs in an age of techniques heightened by emergencies. Before returning to these matters it is well to speak further about the nature of advice.

Aspects and Organs of Advice

Phases of advice

Advice, drawing upon a society's resources of knowledge, is at once less and more than knowledge. It is selective information brought to bear in the context of action. Sometimes facts that are sought or offered may be of the sorts called objective. In addition to the data and inferences of technology and science, these may also include circumstantial details about the unwritten ways of the marketplace or professional life. Sometimes the relevant information may be of the kind called subjective, having to do with people's attitudes or potential reactions.

There is a difference between facts at hand and facts that come from fresh inquiry, which often by necessity is elaborate and protracted. Advice uses both kinds in posing alternatives, arraying arguments, and advancing judgments. It must avoid a double risk. What is at hand may be sufficient and yet be slighted. At times, however, reliance on the facts at hand—as in so many hearings—may leave the assumptions untested and the larger realities unexplored. A phase of this side of the danger, in the words of Henry A. Kissinger, is the chance that the reputable people who are chosen as advisers "freeze at the level of the experience or effort that gained them their reputation."[4] Advice is not decision but it must have something of decision's temper. David Bell, when budget director in the Kennedy Administration, reflected the executive's need when he testified that "the President and those who work with him are very impatient if a paper comes up with the pros and cons neatly labeled, but with no recommendation, no conclusions, nothing to chew on."[5]

The advice-gathering capabilities of the American legislative com-

[4] Henry A. Kissinger, "The Policy Maker and the Intellectual," *The Reporter*, Vol. 20 (March 5, 1959), p. 32.

[5] 87th Cong., 1st Sess. Senate Committee on Government Operations. Hearings before the subcommittee on national policy machinery, "Organizing for National Security," Vol. 1, p. 1178 (August 1, 1961).

mittee system are not belittled by stressing the administrative aspects of the advisory process. Even in the state governments interim committees partly offset the effects of short, biennial sessions. In a recent year, New York State spent more than two million dollars in the work of forty such committees.[6] The original hopes for legislative councils have hardly been realized since Kansas broke ground in 1933. Nevertheless, the varied application of the idea in forty-two states (according to a recent reckoning by Frederick H. Guild, a pioneer in the movement) has been a significant contribution to policy-making.[7] Nationally, the often massive assemblage of information by the congressional committees has faced two hazards: the limitations of the evidence when facts at hand are in large measure presented orally, and possible distortion through the volunteer appearance of witnesses whose credentials are scarcely examined.

Deficiencies of the first kind were noted also in the British royal commissions. "In general," declared Nicholas Mansergh in 1940, "it appears that the examination of witnesses, which takes inordinate time, yields but meager results."[8] In subsequent years, to be sure, along with a relative shift to departmental and other organs of inquiry, it became customary to require the advance submission of written statements. Nevertheless, as late as 1961, William Robson complained that "too much reliance is still placed in official investigations on the so-called 'evidence' of heavily committed interests."[9] He believed that "independent investigation by disinterested and professionally qualified staff using modern techniques would usually be more successful." As to the other risk in American legislative hearings—imbalance through the haphazard attendance of witnesses—improvements may come with the professional staffing of the committees. Apart from the strengthening of committee procedures, the legislative bodies can on occasion extend themselves through advisory bodies as well as contracts for research. An example was the Advisory Council on Social Security created in 1947 by the Senate Committee on Finance at a strategic time in the evolution of welfare policies.[10]

On the administrative side, dependence on hearings and public

[6] Council of State Governments, *The Book of the States* (1963), pp. 63-79.

[7] Frederick H. Guild, *Legislative Councils after Forty Years* (Southern Illinois University: Public Affairs Research Bureau, 1964).

[8] R. C. Vernon and Nicholas Mansergh, co-authors and editors, *Advisory Bodies* (London: Allen and Unwin, 1940), p. 83.

[9] William A. Robson, "The Present State of Teaching and Research," *Public Administration,* Vol. 39 (Autumn 1961), p. 222.

[10] 80th Cong., 1st Sess., S. Res. 141, July 23, 1947, leading to the Advisory Council's report, issued in the 2nd Session as S. Doc. 208.

advisory bodies as sources of information is partly offset by the increasingly refined ability of a modern government to learn the facts—including attitudes and expectations as facts—through its statistical apparatus, including sampling methods. A considerate government must through knowledge have confidence in the face of the esoteric claims of myriad interests. Well did Emmette Redford say, "Facts—lots of facts, facts about the details of industry operation—are the *sine qua non* of intelligent public control."[11] Administrative hearings for the parties may not in themselves catch the wider and longer perspectives that are of the essence of public interest. The hearings themselves are insufficient guides in the realistic measure of needs and the imaginative projection of policies. Fact-gathering by the national government—coordinated and partly controlled by the Office of Statistical Standards in the Budget Bureau, including review of well above 2,000 questionnaire forms in a recent year—is gaining flexibility through the potentialities of sampling.[12] Nearly all of the forty undertakings of the Bureau of Labor Statistics are samples. The Census has already developed an omnibus and adaptable sampling technique that is available to a wide range of governmental agencies. It is unnecessary here to dwell on the suggestive essays on the administrative uses of polling that followed the article by Henry Wallace and James McCamy in 1940.[13]

A frontier today lies in the judicial cognizance of the findings of sampling techniques.[14] The government's cumulative grasp of both objective and subjective facts is already large and resourceful. The data are being refined in terms that suit the spotty incidence of many national problems. Broadly speaking, a government's statistical and like tools are a phase of advice in a fluid sense of the word. The basic

[11] Emmette S. Redford, *Administration of National Economic Control* (New York: Macmillan, 1952), p. 156. For valuable background, see the pioneer study by Avery Leiserson, *Administrative Regulation: A Study in the Representation of Interests* (Chicago: University of Chicago Press, 1942).

[12] But note continued congressional cavil—reflecting especially small business vexation—as shown in 1964 hearings on "the Federal Paper Work Jungle," 88th Cong., 2nd Sess. H. R. Committee on Post Office and Civil Service, subcommittee on Census and Government Statistics, p. 750. It criticized the Bureau of Statistical Standards for disapproving only 86 of 2,510 report forms reviewed in 1963.

[13] Henry A. Wallace and James L. McCamy, "Straw Polls and Public Administration," *Public Opinion Quarterly*, Vol. 4 (1940), p. 223. For a recent comment, see Adam Yarmolinsky, "Confessions of a Non-User," *Public Opinion Quarterly*, Vol. 27 (1963), pp. 543-48.

[14] See the publication of the Society of Business Advisory Professions, *Current Business Studies No. 19* (October 1954), on "The Role of Sampling Data as Evidence in Judicial and Administrative Proceedings."

information, when reliable and respected, is part of a plural society's apparatus for the congruent guidance of decisions in the growing areas of interdependence. The statistical methods in themselves, however, do not provide for contacts, interchange, and a source of enlistment.

Within the government, the process of interchange in multiple counsel is reflected in many official committees, departmental and inter-agency. The number may be guessed by noting that the Commerce Department, in listing committees that existed early in 1964, mentioned 206 interagency bodies of which it was a member and 26 departmental committees, as against 56 advisory committees—that is, bodies not composed wholly of officials. Speaking generally, it was the policy-preparing involvements of the official committees that invited the sharpest attacks. On the eve of the Kennedy Administration and during its early stages these attacks sometimes merged in a criticism of the precepts and influence of "prevailing administrative theory" in the United States. Walt W. Rostow, soon before he became a high officer in the new administration, declared that the theory made a fetish of relevance, unduly extolling the virtue of consulting all parts of the government that have any relation to a pending action. "A systematic counterattack on prevailing administrative theory, bureaucratic struc-ture, and organizational spirit appears to be in order," he wrote.[15] Such complaints believed that policy was diluted not only by delays but especially by weakening compromises as the price of avoiding dead-locks among persons who were likely to have agency "positions" to defend.

This sort of criticism was expressed more moderately by the sub-committee on national policy machinery under the Senate Committee on Government Operations. "The role of a committee in policy forma-tion," it said, "is essentially critical and cautionary, not creative."[16] It added: "The prime source of policy innovation is the contribution of a responsible individual who wrestles day in and day out with the prob-lems of national security." In a report early in 1961, still accented by the mood of that period, the subcommittee suggested that if committees are used at all they should preferably be *ad hoc* bodies whose members are brought together as individuals rather than as representatives of agencies or units. At bottom, however, it was impossible to disregard the mutual involvements of various parts of the government and the

15 Walt W. Rostow, *The United States in the World Arena* (New York: Harpers, 1960), p. 502.

16 86th Cong., 2nd Sess. Senate Committee on Government Operations. Sub-committee on national policy machinery. Report on "Organizing for National Security. Super-Cabinet Officers and Staff" (November 1960), p. 2.

different components in a decision. In making terms with the inevitable, the Budget Bureau sought by its instructions and influence to limit the existence of committees unless there was a definitely affirmative wish to continue them. The solvent lay in a sense of action, not in less mutual awareness.

Administration as a deliberative and even argumentative process, secreting advice in interagency relations, is sometimes evidenced in units that are deliberately set up to act, and still more widely to speak, for a viewpoint or group that might otherwise be overlooked. The establishment of such units usually reflects the equalizing play of politics. They seek to compensate for the administrative condition that may be called the limited span of attention. Such units take many forms; they mingle advocacy with action in different proportions and in diverse ways. The device may be a single officer for minority group relations in a public housing agency. Or it may be an institution as extensive as the Small Business Administration in the national government. It is equipped to provide loans and other services in its own right. Much of its work, however, is representative in relation to other parts of the government, notably the Defense Department. In the circumstances of big government and a marketplace of giants it would be a counsel of perfection to condemn such a mission as a clumsy expedient in seeking to promote a symmetrical national development.

A strong case exists for a degree of detachment in the relation of organs of advice to arenas of action. Strong also is the argument that creative thinking finds both its assignments and its clues in the crises of decision. McGeorge Bundy, the President's special assistant for national security affairs, made the point in a talk during 1963 on scientists in national policy. He could hardly be doubted when he spoke of the need for continuity and experience, saying that "nobody ever made a lasting contribution to government by one visit to Washington."[17] The gist of his challenge to advisers lay in the further remark: "What really bends the processes of government is continuous, sustained, and intensive effort, generally uncertain at the beginning of what its exact final outcome will be, always responsive to the situation as it is, and continuously aware of the need to be on top of that situation, and not some abstract plan of what ought to be, or was when one once knew it, or would be if the people in Washington had more sense." Moreover, Mr. Bundy said, it is hard to give useful advice "if you do not know what they are trying to do."

[17] McGeorge Bundy, "The Scientist and National Policy," *Science*, Vol. 139, No. 3557 (March 1963), p. 807.

It is doubtless a sound ideal that looks for a main answer to the problem of detachment in a type of executive, constantly primed by imminent decisions but who, free of the illusion that just extra hours on masses of detail are enough, spares himself for the wide, long view. The launching of the Marshall Plan was the story of an imaginative grasp of an impending crisis that was still avoidable, confirmed by a quick but careful analysis, followed by a period of government-wide, team-like planning with the additional support of a public advisory body.[18]

Collegial versus individual advisers

So far as advice in personal form is sought or formal provision is made for its reception from outside the government, the question may arise of the preferability of individual consultants rather than committees. In recent times the wide use of individual advisers has been prompted by the novelty of many issues, both technological and economic. Their employment has fitted the outlook that disparaged committees where problems should be handled with despatch. The practice has not been free of embarrassing conflicts of interest when individual advisers played a role in decisions.[19] The vogue of such advisers and their seeming indispensability, along with the risks their use entailed, led to a presidential memorandum in February 1962 on the use of individual consultants.[20] This memorandum antedated the final passage of a revision of the conflict-of-interest laws. It sought to interpret the existing legislation in ways that would not unduly discourage the recruiting of exceptional individuals for short or intermittent service. It hinted at the emergent category of "special Government employees" which was embodied in the pending bill on conflicts of interest. The term covered persons who are appointed or employed to work, with or without pay, on a full-time, intermittent, or part-time basis, for not more than 130 days during any period of 365 consecutive days. The prohibitions against conflict of interest do not apply fully to such persons. This feature of the new legislation was dealt with in a presidential memorandum of May 2, 1963.[21] The memorandum (as will be

[18] Joseph M. Jones, *The Fifteen Weeks* (New York: Viking Press, 1955).

[19] *United States vs. Mississippi Valley Generating Company*, 364 U.S. 520 (1961) upheld the cancelation of a contract because of a conflict of interest that involved an individual adviser in the Dixon-Yates negotiations. See Aaron Wildavsky, *Dixon-Yates: A Study in Power Politics* (New Haven: Yale University Press, 1962), pp. 285-92.

[20] Memorandum by the President to the heads of executive departments and agencies, "Preventing Conflicts of Interest on the Part of Advisers and Consultants to the Government," 27 F.R. 1341-48 (February 9, 1962).

[21] Memorandum of the President to the Heads of Executive Departments and

noted later) sought to exclude from the new category all who serve in a "representative" role in behalf of groups or organizations.

The preferability of committees rather than individuals in many advisory relations is implied partly in what has just been said. Moreover, there is profit in the meeting of minds, even those of persons who do not differ in economic or other interests or markedly in training, knowledge, and experience. A new start may be given by the way a member of the assemblage expresses an idea held broadly in common. In talk one achieves a fresh view of his own thought. So, at numerous points in preparing for decisions, groups tend to assemble. There are additional reasons for collegial council. The situation is likely to involve varied interests or disciplines, or different but impinging administrative functions that cannot be called either interests or disciplines. The collisions are not always economic. McGeorge Bundy said in the quoted address: "It is very important that at the crucial points of counsel, judgment, decision, and action, there be more than one scientist involved." Considerations of convenience as well as fairness are still other reasons for employing committees when the involvements are continuous and the need for contact is recurrent. "As distinct from ad hoc arrangements," said a recent British study of advisory bodies, "committees may be said to have four virtues: regularity, comprehensive personal contact, convenience, and formal commitment."[22]

The blend of elements varies endlessly. The purpose may be mainly informational and the accent may be on technical knowledge and judgment. In other situations the stress may be on consulting with those who are affected by a governmental policy; here the purpose may be partly to learn where the shoe pinches, partly to enlist support through this comity, and partly to advertise the program itself. A variation is to choose the advisers from among the users of a governmental service. In still different ways the emphasis may be on offsetting administrative routines by the presence of public members who have no special knowledge or involvement, although they are more likely to be useful if they are both knowledgeable and also concerned about the problem with which the program is dealing. Geographical factors may be prominent among the criteria of choice. In the United States many advisory committees of mixed membership are part of the apparatus of cooperative federalism.

Science as a component of public policy, along with questions of

Agencies, "Preventing Conflicts of Interest on the Part of Special Government Employees," 28 F.R. 4539 (May 2, 1963).

[22] *Advisory Committees in British Government.* A PEP Report. (London: Allen and Unwin, 1960), p. 86.

policy in the public use and support of science, is said to introduce a new dimension. It is a dimension of disciplines, not of interests in the older, primarily industrial implications of the word. Moreover, coteries of disciples may exist within disciplines, at odds about theories and inferences if not about technical facts in themselves. To be sure, scientists have some common stakes, notably their autonomy. Nevertheless Pendleton Herring seemed to overstate the unity when he declared: "Science has become another of the great interest groups and in a free society it has assumed a prominent place in the polity."[23]

STANDARDS FOR ADVISORY COMMITTEES

Antecedents of the executive order of 1962

The executive order of 1962 that set standards for advisory committees was the outcome of a cumulative movement, already partly embodied in a presidential directive of 1959.[24] On the one side it was in line with the wish to make easier the government's ability to draw upon the country's resources of talent. On the other side, in the setting of successive emergencies were anxieties about conflicts of interest in the mingling of public and private affairs, about opportunities for unfair advantage among competitors, about invitations to collusion among competitors, and about the portent of industrial centralization which government patronage might encourage unwittingly. Meanwhile administrative skepticism was mounting about deadwood among committees. Such was the matrix that shaped the effort to deal with the problems of responsibility and representativeness.

Committees for individual industries or industry groups multiplied in emergencies. A pattern for their safer use began to emerge in the Second World War and was projected during the Korean crisis. It included a formula for representativeness, superintended by central offices for advisory committees, with the Justice Department in the background. In the middle 1950's criticism waxed in certain congressional circles. Among its leaders were the members and staff of the antitrust subcommittee of the House Judiciary Committee. The gravamen was the presence at control points in defense agencies of persons temporarily borrowed from business. The prime targets were those who were serving without compensation (WOC's) while being enabled to

---

[23] Social Science Research Council, *Items*, Vol. 15 (March 1961).

[24] Executive Order 11007 (February 26, 1962), "Prescribing Regulations for the Formation and Use of Advisory Committees," 27 F.R. 1875-77. This order elaborated on a presidential directive in 1959 on "standards and procedures in the utilization of public advisory committees by government departments and agencies."

meet their continuing financial obligations by salaries and perhaps other benefits from the concerns from which they were on leave of absence. The vital aspect, of course, was not the nature of the compensation but the background of experience, the affiliations, and the expectations that attended the temporary governmental employment. The symbolism that had gathered around the question of compensation, however, invited the critics to concentrate on demanding that persons employed without compensation should serve in advisory roles only. Enough exceptions continued and enough conflicts of interest appeared even in advisory roles to bring congressional criticism to a head in 1955 and 1956. The indictment spread to the galaxies of advisory bodies.[25] The industry committees, whose number reached a postwar peak in 1956, were the center of attention.

Anxiety about the adequacy of the then existing laws on conflict of interest was present in much of the ferment that has been noted. Simultaneously, however, the need for revision was being urged on the ground that the laws (in part through vagueness) were handicapping the government in tapping the reservoirs of specialized competence which was increasingly required. The recasting that finally became law late in 1962 was in effect a weaving together of the opposing strands of concern. Mention has already been made of the explicit recognition of the new category of "special government employees." The mixture of objectives that entered into the revision was part of the climate of official opinion that shaped the executive order on advisory committees.

Provisions of the executive order

The order commended the institution itself, declaring that "the information, advice, and recommendations obtained through advisory committees are beneficial to the operations of the Government." At the same time it spoke of the need for "uniform standards" "in order that such committees shall function at all times in consonance with the antitrust and conflict-of-interest laws." The order included the advisory use of committees not formed by the government itself but only during the period of consultation with them. It did specifically except advisory committees "composed wholly of representatives of State or local agencies or charitable, religious, educational, civic, social welfare, or

[25] 84th Cong., 2nd Sess. H. R. Committee on the Judiciary. Antitrust subcommittee. Interim Report on WOC's and Government Advisory Groups (Committee Print 1956). Earlier, in a report on "the mobilization program," the subcommittee had criticized features of the advisory committees. 82nd Cong., 1st Sess., H. Report 1217 (October 19, 1951).

other similar nonprofit organizations," and any local, regional, or national committee "whose primary function is that of rendering a public service other than giving advice or making recommendations to the Government." The wide coverage was shown in the definition of "advisory committee" to mean "any committee, board, commission, council, conference, panel, task force, or other similar group, or any subcommittee or other subgroup thereof, that is formed by a department or agency of the government in the interest of obtaining advice or recommendations, or for any other purpose, and that is not composed wholly of officers or employees of the Government." Thus the provisions reached bodies of mixed membership even when the outside persons were in the minority.

Control was sought partly by requiring the specific approval of the agency head for the formation or use of any advisory committee that was not created directly by law. A two-year limit was put on the life of all nonstatutory advisory committees unless prolonged by specific approval of the agency head. An additional control was sought in a declaration: "Unless specifically authorized by law to the contrary, . . . determinations of action to be taken with respect to matters upon which an advisory committee advises or recommends shall be made solely by officers or employees of the Government."

Particular provision was made for the industry committee type, defined as "an advisory committee composed predominantly of members or representatives of a single industry or group of related industries, or of any subdivision of a single industry made on a geographic, service, or product basis." As to their makeup, the order said: "Each industry committee shall be reasonably representative of the group of industries, the single industry, or the geographical, service, or product segment thereof to which it relates, taking into account the size and function of business enterprises in the industry or industries, and their location, affiliation, and competitive status, among other factors." The order implied that trade association executives should not be members.

The procedure of committees was subject to certain standards, with added care about the industry committees on some points. Meetings could be held only at the call, or with the advance approval, of a full-time salaried officer of the department or agency, and with an agenda formulated or approved by him. All meetings must be chaired by, or conducted in the presence of, a full-time salaried official, who could end a meeting whenever he considered adjournment to be in the public interest. Minutes were to be kept, certified to by a full-time salaried officer. In the case of industry committees, a verified transcript of the proceedings was required, subject to waiver in certain respects.

Records were to be furnished to the Attorney General, who might ask for fuller documentation. Annually each department or agency must publish, in its yearly report or otherwise, a list of all committees used by it during the year, showing the functions, membership and affiliations, and the dates of meetings. The full requirement, however, might be waived by the agency head. Departmental practice soon showed that a majority of the agencies would take advantage of the option to omit publication of the voluminous details. It was not yet evident how much use would be made of the permission to omit the procedural requirements, except for industry committees, on the basis of a formal determination that compliance would interfere with a committee's proper functioning or be impracticable and that substitute provisions existed to ensure that committee operation was subject to government control and purpose.

The number of committees

A measure of the number of advisory committees became available in their recurrent listing by all departments and agencies under a common though loose definition. Any total reckoning is subject to the obvious qualifications that attend an overall figure for things so particular and so shifting. The exact numbers do not matter; the scale is significant. The lists that were available in the first two years under the executive order showed a total of about 900 advisory committees. Only a dozen of 40 departments and agencies did not list any committees. Of the grand total, 739 were in the departments. In point of numbers, Health, Education, and Welfare led with 229; the Public Health Service accounted for 191 of these, 135 being grant-reviewing bodies under the National Institutes of Health. Agriculture followed with 218, of which 44 were national in scope. Defense had reduced its advisory committees to 86. Interior had a total of 85, including 63 district and state boards in connection with land management. The Commerce Department's total was down to 56 (with only 6 industry committees left under the Business and Defense Services Administration in 1964); the State Department, including the Agency for International Development, was using 28; the Labor Department, 21; the Treasury, 15, 6 being committees of outside bodies which were consulted on debt management. The Post Office had a single general advisory body. Among the independent executive agencies, with a total of 112, the National Science Foundation led with 40 advisory groups and the Atomic Energy Commission with 19, followed by 16 in the Veterans Administration, 15 in the Federal Aviation Agency, 8 in National Aeronautics and Space Administration, 6 under the United States Information Agency, 5 under Housing and

Home Finance, and two central committees in the Selective Service System. The single national committee of the Small Business Administration ramified in regional and state advisory councils. Among the regulatory commissions, only a minority indicated the use of advisory committees: 14 under the Federal Power Commission; 8 under the Interstate Commerce Commission; 7 under the Federal Communications Commission, a single one with task groups under the Civil Aeronautics Board. The total was completed by less than 20 in the various parts of the Executive Office, including 7 in the Office of Emergency Planning. The overall figure of about 900 did not include numerous bodies with partly administrative duties under law, like some 30,000 community and county committees in the Agricultural Stabilization and Conservation Service and several thousand that aid in the loan programs of the Farmers' Home Administration.

Comparisons over time are risky. In the late 1930's, on the basis of a fairly strict definition, a figure of less than a hundred was given by Norman Gill in a survey for the National Resources Board.[26] In 1956 the replies gathered in response to a congressional questionnaire showed a total of about 1,000, excluding about 500 stand-by industry committees for defense mobilization.[27] A comparison with the situation in another industrial country was aided by the British survey in 1960, already mentioned. It put at 484 the number of bodies attached to departments of the central government in an advisory capacity, containing nonofficial members, and of a standing rather than temporary character. It should be noted that the bodies thus embraced included some "committees for independent administration" like the University Grants Committee. In reckoning the total at nearly 500, the survey discounted the figure of 600 committees that had been given in the already mentioned study of advisory bodies published in 1940; it believed that 200 or so would be more comparable. On this question of scale perhaps it would be enough to say that advisory committees are always numerous if it were not for the value of some measurements in connection with vigilant pruning as an aid to the vitality of the system.

[26] Norman Gill, "Permanent Advisory Committees in the Federal Government," *Journal of Politics*, Vol. 2, No. 1 (February 1940), pp. 411-35, which in summarizing his study identified 82 "permanent" advisory committees. See also David S. Brown, "The Public Advisory Board as an Instrument of Government," *Public Administration Review*, Vol. 15 (Summer 1955), pp. 196-204.

[27] 84th Cong., 2nd Sess. House Committee on Government Operations. Replies from Executive Departments and Agencies to Inquiry regarding the Use of Advisory Committees, January 1, 1953 to January 1, 1956. (Committee Print in several parts, 3,478 pages, 1956).

The executive order, as has been noted, set a limit of two years for any advisory committee unless the law provided otherwise or unless the department or agency head, not later than 60 days before the end of the period, determined specifically that the committee's continuation was in the public interest. In getting the control system started, the order stated that all advisory committees in existence at the time it was published, February 27, 1962, should be regarded as having been created on July 1, 1960. Much would depend upon the sustained alertness of the departments, which were invited to issue and administer supplementary rules, as also upon the handling of conflicts of interest under the revised law. The crucial question is not sheer numbers, less or greater; it is the avoidance of deadwood through constant attention as a responsibility of central management. A possible disadvantage in the permanent establishment of particular committees by law is the risk of lessening the scope for this salutary watchfulness. What has been said does not apply to the statutory provisions for the appointment of advisory committees at stated future dates as a method of periodical appraisal, as has been done for phases of welfare administration.

THE COMPOSITION OF ADVISORY BODIES

A sense of relevance and an impulse toward equipoise, together with an appeal to various sorts of prestige, shape the makeup of most advisory committees. The criteria may or may not be categorized and avowed. In the absence of legislation, the administrator inevitably has some classification in mind. It combines his awareness of the ramifications of his work with his strategy for the handling of pressures. Statutory provisions, bowing to an ideal, sometimes seek to enlist experience without affiliation; oftener they are frankly accepted together. There are indeed crucial differences in the leeway that may exist in the practice of group nominations, both as to the organizations that are designated and how they are approached and as to the number of names submitted.

Moreover, the shades of relationship between an advisory committee member and an organization, like the shadings in the position of an organization within a group that it purports to represent, elude a realistic classification. The member may serve without specific instructions, exercising judgment in fulfilling his group obligation, or he may be controlled by more or less constant instructions. It is the latter situation especially that discredits functional group representation. Leeway is indeed of the essence. Yet flexibility may have dangers for the administrator. In controversial fields where hard-driving public purposes are at stake—perhaps in the drafting of a bill or in writing regulations—

the administrator must be able to carry consultation to the brink of "negotiation" (as Professor Eckstein called it) without falling into the trap of an undue concession.[28] A partial corrective is at hand when advisory bodies are composite. It has been well said that "the most powerful argument for or against a group is the attitude of another group."[29]

It is interesting to note how frankly the fact of group representation in many advisory bodies was recognized in recent official statements. In the United States the avowal was explicit in the presidential memorandum of May 2, 1963, already mentioned. This document took account of the 1962 revision of the laws on conflicts of interest, which had given statutory recognition to the category of "special government employees." The memorandum faced the question of the extent to which members of advisory committees, as well as individual consultants, were "special government employees" exactly as if they were "serving the sponsoring department separately or individually." This ruling made it necessary to distinguish between "consultants and advisers," including committees, and "persons who are invited to appear at a department or agency in a representative capacity to speak for firms or an industry, or for labor or agriculture, or for any other recognizable group of persons, including on occasion the public at large." The memorandum stated that a person who, individually or as a committee member, appears in order "to present the views of a non-governmental organization or group which he represents, or for which he is in a position to speak, does not act as a servant of the Government. . . . He is therefore not subject to the conflict of interest laws." To be sure, he should observe the canons of ethical conduct.

The foregoing distinction left the tricky question of knowing when a person was acting in a "representative" capacity. The memorandum gave some suggestive clues. Thus, although the receipt of compensation from the government for services as an adviser or consultant indicated that the person in question was a "special government employee," it did not follow that payment of travel expenses with a *per diem* allowance made the recipient an employee. Another clue was the fact that a consultant or adviser who acted singly was rarely serving in a "representative" capacity. Yet not all committees were "representative." The memorandum pointed to some clues in the method of appointment. When a person was named to an advisory body upon the recommendation of an

[28] Harry Eckstein, *Pressure Group Politics. The Case of the British Medical Association* (Stanford: Stanford University Press, 1960), p. 22.

[29] J. R. Stewart, *British Pressure Groups. Their Relation to the House of Commons* (London: Oxford University Press, 1958), p. 43.

outside group or organization this fact tended "to support the conclusion that he has a representative function." As to the significance of the ability of representatives to bind or not to bind their organizations, the important thing, said the memorandum, "is whether they function as spokesmen for non-governmental groups or organizations and not whether they can formally commit them." The practical thought behind the quoted language was clear. Enough remained cloudy to sharpen the responsibilities of committee management.

Mention has been made of the fact that the executive order permitted the controlled use of committees which the government does not form. The arrangement is inherently ambiguous; in practice it could compromise the objectives of the order from the standpoint of both responsibility and representativeness. Yet the option is necessary to tap the country's full resources of counsel and criticism. When an independently technical judgment is needed it is fitting, for example, for the Census Bureau to take advice from a standing committee of the American Statistical Association. Different considerations are at stake when the Treasury consults with the Committee on Government Borrowing of the American Bankers Association.

PROBLEMS OF SCOPE AND LEVEL

Defining the assignment

The setting of the agenda for advisory committee meetings was to be a main control under the executive order of 1962. In the conduct of industry advisory committees, notably, it was a safeguard against collusion, as in price-rigging, or access to improper information, such as knowledge of certain governmental intentions or the private affairs of competitors. Nevertheless the control of the subject-matter of committee discussion touches an important problem in the art of constructive advice. The crux is likely to lie in the framing of the problem. One side of it was suggestively stated by Secretary of State Rusk when he said, "The first and sometimes most difficult job is to know what the question is."[30] He went on to say that "when it is accurately identified it sometimes answers itself." In any case, "the way in which it is posed frequently shapes the answer." Precisely for this reason the essence may lie in the ability of the adviser or advisory group to redefine the issue. The need may become apparent only after some exploring of the original assignment. A lesson in the value of flexibility was given by the

[30] Secretary of State Dean Rusk in a talk on February 20, 1961 to State Department Officers, reprinted in *Selected Papers*, compiled and published by the subcommittee on national policy machinery of the Senate Committee on Government Operations, 87th Cong., 2nd Sess., 1962, p. 26.

so-called Gaither Committee. In form it was a citizen panel under the science advisory committee, then attached to the Executive Office unit for problems of emergency planning. The inquiry was touched off by the proposal from the officials in charge of civilian defense which called for a program costing $40 billion. The inquiry became fruitful because the panel broadened the issue into an appraisal of the country's total defensive posture, needs, and capabilities.[31]

To be sure, advisers cannot succeed if they lose touch with the administrator's problem; they are likely to fail when they become combative. An advisory committee's access to information is partly a question of formal legal right, on which provisions vary among the minority of committees that have a direct statutory basis; it is partly a matter of facilities, including the extent to which committees have staffs of their own; mainly it is a matter of good sense on both sides. Situations do arise that call for sharp comment, carried to the appointing authority above, but ordinarily effective advisory relations depend upon mutual confidence that respects alike the nature of administrative responsibility and the autonomous quality of advice.

Difficulties faced by general advisory bodies

Advisory bodies have an advantage when their scope is limited and relatively technical. They are inherently disadvantaged when attached as standing bodies for overall counsel to an agency or unit as a whole. In such circumstances, amid the pressure of administrative decisions, items for the agenda are likely to be history when the committee meets. The sessions are padded with descriptive lectures. It may happen, therefore, that administrators become irked and the advisers frustrated and indifferent even when they cherish the honor of membership and attend through habit or curiosity. The difficulties that are likely to mark a standing, general assignment were illustrated in the story of the advisory committee established by law in connection with the program of foreign economic aid in 1948 and after. The statute required monthly meetings. David S. Brown has told of the dwindling attendance amid growing frustration, in the face of an indifferent administration, while the committee staff joined in an almost pathetic attempt to find something for the committee to do.[32] A job was invented in the form of a study of trade and tariff policy which in the circumstances of the time passed almost without notice.

[31] See Morton H. Halperin, "The Gaither Committee and the Policy Process," *World Politics,* Vol. 13 (April 1961), pp. 360-84.
[32] David S. Brown, *The Public Advisory Board and the Tariff Study.* The Inter-University Case Program, No. 30 (University, Alabama: University of Alabama Press, 1956).

It would be false, however, to assume that skillful administration cannot make constructive use of general advisory bodies. To be truly seen, moreover, they must be appraised sympathetically, attentive to the inductive processes of policy and its timing. Mort Grant doubtless was thinking of these aspects of the work of general advisory bodies when he wrote, a bit too mordantly: "One can readily set forth a score of reasons for the existence of advisory bodies only to conclude that they invariably relate primarily to the supposed by-products of advice rather than to advice itself."[33] The PEP study drew a line that is relevant here in distinguishing between "consultative" and "technical" committees. As to the former it remarked that "those who look for definite results and decisions from the work of consultative committees will not find them; but to do so is to mistake their function." At the least, they help administrators to take the temperature. "To ignore the value of this," declared the study, "is to practice blindfold the art of the possible." The word "possible" was used in the minimal sense of practicality in the setting of politics and group opinion. It has a wider meaning. Sometimes new possibilities are suggested. Even when nothing is proposed that has not been thought of within official ranks, the effect of its presentation by outside advisers may be to recall it in a new perspective and to galvanize attention in a way that amounts to fresh thinking.

Executive leeway

The flexible role of the chief executive is indispensable in eliciting advice and enlisting attention.[34] The President needs leeway in using special assistants for exploratory work, in convening conferences, and in appointing committees. For many purposes such leeway must extend to undertakings that are not specifically authorized by the Congress. The availability of funds, including the ability to draw upon the services of the departments and agencies, is more important than compulsory powers.[35] Various aging restrictions still complicate matters. A long-standing proviso about commissions of inquiry was supplemented in 1909 by the declaration that no money could be used or personnel

[33] Mort Grant, "The Technology of Advisory Committees," *Public Policy*, Vol. 10 (Cambridge: Harvard University Press, 1960), pp. 92-108, at 92.

[34] Paul H. Appleby, *Morality and Administration in Democratic Government* (Baton Rouge: Louisiana State University Press, 1952), p. 134.

[35] Carl Marcy, *Presidential Commissions* (New York: Kings Crown Press, 1945), p. 100. In this connection, however, it should be noted illustratively that the Temporary National Economic Committee—a joint legislative-executive body in the late 1930's—"decided to subpoena every witness who appeared . . . to avoid discrimination." David Lynch, *The Concentration of Economic Power* (New York: Columbia University Press, 1946), p. 68.

assigned for advisory bodies unless authorized by law. The binding effect was largely avoided by the sensible ruling that the authorization need not be explicit. A different sort of prohibition in 1944 forbade the use of public funds for any advisory body, including one created by executive order, after it had been in existence for a year unless meanwhile Congress had made an appropriation for it. This check was modified in 1945 by exempting interagency bodies in the work of which the personnel from the agencies received no extra compensation. Apart from the interagency loophole, two sources of support have been at hand in discretionary funds given routinely to the President for staff assistance on "special projects" and for "emergencies affecting the national interest, security, or defense." These funds have amounted yearly to less than $3 million. Moreover, budget officers are cautious about their use in the face of possible later questioning by Congress. Private financing is possible.[36] In an age of foundations, the demarcation between public and technically private funds is indeed unreal for many purposes. Nevertheless it is not desirable that the President's advisory initiative should be dependent upon private funds.[37] In short, the presidential scope in arranging for consultation is wide; for matters great and small it finds hundreds of channels within a single term. Withal, the leeway should be even greater.

To say this is not to question the need for direct congressional support of large undertakings; nor is it to overlook the mingling of congressional and executive auspices in many types of inquiry. The possibilities of a composite pattern was shown in the Hoover Commissions, which combined congressional and executive initiative in building a bipartisan membership from within and from outside the government. The balance sought in such a body may be marred (apart from the inattention of busy legislators) by the extent to which the work devolves upon task groups and the selectivity that enters at that level.[38] The blending of legislative and executive auspices can take many

[36] In the Hoover Administration it was said that all but seven of thirty-eight presidential commissions were privately financed. Carl Marcy, *op. cit.*, p. 31.

[37] The Presidential Transition Act, P.L. 88-277, 78 Stat. 153, March 7, 1964, sec. 3, authorized the General Services Administration to provide the President-elect and the Vice President-elect with suitable quarters, compensation of office staffs, and other assistance.

[38] In the final report of the Second Hoover Commission, June 1955, pp. 26-31, Rep. Chet Holifield complained that "in both the first and second Hoover Commissions the basic investigations and reports were undertaken by so-called task forces appointed mainly by the chairman . . . determining for themselves the scope of their inquiries, making their own findings and recommendations, and, in certain cases, influencing agency action without the knowledge or approval of the Commission."

forms. Two sizable inquiries in recent years—on outdoor recreation and on the review of the public land laws and their administration[39]—illustrated the plan of drawing the congressional members on a bipartisan basis from the relevant standing committees. In both cases the composite body was supplemented by departmental liaison officers and an advisory council which consisted of these officers and persons drawn from many cognate fields of enterprise, state and local administration, and civic leadership as sketched suggestively in the law.

An Unstructured Base

At the outset it was said that, while a monopoly of access must be avoided, advice may need sufficient structuring to ensure fair as well as abundant counsel amid complicated interests and issues. In conclusion the stress should be on the importance of an unstructured condition in the underlying advisory processes of a resilient and progressive society. Creative thinkers, lonely often, are its prime movers. Its invaluable institutional apparatus is an educational system of many elements which, with instruction as its direct responsibility, conducts research as an adjunct. Along with their mutually galvanizing interaction, at the cost of some pain for the individuals involved in a double responsibility, the very indirection is a protection for spontaneity in choosing the questions that are worth asking and for freedom to speculate about them.

It is from this standpoint that the impact of governmental contracting for research and development should be considered. By the middle 1960's, in a total of $15 billion spent for research and development by the national government, about one-tenth was for research that could be called basic. In the overall total, the bulk was spent in contracts with private industry; about 20 per cent through the government's own establishments; and 13 per cent through universities and other non-profit institutions. This is not the place to discuss the significance of novel research organizations, whether of the "agency adjunct" type or otherwise. It is of the educational system that we are speaking. The need for massive governmental support is not denied. In the future, the constructive line will be further to replace contracts by grants and, still more fundamentally, to gear the grants into the overall educational operation.[40]

[39] P.L. 85-470, 72 Stat. 238, approved June 28, 1958; and P.L. 88-606, 78 Stat. 982, approved September 19, 1964.
[40] The Report to the President on Government Contracts for Research and Development (the "Bell Report") recommended "grants to support broader programs, or to support the more general activities of an institution, rather than to tie each allocation to a specific objective."

· 11 ·

Bureaucracy in a Democratic Society

VICTOR A. THOMPSON

Bureaucracy has been defined in many ways—as government by non-elected officials, as administration in the interests of the administrators, as a disease of large organizations, as a highly rationalized kind of organization, as all governmental activities other than those of the courts, the legislature, and the chief executive. It is in this last sense that I intend to use the term. I wish to investigate the qualities of public administration in a modern, industrialized democracy.

Industrialism and democracy are both important variables determining the qualities of public administration, but industrialism is the more potent. The differences between administration in the United States today and in 1800 are greater than the differences between administration in the United States and Russia today.

Certain qualities of an industrialized society are especially important in determining the nature of its public administration.[1] Of first importance is the fact that such societies generate and use enormous amounts of technical and scientific information. This fact affects all institutions of the society—education, religion, the family, interpersonal relations, organization and management, government, etc. Industrialism's insatiable demand for trained people eventually breaks down old social barriers such as caste and class. A particular set of institutional norms or standards comes to characterize the society, distinguishing it from agrarian societies. Rationalism tends to replace tradition. More and more, rewards and services are distributed according to impersonal, universalistic criteria rather than particularistic ones like family, tribe, religion, nationality, etc. The society comes to feel that status and function should be distributed according to achievement rather than ascription—according to what you can do rather than who you are.

[1] See Fred W. Riggs, "Agraria and Industria—Toward a Typology of Comparative Administration," in William J. Siffin, ed., *Toward the Comparative Study of Public Administration* (Bloomington, Indiana: Indiana University Press, 1959), pp. 23-116.

Education becomes universal. Geographical and social mobility increase markedly.

All of these changes are associated with profound changes in social organization. Intimate, locality-bound, primary groupings of people give way to association based upon specific common interests. Enterprise is released; a great differentiation of goals and values occurs. The particularistic interests of family-type organizations in special privileges, in places, positions, and status, tend to be replaced by universalistic interests of associational groupings in policies. Multipurpose structures lose ground to special-purpose ones. Individuals become functionally differentiated and highly interdependent. New needs arise out of this interdependence. Some are met by a great expansion of associational groupings, others by government. The functions of government expand enormously, and it becomes a matter of intense interest and concern to the whole citizenry.

The mobilized population, great interdependence, vastly improved communication and transportation, and a much improved technical arsenal of government, all combine to increase the impact of government on the ordinary citizen. In a democracy, this greater potential weight of governmental activity is balanced and disciplined by the existence of a technically competent, interested, and appropriately organized citizenry buttressed by various constitutional devices. Both are important. A constitution without a qualified and interested citizenry produces formalism. A qualified and interested citizenry without constitutional guarantees is likely to be repressed, creating dangerous social tension. One of the unanswered questions of political science is whether industrialism is ultimately compatible with a repressive (nondemocratic) government. Personally, I think it is not.

THE DOCTRINAL BASIS OF BUREAUCRACY

The doctrinal basis of bureaucracy is more confused and complex in a democracy than in a nondemocratic government. Modern bureaucracy everywhere starts with a monistic, normative underpinning. Public officials were originally servants of a king. Later, both king and officials were considered to be servants of the state or nation. The advent of popular sovereignty substituted "the people" for king or state. In all of these cases, the bureaucracy is considered to have an owner who makes payments to officials in return for their undifferentiated time and effort. Thus, the bureacracy is considered to have a goal, that of the owner.[2] It is considered to be a single, monolithic tool;

---

[2] This doctrine constitutes the dominant normative theory of all modern bureau-

and good administration consists of making this tool predictably and reliably responsive to the wishes of the owner. This result is sought through a hierarchy of authority. Authority to act comes down from the very top, and only from the top, by means of delegation, and responsibility is directed up the hierarchy, and only up the hierarchy, from lower to higher official. No official is to have authority or rights apart from that granted him by his superior officer and such grants are revocable at will.

Unquestioning obedience is emphasized in such a system. There is no room for employee rights, which would conflict with the owner's interests. In fact, there is no place for conflict in such a system and no bargaining or negotiating devices for settling conflicts have to be provided.[3] Administration is harsh and replete with pathologies. Employees treated without dignity can hardly be expected to pass on humane and dignified treatment to clients. However, the purpose of this bureaucratic system is to achieve the interests of the owner, not those of employees or clients.

In a democracy, the owner is "the public," and "his" interest is called the "public interest." Democracy, therefore, does not necessarily soften and humanize this owner-tool concept. Much depends upon how the "public" is conceptualized. If the public is considered to speak solely through the single voice of an elected assembly or a dominant political party, the essentially hierarchical and monistic nature of this system is not greatly altered by democracy. People who take this point of view are likely to consider the democratic political process solely in terms of parties and elections and to be great admirers of a strong, two-party, parliamentary system on the British model. They tend to reify the public and the public interest or, at the very least, to glorify majorities.

Associated with democracy historically, though perhaps not logically, is a great emphasis on individual and group rights. From this tradition comes a different administrative doctrine, a pluralistic one. The owner of the bureaucracy, the public, is conceived in terms of concrete individuals and groups of individuals with interests which they urge upon government. This public expresses itself in many ways. It expresses itself through parties and elections, the courts, the chief executive, the legislature, committees of the legislature and individual legislators, the communication media, and, most important of all,

cratic organizations, public and private. See Richard M. Cyert and James G. March, *A Behavioral Theory of the Firm* (Englewood Cliffs, New Jersey: Prentice-Hall, 1963), pp. 27-28.

[3] Victor A. Thompson, *Modern Organization* (New York: Knopf, 1961), pp. 122-28.

through access to all of these by organized associations of interested citizens. This pluralistic doctrine, though frequently invoked, is not well integrated into our administrative philosophy. For many people, the interest group is still tainted with illegitimacy. The dominant administrative doctrine in this country, as elsewhere, is still the monistic, hierarchical one.

Regardless of formal administrative doctrine, the actual patterns of administration in democratic industrial countries are pluralistic. Governmental activities occur in response to demands of interested citizens organized into functionally differentiated associations. As noted above, industrial society produces, and depends upon, such a citizenry. In a democratic society, this situation produces an intricate, pluralistic pattern of group politics. The governmental response to such politics is inevitably pluralistic as well. The bureaucracy, therefore, is not a monolithic tool of a single owner but a highly fragmented set of institutions, replete with conflict and often working at cross purposes.

In the democratic, industrialized countries of the West, the pluralistic political system developed first, and the bureaucratic system arose in response to it. Politics came before administration. In many other countries of the world, and especially former colonial countries, administration developed first. It developed as a tool of a single source of power—a modernizing autocrat, a totalitarian party, a colonial secretariat. A monolithic bureaucracy arose before there was a developed, pluralistic, political system to direct and control it.[4]

In the United States, the fragmentation of the bureaucracy is reinforced by the separation of powers, by constitutional and political federalism, and by many checks and balances written into the Constitution. Although the resulting lack of integration in the bureaucracy is deplored by many people sincerely dedicated to the monistic doctrine, others believe it is a source of strength, not weakness. It forces a coping with problems, and negotiation and compromise. It provides checks and balances within the bureaucracy with its inevitable combination of legislative, executive, and judicial functions. Although this fragmentation is probably greater in the United States, because of its particular constitutional traditions, it is healthily extensive in all democratic, industrial countries.

Whereas a past tendency toward class recruiting has undoubtedly introduced a certain unity into administration in many Western democracies, the advance of industrialism is rapidly eliminating this

---

[4] This theme is touched upon by several of the writers in Joseph LaPalombara, ed., *Bureaucracy and Political Development* (Princeton, New Jersey: Princeton University Press, 1963).

agrarian residue as it has almost completely done in this country. As noted above, industrialism's insatiable demand for trained personnel cannot long tolerate such restrictions on recruitment. It is true that a certain formal unity within the bureaucracy is provided by the common legal conditions of employment, but whatever behavioral significance this has had is rapidly disappearing as the professionalization of work encourages movement between governmental and nongovernmental positions, gradually equalizing the conditions of employment.

The growth of employee rights of various kinds has further dented the monistic structure of bureaucracy. It breaks the owner's monopoly of right, introducing formally a pluralistic element. Adjudicating devices within the bureaucracy become necessary. The owner must negotiate with his tools. This development has not come about as a result of modifications in the dominant bureaucratic doctrine. Such rights have been wrung from reluctant managements through essentially political activities of employees. These rights represent the government's response to the demands of a particular set of organized interests—in this case, those of public employees. It would seem to me that similar developments will eventually occur in nondemocratic, industrial countries as a necessary managerial response to the problem of maintaining morale among employees undergoing rapid upgrading.

American bureaucracy has not been a leader in extending rights to employees. Great Britain and other West European countries have gone further. These facts tend to support my belief that this extension of employee rights has not been a result of doctrinal development. Although there is probably a causal relation between humane treatment of employees and humane treatment of clients, this result is irrelevant to the dominant bureaucratic doctrine which seeks only the interests of the owner—the public—through rigid hierarchical discipline and control.

CONTROL AND RESPONSIVENESS

Differences in the problems and mechanisms of control distinguish public administration in a democratic, industrialized country from administration in both nonindustrialized and nondemocratic countries. The monistic, owner-tool doctrine lends itself to a search for control and responsibility through the hierarchy of authority. If each official is sufficiently responsive to the wishes of his superior officer, ultimately the whole bureaucracy is controlled by the wishes of its owner, the public, through the top elected body.[5] In its extreme form, this view

[5] See Charles S. Hyneman, *Bureaucracy in a Democracy* (New York: Harper and Brothers, 1950), and Carl J. Friedrich, *Constitutional Government and Democracy*, rev. ed. (Boston: Ginn & Co., 1950).

holds that there can be no administrative responsibility to the public except through strict hierarchical responsibility. In the United States, with its constitutional separation of powers, an unanswered question connected with this viewpoint is whether the ultimate hierarchical responsibility should be to Congress or the President.

There are serious limitations to hierarchy as a control device. The technical information and calculating capacity within the hierarchy of modern, technically complex administration is inadequate to this task. Information sent up through hierarchical channels is highly edited and often unreliable. These limitations are operative whether the top hierarchical position is considered to be the chief executive or the legislature. Serious efforts to overcome these limitations lead to gimmickry like administrative spy systems. These devices do not solve the problem of control but rather shift it. If they become large enough to gather and master the information needed for a thorough hierarchical control, the problem then becomes how to control the spies. Assuming that the problem of information could be overcome, a really successful system of hierarchical control would require a posture of dedicated conformity throughout the administration. Such a posture would dry up initiative and prevent responsiveness to clientele.

Beyond the question of the ability to control is the question of interest in control. Legislative constituencies are rarely policy constitutencies in the highly mobile, interdependent, functionally differentiated industrial society. They are area-bound, communal, and tend to generate particularistic interests in special privileges, recognition, exemptions, favorable treatment, etc. *Policies* associated with areas or localities are for the most part dealt with by local governmental jurisdictions.

Although the chief executive has policy interests, they are very limited. He can muster the information to control only a few policy areas, and his political needs are met with only a few areas of policy control.[6] Consequently, most policy is not only beyond his ability to control but also beyond his interest. The important function of centralizing authority in a hierarchical arrangement is not control of policy but providing a legitimate means for interfering in policy whenever it seems politically desirable to do so. It is politically desirable to do so whenever politically important interests have not been satisfied in the policy-making process.

The two indispensable ingredients of control lacking in the hierarchical device are provided by the citizenry in the democratic indus-

---

[6] See Peter Woll, *American Bureaucracy* (New York: W. W. Norton, 1963) Chaps. 4 and 5.

trialized society. It is highly organized into associational (noncommunal) interest groupings oriented to policies rather than places for their members. Such an organized citizenry provides laterally the ingredients missing from hierarchical controls—technical competence and interest in every conceivable aspect of policy. The great superiority of administration in industrialized countries as compared with that in underdeveloped countries is largely due to the existence in the former of a technically competent, interested, organized, policy-oriented citizenry. Such a citizenry can and will confer prestige and other rewards for the faithful, humane performance of duties and punish the converse.

In the pluralistic, democratic, industrialized society, policy constituencies tend to be administrative ones. Administrative organizations and activities have appeared in response to the public policy needs of the society—needs which could not be met by the more traditional constitutional organs of government. Inevitably, therefore, administrative activities combine the older functions of legislation and adjudication because these functions are necessarily involved in policy-making. Interests in policy shift to these administrative policy-making centers, creating administrative constituencies which are both able and willing to participate in policy-making, to evaluate the result, and to reward or punish the policy-makers.

Administrative constituencies are highly representative of the interests involved. These interests consist of other affected administrative units, clientele, the communication media, the hierarchy, and strategically located members of the legislature. Occasionally, party interests must be represented. The policy-making unit seeks a consensus among any of these that manifest an interest, or at least the largest, most viable coalition possible. Negotiation and compromise are required, and elaborate searching or clearance devices are employed to assure that all interests have been consulted. If any politically important interest is overlooked, or if interests broader or beyond the administrative constituency are involved, the centralized authority of the hierarchy can be employed to shift the matter to a level which includes this broader constituency. The hierarchy is thus employed, not to enforce conformance to the monocratic owner's goals, but to search out other, overlooked interests in a pluralistic society.

The administrative official must seek political support from his constituency. He cannot rest his case solely on the approval of a superior officer or any other single element in that constituency. Consequently, the administrative official in a democratic, industrialized society is more involved in value choices, in politics, than his counterpart in a dictatorship where the support of a superior carries much more weight, and the citizenry is not allowed to organize freely. Theoretically, therefore, we would expect a democratic public administration to be more concerned with the value orientations of its employees than administration in a dictatorship. The fact that such is not the case testifies, among other things, to the reliance placed upon an interested, pluralistically organized citizenry as a control over administration. Those commentators who see democratic administrative responsibility as arising chiefly out of the personal value commitments of public employees miss this central feature of modern democratic society.

The fragmented nature of public administration in modern democratic society causes some to point with pride and others to view with alarm. Whereas I am arguing essentially that watchfulness and not complacency is the proper citizen attitude toward public administration, I cannot agree with the alarmists who constantly cry for more integration. What or whose is the integrated value system to be promoted by a more integrated administration? The "public interest" does not define itself, and I am sure that the oligarchical elements involved in our fragmented policy-making are more visible and subject to criticism than would be those involved in defining a reified "public interest." Nevertheless, there are problems in our system of citizen control and improvements are needed. Many interests are not represented and some are overrepresented. We have some peculiar notions as to what constitutes an interest and hence gives a group standing. Very often it seems that if a group cannot show some economic interest its views are not taken seriously. Consequently, the views of the highly informed and "disinterested" sector of our population have less weight in many matters than they might have.[7] More attention to the question of representation is indicated. Better publicity concerning access and contacts would help, as would conflict-of-interest regulations and similar devices. In short, we must take public administration seriously and seek the values and objectives of democratic government through the bureaucracy as well as through parties, elections, and legislatures.

The Appropriation of Administrative Resources

In agrarian societies, the particularistic interest of familistic, communal, social organizations in places and privileges for their members resulted in strong tendencies for administrative resources of office,

---

[7] This lack of standing seems to be partly the basis for the weakness of organized support for foreign aid. See, for example, Andrew Eliot Rice, "Building a Constituency for the Foreign Aid Program: The Record of the Eisenhower Years" (unpublished doctoral dissertation, Syracuse University, 1963).

authority, material, and subordinates to become personally attached to officials. Offices were often inherited or bought and sold. Authority often became the personal property of an individual to be used to grant favors, punish enemies, or enrich its possessor. The overriding importance of personal dignity and social status in these hierarchical societies made it virtually impossible to use offices and employees in a rationalistic, instrumental way. Involved in this problem was the difficulty of separating person and role. Important personal needs were met by assimilating the role to the person.

In the modern industrialized society, great social and geographical mobility plus education has made it possible and inevitable for a person to play many social roles and to change roles frequently. It has become possible to distinguish role and person. Administrative norms have arisen which distinguish the public from the private, the office from the person.[8] Although these norms are more thoroughly and more generally accepted as industrial society evolves, such was not always the case, and elaborate procedural devices to prevent the personal appropriation of administrative resources were everywhere installed in early modern governments and are still here today. Stringent budget, accounting, property, and other controls everywhere in governmental administration, from the Inspector General system of the Military to the "secret" observation peepholes of the Post Office, testify both to the past practice of personal appropriation of resources and to the revulsion against this practice in an industrial era. This distrust of public officials and the procedures and devices through which it manifests itself are probably more ubiquitous in dictatorship than in democracy, but they are very much present in both. The problem and the response to it have given modern management an almost morbid preoccupation with control and procedures to secure it.

Great changes have occurred, and modern management is much freer to use public employees (and clientele) in an instrumentally efficient manner. Standard procedures and uniform regulations are possible because administrators need consider only what is instrumentally effective and need not take into account the social position or status of each employee or client. Public officials are no longer precious, a group apart, enjoying special position and privileges. Sinecures have all but disappeared. Officials are servants of the public, not the king or the state. Statolatry has consequently declined considerably. All of these things bring the citizen and the official closer together, greatly easing

[8] See Max Weber, *The Theory of Social and Economic Organization*, trans. A. M. Henderson and Talcott Parsons, ed. Talcott Parsons (New York: Oxford University Press, 1960).

citizen access to the latter. Efficient and effective administration finally become possible.[9]

Nevertheless, the separation of person and office is not complete, and I believe it never will be. Deep personal needs remain. Individuals will try to make personal use of administrative arrangements, positions, powers, and other resources for a very long time to come. However, in the modern period this problem takes on much more subtle forms than gross theft, bribery, nepotism, etc. Whenever administrative action represents a response to personal or group needs generated within the bureaucracy rather than to the needs of the public, however defined, there has been some administrative appropriation of administrative resources.

This problem is exceedingly complex because certain manifestations of administrative self-indulgence are clearly within the tolerances of public attitudes and administrative norms. Despite the predominance of the owner-tool doctrine, the community generally does not demand that its public servants be literally tools. Certainly, conditions of work not too inferior to general community standards fall within the limits of an admittedly legitimate administrative interest. A certain amount of organized activity to promote this interest is conceded to be legitimate (but not as much as would be conceded to the private sector). The problem of the illegitimate appropriation of administrative resources arises when administrative self-indulgence begins noticeably to affect public policies. A few brief examples of the latter will show that a technically competent, interested, and organized citizenry provides the best protection against these subtle perversions.

In recent years we have learned much about real behavior within administrative undertakings, as opposed to prescribed behavior. We now know that organizations are not just instruments. They can also be regarded as political systems in which policies are sometimes made or vetoed with an eye chiefly to the power or position advantage of a group or an ambitious individual. Contrasting to the monocratic structure of the formal organization is the luxuriant pluralism of the informal one in which cohesive groups develop and pursue interests and goals of their own. Information and cooperation are extended or withheld with the idea of protecting and promoting these informal group goals.[10]

Hierarchical control is relatively ineffective in dealing with these

[9] See E. Strauss, *The Ruling Servants* (London: George Allen and Unwin, 1960).

[10] These processes operate with equal strength in private "bureaucracies." See Tom Burns and G. M. Stalker, *The Management of Innovation* (London: Tavistock Publications, 1959), and Richard M. Cyert and James G. March, *op. cit.*

phenomena. It lacks both the information and the interest to do so. It is dependent for information upon the very processes in question, and its interest in controlling the phenomena is compromised by virtue of the fact that hierarchy is itself involved in them. Among the prizes around which this internal struggle revolves are managerial positions. Here again, tolerable limits can be imposed on this internal political activity only by the constant attention and intervention of technically competent lateral interests, aided by a free press.

Although society may have evolved from status to contract, interest in personal status within organizations is still strong, and a thriving, localized status system exists in every bureaucratic organization. Whereas status formerly depended upon birth, today it depends upon the roles one manages to adopt. High status roles, therefore, have a tendency to stick to people like flypaper, perpetuating many of the inflexibilities of management in an agrarian, caste society. Person and role tend to become fused. The rational adaptation of administrative means to public policy ends is deflected proportionately.

The personal appropriation of administrative resources involved in providing symbols of status rank and manifestations of deference is kept in check in a democracy by an interested, taxpaying citizenry, operating both through the press and through an elected legislature. More important than the use of resources purely as symbols of rank is the distortion of rational policy-making which accompanies status, now as in the feudal past. The flow of information and communication is distorted, as is the correction of errors and the initiation of ideas and suggestions. To deal with this problem, a citizenry that knows what it wants and has the technical capacity to evaluate official action is especially important, as is decentralized and fragmented policy-making. To rely upon the hierarchy of authority to control these perversions due to status behavior is almost a contradiction in terms because an organizational status system is almost synonymous with the hierarchy of authority.

The administrative appropriation of administrative resources in volves a conflict between administrative interests and public goals. One such conflict, universal in the modern era, is the conflict between policy and administrative feasibility. The clientele (or public) is primarily interested in policy goals, but officials must always be interested in feasibility as well, because resources are always limited. The scale of feasibility is a scale of effort. To say that a proposed policy is administratively infeasible is to say that it would be administratively difficult. It is understandable that the official should wish to avoid implementing such a policy. Should he nevertheless be required to do so, he can be expected to shift as much of the cost to the clientele as he can. The public presentation of a program will be couched in terms of its ideal policy goals, but the actual performance will also be governed by considerations of administrative feasibility (least effort). Thus, there is always a gap, more or less wide, between the ideal and the actual, between the administrative self-presentation and the administrative reality.[11] Until robots take over administration, this gap will remain. The problem, again, is to keep it within tolerable limits.

As in other matters, hierarchical control is greatly limited in protecting policy interests from feasibility interests. In the first place, hierarchy shares these latter interests. In fact, the impact of feasibility considerations is probably greatest on the managerial hierarchy. The extra effort required to push back the boundaries of feasibility will fall especially heavily upon it. In the second place, the feasibility argument appears particularly as an expert, nonpolitical one, and the managerial hierarchy is especially defenseless against such arguments. It simply does not have the technical knowledge to rebut them. Thus, here as elsewhere, the importance of technically competent lateral controls in the form of organized interests is apparent. Chiefly in them will we find both the interest and technical ability required.

A related question is the extent to which the bureaucracy becomes independent of political control by virtue of its great concentration of expertise—the extent to which there is real discretion in the administration. I should say that the amount of independent discretion enjoyed by a bureaucracy would depend first upon the degree of dependence of the society upon advanced technical knowledge (the degree of industrialization), and, second, upon the extent to which control was sought through the hierarchy of authority. The principle of expertise is specialization. The principle of hierarchy is generalization. Thus, the more technical, complex, and voluminous the information (technologies) upon which an organization depends, the less effective are hierarchical controls. In a democratic, industrialized country, this problem is approached largely through the lateral controls exercised by the organized citizenry. Further improvement of this representative process would increase this control.

Some bureaucratic independence exists, and I suspect it will increase with the increasing technical complexity of our age. A nondemocratic country must depend upon hierarchical controls. A tremendous

[11] See Erving Goffman, "Characteristics of Total Institutions," in Maurice R. Stein, Arthur J. Vidich, and David Manning White, eds., *Identity and Anxiety* (Glencoe, Ill.: The Free Press, 1960).

hierarchical effort is required, using devices which would not be tolerated in a democracy—terror, extremely heavy penalties, spy systems of several kinds, constant propaganda, duplicating administrative organizations, etc. Even with a strenuous effort of this kind, I suspect that there is more independent bureaucratic discretion and more personal appropriation of administrative resources in a modern dictatorship than in a modern democracy. The wide dispersion of personal power in the bureaucracies of underdeveloped agrarian countries, dictatorships or otherwise, reflects itself in the widespread incidence of graft.

Some commentators in modern democracies urge a greater administrative initiative in policy, but I do not believe this need is at all obvious. In countries with little development of their political systems, the bureaucracy will indeed play a large role in policy initiation. It would seem to me that a much smaller part in policy initiation needs to be played by bureaucracies in Western democratic countries with their highly developed political systems. The more appropriate policy role for a modern democratic bureaucracy is the role of policy broker, seeking consensus, compromise, and agreement, and promoting coalitions of interests.

Administrative action in the modern world is impersonal and institutional. It is not the product of one person's mind or heart. It reflects the concerns of all legitimate interests in the appropriate administrative constituency. Elaborate horizontal clearances and coordinating procedures assure this broad scanning of proposals before action. Furthermore, administrative action is expected to be (and usually is) objective, impersonal, unsentimental, occasioned by universalistic criteria rather than particularistic personal appeals or sympathies. To protect against charges of subjectivity or personal favoritism, considerable documentation is collected before any action is taken. All of this preparation takes time and frequently leads to charges of bureaucratic red tape.[12]

This impersonal, objective, institutional approach to action, while demanded by the norms of an industrial society, is somewhat at war with basic sociopsychological needs of individuals, most of whom have been socialized in primary groups where personal loyalty and action is stressed. Clienteles press for particularistic treatment, and many are tempted to use primary relations with officials to secure it. Reciprocally, officials may be tempted to appropriate authority to their personal use so that such particularistic requests can be granted (or denied). The desire for money side payments need not be behind this conversion of

[12] See Paul H. Appleby, *Morality and Administration in Democratic Government* (Baton Rouge: Louisiana State University Press, 1952).

institutional power to personal use. In fact, in the modern age it is probably more likely to be the understandable human need to be rewarded with gratitude or admiration.

Consequently, administrative assurances are sometimes given which cannot subsequently be redeemed. They cannot be passed through the impersonal, objective, institutionalized decision-making process of the bureaucracy. Generally speaking, if an individual administrative official has the personal power to grant or withhold favors, he has managed to appropriate administrative power to his personal use. One of the hardest lessons modern industrialized man has had to learn is neither to demand nor to promise special favors. Here again, the best defense against such feudal practices is an alert, interested, and organized citizenry, backed up by a free press. For although individual members of such groups have these particularistic needs, the associational group does not. Its interests are universalistic and, in fact, it could not survive if it pressed particularistic demands. It would break apart due to internal bickering and jealousy.

The search for special favors and for the power to grant or deny them, so common and general in agrarian society, will finally disappear only (if ever) when the evolution of modern man is complete. Perhaps, as long as the family continues to exist in some form, however diminished, the belief that some person can grant one's wishes if he so desires will continue to exist. However, a comparison of both clientele and official behavior in feudal with modern times, or in underdeveloped countries with industrialized ones, shows how very greatly modern man has changed in this respect.

THE QUALITY OF PUBLIC EMPLOYMENT

In agrarian society, public employment carries great prestige. It is one of the few honorific occupations—in fact, one of the few kinds of occupation, honorific or otherwise. In industrial society, the vast increase in technology and the great functional differentiation, enterprise, education, and mobility create a world of other opportunities for social function and status. The prestige of public employment declines proportionately. Although it is higher in Western Europe than here, it is declining there as well. It is still very high in underdeveloped countries where few other career opportunities exist. Whereas recruitment was formerly based on caste or class, industrialism has been unable to tolerate such restrictions. Consequently, caste or class bureaucracies are on their way out.

Some notions of the higher ethical nature of public employment still persist. In support of these notions the different standards of interorganizational influence as between business and government are frequently mentioned. This contrast is not as clear-cut as it is often pictured. In the United States, devices used by the bureaucracy to influence Congressmen, such as Reserve Officer commissions and expense-paid junkets, would not be publicly condoned in business lobbying. The V.I.P. treatment accorded Congressmen and the almost sycophantic receptiveness to their particularistic importunities hardly square with our universalistic, egalitarian norms of official conduct. Besides, it is likely that the standards of interbusiness influence methods are changing in the direction indicated by the norms of industrial culture. I suspect that the personal exploitation of strategic positions and powers by purchasing agents, for example, is on the decline.

Some people have said that public administration in a democracy, as contrasted with private administration, takes place in a "goldfish bowl." It must be remembered that the interests of citizens in a modern society are intensely involved in governmental action and that a democratic public feels it has the right to know what *its servants* are doing. However, this distinction between public and private administration is also declining as the clientele interest in business decisions, and the legitimacy of that interest, increase. When business decisions have a greater and greater impact on society, the only thing which keeps the society from demanding some voice in them is an ideology which teaches that it is none of the society's business. The power of this ideology has been on the wane in this country for the past eighty years, at least.

Among the functions a society must perform to survive is the socialization of its members into important roles they must perform. For bureaucracy, the two especially important roles are public official and client. In past agrarian societies, clients (the citizens) were taught deference and fear of public officials. They were taught the proper rituals and ceremonies of approach and address, of speech, posture, facial expression, and manners. Officials were taught the majesty of sharing the power of the king or the state. They were taught haughty manners for dealing with subordinates and clients; they were taught to look down upon the citizen. They formed a class apart, distinctive by clothes, manners, and speech. All of this was reinforced by the rigid class system of the society and the practice of class recruitment.

In the modern industrial society there seems to have been, perhaps understandably, a reaction against the role of public official. People—clients—are taught to deprecate them as seekers for security without enterprise or ambition; as lazy eaters at the public trough; as inefficient and less able than other people, possibly failures elsewhere. This kind

220 VICTOR A. THOMPSON

of client socialization seems especially to occur within the middle and upper classes of society. The older agrarian attitudes of fear and deference are still quite prevalent among the lower class. Downgrading of the public official is also occurring in Western Europe and in other countries where growing industrialization is creating an increasing number of alternatives to public employment.

There is no special process of socialization into official roles in modern society. Most people learn how to play roles of superior and subordinate. I have noticed both here and elsewhere a certain contempt and lack of understanding of politicians on the part of public officials. This may be a reaction to the particularistic demands of politicians upon administration in an age dedicated to achievement norms and universalistic criteria. It may also be partly a residue of the long struggle to achieve the merit system.

As noted earlier, human beings are not likely soon to become completely domesticated to the universalistic, objective, rational, impersonal norms of an industrial society. They continue to have needs for individualized treatment. One way these particularistic needs are pursued is through elected representatives, especially legislators. The modern legislator is a representative of a communal, area-bound constituency rather than a policy one. Although this fact does not prevent him from developing policy concerns and representing policy interests, it nevertheless means that many of his demands upon the bureaucracy are of a particularistic, special-treatment nature.

To the administrative official thoroughly socialized in modern administrative norms of conduct, such demands upon him can only appear contemptible. They are "just politics." Yet the needs back of these demands are real, and the politician's political needs which impel him to press these demands are likewise real. The virtue of modern administrative norms lies not in their philosophic beauty but in the fact that they meet the needs of an industrial society. The limits of their utility are set by their need-satisfying power. It may be that some officials (and students of public administration?) are a bit too priggish. Politics is an honorable activity, and it must occasionally call upon administrative resources. Modern public officials generally need more understanding of the needs of politicians. One of Paul Appleby's many great accomplishments was to further that understanding.

In the agrarian past, government work was largely clerical desk work, concerned mostly with the operation of administrative procedures. The only pre-entry preparation required in most cases was reading and writing and sometimes arithmetic. As Jackson said, the work was simple enough so that most faithful party supporters could perform it. Government employees were largely white-collar unskilled or semiskilled. Such employees ("desk class") were highly dependent upon their procedures, programs, and organizational units for status and function. They had little interorganizational mobility. Their educational backgrounds (or lack of them) were all much the same. All of these things provided the basis for a certain unified, bureaucratic interest and gave a conservative, authoritarian quality to administration.

These simple technological conditions have passed. Administration today is based upon an exploding and already astronomically large volume of information. Jobs and individuals are being rapidly upgraded. A larger and larger proportion of government positions require long periods of pre-entry preparation. The desk class is fast disappearing. Government employs an increasing proportion of professionals and subprofessionals. In the American federal service almost half of the incumbents of the highest grades (GS-14 and above) started their careers as professionals, not as desk workers.

These changes are rapidly changing the character of public employment. Interorganizational mobility is increasing rapidly. Movement between governmental and nongovernmental jobs is increasing. Under these circumstances, authoritarian managerial practices have become obsolete. There is much less inclination to intense organizational and program loyalty, and the basis for a general civil service loyalty has simply disappeared. Professionals are loyal to their profession first of all, and look to peers for personal evaluation rather than to superiors. The hierarchy of authority as an instrument of control and policy initiation is bound to grow even weaker, its eventual form and function being still a matter of conjecture. As functional differentiation and professionalization continue to expand under the impact of exploding technical and scientific knowledge, the importance of the technically qualified and interested elements of the administrative constituency, as controllers and evaluators of administrative action, increases apace. Of these elements, the technically competent, interested, organized citizenry is foremost.

Associated with all of these changes is a growing administrative interest in courteous, sympathetic treatment of clients and their problems. This interest often manifests itself as an emphasis on "good public relations." Training programs stress the importance of good relations with the clientele. As is appropriate in a liberal democracy, the individual citizen is to be treated with dignity and given satisfaction if possible. He is to be taken seriously. Although these aims are not always reached, I think it correct to say that they have become incorporated into the role of the modern administrative official.

In this period of flux, with all of these changes occurring, the

concept of a "public career," a "career in public administration," seems
to be weakening. It suggests a special group of "servants of the state,"
so uncongenial to modern democracy. After all, we do not speak of a
"private career." A profession of management is not now possible
because, with managerial progression still the dominant definition of
success, managerial positions must be left open to all. If something
approaching a profession of management finally evolves, I suspect
managers will move freely between public and private employment
even as other professionals tend to do now.

BUREAUCRATIC SECRECY

Carl Friedrich has argued that one of the benchmarks of modern
bureaucracy is an addiction to secrecy. A certain amount of administrative secrecy is clearly indicated by the circumstances and hence
falls within limits of legitimacy. Such is secrecy in some aspects of
law enforcement and in military affairs. I am concerned with an
administrative interest in carrying secrecy beyond these limits of general acceptability. Such an interest exists and I would like to examine
some of its bases.

One source of the interest in secrecy in modern bureaucracy can
be found in the depersonalizing of power which has come about.
Administrative decisions are institutional, not personal. This fact gives
a quality of tentativity to administrative action. Any assurances given
are quite likely to be overidden later. This fact causes the wise official
to avoid saying too much.

Another source of the interest in secrecy is the universal administrative concern with administrative feasibility. Though a premise of
all administrative decisions, feasibility is often not an acceptable reason for action to publics intensely interested in policy. Consequently,
there is a strong tendency to conceal this basis of action. The organization must present an idealized version of itself even though the
bases of its action cannot always be idealistic.

The internal political struggles for power and position have to be
hidden. Such independent administrative interests are not accepted
as legitimate by a public which expects the bureaucracy to be a tool
of its interests. Furthermore, the personal appropriation of power and
position is simply contrary to modern administrative norms of action.
It is immoral. Consequently, the taint of personal (or subgroup)
interest, usually to be found somewhere in any administrative action,
must be carefully concealed.

The actual independence from hierarchical controls, and the control power of lateral interests, do not square with the dominant owner-

tool doctrine and therefore have to be camouflaged. An elaborate dramaturgy is used to hide these necessary departures from the dominant stereotypy.

The administrative norms of an industrial society, as sketched above, are strict and somewhat at odds with personal needs. Our own agrarian past is very close to us, and we have not yet been fully socialized into the requirements of an industrial society. Consequently, departures from these norms often seem to be necessary for practical reasons, or for reasons of human compassion, or to discharge the obligations of primary relationships not yet fully articulated with the administrative obligations of an industrial, urban era. Some conflict of norms, of obligations, persists, although to nowhere near the same extent as in the newly modernizing, agrarian, underdeveloped countries. In these latter countries, this conflict of norms creates an anomic situation in which individual officials can appropriate considerable personal power to use as personal expediency dictates, now according to one set of norms, now according to the other. In industrial societies, the occasional departure from modern bureaucratic norms of official conduct is not publicly acceptable and therefore must be hidden or distorted beyond recognition by elaborate rationalizations and semantic confusion.

In the clerical, desk-class bureaucracies of agrarian society, much of the power of public officials derived from their monopoly of knowledge about complex government procedures and requirements. The "professional expertise" of bureaucrats to which Max Weber referred was expertise in such procedures and requirements. Preparation for government service was often the study of these procedures in schools of law. Consequently, this clerical, desk-class officialdom was interested in both complexity and secrecy, the main sources of the citizens' dependence upon officialdom and hence the main sources of officialdom's power.

This kind of secrecy is associated with a desk-class bureaucracy. A professionalized bureaucracy, such as is emerging in industrial society, may have no less secrecy but there will be a less pernicious basis for it. It seems to me that professional secrecy, beyond the sources of secrecy discussed above, has two primary bases: (1) considerations of the good of the client, however mistaken; and (2) an unwillingness to make the effort to translate the technical bases of action into layman's language.

An industrial citizenry, as we have observed, is intensely interested in administrative actions and the bases for them. In a democracy, such a citizenry constantly battles bureaucratic secrecy, attempting to hold it within tolerable limits by means of interest organizations, legislatures (especially legislative committees), and a free press. In a modern dictatorship, bureaucratic secrecy reigns largely undisturbed.

The Individual and the Bureaucracy

Up to now I have said a good deal about the organized citizenry but relatively little about the problems of the individual citizen as he faces the bureaucracy. The stringent norms of conduct and the impersonal, institutionalized character of administration in an industrial society conflict with persistent needs for particularistic, personal, individualized treatment.[13] The problems or conditions of the individual rarely match perfectly the abstract, universalistic criteria of modern administrative action. Furthermore, the impersonal, institutional decisional processes, plus the need for documentation to defend against charges of personal favoritism or arbitrariness, often result in considerable delay in dealing with the individual's requests or inquiries. Administrative clearance procedures, including hierarchical clearance, stress the veto and neglect affirmation. A "no" ends the matter; a "yes" must frequently go higher. The individual seems to be able to find many who can say "no" but no one who can say "yes," leaving him with a feeling of powerlessness.

Authoritarian management resulting from the owner-tool doctrine plus the desk-class bureaucratic orientation often resulted in the past, and still does occasionally, in a certain pathological quality in administration. This pathology was (and is) characterized by excessive official aloofness and disinterest, unwillingness to change, reification of administrative procedures to the point of sacrificing governmental goals, excessive delay and buck-passing, petty officiousness and self-importance. It is my belief that this pathology results from the personal insecurity of officials in the authoritarian, monocratic organization.

How is the individual citizen protected in his contacts with such a milieu? In past agrarian cultures, many individuals were protected by primary ties to officialdom, by personal contact with important people. Others could get protection of their individualized interests by means of various kinds of payments to officials who characteristically had managed to appropriate official power to their personal use. These methods have declined in potency as modern norms have rendered them unethical. Now they constitute "graft," "corruption," nepotism, favoritism, all terms of negative connotation. Later, partisan

[13] On this point, see especially Talcott Parsons, *The Social System* (Glencoe, Ill.: The Free Press, 1951), pp. 268-69.

political activity provided personal protection, but this, too, is becoming unethical; it is "spoils," "politics," etc.

A system of administrative law has developed, defining the limits of official powers and appropriate administrative procedures for assuring fair play and interpreted and applied through judicial processes. Although administrative law provides some important protections, it is too slow, cumbersome, and expensive to do much more than scratch the surface. Administrative appeals to higher authority are usually formally available but work poorly. The technical information to reverse a lower decision is often not adequately available, and the interest in doing so is weak because of the dependence of higher officials upon the loyalty and cooperation of the lower. Maintaining the health of the administrative organization as a cooperative system is more important administratively than making one disgruntled citizen happy again.

In the present period, some individual protection is afforded through the individual's interest associations, but such associations are primarily concerned with policies of universal interest to all people similarly situated. Should they go far in pushing the particularistic interest of an individual, not only would they jeopardize their own internal unity, but they would compromise their effectiveness with the bureaucracy in promoting the policy interests of their members.

It seems that the best protection for the individual in the recent past and possibly the present is the personal intervention of legislative representatives, and the constant concern of a free press with newsworthy cases of individual "injustice." The particularistic importunities of legislative representatives still perform a needed function. A completely rationalized, objective, impersonal, universalistic, "efficient" administrative performance will not yet be tolerated by modern publics. We are not so different from "backward" peoples as we like to think. In the United States, it appears that most people prefer a public administration which is not too "efficient," and which they can therefore regard as human and benign.

In a modern dictatorship, the protections derived from organized interests, a free press, and legislative representatives are lacking. In such countries one would expect public administration to be less humane, more dominated by the intellect than the heart. In colonies where modern colonial powers have installed a modern administration governed by the stringent norms of an industrial culture (and strangely out of place in an agrarian society), the individual may have no protection at all. Frequently the perception of individual injustice expands until a kind of amorphous, anomic political action forces some official concern and reform. Fiats lead to riots.[14]

With the decline of the desk-class "bureaucratic" orientation and the growth of a professional one goes a decline in bureaucratic pathology. Furthermore, the awesome ceremonies and rituals of interpersonal relations in an agrarian age have all but vanished. The role of public official is changing to include norms of sympathetic and helpful treatment of clients and a professional interest in their problems. Such an interest, though impersonal, is benign rather than the contrary. Consequently, I believe the administrative treatment of individuals is improving in industrial countries, democratic or otherwise. However, in democracies, the individual has the additional protections outlined above and a much greater number of alternatives to governmental action for meeting his needs.

In this essay I have argued that both industrialism and democracy are important variables determining the quality of public administration, but that industrialism is the more important one. I have implied that public administration is not an abstract product of eternal human reason but the product of cultural evolution. In depicting this evolution I hope that I have not implied a sharp qualitative difference between modern industrial man and feudal agrarian man. Great character changes have obviously occurred, but there is much of feudal man in modern man. The evolutionary changes are matters of degree. There is continuity between the past and the present. Man's culture, and consequently his character, constantly change. We are not approaching the end of any teleology. Man and administration in the future will be as different from those in the present as they are from those in the past. There is enough of the old in our culture so that we should have little difficulty understanding the administrative problems of less industrialized countries.

Perhaps the most pressing problem of public administration in the Western democracies is the formulation of an administrative doctrine, a normative theory, that squares more closely with the administrative facts of an open, pluralistic society. Once this is accomplished, long-deferred administrative reforms will become possible and many apparently insoluble problems will either become soluble or simply disappear. The pace of scientific and technological growth and change may not allow us to defer this matter much longer.

[14] Reports of inquiries into colonial riots will often show this pattern. See, for example, the *Report of the Commission of Inquiry into Disturbances in the Eastern Province, 1960* (Entebbe, Uganda: Government Printer, 1960).

IV. INTERNATIONAL PUBLIC
ADMINISTRATION

•

· 12 ·

Conjectures on Comparative
Public Administration

LYNTON K. CALDWELL

"Probably no practice—certainly none of any importance—can ever be directly copied from one government and
simply applied to another. There is value in comparisons, but
the value is in stimulating some development which had nowhere before existed in precisely the same form or manner."

PAUL H. APPLEBY
Public Administration in India:
Report of a Survey, 1953

This essay is an examination of the current state and probable course
of comparative studies in public administration. Its purpose is to
ascertain, as best one observer may, in what directions the comparative study of public administration is moving. It will do this by giving
special attention to the "movement" called "comparative public administration," which is to be distinguished as a self-conscious and contemporary aspect of the comparative study of public administration.
Such conclusions as it may reach will be conjectural, for the circumstances do not make for precision forecasting. But whatever the future
of comparative public administration as method or as "movement"
may be, it will obviously have arrived there by way of its present
state of affairs. And so, in order to find out where comparative public
administration is going it will be useful to have at least a brief look
at where it has been and where it is now.[1]

[1] Representative of a much longer list of published writings describing the state
of studies in comparative public administration are: Heady, Ferrel, "Comparative
Public Administration Concerns and Priorities," in Ferrel Heady, ed., *Papers in
Comparative Public Administration* (Ann Arbor: University of Michigan, Institute
of Public Administration, 1962); Riggs, Fred W., "Trends in the Comparative
Study of Public Administration," *International Review of Administrative Sciences,*
Vol. XXVIII, No. 1 (1962), pp. 9-15; Shor, Edgar L., "Comparative Administra-
tion: Static Study Versus Dynamic Reform," *Public Administration Review,* Vol.

CONTEXT OF COMPARISON

The older pre-World War II comparative public administration was largely (but of course not exclusively) focussed on Western democratic societies, and relied principally upon paralleling or analytic studies for its data. It had an historical dimension exemplified in Walter R. Sharp's study of the French bureaucracy[2] and in Leonard D. White's *Civil Service Abroad*[3] and *Civil Service in the Modern State*.[4] Indeed the "older" comparative administration blended imperceptibly into administrative history. It was thoroughly consistent for Leonard White, who may be fairly described as a "founder" of comparative public administration, to have made his final and perhaps greatest scholarly contribution in his studies of the administrative history of the United States.

The newer postwar comparative public administration incorporates a greater diversity of methods and subject matter derived from sociology, cultural anthropology, and organization theory. Its field of inquiry has been primarily in the so-called new or "underdeveloped" nations. Overseas service in international assistance programs and availability of foundation money for study of the new nations have pushed scholars toward the comparative study of the process of development. And indeed, "development" affords a focus that Dwight Waldo argues would be useful "to bring into useful association various clusters of ideas and types of activity that are now more or less separate and help clarify some methodological problems."[5] "Development" would become an integrating concept for the comparative study of public administration.

In Waldo's words, "The enterprise of Comparative Public Administration would benefit from a 'lowering of its sights,' a narrowing of its perspective, a closing of the gap between its models and field research."[6] To understand this evaluation we must distinguish between the comparative public administration "enterprise" or "movement" and the comparative study of administration, public or otherwise. The two

XXII (September, 1962), pp. 158-64; Siffin, W. J., "Toward the Comparative Study of Public Administration," in W. J. Siffin, ed., *Toward the Comparative Study of Public Administration* (Bloomington, Indiana: Indiana University Press, 1957); Waldo, Dwight, *Comparative Public Administration: Prologue, Problems and Promise*. Papers in Comparative Public Administration Special Series: No. 2 (American Society for Public Administration, 1964).

[2] *The French Civil Service: Bureaucracy in Transition* (New York: Macmillan, 1931).

[3] New York: McGraw-Hill, 1935.

[4] Chicago: University of Chicago Press, 1930.

[5] *Op. cit.*, p. 27.

[6] *Ibid.*

things are not the same, although the latter includes the former. The "enterprise" includes the group of political scientists and students of public administration who since about 1952 have led the "movement" for comparative public administration in American universities. The formal expression of the movement and its leadership has been the Comparative Administration Group (CAG) of the American Society for Public Administration.

What is this movement? Waldo has described it by indicating its disciplinary orientations and conceptual foci. I propose to add my personal interpretation, derived primarily from first-hand observation of the movement, to his analysis of the literature. This appraisal is based less on analysis of the papers, reports, and models that have resulted from the movement than on a distillation of innumerable meetings, conferences, and conversations in which many of the ideas and efforts that have characterized the movement had their genesis.[7]

Waldo's phrase, "self-conscious movement," suggests group commitment to an objective. As with most group efforts, the goal perceptions of the CAG have changed over a period of time. The change, however, is in emphasis and in degree; the original motives have not consciously been displaced. Comparative public administration in its postwar expression has been a reform movement and has at times been characterized by a kind of missionary zeal. The object of reformation was prewar academic public administration, which, largely circumscribed by American assumptions, was of uncertain relevance to the kinds of administrative problems appearing in the newly emerging nations of the excolonial world. Subsidiary and shorter-term objectives have been defined in the course of the movement. But its ultimate purpose has been to hasten the emergence of a universally valid body of knowledge concerning administrative behavior—in brief, to contribute to a genuine and generic discipline of administration.

Members of the movement might differ regarding the probability of attaining this goal. There has been virtual unanimity regarding the ecological uniqueness of each administrative system and the fallacy of assuming that principles and procedures that have proven effective in one country can be applied unmodified to obtain comparable results

---

[7] First-hand exposure to the actual discussions and debates among participants in the "movement" would reveal a greater diversity of viewpoint and tentativeness of opinion than might be deduced from an examination of the published writings. For example, Edgar L. Shor's *Memorandum of Discussion on Scope and Methods in Comparative Administration–CAG Program Committee Meeting, Chicago, December 27-29, 1962 Annex A-1* (mimeo), captures some of the variety of viewpoint and give-and-take in discussion that has characterized the development of the comparative public administration movement.

in another environment. This has not, however, led to an inference that each system of public administration is unique in all respects, or that no principles of administrative behavior hold true (although perhaps in different ways) throughout all forms of government. But the proposition that there are universal principles of administrative behavior has been too formidable to research head-on and all at once. The contribution of the movement has therefore been more to demonstrate what was patently *not* universal or generically true than to identify general principles.

This latter preoccupation has given the movement the appearance of a commitment to diversity. There has also been, as Waldo has observed, "a conscious attempt not to presume the American or Western 'ways of doing things' are 'better.'"[8] This, however, has been largely a corrective to the seemingly built-in bias with which Americans have often approached administrative organization and behavior abroad. There has been equal resistance to the proposition that British, French, or Russian ways are intrinsically better than any other, but no disposition to conclude *a priori* that whatever is, is best.

Evidence that amidst diverse societies there was no one best way to administer public affairs has been basic data in the reform of the older conventional public administration in the United States. And it was this more cosmopolitan and comprehensive approach characteristic of the new comparative public administration that led Paul Appleby to recommend that the study be pursued in the then-to-be-established Indian Institute of Public Administration. This approach he hoped might avoid the "familiar danger" that the literature of Indian public administration "may too quickly turn to seeking general theory and principles based too exclusively on structures and procedures conventional here."[9]

Concern with the variables of administration has also been a consequence of the ecological analysis that has characterized the movement. Administrative systems differ from one another as they are shaped to the changing needs of particular societies. Discovery of the influence of the diverse societies of the underdeveloped nations upon administrative organization and behavior in their governments was a major stimulant to the emergence of the new comparative administration. And it was the rapidly changing character of these societies that induced a special concern with processes of change and development. Thus the subsidiary interests of the movement in diversity, in variables,

[8] Waldo, *op. cit.*, p. 21.
[9] *Public Administration in India: Report of a Survey* (New Delhi: The President's Press, 1953), p. 62.

in ecology, and in development are consistent with its guiding philosophy and ultimate objective.

The focus upon development, which Dwight Waldo recommended to the movement, is a point of convergence toward which it has in fact been tending. Concern with development as an integrating concept grew naturally out of the preoccupation of the movement with the emerging nations. This natural evolution was greatly reinforced by the decisions of several of the large foundations, notably Rockefeller, Carnegie, and Ford, to make a generous commitment of funds to study the problems of the underdeveloped nations. The coincidence of foundation support and research interest made possible the Ford Foundation grant in 1962 to the American Society for Public Administration on behalf of the Comparative Administration Group. The Ford grant gave operational strength to what had hitherto been only an intellectual movement. The CAG could and did take measures to realize its objectives through summer seminars, study groups, a newsletter, publications, grants to assist research and teaching and a comprehensive review of the needs and opportunities for the study of development administration in the United States.[10]

Interest in comparative studies in public administration as applied to the United States has not been notable. An attempt to publish a comprehensive, paralleling, if not strictly comparative, set of studies of American state government and administration withered through, among other causes, lack of interest. More successful has been a series of studies of efforts toward metropolitan government coordinated by York Willbern.[11] The studies in comparative administration by James D. Thompson and his associates were not in a strict sense in public administration;[12] but they represent the most conspicuous attempt outside the comparative public administrative movement to consciously apply comparative methodology to the study of general administrative behavior.

Comparative studies in public administration have used historical, biographical, and legal data extensively. But paradoxically the tendency to direct comparative studies toward the underdeveloped coun-

---

[10] See the following reports published by the Comparative Administration Group: (1) *Interim Report for December 1962* by Fred W. Riggs, 21 pp., ditto, plus annexes; (2) *Second Annual Report 1963-64*, June, 1964, 14 pp., mimeo; (3) *Development Administration: Report by A Special Committee*, June, 1964, 84 pp., mimeo.

[11] Metropolitan Action Series. (Bloomington: Indiana University Press, 1961————).

[12] *Comparative Studies in Administration* (Pittsburgh: University of Pittsburgh, 1959).

tries may create an impression that the historical perspective has been neglected. In some respects it *has* been neglected, although Braibanti, Eisenstadt, Freeman, Hoselitz, Riggs, and Spengler among others have drawn extensively on historical data in studies that are basically comparative. Researchers in comparative public administration did not, until recently, give major consideration to comparison in historical depth of administrative development in Western Europe or between Western and non-Western industrialized States. A number of studies now under way (for example, those by Robert Holt) will help to rectify this imbalance. And, of course, significant comparative research in the origins of Western administration has occurred, such as the comparative studies in field administration undertaken and directed by James W. Fesler.[13]

Outside of the comparative public administration movement the combination of historical and comparative method has not flourished in the study of public administration. In contrast, among students of American business, historical research, much of it essentially administrative and comparative in context and method, has flourished. Not so in the academic study of public administration. The high tide of behavioralism with a strongly contemporary focus seems to have all but inundated the interest in comparative biographical and historical studies that was showing promise as late as the early 1940's. The congruence of comparative and historical approaches to the study of administration that seemed natural to Leonard D. White and was exemplified in his work has failed to interest a later generation of scholars. The case method approach to public administration remains a possible example of the utilization of historical data and research methods for comparative purposes. But it is by no means certain that the members of what may be called the case method movement would accept a description of their work in these terms.

Some Conceptual Problems

Among the problems of concept and methods inherent in comparative studies three have been selected for attention here. These are, in fact, groups of related problems and other observers might view them in some other way. With particular but not exclusive reference to the comparative public administration movement, these problem

---

[13] E.g., "French Field Administration: The Beginnings," *Comparative Studies in Society and History*, Vol. V (October 1962), pp. 76-111; Robert C. Fried, *The Italian Prefects* (New Haven: Yale University Press, 1963); Herbert Jacob, *German Administration Since Bismarck: Central Authority versus Local Autonomy* (New Haven: Yale University Press, 1963).

groups may be designated as: (1) comparability, (2) commensurability, and (3) relevance.

Comparability continues to be the number one pervasive and perennial problem of comparative studies. The entire rationale for comparison rests on the assumption that there are similarities (and differences) among given bodies of data that can be defined, and regarding which significant generalizations may be made. At the root of the comparative method lies the question of what factors are significant—what factors or aspects of a system or situation are critical to an understanding of its existence or its behavior? One explanation for low interest in the historical or legal aspects of comparative study has been the belief that the yield of empirical data useful to the answer of these questions is likely to be relatively meager. Behavioralism has largely monopolized the approaches to comparative study because its techniques and its concern with functions and relationships has seemed more likely to yield meaningful concepts and data than the older methods of institutional comparisons. As between the dichotomy often postulated between functional and institutional approaches to administrative phenomena, the behavioral emphasis obviously favors the functional.

Acceptance of a behavioral approach to comparative public administration puts one on the road but does not take one very far toward identifying its relevant data. There are many ways of examining behavior and many variables to be dealt with in the process. Although the behavioral approach of the comparative public administration movement is also ecological, it has not as yet led to any notable empirical analysis of ecological influences that would explain (not merely describe) the differences among administrative systems. The most explicit effort to present an ecology of public administration has been made by Fred W. Riggs.[14] Ecology, as Riggs has employed it, has been more a concept or way of looking at administrative behavior than a tool of empirical research. But without the concept or idea, the appropriate tools of research are not likely to be developed. The influence of ecological thinking appears to be making headway, and Riggs is in all probability right in believing that the most significant comparative research in the future will be ecological. Nevertheless the comparative public administration movement has as yet shown little tangible accomplishment in ecologically oriented research.

Two explanations may be given for this state of affairs. First, students of administration have been unable to undertake field studies

[14] *The Ecology of Public Administration* (New Delhi: Asia Publishing House, 1961).

in the depth, breadth, and number required to yield the raw materials of really significant ecological research; hence there has been no convincing demonstration of the value of the ecological approach. Second, the movement, as seen by some observers, has been bemused with model-building and methodology, developing deductive rather than inductive theories of administrative behavior. It would be unfair to imply that the model-builders have sought to substitute armchair thinking for field research. There has been unanimity throughout the comparative public administration movement that more and better field work is needed. But the high cost of field work and the relative scarcity of funds has, in effect, forced scholars to do what they could do within budgetary limitations. Model-building costs little.

Although some observers have believed that the movement has been in danger of diverting itself into exercises in modelsmanship, a case for model-building can be made.[15] One argument for models is that they may help discover the questions that empirical inquiry should ask. In this respect they bear some analogy to machine models, constructed to test ideas developed on the drafting boards. Another argument is that they help to reveal the relationships among data—to organize the knowledge accumulated by many different researchers into coherent form. A third argument rests on their utility in teaching —in helping students conceptualize the complex interrelations that characterize administrative systems.

The foregoing arguments make sense only if the models are somewhere near valid. It may also be argued that premature model-building can lead a researcher into error; that models may be logically consistent, may appear to offer accurate analogies to actual situations, and yet be false representations of what really happens; and that they offer a tempting substitute for the tedious and time-consuming work of empirical research.

Whatever balance one strikes for or against model-building, the models do demonstrate the great difficulty of conceptualizing the administrative process in a crosscultural context. What do the models represent? For the most part they are intended to describe processes rather than organizations, psychosocial conditions rather than func-

[15] E.g., Alfred Diamant, "The Relevance of Comparative Politics to the Study of Comparative Administration," *Administration Science Quarterly*, Vol. V (June 1960), pp. 87-112; Fred W. Riggs and Edward W. Weidner, *Models and Priorities in the Comparative Study of Public Administration*. Papers in Comparative Public Administration Special Series: No. 1 (American Society for Public Administration, 1963). Note also Glenn D. Paige, *Proposition Building in the Study of Comparative Administration*. Papers in Comparative Public Administration No. 4 (American Society for Public Administration, 1964).

tioning institutional structures. The models developed by Fred Riggs are most accurately understood as abstract descriptions of social change and of the matrix of social relationships in type situations that strongly influence the character of government and public administration.

Commensurability is of course one of the problems of comparison and one that frustrates the construction of models and typologies. How can the trends, values, and relationships inherent in every administrative system be quantified? If they cannot be quantified, can they be compared? How much and what kind of quantification is necessary for comparative measurement? What mathematical concepts or methods have greatest relevance to the comparison of dynamic social systems? Have mathematicians potential contributions to make to comparative public administration?

In part the deficiency in empirical comparative research into systems of public administration may be attributed to the formidable task of manipulating the enormously complex, voluminous, and scattered data. Computer technology may resolve this difficulty, if the data can be defined and reduced to terms amenable to meaningful comparison. It is hardly to be expected that the way to do this will be discovered all at once. As with most other research technologies, many trials and some errors will be necessary to obtain satisfactory results. An analysis of experience with the Human Relations Area Files might prove instructive in indicating how the raw materials for the comparative study of public administration should (or should not) be collected and classified. Computers cannot begin to yield meaningful results until their work has been conceptualized and the validity and utility of the data inputs have been established.

This leads us to the third problem area in conceptualizing the comparative study of public administration—the ultimate problem of relevance. It matters little if precise correlations may be obtained among classes of data if the results add nothing to understanding. But the problem of relevance is also a problem of purpose. What is it that one wishes to know about administrative organizations and administrative behavior? The question of relevance has no meaning in the abstract; it must be joined to a goal or purpose that at least in theory will enable one to determine what relates to it and what doesn't. Here is an area in which unvoiced purposes and unsensed assumptions lie like hidden shoals beneath the surface of research designs. Cross-cultural studies are particularly vulnerable to built-in biases. An obvious reason is that superficial similarities lend themselves to misinterpretation by researchers consciously or subconsciously trying to prove a thesis. Rigorous and comprehensive searching and testing of relevance are necessary to prevent inadvertent loading or omitting of significant data.

The comparative public administration movement shows some subjective tendencies that could prejudice the conclusions of its researchers. Particularly in dealing with the idea of development there is a liberal, optimistic tenor in the literature with which "right-thinking" people will surely sympathize but which rigorous-minded skeptics may term "wishful thinking." One sometimes feels that, despite disclaimers to the contrary, an idealized, liberal, more thoroughly socialized American society is the model from which the comparative public administration movement derives its norms. "Development" as the term is commonly used in the contemporary literature of political-economy is heavily value-laden. If the efforts of the movement are to assist the process of development, the relationship between research and promotion becomes less certain. Could it be that the movement that began as an effort to remedy one species of provincialism (traditional public administration) might end by confirming another equally culture-bound concept (conventional development theory)?

Overcommitment to particular research approaches or techniques is a notorious cause of mischief in research efforts. Overemphasis in some respect implies underemphasis in others. The heavily political science-sociology orientation of research in comparative public administration and the commitment to behavioralism has left some large areas of inquiry relatively unexplored. Two of these research areas— the historical and the geographical (particularly in its biophysical aspects)—deserve some comment. In addition, there has been less integration of economic development and comparative public administration thinking than the vigorous research efforts in the respective fields might lead one to expect. However, some of the language and concepts of the development economists (W. W. Rostow, for example) has been taken over by comparative administration researchers; and collaborative efforts among students of economic and political development appear to be increasing.[16]

The relative neglect of historical studies and historical methods may deprive comparative public administration of some of the most

---

[16] For example, Ralph Braibanti and Joseph J. Spengler, eds., *Tradition, Values, and Socio-economic Development* (Durham: Duke University Press, 1961); Albert O. Hirschman, *Journeys Toward Progress: Studies of Economic Policy-Making in Latin America* (New York: Twentieth Century Fund, 1963); and Bertram M. Gross, ed., *Action Under Development Plans: A Report on the 1964 Minnowbrook Seminar*, CAG Occasional Papers (American Society for Public Administration, 1964).

revealing and meaningful data that behavioral studies are designed to seek. Access to critical documents and to the opinions and recollection of participants in important public events can often be had only after the passage of time. The predominant contemporary-to-future orientation of the comparative public administration movement may work against the fullest exploitation of available research data and may possibly result in the loss of valuable insights and perspectives. This neglect of the historical dimension is a relative matter, however, as historical depth has characterized the writings of Riggs and Fesler and a number of the CAG summer institute papers.

Although committed in principle to an ecological approach to comparative studies, surprisingly little interest in the biophysical aspects of administration or development has been evidenced in the comparative public administration movement. This may be merely another illustration of the generally recognized problem of communication among the sciences. But it may also be that the members of the movement understand ecology largely in sociological terms; that they have no great interest in, for example, the reciprocal influences between development and the biophysical environment. Here is an instance of where regard for disciplinary boundaries may stultify the growth of concepts and of research.

Nevertheless the comparative public administration movement has been conspicuously free from deliberate exclusiveness, intolerance, or snobbery in relation to the broad range of comparative methods by which public administration can be studied. Allocation of funds by the Comparative Administration Group has necessarily been influenced by the terms, implicit as well as explicit, in the Ford Foundation grant. Thus, although the CAG has inclined toward a liberal rather than restrictive interpretation of the purposes of the grant, there are unquestionably areas of comparative research in which many of its members might have interest and sympathy but which could not or would not receive financial support from the Group. Development is the password, and development of the administrative institutions of the newly emerging nations is the focus.

To the extent therefore that the comparative public administration movement is identical with the CAG and that the concerns of CAG are determined largely by the terms of the Ford grant, the scope of comparative public administration is likely to be narrowed to the development process, as Dwight Waldo suggested it should. To the extent that comparative public administration becomes understood to be the crosscultural and international study of development, some problems of concept and method are solved by arbitrary elimination.

Nevertheless the more difficult problems of method remain. And in any event the comparative study of administration will continue to include the areas remaining outside the purview of the movement. What then appears to be the outlook for comparative public administration in the period ahead?

A CONJECTURAL FORECAST

The movement called Comparative Public Administration faces now or will soon face a dilemma. If it concentrates its focus on development administration to the exclusion of all else, its purview will in fact cease to be comparative public administration. It will have transformed itself into a development administration effort in which the use of comparative methods would be secondary to a substantive objective—to understand the development process. The comparative method would thereafter have neither more nor less relevance than it would have for the study of any process or behavior that was found in a crosscultural or international context. If the name "comparative public administration" were still attached to this effort it would, like the smile of the Cheshire cat in Alice-in-Wonderland, remain after the substance of the thing itself had faded away.

On the other hand if the movement affirmatively broadens its scope to include all possible comparative studies of administration, it might well lose the momentum that it has acquired since the Ford grant made possible the program sponsored by the CAG. But if no gestures are made toward a more inclusive definition of its interests, it may confirm the opinion now held by some critics that it is a highly specialized, almost esoteric effort with little practical value for the person who wants to know how administrative institutions really work.[17] The CAG, particularly through its summer institutes, has steered a course between these extremes and has been hospitable to a wide range of application of comparative methodology including the historical. Thus, the present response to the dilemma is to hold a near-middle position, edging, however, toward the development side.

Whether the movement can or will continue to follow this modified middle course can only be conjectured. Much depends upon the attitude of its financial benefactors. In the game of grantsmanship the grantors call the turns. If the Ford or other foundations that may assist the movement insist on a narrowly construed development focus they

---

[17] But the practical implications of research in comparative and development administration are set forth by Fred W. Riggs in "Relearning an Old Lesson: The Political Context of Development Administration," *Public Administration Review*, Vol. XXV, No. 1 (March 1965), pp. 70-79.

may destroy the effectiveness of the effort they purpose to aid. At present the CAG, as the institutional expression of the movement, can justify an emphasis on the development process. The needs of the times and the availability of research opportunities and of supporting funds add confirmation to the logic of this emphasis. But if the emphasis is to avoid a progressive narrowing that would diminish the influence and vitality of the movement it should be adopted by the CAG in a manner calculated to clarify its relationship to the broader aims of comparative study—that is, if those earlier aims are indeed still the objectives of the movement.

It is of course easily possible that the comparative public administration movement may evolve altogether and completely into a study of development. Its ultimate destiny therefore might be quite different from its original purpose. But it may be argued that the shift of goals is justifiable, in addition to the reasons detailed above, because the initial objective has been substantially achieved. Conventional public administration in the American academic context has been reformed or at least greatly broadened in outlook. The culture-bound assumptions of much of the pre-World War II public administration have been displaced by a less assured but more sophisticated attitude toward the study of administrative behavior. For this change the comparative administration movement deserves credit. How much cannot easily be determined, but such adjectives as "considerable" or "substantial" are surely justifiable.

There have, however, been other influences at work upon the old-fashioned public administration. Not the least of these has been systems theory, which has in the writer's judgment changed the orientation of administrative studies more profoundly than have the theories growing out of comparative methodology. These two influences are not mutually exclusive. The open-systems approach has influenced studies in comparative administration particularly in conceptualizing environmental influences and the interactions among social and political groupings in developing countries. However, by providing a common vehicle for the study of organizational behavior in a great variety of contexts, systems theory threatens the very basis for the study of public administration (or business administration) as it has been conceived for the past half-century in American universities.

Although there is an aspect of the study of public administration that will probably always remain inseparable from the study of government or political science, the logic of systems theory is to place the study of administrative behavior in a much broader context. The study of organization science and of administration as a generic social process may in the coming decade absorb much of the intellectual effort hitherto expended in the study of administration within the special contexts of business, government, education, social work, or public health. In short, we may find that these special areas of administrative study become more and more professionalized applications or subdivisions of the larger generic disciplines of organization and administrative science.

But there is also the possibility, indeed the probability, of new research concepts and foci emerging to change the character or direction of contemporary trends. Our understanding of organizational and administrative behavior will always depend in some respects upon our understanding of human beings. To this understanding physiologists, psychologists, psychiatrists, and many others will continue to bring new insights and new findings. Some significant work already being done on the psychological and personality aspects of development has been surveyed in a paper prepared by Alfred Diamant for the 1963 CAG summer seminar at Indiana University.[18] The factors that govern personality development, motivation, and interaction among individuals are still only dimly perceived and yet administration in essence is simply an organized and directed process of interpersonal interaction. The importance of man's inner qualities to his outward organized conduct was surely in Paul Appleby's mind when at the conclusion of his first Indian report he wrote:

> The difference between one organization and another organization can never be appraised exclusively in analytical terms, or in terms of organizational and administrative theory, no matter how perceptive these analyses are. Great significance must be attached to the spirit of those who are members of these organizations.[19]

Unless revitalized by new insights or concepts comparative public administration, like an old soldier, may be in danger of fading away: first, because it may, in becoming developmental, cease to be primarily comparative or public; and second, because its public emphasis may be rendered irrelevant not only by the development approach (which necessarily embraces all the organized effort in a country), but even more by a systems-inspired generic theory of administration that does not accept the simple public-private dichotomy as a valid approach to the realities of organizational behavior.

---

[18] *Political Development: Approaches to Theory and Strategy*, CAG Occasional Papers (American Society for Public Administration, 1964), pp. 45-55.
[19] Appleby, *op. cit.*, p. 66.

I certainly do not predict the disappearance of the comparative public administration movement in the decade ahead. To do so when the movement is enjoying unquestionable achievement and success would seem rash perversity. And yet continuation of the trends prevailing within and relating to the comparative movement seem almost certain to bring about its ultimate transformation or disappearance. Would the movement then have failed, having reached the apogee of success? Would the efforts of those who guided or supported its efforts have been misguided or misplaced? I think not.

If the comparative public administration movement fully accomplishes its purpose it will have contributed elements of content and viewpoint to the generic study of administration. It will in fact have blended itself into the main current of administrative study and a separate identity as a self-conscious movement will no longer be necessary. The generation of scholars who have constituted the movement will have made their point. The newcomers, accepting the cross-cultural cosmopolitanism of Riggs, Heady, Weidner, Diamant, and many others as given, will surely move ahead to explore administrative behavior from other viewpoints and in other ways.

But the comparative study of administration, as distinguished from comparative public administration, will no doubt remain a useful method of learning and teaching about organizational and administrative behavior. It is possible that computer technology may greatly increase the number, complexity, and significance of comparative studies in the years ahead. Ultimate transformation of the movement would not signify disappearance of its methodological contributions. Rather the reverse. The success of the movement that would permit its dissolution would leave a rich legacy of verified methods of research, of conceptualizations of the common elements of organizational behavior, and of accumulated field data that could be drawn upon by students of development and of administration for many years to follow.

In the aggregate these conjectures seem both realistic and optimistic: realistic regarding the possible future course of the comparative public administration movement, optimistic concerning its outcome. As an intellectual movement comparative public administration will have paid off. It has already done so in part, and, if present financial support can be maintained, will continue to do so in the future. Field research to test its theories and enlarge its fund of relevant data is its greatest need. The foci of comparative studies in administration will in all likelihood be those of research into administrative behavior generally. Among the many aspects of administration on which attention will be centered, two seem almost certain to command major attention and to influence the character of comparative studies. They are the systematic complex within which administrative organizations function—their outer environment—and the aspects of motivation and personality in interaction that shape the inner lives of organizations, the orderly activation of which is the process of administration.

The ultimate test of the value of comparative studies of administration in and beyond the comparative public administration movement will be their effect upon administrative practice. Inherently a practical affair, administration is one of the uniquely human arts and processes that is amenable to improvement. The ultimate value of comparative public administration will therefore be "in stimulating some development which had nowhere before existed in precisely the same form or manner."

· 13 ·

Public Administration and Nation-Building

DONALD C. STONE

The worldwide commitment of new nations and low-income countries to achieve, virtually overnight, higher levels of economic and social development has given a new dimension to traditional concepts of public administration. The conferees at San Francisco did not foresee that more than forty new States would join the United Nations within twenty years of its founding. Nor was the public administration profession equipped to define the problems, elaborate the strategy, and concert the many talents required in nation-building.

The formulation and implementation of strategies and programs for the modernization of a nation without doubt present the greatest single challenge to public administration. But because public administration theorists and practitioners in the past were preoccupied with administrative services, juridical processes, and behavioral phenomena, the field of nation-building was left largely to others, principally to economists. The latter have approached the task of development as though it were primarily a matter of economics, rather than a blend of elements and processes—political, social, cultural, economic, and administrative. Development strategies and programs involving multidisciplinary elements obviously cannot succeed if they are restricted to the concepts and tools of a single discipline.

As long as development efforts were in initial stages, the inadequacies of economic planning as commonly practiced were not discerned. But time moved on, and the lack of results began to track down the politician who alone had to carry the burden of failure. All too slowly it is being realized that plans, programs, and projects are not self-implementing, that implementation requires administration.

Preoccupied with administrative procedures and behavioral phenomena, the public administration profession as a whole has not been in the vanguard of modern man's exciting efforts to improve conditions of life. These efforts have provided a vast amount of data for empirical analysis and many lessons and guidelines for a new breed of nation-builders. But, while many sideshows were packed with professionals watching their favorite medicine men perform, the main show for public administration—nation-building—was not rehearsed and drew no audience.

Paul Appleby was one of the few who foresaw the central role of the public administrator in nation-building. His concern for oppressed people, for social justice, and for economic welfare, together with his keen appreciation of political and social interaction, made him especially sensitive to the needs of men and developing nations. Fortunately, many persons grappling with the problems of low-income nations are now developing the same sensitivity. Moreover, foundation grants and technical assistance assignments are enabling scholars to engage in empirical research leading to the publication of a valuable body of literature.[1]

Administration's Adaptable Role

Public administration is the process by which objectives are defined, plans and policies formulated, institutions created and managed, human energies mobilized, resources utilized, and changes effected. It is linked with and sustains political action, and it utilizes whatever knowledge and skills may be required for a particular objective. Historically the subject was viewed in much narrower or more specialized terms. Some writers endeavored to draw a sharp line between politics and administration, insisting that administration is not concerned with policy and that policy should be left to politicians to formulate in legislative bodies. Most theoreticians have not treated administration as a developmental or operationally oriented field. Evolving in most universities as a fragment of political science, public administration teaching and research has occupied itself with governmental structures, administrative procedures, and, more recently, with decision-making and human behavior. Personnel, budgeting, accounting, purchasing, planning, and managerial processes have been its distinctive elements. Yet, if any field requires a multidisciplinary and multiprofessional approach, it is surely public administration.

Over the years, administrators in most countries have engaged in social and economic reform or in trying to prevent it, or in waging war or in trying to prevent it. They have not limited their concerns to instrumental tools. Of necessity, they have been concerned with strat-

[1] Saul M. Katz and Frank McGowan, A Selected List of U.S. Readings on Development, Prepared for the United Nations Conference on the Application of Science and Technology for the Benefit of the Less Developed Areas, Agency for International Development (Washington, D.C., 1963).

egy, policy, programs, and the substance of what has to be accomplished. Even though they may not have viewed themselves as administrators in the scholarly or professional sense, they have had to either master administrative fundamentals or watch their efforts collapse.

Systematic study of public administration started auspiciously in the early part of the twentieth century with a focus on the performance of municipal services and as a search for better ways of operation. Attention spread to state and national levels. Soon, however, sponsors of governmental research and education infected the function of administration with the assumption that efficiency, rather than the provision of essential conditions, facilities, and services, was administration's purpose. The popular doctrine was, "the less government, the better."

During the 1930's, dynamic political and administrative action to accomplish rapid social and economic modernization in the United States foreshadowed the nature of the processes which, thirty years later, would be found indispensable to nation-building. The programs of those years were the products of social reformers. They reflected an "operational" approach to societal change, an approach which embodied political, social, legal, and administrative, as well as economic, elements.

As in contemporary nation-building, the development programs of the 1930's required fundamental structural, institutional, and behavioral changes in major aspects of society. They entailed the formulation and execution of policies, plans, programs, and projects on a dimension capable of producing sweeping economic and social results. This is the process, essential at any time and in any place, through which the polity of a country, responding to human aspirations and values, takes action to achieve modernization goals.

Having served as a consultant in establishing nearly all the new agencies in the 1930's, I can testify to the sustained efforts which went into the formulation of policies and programs, the design of organization, and the multitudinous steps required to execute operations. The concept that, at the highest levels, the politician and the administrator must be combined into the same person, the political executive, was both widely accepted and well demonstrated. In this period of social stress and change, the crucial importance of administration as the vehicle for implementing plans, programs, and projects could be clearly discerned. But the lessons were largely overlooked by a growing public administration profession preoccupied by gadgetry and routine.

One of the bold persons who saw public administration in its broader perspective was Paul Appleby. He asserted that public administration is an instrument of policy formulation and actively related to societal achievement.

> Public administration is policy-making. But it is not autonomous, exclusive or isolated policy-making. It is policy-making on a field where mighty forces contend, forces engendered in and by the society. It is policy-making subject to still other and various policy-makers. Public administration is one of a number of basic political processes by which this people achieves and controls governance.[2]

He placed stress on words of action. To him, public administration was policy-*making*, decision-*taking*, *administering*.

> The carrying on of government (*development*) involves action. No matter how many studies may be required, government in the final analysis is action—organized action. Persons in high position must have a sense of action. They must have a feeling of the need for decisions to get things done.[3]

During World War II, the United States and other countries found it necessary to mobilize national resources for an all-embracing purpose. Entire economies required major adjustment. For the first time, the importance of creating administrative capabilities sufficient to formulate and discharge comprehensive plans, programs, and projects to achieve major societal and economic goals was appreciated. Wide consensus on objectives, policy formulation, program planning and scheduling, operational administration, and control with democratically applied sanctions became the order of the day. Here was administered government and economic action on a new scale. Especially noteworthy is the fact that war mobilization was carried through with a minimum impairment of citizen freedoms.

While too close to the administration of the war to be objective, I am convinced, in retrospect, that a major factor in the extraordinary speed with which the United States created massive military capabilities and all of the supportive productive, economic, social, educational, health, and informational elements was due to its having effective planning and administrative management organs staffed with

---

[2] Paul H. Appleby, *Policy and Administration* (University, Alabama: University of Alabama Press, 1949), p. 170.

[3] As quoted by Robert S. Herman, "Paul H. Appleby: An Impressive Legacy," Reprinted from the *Indian Journal of Public Administration*, Vol. X, No. 1 (January-March 1964), p. 6.

multidisciplinary personnel both in the Executive Office of the President and in the war agencies. Paul Appleby was deeply involved in these tasks of war administration, and subscribed to this view. The general historical account of this effort, written in the Bureau of the Budget's Historical Reports on War Administration,[4] as well as in the administrative histories of military and civilian war agencies, could be read with profit by today's nation-builders.

We now have had over fifteen years of sustained technical and economic assistance for nation-building and modernization purposes. While modest efforts reach back to the late 1930's, the first major postwar illustrations of nation-building were the programs to reorient and reconstruct the societies of Germany and Japan. In retrospect, these might have been far more effective if multidisciplinary administrative competences for such tasks had been more systematically nurtured.

Several aspects of the Marshall Plan—without doubt the nation's most successful international assistance program—contributed significantly to our knowledge of development administration.[5] This program and early development efforts in Korea, China, and Southeast Asia demonstrated:

(1) The importance of attitudes and morale; the dependence on hope, determination, and readiness to sacrifice when goals are compelling; the sense of unity and purpose gained from joint commitments; the need for wide citizen participation in any program of social and economic change.

(2) The role of political leadership in delineating and dramatizing objectives and major policy, in committing resources, in reconciling conflicting interests and values, in leading and sustaining the administrative apparatus to implement the entire operation.

(3) The value of comprehensive planning in which economic, social, physical, administrative, and other elements are meshed. (The Economic Cooperation Administration initiated the concept of the "country program," and demonstrated the methodology of preparing such programs in Europe and especially in Southeast Asia. These were important contributions to nation-building.)

(4) The essentiality of creating administrative capabilities as part of the social capital required to formulate and execute strategies, plans, programs, and projects.

[4] Bureau of the Budget, War Records Section, *Development and Administration of the War Program by the Federal Government* (Washington: U.S. Government Printing Office, 1946).

[5] Harry Bayard Price, *The Marshall Plan and Its Meaning* (Ithaca, New York: Cornell University Press, 1955). Published under the auspices of the Governmental Affairs Institute, Washington, D. C.

(5) The contribution of technical cooperation by the assignment of external experts to a country and by organizing field visits, training programs, and conferences in the United States and third countries.

(6) The special need for technical exchange and assistance in creating capabilities in planning, organizing, and executing development programs and projects; the fact that such assistance, if properly conducted, is not an affront to sovereignty or sensibilities.

(7) The dynamics of achieving higher standards of living through a three-way sharing of the benefits of higher productivity among workers, consumers, and owners of enterprise.

(8) The indispensability of a United States international cooperation or development agency having in its top posts development generalists who are also capable political executives able to concert the talents of specialists into a team operation without any one group gaining dominance.

Recent U.S. approaches to development administration have benefited greatly from this accumulated experience, including that of the "Point Four" program which reflected a different and much narrower approach and omitted many essentials of nation-building. The necessity of using a mixture of tools to facilitate development in a country (loans, grants, surplus commodities, technical information, advisory services, and training) has been fully demonstrated. Development now is recognized as a comprehensive social, economic, political, and administrative process which demands not only sound economic and fiscal measures, but also programs and projects capable of bringing about change. Macro and micro elements are being integrated. Programs and projects increasingly are related to an overall development strategy and to the achievement of balance among such sectors as agriculture, industry, public works, education, and public health. Through improved analytical methods, projects can be planned and balanced to derive optimal use from available resources.

Despite all the lush laboratories of experience from which the public administration profession can draw in creating the educational and research underpinning for nation-building, few persons have elaborated on either the potential or the methodology. Little has been done to translate the achievements of the depression, war, and postwar years into a body of useful knowledge applicable to nation-building tasks. In the United States and in countries developed with American help, most public administration curricula seem remarkably oblivious to this body of experience or to the substance of development itself.

Thus, when United States assistance in the 1950's began to focus upon the newly independent and emerging nations, there was little reserve manpower, technology, or institutional capability on which to draw. The most experienced personnel were within the United States aid agency, or had left the field. Since the dominant economic processes of the Marshall Plan were not applicable to the new countries, even this important resource proved less than adequate. The United Nations had approached the problem largely in a fragmented way, and its agencies dealt only with specialized sectors.

PRECONDITIONS AND CAPABILITIES FOR NATION-BUILDING

It is a common assumption in independence and revolutionary movements that conditions of life will improve once external rulers or internal despots are "eliminated." Yet most political reformers and liberators inevitably are so preoccupied with criticizing or overthrowing the former régime and with winning public support for their cause that they seldom have opportunity to gain the experience or insight essential to implement their commitments. Once the new government obtains power, its initial effort is directed toward maintaining order and subduing dissident factions. Merely keeping the traditional wheels of government turning, primitive though they may be, becomes in itself a staggering task.

The newly won privilege of maintaining law and order constricts the availability of indigenous resources for development. Foreign exchange and tax revenues usually dwindle. Too often the trappings of a modern society are espoused prematurely, excessively sapping available resources. Airlines, monumental buildings, and stadia, and even mass educational facilities, medical schools, and hospitals may be greater economic liabilities than their contribution to social welfare or a sense of national achievement warrants.

To identify urgent undertakings which merit support, the preparation of comprehensive development plans has been encouraged by multilateral and bilateral aid organizations. As a result, planning offices, and five-, six-, and ten-year plans have become almost universal. Some of these plans are little more than lists of projects which interest different factions of the country. Others are essentially economic projections of development levels to be achieved. The assumption has been that development is primarily a matter of economics, and that economists therefore are the ones to formulate plans. Most strategies for development overlook the human values, political realities, social factors, and cultural determinants so crucial to societal change and modernization. Plans are expressed in macro terms, with micro elements missing or only vaguely defined. They fail to incorporate the administrative instruments for policy and program implementation, including discrete projects, essential to achievement. The result too often has been frustration and disappointment over slow development progress.

To embark on programs of rapid social and economic development, there must be a certain extant degree of modernization and institutionalization of the society. This means at least elementary levels of agricultural production, trade, education, and public services. The social and political system and processes of government must be of a character which will support change from traditional patterns of thinking and action, or which can be adapted to this purpose. Nation-building depends above all on a predisposition to change—change from the traditional to new forms of thinking, behavior, association, and action.

A good measure of political and social stability is vital to any orderly change. Political and administrative leaders must have some freedom from daily crises to focus upon those new tasks and processes which produce development. For the new nation, this creates a special problem. The very maintenance of law and order may be difficult once colonial rule is removed and diverse elements begin to struggle for power. Thus the ability to keep the country stable, internally peaceful, and free from external aggression becomes a basic precondition to development.

Along with stability, there must be an awareness of needs or aspirations which are "national," at least to the extent that they are shared by some of the influential elites. These aspirations need to be translated into objectives and goals with political potency. The necessity for political leadership is crucial at every stage and in every ramification of the development process.

Most development strategies entail, to a greater or lesser extent, restricting consumption, postponing improved living conditions, remunerating labor, industrializing, and urbanizing without adequate social overhead. Unless a strategy blends social and political realities and builds on shared values and preferences, it cannot succeed.

A country also must have some administrative capabilities to plan and implement the interacting measures, programs, and projects essential to development, and to create conditions favorable to entrepreneurial investment and corporate productivity. Government structures and procedures evolved for a "law and order" role are inadequate for the dynamics of nation-building. Sufficient political and administrative competence must be achieved to ensure that development goals will be pursued. Countries can make little progress until they create the administrative instruments and acquire the trained personnel to plan, organize, and implement.

The need for more than elementary capabilities to engage in a sustained nation-building operation is illustrated by an inventory of important elements and sectors. The table of contents of any comprehensive plan gives a clue to the complexity of issues and subject matter. The Five-Year Plan of Tanganyika,[6] for example, covers in Volume I: (1) General Development Policy, (2) Productive and Distributive Activities, (3) Economic Infrastructure, (4) Social Infrastructure, (5) General Administration, (6) Manpower, (7) Finance, and (8) Administrative Machinery. Volume II has 13 chapters covering sector programs: agriculture, land settlement, water, commerce, industry, mineral resources, power, tourism, communications and works, local government, housing, community development, labor, education, health, and justice.

In dealing in even an elementary way with these substantive elements, a great amount of factual data obviously is necessary. But most countries do not have a statistical system to produce adequate or reliable data covering these subjects. For example, knowledge of resources—both physical and human—is an elementary need for the development planner and administrator. This calls for an inventory and forecast of manpower resources postulated against the skilled personnel required to implement each sector of a country's plan. In most low-income countries, the information to make such analyses and to formulate programs of action is lacking or difficult to assemble.

The problem a country faces in formulating a national approach to sector development is further illustrated by the forces of tradition which characterize the less (as well as the more) developed countries. Educators, including specialists supplied by technical assistance agencies, naturally are concerned with how to accelerate the number of persons enrolled in the educational system. Education is a good thing. Political leaders promise elementary schooling for the masses, and the people want it. A mighty force urges the allocation of funds to large-scale programs for teacher training and for school construction to accommodate sharply rising enrollments. But the magnitude of financial resources required for such an educational advance drains off funds essential for the development of basic industries, irrigation, electric power, and railroads. While mass education contributes to social and economic capital, there may be many more critical development needs.

One of these is the strategic necessity to accord high priority to

[6] The United Republic of Tanganyika and Zanzibar, *Tanganyika Five-Year Plan for Economic and Social Development, 1st July, 1964—30th June, 1969* (Dar Es Salaam, 1964).

the vocational, technical, and professional education essential to development operations. Unless a country has the capability to produce data which show the availability and needs of skilled personnel, unless it incorporates into its development program those measures for the education sector which will produce skilled personnel, development projects in all sectors will stagnate. Here is a precondition which can be accomplished only by internal perseverance with prudent utilization of external assistance.

Another difficulty in creating a viable growth economy is the limited size and poor competitive position of many of the less developed nations. How can a country with a population of one or five million create the administrative and social infrastructure and productive resources to cope with its primary needs? Its national tax yield must be devoted first to the cost of governance and elementary public services, and there will be little or no excess for development. The cost of participation in international organizations and conferences incumbent on a modern state—an insignificant item in the budget of the United States—becomes a heavy burden to a Mali or an Afghanistan. Furthermore, interdependence requires regional cooperation in world economic relations. Apart from simple cost, all this entails high political and administrative sophistication—two very scarce commodities.

POLITICAL PREREQUISITES OF NATION-BUILDING

Although the tasks of political leadership vary greatly according to circumstances, there are important common requisites. Rapid societal modernization affects the lives, behavior, and interests of all elements of a society. Elites, fearful of losing their special status, resist change, while peasants and workers, subject to depressed economic and social conditions, do not understand how to work for change. The burden of leadership, then, falls on those concerned persons among the intelligentsia, limited middle class, and dissident groups who have enough knowledge and political skill to elicit support from a significant segment of the population. If this leadership fails to emerge, the communist, fascist, or military extremes may become the only apparent alternatives.

Above all, there is the need to unify the centrifugal forces of differing class interests, race, tribe, religion, and ideology. The political leader's job is to dramatize goals, programs, projects, and incentives in a combination that enlists support sufficient to sustain development while law and order are maintained without excessive repression.

Appeals to nationalism and national achievement are a means of fostering unity for development. The politician demands that his nation be respected, that it share in world resources and opportunities, and that it meet the challenge of superior achievement with competitive countries. Communist countries often find it convenient to subvert Marxist-Leninist doctrine to the rallying force of aggressive nationalism. These methods easily lead to the age-old stratagem of fostering fears by fabricating or magnifying external dangers, evoking so-called threats to national progress from internal or external "enemies." Countries with high living standards provide leaders of new nations with more than enough precedents for rationalizing such behavior.

Although the politician is the pivotal figure in a country's development, countries most in need of economic and social advancement generally have the least developed political processes. Societies emerging from colonial status have had little opportunity to acquire political sinew and self-reliance. Their immediate problem is to create a sufficiently strong political foundation for government survival. They must meet elementary standards of public service. To achieve these necessities, and at the same time show aggressiveness in fulfilling aroused expectations, the new leadership strives for alluring, and often unattainable, goals. Efforts to precipitate this leap from a traditional to a modern industrialized nation may create more stress than the country can absorb without incurring disastrous internal conflict. Dissident forces, with a view to seizing power, often foster chaos to discredit whatever stabilizing leadership may exist.

The preparation of a viable national development plan is a chastening experience for heady politicians. It also provides them opportunities to win public support. In new countries especially, politicians gain and consolidate power through popular anticipation that reforms will be achieved and conditions improved. People desire and take pride in achieving a better life, schools, roads, markets, hospitals, and other benefits of modern society.

Combining goals and projects which have high popular appeal, even if of questionable economic value, with goals and projects which effectively utilize resources for purposes that genuinely contribute to development constitutes sound strategy on the part of an aspiring politician in any nation. Hard work and sacrifice are essential, but people will respond if they sense sincerity in their leaders and feel they have a real part in the endeavor.

An aim of the political process, therefore, is to achieve and sustain an adequate degree of public support for the nation-building goals. This is not as difficult in a monolithic political system as it is in an environment of freedom where two or more political parties or factions may espouse different goals and approaches. But even totalitarian régimes have their share of problems in inducing unified support for programs. To achieve support, capable politicians dramatize development goals and aspirations, the steps to fulfill them, and the national and individual advantages of doing so. This requires the formulation of an ideological or philosophical rationale for development which will appeal to diverse elements within the population.

Political education will help achieve these goals. Creation of a general understanding of the processes of self-government and of the role of local communities is an important ingredient in nation-building. Even though the establishment of a formal school system is a slow process, students at least can be provided textbooks which feature their own country's constitutional history and government. Among the tools for political education are literacy primers, rural and community development programs, health and sanitation training, agricultural extension services and cooperatives. Special institutes in citizenship, social action, and political education can be designed for various groups.

A number of international organizations are contributing to this process, but the range of available instruments to achieve political education in its broader aspects still is limited. Since it is possible to provide technical assistance in public administration without threatening a country's sovereignty, it also would seem feasible to advise on the initiation of political education programs. This sort of assistance may carry special labels, and usually will be most effective if incorporated into readily acceptable programs. More frontal approaches may be left to international agencies, private foundations, or universities.

Political action in the formulation and implementation of development undertakings involves the full cycle of political-legislative-administrative-citizen participation activity. This in itself is a potent exercise in political education. In addition to creating a climate for effective planning and administration of development operations, political leadership also must sustain such action. This calls for effective interplay and a close relationship between the political process and the agencies of development administration. One objective in this interplay is a realistic relationship between the legislative and administrative branches of the government. Unless the functions of each and the manner in which they work together are clearly identified and regularly policed by either legal action or citizen criticism, the tendency will be for political and legislative leaders to encroach upon and disrupt the administrative process, and for administrative officials to usurp legislative functions. Insufficient attention is accorded to the meaningful articulation of the political and administrative processes and to securing a commitment to them. This commitment should be so publicized and sustained that people come to understand and respect the processes and the relationships implicit in them. They must become an esteemed and practical part of prevailing political values.

The difficulty of accomplishing this is compounded by misguided efforts to transplant systems from societies with radically different conditions. It seems easier to copy than to invent. Moreover, the human tendency is to assume that what one person knows, no matter how restricted his own experience, is what others need. Acting upon this impulse, colonial officers carried the patterns of government and administration from their home countries to distant lands. Today, many technical assistance "experts" (which may mean only that a person has detailed knowledge of how matters are handled at home) engage in the same process. Here is a lush pasture for relevant research and education to make a comparative evaluation of previous experience. Penetrating assessment of the innovations and adaptations most likely to succeed under conditions prevailing in countries undergoing rapid social change would be of great value to nation-builders.

Finally, political leadership must sustain the administrative decision-makers as the development process continues. The task of creating an environment in which policy formulation, operation, and evaluation are accelerated requires effective legislative-administrative relationships. Dynamic and effective administration flourishes in a climate of freedom where administrative officers can make unpopular decisions or mistakes for which they may be criticized without being sacrificed. Administrators under such circumstances require political protection, and this protection depends on a political system which maintains a broad consensus for national development goals.

In many countries, political support and protection are lacking. Administrative officers at all levels refrain from taking stands, signing documents, formalizing decisions, or in any way exposing themselves to possible criticism. A common result of such insecurity and timidity is the passing of decisions on very minor matters up the administrative line until a cabinet finds its agenda contains such items as "Should Mr. Mombezie be authorized to spend five months under a UN fellowship examining development planning techniques elsewhere?" or "Should the city government of Regresso be permitted to install a filtration unit in its water system?" A political system effective in decision-making is as basic a prerequisite of societal change and development as is an action-oriented administrative process.

ADMINISTRATIVE PREREQUISITES OF NATION-BUILDING

In due time, politicians must deliver results. This requires administration—the interacting processes of formulating, evaluating, selecting, programming, scheduling, organizing, managing, and coordinating plans, programs, and projects. The primary obstacles to development are administrative and political, not economic. Yet, even when political stability and leadership are relatively favorable, countries of low income generally lack the essential administrative capabilities for sustained development. As indicated earlier, they do not have the manpower with adequate experience or training to design and establish the institutions, processes, and operating systems essential to implementation.

A crucial administrative step is the creation of a realistic and operationally feasible development plan. Vague programs and projects or analyses of economic and fiscal trends do not constitute a plan. Projections or economic models of desired increases in national income, agricultural and industrial production, education levels, trade, tax revenues, foreign exchange, investment, and similar matters standing alone also are insufficient. Nor may planning activities be confined to those undertakings which receive external aid or special earmarked revenues.

Comprehensive plans for nation-building objectives must deal not only with a country's economic and social goals but also with its policies and programs for utilizing all resources, internal and external. Plans must include or be supported by definitive programs and projects for each sector, i.e., infrastructure, agriculture, education, health, village and community development, urban development, and industrialization. They obviously should be based on a realistic assessment of resources and of implementation capabilities.

A common deficiency in development plans and programs is the inadequate attention paid to the private sector. Plans cover government programs but seldom focus on the policies, services, and projects necessary to create conditions and inducements for maximum investment, production, and productivity by private individuals and enterprise. Measures to create a climate for entrepreneurial activity are as important and essential to a development plan as are physical infrastructure or educational programs.

Plans suffer from the inability or disinclination of planning agencies to involve operating ministries, field units, and regional and local governments. Planning is done almost totally from the top down, rather than from the bottom up, within the framework of centrally established goals, policies, resource availabilities, and financial inducements. The fact that most development plans are largely "nonfunctional" reflects these deficiencies. For instance, most plans do not incorporate the organizations, procedures, and other instruments essential to their implementation. Planning staffs are insufficiently concerned with the political and administrative measures involved in executing programs and projects.

These deficiencies are not surprising since it is always easier and more pleasant to develop projections or proposals than it is to fulfill them. Administration is hard work. Moreover, planning agencies are staffed almost exclusively with economists, statisticians, and other technical personnel. If development requires political, administrative, and social processes, then planning agencies must be staffed with personnel capable of dealing with these processes. This necessitates a change in the assumptions and technologies now utilized by bilateral and multilateral assistance agencies, universities, and foundations, as well as by developing countries.

Policies and programs require a set of actions to realize definitive projects, services, and activities. If plans state that cocoa, cotton, or rice production is to be increased, there must be a program to improve the quality of seeds, to apply better fertilizer, to irrigate more land, to educate more extension service agents. To fulfill a program, there must be specific projects and activities to make it operative. Here the development process usually begins to dry up. Examination shows that the overriding cause is the failure—or the inability—of governments to design, schedule, evaluate, manage, and control projects. In many countries, essential competences for project administration are virtually nonexistent. Development plans make no provision for creating these competences, and few external advisers are capable of helping to remedy this deficiency. A combination of actions to create these administrative capabilities is then a major precondition to nation-building, and one which assistance agencies and developing countries should tackle with massive energy.

One of the best, easiest to effectuate, and least-used tools for development administration is the budgetary process. Planning, budgeting, programming, and project authorization and control comprise an interrelated set of processes: at least they *should* be interrelated. Few countries, however, have achieved such a satisfactory arrangement. Plans, programs, and projects should be formulated in terms of both capital and current budgets. It would seem obvious that all financial resources available for application to development purposes would be covered in a country's budget, but often important categories are omitted. Also frequently ignored in the budget process are earmarked revenues, monies derived from internal borrowing, funds of financial institutions available for investment in developing purposes, earnings of public enterprise, and external loans and grants.

All the fiscal resources of a country need to be budgeted and authorized as formal steps in the implementation of programs and projects. Forecasts of the public resources necessary to induce private savings and investment must be taken into account. Estimates of temporary loss of income through special inducements to new industry and immediate and ultimate increases in revenues yielded by higher levels of private productivity also must be considered.

The contribution of a country's budget system to development administration depends largely on whether it is viewed as a fiscal or as an administrative process. When budgeting is a function of a ministry of finance, the budget tends to become a fiscal and accounting rather than a policy formulation and program decision-making instrument. Regardless of its organizational location, budgeting should be considered an administrative instrument indispensable to the head of state, to each minister, and to all principal administrative officers in achieving effective program and project development and implementation. The best results can be achieved most easily if the budget office is attached to the chief executive.

The role of the chief executive and the structure of government thus affect the ability of a country to formulate and implement development plans. If the planning, budgeting, personnel, and administrative management or administrative improvement agencies all can be attached to the office of the chief executive or embraced within cabinet machinery under a parliamentary system, effective utilization and coordination of these vital administrative tools is facilitated.

Such coordination needs to extend from the center to the ministries, and then to field establishments. Only through carefully assigned arrangements will there be unity of action among the offices, departments, and institutions responsible for overall planning and financing of programs and projects, and those operating agencies responsible for their execution. For example, sufficient funds may not be budgeted or allocated to finance a project, the personnel required may not be authorized, essential loan funds may be unavailable, foreign exchange necessary for importation of equipment or materials may be denied, materials may be unduly delayed at customs, or other administrative roadblocks may stop or seriously impair the project. With proper administrative resourcefulness these obstacles can be minimized, or avoided altogether. Yet in only a few countries have there been established effective systems of scheduling, progress reporting, and evaluation. Generally absent is the staff to supervise the execution of programs and projects, to identify and remove difficulties, and to ensure that approved projects, programs, and activities are actually launched.

The problem may be exacerbated by lack of synchronization between central government action and projects and services conducted in the field. Highways may not be planned in relationship to industrial undertakings. Or, in an agricultural production program, the departments responsible for storage, transport, and marketing facilities may fail to perform their individual undertakings to permit the several elements to mesh.

Diffusion of governmental structures generally complicates efforts to produce unity. New ministries, agencies, and public corporations to carry out development functions have been superimposed on tradition-oriented governments without careful review of the entire structure for new objectives. The result is a multiplicity of organs, duplication of function, and diffusion of responsibility which renders impossible effective coordination in policy formulation, plan preparation, and program implementation. Similarly, countries often attempt to administer public and quasi-public enterprises on the basis of traditional governmental controls, or to provide these enterprises with such a degree of autonomy that they no longer are accountable to the public interest.

The problem comes into agonizing focus when developing countries endeavor to coordinate national, regional, and local governmental roles while at the same time fostering a maximum of local self-government. The point where responsibilities of national ministries end and local governmental initiative begins is universally fuzzy. Seldom has it been specifically defined. Cities and other local governments are infrequently consulted and involved in the formulation of development plans and operations.. Nor are they given sufficient operational authority, tax powers, conditional grants, or opportunity to organize local programs that would make a significant contribution to overall development. Little recognition is given the fact that urban development, with its infrastructure and services, is an essential element in industrial development. Working out these administrative problems and processes must be done in each country with reference to its distinctive traditions, values, resources, and capabilities. The approaches and methods to produce change must be compatible and effective within each country's particular culture and environment.

Throughout, the administrator or adviser must have some understanding of the processes of inducing change—how to foster or set in motion the forces and activities that will effect change. This means planning, changing attitudes, winning support, organizing, implementing, and evaluating. In the context of development, this process can appropriately be called "institution-building." Institution-building begins with a formal commitment to the objective to be accomplished. It entails the creation of the organizations, services, systems, practices, or relationships which evidence that change in fact has taken place. The objective may be a school, a water distribution system, a credit agency, a tax program, or any organized effort requiring acceptance and response.

Institution-building illustrates the interdependence of the administrative and political processes as they act and react upon each other in the larger context of nation-building. For example, the same channels that the politician uses for establishing popular needs and aspirations in a particular sector also may be used by the administrator in establishing the organizational infrastructure to meet those needs and in evaluating their fulfillment. This is dynamic interaction in a society where popular needs must be transformed into programs, and where programs must be realized in such a way that "higher" needs will emerge. Establishment and recognition of a system in which change can succeed will enable a population to participate actively in the developmental process of nation-building by giving it a vehicle for articulating its desires to the politicians and administrators of a government which not only listens but acts.

CREATING ADMINISTRATIVE CAPABILITIES

Is it any wonder that newly independent and other low-income countries encounter many difficulties in mounting a sustained national development effort? Few industrialized countries possess sufficient political competences or administrative capabilities to cope with their development problems or to engage effectively in economic and technical assistance. When the limited educational systems, the lack of effective civil services, and the scarcity of trained manpower are considered, one marvels that progress is not more painful than it actually is.

The leadership of both developing countries and external assistance agencies must take the first step in overcoming such deficiencies by recognizing the true character of the problems to be solved and by creating the competences to meet them. Many obstacles would be removed more quickly if the formulation and implementation of development plans, programs, and projects were viewed as social action and administration operations, not as self-implementing economic and financial commitments. When administrative means to carry out politically tested plans and programs are built into the plans themselves, and when essential administrative instrumentalities and competences become primary steps in implementation, development plans have a far greater prospect of success.

A second and related step is the authorization of the planning agency, on behalf of the chief executive, to exercise central coordination and direction of plan administration. Other staff agencies, such as the budget and administrative management offices, have crucial roles to play in this responsibility. Teamwork is vital. In the planning agency, however, a distinctive staff should be charged with the surveillance and coordination of plan and program execution.

The third step is the activation of programs to strengthen the organization and management of ministries and all other operating units. The highest priority must be given to creating capabilities to formulate and manage programs and projects, and to improve the effectiveness of planning and programming, budgeting, personnel administration, and supervision in all agencies. A continuous program of administrative improvement headed by an administrative management chief is essential.

The fourth step is the upgrading of regional and local governments through greater involvement in program preparation and execution. Village or community development, urban development and industrialization, and regional efforts through provinces or states must be fostered, coordinated, and supported. Competence in project administration is the key to results at this end. Here again, administrative management and training programs to create internal capabilities are essential.

Once this groundwork is established, the fifth step is the continuous and effective evaluation of the validity of plans and their constituent programs and projects. The instruments of evaluation must be incorporated into the system in both the operating departments and the central planning machinery. Also involved here is a formalized system of inspection and progress reporting. Without these, the means for knowing when to take corrective measures will be lacking. The by-products of such evaluation and review will help develop capable personnel by involving them in all steps of the development process.

The last and most essential step is the acquisition of personnel technically qualified to perform the various functions. The problem of recruiting, educating, and developing managers, program experts, and technicians capable of administering development programs and other public services is critical in every country. Traditional educational systems and patterns of life inhibit change, and the initiation of manpower policies and projects requires sustained political and administrative effort. Manpower requirements in the private as well as the public sector must be met. In addition to assessments of personnel needs and resources, programs must be carried out to provide the necessary education and training and to introduce effective personnel practices in areas crucial for expediting development.

Creation of a competent civil service lies at the heart of establishing capabilities. Legal sanction and administrative resourcefulness are needed in formulating policies and procedures governing recruitment, promotions, conditions of work, training, and discipline. This requires an appropriate balance between protection of the individual civil servant and authorization of administrators to utilize personnel most effectively on the basis of administrative requirements.

Nation-building thus requires new types of knowledge and skills. An examination of the administrative obstacles to development in any country will reveal serious shortages in personnel who possess the essential blend of administrative and technical competences. If these shortages are matched against educational and training programs, it will be found that the latter are not geared to producing the knowledge and skills required. New curricula and improved teaching methods are required for pre-service and in-service development administrators and technicians, project designers, managers, expediters, and many other categories of personnel.

Much point is made by development planners of the necessity for constraints on consumption as a requisite in capital formation. Administrative capital is as important in nation-building as capital formation is in industrial enterprise. A willingness to give temporary leave for training to critical personnel even though inconvenient, is equally essential. Federal, state, and city governments in the United States with their lush personnel resources might well demonstrate the efficacy of this principle.

Likewise, a more solid underpinning of research is essential, especially for examining the foregoing administrative problems. Such research would contribute to solving particular problems and would result in valuable materials both for teaching purposes and for operational guidance.

Steps along these lines are steps which Paul Appleby would have supported. Education to meet changing challenges was an important part of his life's work. And just as his vision has enabled us to take giant strides in understanding and influencing the process of nation-building, so must we now be no less enterprising in our efforts to educate able young men and women to help govern the nations he helped to build.

· 14 ·

Administration and Policy in International Technical Assistance

HERBERT EMMERICH

In treating a topic such as this, as broad, as baffling, as complex, and as controversial, particularly in a short paper, I shall adopt a self-deny-ing ordinance. In spite of temptation to wander off into the complexities of high American foreign aid policy, I shall confine myself to a discus-sion of one phase, that of international technical assistance, and in fact to the aspect of the latter topic which has to do with the dispatching of technical advisers (or experts as they are called in the United Nations family) from one country to another. Since I shall base these observa-tions primarily on my own experience, observation, and reflection and only secondarily on the literature, it is appropriate that I focus on the area in which I had the most opportunity to observe technical assist-ance. Thus I shall emphasize the multilateral programs.

The choice of the word "policy" rather than "politics" is deliberate, and is not consciously due to the fact that in my six years at the United Nations I learned that these two words in the French and Spanish languages were synonymous. The forces that govern international tech-nical assistance at any time (and these forces are in a constant state of flux) can accurately be designated as *policy*, for they are more closely related to the current operating policies of the donor agencies (and even more narrowly to those of their technical subdivisions) than to the grand announced political positions of the donor organiza-tions and governments. Nor was I uninfluenced by the use of the words "policy" and "administration" and their intertwined relationship in one of the main writings of the man whom these essays honor.[1]

Although I have opinions on most of them, I shall withhold comment on the major political questions treated in such books as *Why Foreign*

[1] Paul H. Appleby, *Policy and Administration* (University, Alabama: University of Alabama Press, 1949).

Aid?, in which one finds a wide range of viewpoints and doctrines on the basic philosophy, purpose, and effectiveness of American foreign aid programs, running the full gamut of such concepts as "down the drain," "do-gooding vs. national self interest," "winning the cold war," and "saving the peace."[2]

EXAGGERATED EXPECTATIONS OF TECHNICAL ASSISTANCE

Technical assistance is a never-never land in which both the donor agencies and the receiving countries expect miracles. The expectations and goals are no less chimerical than the means employed to realize them.[3] In too many cases the attempt is being made, by means of a bountiful alchemy, to transmute countries overnight from the conditions of the paleolithic or early bronze age into all the golden glories of the high-technology welfare state. And this is to be done with human consideration and by democratic methods. Even the slightest familiarity with history would throw doubts on the validity of such expectations. The history of the advanced countries is largely the story of the accumulation of knowledge, technical capability, productivity, and capital, not to mention a capacity for self-government, after centuries of ignorance and cruelty and ruthless exploitation of human beings and natural resources under despotic rule.

Nor can too much of the arrested development of great parts of the world be charged predominantly to the colonialism of the great powers. Development was accelerated under colonial rule, particularly in some of the great cultures of Asia; and countries like India, as Paul H. Appleby testified, had been amazingly well prepared for independence and self-government by their colonial masters.[4] But there were profound cultural, physical, and ethnographic roadblocks which kept vast parts of human society in a retarded state even before colonial rule began. These took many forms and were due to a variety of causes, many of which we do not entirely understand.

To have a government at all there must be a State and to have a State there must be a country with some elements of a common tradition and ethos. But the craze for nationalism of the second half of the

[2] Robert A. Goldwin, ed., *Why Foreign Aid?* (Chicago: Rand McNally, 1963).

[3] *A Handbook of Public Administration*, United Nations Publication, Sales No. 61.II.H.2. (New York: United Nations, 1961), Part I. Public Administration and National Development, Paras. 15 and 16. Prepared by Herbert Emmerich with the assistance of the Division for Public Administration.

[4] Paul H. Appleby, *Public Administration in India—Report of a Survey* (New Delhi: Government of India, Cabinet Secretariat, 1953), Section I, A General Appraisal.

twentieth century has exceeded all the dire predictions made by Professor Carlton Hayes in his studies on nationalism in the 1920's. Many of the new nations are barely countries at all. In many African nations the people in one region have more in common, in respect to tribal, cultural, and historical ties, with those just across the border than with their own people of other regions, or with the tiny group of European-trained national leaders who have led the movements for nationalism and independence. In Africa many nations are agglomerations of people and tribes in a land area whose boundaries were designated on inadequate maps in a distant chancery a century ago by two gentlemen named Disraeli and Bismarck. In Brazil such countries are called "cartorial states."

Many of the new States that have been admitted to the United Nations would have benefited by a period of a different kind of tutelage, divorced from the self-interest of great powers by an international trusteeship for several decades under the United Nations organization itself. Its Charter contains these very words, but this clause has never been invoked, nor for that matter seriously considered.[5]

Although colonial rule undoubtedly imposed limits on national development in certain colonies, thoughtful Africans today fear that the first stages of independence under exuberant but inexperienced politicians will result in economic and political and administrative retrogression instead of advance and may lead to more despotism than in colonial régimes. In the countries of Asia, with their rich cultural history, there are deep-seated forces of tradition along with religious, caste, and cultural roadblocks to rapid modernization in the village as well as in the town, in the ministries, and in commerce and industry. It is all the more noteworthy that in the face of these obstacles notable and resolute advances are being made.

In the Latin American republics, where independence dates back almost 150 years, effective administrative services have not in the past been an important criterion of the government's prestige.[6] In spite of many obstacles there are signs of hope and evidences of advances in the political and administrative development south of the border. But the implications of the new approach through the Alliance for Progress calls for such profound (if not indeed revolutionary) changes in deep-seated mores and vested interests that our expectations must be geared

---

[5] *Charter of the United Nations,* Article 81.

[6] Herbert Emmerich, "Administrative Roadblocks to Coordinated Development," Chapter XV in *Social Aspects of Economic Development in Latin America,* Volume I, edited by Egbert De Vries and José Medina Echavarría (Paris: Unesco, 1963).

to decades and not to annual budget cycles. In Mexico, which has made the greatest strides, the revolution began more than four decades ago.

The purpose of the foregoing paragraphs is not to offer a counsel of despair but to warn against a whole series of unrealizable and absurd expectations on which technical assistance has proceeded. We must come to have a greater awareness of the interrelationships between the administrative and political fields and their effect on social and economic development. Above all, we must restrain a Quixotic tendency to try to transform these struggling countries overnight into whatever may be the image we have of our own.

MOST TECHNICAL ASSISTANCE IS PUBLIC ADMINISTRATION

Almost everyone engaged in technical assistance work is, whether he knows it or not, engaged to a great extent in public administration. In most cases such persons are either unaware of the fact or find it prudent not to acknowledge it. This astonishing conclusion was borne in upon me in 1962 after Mr. Pierre Juvigny (of the Conseil d'Etat in France) and I had conducted a survey for the Economic and Social Council of the United Nations on the administrative aspects of the United Nations and the Specialized Agencies.[7] Experts in education, health, agriculture, social security, industrial development, administration of river valleys, transportation, communications, and town planning are constantly recommending structures for ministries, personnel systems, accounting methods, and regional and field office arrangements, not to speak of bill-drafting and writing of executive decrees, which have implications far beyond their own fields. As the old abbé said in Molière's comedy, they have been talking prose for years without being aware of it. And this goes on with little or no consultation with advisers in related fields or with the general advisers in public administration. Nor does it take account of the administrative and political structures and functions of the government as a whole. It is encouraging to note, however, that during the survey more and more agencies acknowledged that many of their defeats and frustrations were due to the disregard of these factors; Mr. Juvigny reported a year later that a new spirit is growing toward a more concerted and coordinated attack on these problems.[8]

[7] *Programmes in the Field of Public Administration in the United Nations and Specialized Agencies,* Document E/3630, May 1962 Economic and Social Council, 34th Session, United Nations.

[8] Annex I in *28th Annual Report of the Administrative Committee on Coordination,* Document E/3765, May 1963 Economic and Social Council 36th Session, United Nations.

It is altogether likely that this tendency is not confined to the United Nations programs but can also be found in the bilateral ones. The pressure for predominance of the highly specialized sectoral expert is particularly notable in the United States where such foreign programs as agriculture, education, and health have been watched over and advocated by powerful, well-organized professional pressure groups and their counterpart governmental agencies. The important reorganization of the Agency for International Development in 1961, based on the report of President Kennedy's task force on Foreign Economic Assistance, possibly went too far in reorganizing the Agency on the basis of regional rather than functional predominance, but even so it has not been able to offset these particularistic pressures altogether.[9] Professor Edward W. Weidner in his new and immensely enlightening treatise compares these trends in the United Nations, United States, and the Ford Foundation programs.[10]

The International Bank for Reconstruction and Development and to some extent the International Monetary Fund have had a great influence on administrative structures and procedures. The Fund has prescribed the most minute regulations for national accounting for international monetary transactions in the interest of monetary stabilization. The World Bank has prescribed structures and procedures in great detail as a condition for loans to governments. In many countries whose ministries are unstable, inefficient, or corrupt the Bank encourages the creation of autonomous authorities and corporations and the establishment of earmarked revenue accounts to ensure proper management and repayment of the funds advanced in developing countries. In both institutions the sanctions of withholding funds are powerful tools not available to the ordinary technical assistance expert. Some of them are, however, available to the American adviser when his advice is a condition of U.S. loans and grants. These advisers, fortified by a "dowry" as a high United Nations official once called it, have more influence than a dozen experts without such leverage. The total effect on government structure in such cases is subordinated to the needs of the specific project under negotiation. The question arises as to what extent this is banking and to what extent public administration.

The World Bank increasingly stresses the relationship of its loans and investment to the total development in the administrative, eco-

[9] An Act for International Development: A Summary Presentation, Department of State Publication, 7205 (Washington, June 1961).

[10] Edward W. Weidner, *Technical Assistance in Public Administration, The Case for Development Administration* (Chicago: Public Administration Service, 1964), Chapter 2, "Agencies."

nomic, and fiscal growth of a country. Its series of published country reports lays strong emphasis on the need for good public administration and sound overall fiscal policies. And the studies of Albert Waterston of the Bank's technical assistance group have greatly advanced the understanding of the relationship of administration to national development planning.

There have been notable improvements in the structures and administrative practices of the agencies offering technical assistance as well as of the countries who are its recipients. A great many countries have established special ministries or units on these questions in the central cabinet secretariat or executive office. In the receiving countries these units tend to work more and more in direct contact with the national planning agency and the President or Prime Minister. Some of these structures are described in the report of the International Institute of Administrative Sciences on this topic after three years of study culminating in the discussions of its XIIth Congress in Vienna.[11]

The unawareness of the pervasive common denominator aspects of public administration arises from a number of causes. The principal cause is the high degree of specialization and subspecialization among consultants from the advanced countries who have been the main source of supply for field forces and headquarters direction of technical assistance missions. Some of the specialists have been broad-gauged in their appreciation of national needs, in their willingness to cooperate, and in their dedication to their work in the face of heartbreaking obstacles. But particularly in the field of the United Nations and the Specialized Agencies, I believe the basic structure of the various specialties is too fractionized, and the frequent problems of jurisdiction too hard to resolve on this account. The effort required for a coordinated and concerted attack on a country's problems is too difficult and costly. The missing element has been a broad-gauged public administration approach working in cooperation with and as a coordinator of sectoral efforts—an approach which, Professor Weidner pointed out, has not had the benefit of a specialized agency or of strong organized pressure groups.

The predominant reason why most technical assistance is public administration is found in the fact that the most underdeveloped sectors in an underdeveloped country are the private and local ones. The central government is almost the sole initiator of development and

---

[11] Fernand Vrancken, *General Report on Technical Assistance in Public Administration* (Brussels: International Institute of Administrative Sciences, 1963).

reform, and must find the resources and personnel to carry out programs of all kinds. It is not so much a question of socialist or capitalist ideology, although this factor plays a part in some countries, but more a consequence of the lack of private and local institutions and of economic and political entrepreneurs capable of initiative and decision-making. This imbalance throws an added burden on the central government and particularly on its administrative agencies. The ironic corollary is that the significance of public administration is greatest in the least developed countries.

FUNCTION VS. AREA

It is not strange that public administration advice, *qua* public administration, was one of the last activities to emerge in the United Nations universe. Many of the Specialized Agencies were already on the scene with a long history of successful programs before public administration arrived. Even in 1951 public administration was regarded as a very sensitive area and was approached with great diffidence, in a special incubator of the old Technical Assistance Administration, because Messrs. Hugh Keenleyside (Canada) and Gustavo Martínez Cabañas (Mexico), the heads of that unit, were foresighted enough to realize its growing significance. And it was not until 1959 that public administration was made a permanent unit of the Economic and Social Department of the United Nations. Nor should the contributions in budget and revenue administration of the Fiscal and Financial Branch of the United Nations be overlooked as another strong influence in developing countries for overall fiscal planning and improved financial administration. The Agency for International Development has accelerated its services and has published excellent studies in these fields.

The United Nations administrative structure has taken an opposite course from the sweeping transformation that occurred in the structure of A.I.D. in 1963 from a functional to a regional setup. The Technical Assistance Administration, which had been organized on a regional basis, was merged in 1959 with the Department of Economic and Social Affairs, in which the functional units were controlling. As the Specialized Agencies also are organized to a great extent on a functional basis, this has produced a force for further fractionalizing the dominant policy and operations of the country programs. To some extent, the Regional Economic Commissions (Asia, Africa, and Latin America) in the United Nations are a corrective for this trend, but they too are gradually being organized internally by specialties as outposts of the headquarters structure. The United Nations has large specialized technical assistance units and programs of its own and is therefore handicapped in playing a strong role as coordinator of the Specialized Agencies, over which it has little or no formal powers of control.

The most important point of coordination of the donor agencies is the Resident Representative of the Technical Assistance Board, who also serves as the Country Director of the Special Fund program. In July 1964 the Economic and Social Council, on the initiative of the United States, agreed in principle to unify the administration of the Expanded Program of Technical Assistance and the Special Fund program, with Paul G. Hoffman as director of the combined operation and David Owen as codirector. The U.N. Resident Representatives, the Country Directors of the United States Aid Program, and the Country Representatives of the Ford Foundation are in key positions to be overall country advisers, the statesmen of the donor agencies of technical assistance, the coordinators of the many experts sent by many units at the country level, and the links among the several programs. In addition, the country directors of large donor agencies can, if they are qualified, be the best advisers to their client governments on the strategy of a total plan, both on development policy and on general administration. They can act as a healthy corrective to the pressures and importunities of the high-powered salesmen of the over-specialized sectoral units, and as stimulators of interagency cooperation.

VARIETIES OF POLICY-MAKING

Most of the policy problems of international technical assistance are actually problems of emphasis and are operational in nature. A few examples of policy questions at various levels which confront a program of technical assistance will serve to illustrate the point. There are considerable differences between the policy problems of international multilateral agencies, national bilateral agencies, regional agencies, and agencies at the country level. The last category is by far the most important.

Most of the funds now being expended in the United Nations for technical assistance derive from voluntary contributions by its members to the Expanded Program of Technical Assistance (EPTA) or to the United Nations Special Fund. These aggregate over $100 million a year and are five times as great as they were ten years ago. They are supplemented by services to member States out of the regular budgets of the United Nations and Specialized Agencies.

A leading policy question in the allotment of funds is whether allotment should be by the sectoral quotas of the cooperating agencies (from the top down) or by building up programs country by country (from the bottom up). There has been a definite trend toward the latter method; but the sectoral and specialized pressures in the various units, strongly supported in a number of countries by pressure groups in such fields as health, agriculture, education, labor standards, and social security are still very strong. There is a tendency within the United Nations for every specialized activity to demand the creation of a standing commission of the Economic and Social Council to bring pressure for its cause, and ultimately to advocate the creation of a new Specialized Agency in its field. The latest demands are for Specialized Agencies in the fields of housing and town planning, in industrial development, and in international trade and commerce. Gradual coordination and voluntary cooperation are making progress in the United Nations group, but the time has come to practice birth control in the conception of new Specialized Agencies to avoid further splintering of autonomous sectoral units, lest the underdeveloped countries become completely confused by the multiplicity of specialized advice.

The amount that any one country should receive out of the total United Nations technical assistance resources is a major policy question. So also is the question, to what extent should the receiving country be required to commit itself to a substantial contribution of materials, money, and counterpart personnel as a condition for technical assistance? The EPTA program at first tended to be weak in this respect, but it has been greatly strengthened by the insistence on such commitments on the part of the U.N. Special Fund.

There is a certain amount of lobbying by delegations to the United Nations organs and their subcommittees for technical assistance programs. But this lobbying has been for sectoral programs as much as it has been for country allocations. Most of the salesmanship has been the other way around; it has been practiced by traveling representatives of the Specialized Agencies trying to persuade ministers to accept their wares. A good deal of the debate in the Economic and Social Council and its commissions and committees and in the Second Committee of the General Assembly is on the question of what programs or sectors need emphasis. There are waves of styles and fashions in this regard from year to year just as in the case of the bilateral programs.

One of the last projects of Dag Hammarskjold was his espousal of a policy approved by the General Assembly in 1959 to send operating and executive officials to newly independent countries to help fill the void created by the departing colonial officials until such time as the country could train its own nationals to fill these posts. In the first year of this program, Mr. Hammarskjold approved each appointment personally. It has come to be called the "OPEX Program" and has grown rapidly, although it is fraught with problems and difficulties. EPTA funds as well as regular funds are now available for operational posts as well as advisory ones, but they tend to be allotted for posts of technical managers rather than of general administrators. UNESCO and to some extent the World Health Organization have undertaken to provide teachers, doctors, and nurses in the employ of the requesting country and paid in part by them, but generously supplemented by funds of the United Nations Agencies. To make this program a success, a more determined effort needs to be made for the training of nationals to replace OPEX officials, lest they be required to remain in the country indefinitely. Although the means available will never satisfy the growing demand, this kind of assistance will become a major part of the multilateral effort to replace the thousands of European colonial officers still on duty, particularly in African countries. The financial commitment to pay their share of the costs of these officers lays a heavy burden on such countries.

In the United Nations, policy questions may be said to be primarily operational and administrative rather than political, though occasionally national politics of donor countries influence the United Nations program. This is particularly true where the super powers are concerned. The U.N. sponsored a working party on the administration of government corporations in Rangoon in 1956. The U.S. Government was unwilling to send an American representative on the ground that it would be supporting creeping socialism by discussing it. Countries under communist influence distrust American experts in oil exploitation for fear their reports will be biased in favor of U.S. oil interests. The U.S. Department of State during the 1950's viewed with alarm the operations of the United Nations Regional Economic Commission for Latin America. I could never ascertain whether this was because its Secretary, Dr. Raoul Prebisch (Argentina), was suspected of recommending too much government intervention and too little private investment, or whether it was because he was suspected of advocating less dependence on investment and trade with American interests. (I have never found evidence to prove either suspicion.) A little over a year ago there was a tremendous fuss in Congress because the U.N. Special Fund had agreed to finance some preliminary surveys of the livestock industry in Cuba. It is difficult for Congressmen and Senators to accept the fact that, notwithstanding the United States contribution of 40 per cent of the Expanded Program and the Special Fund, our voice in the expenditures is only one and that the United States cannot veto a U.N. program even to a country on which it has placed embargoes. This comes nearer to being a hot political issue at home than anything else one can think of vis-à-vis U.N. technical assistance.

Regional programs have been more promising under United Nations auspices than under bilateral programs or under the auspices of the Organization of American States. One of the notable examples of this is the growing influence of the Agreement for Economic Integration in the Central American States, a replica in miniature of the European Common Market undertaking. The Governing Committee of those States supports, among other projects, the Advanced School of Public Administration in San José, Costa Rica, with substantial aid from the United Nations. This school has now converted its program almost entirely to training at high levels in the administration of economic integration and national and regional development for the five Central American Republics and for Panama.

Generalizations regarding the Alliance for Progress must be made with caution. In spite of the overwhelming proportions of the funds and resources contributed by the United States, the country programs now are submitted to the scrutiny and approval of committees in which Latin American members have an equal voice. Thus the "Nine Wise Men" have been replaced by a "Committee of Seven," modeled somewhat after the O.E.E.C. which proved to be so effective in connection with the Marshall Plan in Europe. The Alliance is much more multilateral than is generally realized. Its policies have reform implications which are almost revolutionary in regard to taxation, land reform, sound budgeting and administration, and prudent development planning and investment. It may be wise, therefore, for the United States to share responsibility for their scrutiny. However, the severe conditions to be met, when added to the cumbersome sequence of multiple clearances, greatly increase the length of time before country programs and projects can secure approvals. The Alliance is one of the most fundamental and serious efforts to combine development, stabilization, and reform with foreign aid and technical assistance, and the initial rate of performance and expenditure must necessarily be slow. In this case too, unrealistic expectations and impatience have been the causes of most of the criticism.

A growing interest in budget and general public administration is being fostered by the U.N. Regional Economic Commissions of Africa, Asia, and Latin America. And regional organizations like O.E.C.D. in Europe are stepping up their programs as joint donors of technical assistance work. Countries must not be flooded by such a host of foreign experts that they exhaust national counterparts. British Guiana could provide a pretty little case study in this regard.

By far the most important element in the relationships of policy and administration is at the country level. But this topic is so complex and has so many variables that a brief comment can do no more than indicate its nature. Paul H. Appleby reminded us that it is not possible to decentralize authority and operations until top policy has been formulated at the center. The governments of developing countries face the awesome task of assuming major responsibility for making broad national policy decisions. At the same time there is imperative need to decentralize a considerable range of choice within this policy to ministries, field forces, and local authorities, and where possible to private initiative, as fast as capable personnel and institutions become available. National policy must be overall policy and the sectoral pressures need to be subordinated to it. There is need for the new political leaders and "enterprise-minded" administrators to concentrate on national development and to avoid excursions in the field of chauvinism and external aggrandizement. Finally, care must be taken that a proper relationship is established between the political leaders and the career service, which should neither dominate the final decisions nor be disregarded in their formulation. Advice on these concepts, if effective help can be given at all by extranational consultants, must come from persons who have broad-gauged backgrounds in policy and administration. It cannot be expected to derive from the specialized and sectoral fields nor even from narrow administrative technicians.

NATIONALITIES OF TECHNICAL ASSISTANCE EXPERTS

The question of the nationality of technical assistance missions is both a political and an operational problem. At the nascent stage of independence, many countries do not want their old colonials, though interestingly enough this aversion seems to wear out in a few years. Even Belgian consultants are returning in considerable number to the Congo. The British still have over 20,000 colonial officials in posts abroad. As countries develop able professionals there is an increasing tendency to recruit in the region. This is quite marked in Asia, the Middle East, and in Latin America. Egyptian advisers have been in demand in Arab countries while Israeli advisers have been sought in Africa below the Sahara. In many cases countries appreciate a qualified expert who has come from a country that is itself going through the developing process and whose expertise is neither too advanced nor too specialized.

The entire field of training presents a special problem for a technical assistance donor agency. How much should be invested in sending technical assistance advisers and how much in training nationals abroad? What and how much training should be offered abroad and at home? How shall those to be trained be selected and what assurance is there that they will be properly assigned and utilized upon their return; indeed, what assurance is there that they will return? There is a close relationship between advisers and training but in the United Nations program this has not always been well correlated. The problem of national susceptibilities also arises regarding the countries to which fellows for training abroad are to be sent. The United Nations has not had the advantages (or headaches) which the United States acquired by contracting with a university for work within a country and for sending its fellows for training at that university. In fact, except for the World Bank and the Special Fund, the contracting device has been but rarely used in United Nations technical assistance. In the case of those agencies contracts have been employed mostly for engineering and resource surveys preliminary to investments and loans.

The bilateral agencies have the handicap that their motives are always suspect even when the individual expert is genuinely free of national bias. There is always the question of whether the advice they give is entirely in the interest of the recipient country rather than being based on the national interest of the expert's homeland. The new-country politicians are suspicious and even hostile and often very unfair in their judgments on these matters. Their state of mind is undoubtedly influenced by Communist propaganda. A Soviet expert once said to me that he knew U.S. nationals in the service of the United Nations reported daily to their embassies for instruction, so why shouldn't he?

Should the technical advisers be members of a career corps with permanent tenure, subject to transfer from country to country? The continuous recruitment effort that goes on in the absence of such a corps is time-consuming and costly. The national burden assumed in letting permanent employees go for extended periods is a great one. There continues to be a place for a small cadre of career people, and the United Nations has recognized this fact by creating a very few posts in the category of "program expert." But I am convinced today that the great majority of advisers must be recruited on an *ad hoc* basis, in terms of their suitability for the job to be done and their adaptability to a given culture. The skills and specialties required vary from year to year, and no donor agency can assure continuous employment to the great variety of specialists needed in technical assistance. Furthermore, there are some disadvantages inherent in career appointments, even when these are not in the category of the man who cannot adjust at home. The consultant forever abroad runs the danger that he will get out of touch with professional and scientific progress in his own field and needs the refreshment of returning to his home base from time to time.

POLITICAL DEVELOPMENT: A NEW RESEARCH INTEREST

American political scientists, particularly, in their studies and writings have recently been stressing the importance of political development in the total spectrum of national progress. Paul H. Appleby, referring to his experiences in India, said in 1962 at Wayne State University: "I am most of all an administrator, and in the past I have talked most about administration. I certainly realize that administrators have important roles in the grand coordinating effort to which I am directing attention. But the more I see things, the more crucial I see the more frankly political structures and functions to be—most notably a good party system."[12]

I strongly doubt whether foreign advisers on political questions will be in great demand in international technical assistance. National susceptibilities are too great on these matters and most countries (except those which have capitulated to Soviet or Chinese Communist influence) will seek out their own nationals to advise them. My conclusion here is that top public administration advisers, particularly the chiefs of missions, need to have broad backgrounds, by training or experience or both, in political and administrative institutions of a number of countries (including of course their own). They should not be highly specialized experts in one small subdivision of the staff functions of public administration.

More promising is the field of training the nationals of developing countries to be political advisers and leaders. In this field American political scientists have a special contribution to make, but it should be made in a multilateral framework. I believe that an international school of "democratics" (a word coined by Richard S. Childs of the National Municipal League), with a multinational faculty, would be a useful addition to the growing list of schools and institutes. One can think of many fields in which such a school could offer education and training in comparative politics and administration and their interrelationships, as well as in methods of applied and operational research. Among such fields are constitutional law, judicial administration, presidential and parliamentary systems, executive-legislative relationships, cabinet secre-

---

[12] Paul H. Appleby, "Making Sense out of Things in General," reprinted in *Public Administration Review*, Vol. XXII, No. 4 (December 1962), p. 178.

tariats or executive offices, bill drafting, public opinion, statistical sampling methods, civil-military relationships, political parties, voting behavior, and election administration. Such questions as political officers—career services relationships, the relation of governmental units to private enterprise, autonomous corporations and local authorities, cooperatives, advisory boards, interest groups, and community development groups might also be studied. In many developing countries such simple processes as secretarial services to governmental committees, including the preparation of agenda papers and keeping of minutes, are imperfectly understood.

THE APPLEBY MISSIONS TO INDIA: CONCLUSION

Paul H. Appleby's four missions to India provide a classic model of high administrative-policy–oriented international technical assistance. They had all these ingredients of success which, alas, so many administrative missions lack:

(1) The sponsoring agency, which in each case was the Ford Foundation, paved the way for the missions, supported them during their stay in India, and helped the Government to follow up and implement many of the recommendations.

(2) Through the personal interest of the Prime Minister and the cooperation of the Cabinet, the receiving country committed itself at the highest political levels to complete accessibility and full support, including the provision of able counterparts from a civil service of high prestige and intelligence.

(3) Above all, the inspired choice of such a rare combination of administrator, philosopher, statesman, and teacher as Paul Appleby ensured the success of the missions. As such a combination of qualities can rarely be found, the choice of the senior adviser remains the hardest part of the model to duplicate.

Appleby not only had the seniority and temperament which appealed to the Indian people and the experience and prestige necessary to deal with ministers of state and high civil servants; he identified himself with the developmental aspirations of the government, praised the excellences he found, and had the insight and courage to point out administrative shortcomings. One is particularly struck, in view of the abstract quality of his other writings, with the precision and detail of his comments on administration in India. He perceived the close relationships between national policies and administrative structures and procedures, and had the skill to show how good "nuts and bolts" techniques could expedite broad programs of national development down to such details as the methods of handling of state papers. He was the rare generalist who appreciated the work of the specialists. He and his wife traveled throughout the country with boundless curiosity and a rare spirit of empathy, and made fast friends in many sectors: among the new politicians, with members of the venerable and powerful civil service, in the universities, and in private life. The final test of his success was that he was thrice recalled after the first visit, that his reports became subjects of wide discussion, and that after his return to the United States streams of visiting Indians continued to make respectful pilgrimages to his home for continued contact and inspiration until his last days.

As the developing countries continue to demand and the United States, the United Nations, and other program sources continue to supply international technical assistance, the utility of this kind of high level mission will be more and more appreciated. Its distinguishing features are its emphases on the relations of administration to policy, and of the impact of the overall, coordinating skills on the sectoral and specialized ones. The Appleby mission reinforces the hope that "Technical Assistance" more and more will become "Technical Cooperation" and that the "Development Decade" will become the "Century of Development." It is the classic case which exemplifies how donors and recipients can work together with mutual respect and tolerance in one of the most difficult and challenging enterprises ever undertaken by mankind.

V. SOME ENDURING CONCERNS

•

· 15 ·

Ethics and the Public Service

STEPHEN K. BAILEY

When Paul Appleby was asked to deliver the Edward Douglass White lectures at Louisiana State University in the Spring of 1951, he chose as his topic *Morality and Administration in Democratic Government*. He preferred the term "morality" because he did not wish to suggest his lectures were "either a treatment in the systematic terms of general philosophy or a 'code of administrative ethics'."[1] His attempt instead was to cast the light of his uncommon wisdom upon what he considered to be the central ethical and moral issues of the American public service. These issues centered upon the felicitous interaction of moral institutional arrangements and morally ambiguous man.

In some ways *Morality and Administration* is a disconcerting book. The essays are discontinuous. Each one is chocked with insight, but in the collection viewed as a whole, theoretical coherence and structure emerge implicitly rather than explicitly. Some inherently ambiguous terms like "responsibility" are clarified only by context. The final chapter, "The Administrative Pattern," is not the logical fulfillment of the preceding chapters. It stands beside the other essays, not on top of them. Furthermore, in spite of the highly personal connotation of the word "morality," Appleby spent most of his time discussing the effect of the governmental system upon official morality rather than vice versa. He saw in the American governmental system a series of political and organizational devices for promoting ethical choices. The most serious threats to the "good society" came, in his estimation, not from the venality of individuals but from imperfections in institutional arrangements.

His normative model ran somewhat as follows: politics and hierarchy force public servants to refer private and special interests to higher and broader public interests. Politics does this through the discipline of the majority ballot which forces both political executives and legislators to insert a majoritarian calculus into the consideration

[1] Paul H. Appleby, *Morality and Administration in Democratic Government* (Baton Rouge: Louisiana State University Press, 1952), p. vii.

of private claims. Hierarchy does it by placing in the hands of top officials both the responsibility and the necessity of homogenizing and moralizing the special interests inevitably represented by and through the lower echelons of organizational pyramids.[2] Both politics and hierarchy are devices for assuring accountability to the public as a whole. The public makes its will known in a variety of ways and through a variety of channels, but its importance is largely in its potential rather than in its concrete expressions. "Its capacity to be, more than its being, is the crux of democratic reality."[3] Politics and hierarchy induce the public servant to search imaginatively for a public-will-to-be. In this search, the public servant is often a leader in the creation of a new public will, so he is in part accountable to what he in part creates. But in any case the basic morality of the system is in its forcing of unitary claims into the mill of pluralistic considerations.

The enemies of this normative model, then, are obvious: they are whatever disrupts politics and hierarchy. For whatever disrupts politics and hierarchy permits the settlement of public issues at too low a level of organization—at too private a level, at too specialized a level. As Madison saw in Federalist 10, bigness is the friend of freedom. But Appleby saw more clearly than Madison that bigness is freedom's friend only if administrative as well as legislative devices exist to ensure that policy decisions emerge out of the *complexity* of bigness rather than out of the simplicity of its constituent parts. The scatteration of power in the Congress, the virtual autonomy of certain bureaus and even lesser units in the executive branch, an undue encroachment of legal and other professional norms upon administrative discretion, the substitution of the expert for the generalist at the higher levels of general government, the awarding of statutory power at the bureau rather than at the department level, the atomized character of our political parties—these, according to Appleby, are the effective enemies of morality in the governmental system. They are the symptoms of political pathology. "Our poorest governmental performances, both technically and morally," he wrote, "are generally associated with conditions in which a few citizens have very disproportionate influence."[4]

---

[2] The intellectual as distinct from the moral implications of hierarchy have been suggested by Kenneth Underwood in his contention that "the policy-making executive is to be distinguished from the middle management-supervisor levels most basically in the excessively cognitive, abstract dimensions of his work." See his paper, "The New Ethic of Personal and Corporate Responsibility," presented at the Third Centennial Symposium on *The Responsible Individual,* April 8, 1964, University of Denver.

[3] Appleby, *op. cit.,* p. 35.

[4] *Ibid.,* p. 214.

He felt that "the degradation of democracy is in the failure to organize or in actual disintegration of political responsibility, yielding public interest to special influence."[5]

Here, then, is the grand design. Government is moral in so far as it induces public servants to relate the specific to the general, the private to the public, the precise interest to the inchoate moral judgment. Within this context, a moral public decision becomes one in which "the action conforms to the processes and symbols thus far developed for the general protection of political freedom as the agent of more general freedom; . . . leaves open the way for modification or reversal by public determination; . . . is taken within a hierarchy of controls in which responsibility for action may be readily identified by the public; . . . and embodies as contributions of leadership the concrete structuring of response to popularly felt needs, and not merely responses to the private and personal needs of leaders."[6]

It is no disparagement of Paul Appleby's contributions to a normative theory of democratic governance to point out that he dealt only intermittently and unsystematically with the moral problems of the individual public servant. The moral system intrigued him far more consistently than the moral actor. All of his books and essays contain brilliant flashes of insight into the moral dilemmas of individual executives, administrators, and legislators, but there emerges no *gestalt* of personal ethics in government. One can only wish that he had addressed himself to a systematic elaboration of the personal as well as the institutional aspects of public ethics. For the richness of his administrative experience and the sensitivity of his insight might have illuminated uniquely the continuing moral problems of those whose business it is to preserve and improve the American public service.

Perhaps, without undue pretention, this memorial essay can attempt to fashion a prolegomenon to a normative theory of personal ethics in the public service—building upon and elaborating some of the fragments which Appleby scattered throughout his writings and teaching.

Appleby's fragments suggest that personal ethics in the public service is compounded of mental attitudes and moral qualities. Both ingredients are essential. Virtue without understanding can be quite as disastrous as understanding without virtue.

The three essential mental attitudes are: (1) a recognition of the moral ambiguity of all men and of all public policies, (2) a recognition of the contextual forces which condition moral priorities in the public service, and (3) a recognition of the paradoxes of procedures. The

[5] *Ibid.*, p. 211.
[6] *Ibid.*, p. 36.

essential moral qualities of the ethical public servant are: (1) optimism, (2) courage, and (3) fairness tempered by charity.

These mental attitudes and moral qualities are relevant to all public servants in every branch and at every level of government. They are as germane to judges and legislators as they are to executives and administrators. They are as essential to line officers as to staff officers. They apply to state and local officials as well as to national and international officials. They are needed in military, foreign, and other specialized services quite as much as they are needed in the career civil service and among political executives. They, of course, assume the virtue of probity and the institutional checks upon venality which Appleby has so brilliantly elaborated. They are the generic attitudes and qualities without which big democracy cannot meaningfully survive.

MENTAL ATTITUDES

The moral public servant must be aware of the moral ambiguity of all men (including himself) and of all public policies (including those recommended by him). Reinhold Niebuhr once stated this imperative in the following terms: "Man's capacity for justice makes democracy possible, but man's inclination to injustice makes democracy necessary."[7] American public ethics finds its historic roots in the superficially incompatible streams of Calvinism and Deism. The former emphasized a depravity which must be contained; the latter emphasized a goodness which must be discovered and released. The relevance of this moral dualism to modern governance is patent. Any law or any act of administrative discretion based upon the assumption that most men will not seek to maximize their own economic advantage when reporting assets for income tax purposes would be quite unworkable. But so would any law or any act of administrative discretion which assumed that most men would use any and every ruse to avoid paying taxes at all. Similarly, any administrative decision threatening the chances of reelection of a powerfully placed Congressman almost inevitably invokes counterforces which may be serious both for the decision-maker and for the program he or his agency espouses. But administrative decisions fashioned totally out of deference to private ambitions and personal interests can negate the very purposes of general government and can induce the righteous reaction of a voting public.

The fact is that there is no way of avoiding the introduction of personal and private interests into the calculus of public decisions.

[7] *The Children of Light and the Children of Darkness* (New York: Scribners, 1944), p. xi of Foreword.

As James Harvey Robinson once wrote, "In all governmental policy there have been overwhelming elements of personal favoritism and private gain, which were not suitable for publication. This is owing to the fact that all governments are managed by human beings, who remain human beings even if they are called kings, diplomats, ministers, secretaries, or judges, or hold seats in august legislative bodies. No process has been discovered by which promotion to a position of public responsibility will do away with a man's interest in his own welfare, his partialities, race, and prejudices. Yet most books on government neglect these conditions; hence their unreality and futility."[8] The most frequently hidden agenda in the deliberations of public servants is the effect of substantive or procedural decisions upon the personal lives and fortunes of those deliberating. And yet the very call to serve a larger public often evokes a degree of selflessness and nobility on the part of public servants beyond the capacity of cynics to recognize or to believe. Man's feet may wallow in the bog of self-interest, but his eyes and ears are strangely attuned to calls from the mountaintop. As moral philosophy has insistently claimed, there is a fundamental moral distinction between the propositions "I want this because it serves my interest," and "I want this because it is right."

The fact that man is as much a rationalizing as a rational animal makes the problem of either proving or disproving disinterestedness a tricky and knotty business. "I support the decision before us because it is good for the public," may emerge as a rationalization of the less elevated but more highly motivational proposition: "I support the decision before us because it will help reelect me, or help in my chances for promotion, recognition, or increased status." But the latter may have emerged, in turn, from a superordinate proposition: "Only if I am reelected (or promoted) can I maximize my powers in the interests of the general citizenry." Unfortunately, no calipers exist for measuring the moral purity of human motivations.

But, in any case, few would deny the widespread moral hunger to justify actions on a wider and higher ground than personal self-interest. In fact, the paradox is that man's self-respect is in large part determined by his capacity to make himself and others believe that self is an inadequate referent for decisional morality. This capacity of man to transcend, to sublimate, and to transform narrowly vested compulsions is at the heart of all civilized morality. That this capacity is exercised imperfectly and intermittently is less astounding than the fact that it is exercised at all. Man's capacity for benevolent and disinter-

---

[8] *The Human Comedy* (London: The Bodley Head, 1937), p. 232.

ested behavior is both a wonder and a challenge to those who work below, beside, and above him. It is in recognition of this moral reality that Appleby wrote in one of his most eloquent statements that "the manner and means of supporting one's own convictions, including inventiveness in perceiving how high ground may be held, are one measure of skill in the administrative process."[9]

But appeal to high morality is usually insufficient. It is in appreciating the reality of self-interest that public servants find some of the strongest forces for motivating behavior—public and private. Normally speaking, if a public interest is to be orbited, it must have as a part of its propulsive fuel a number of special and particular interests. A large part of the art of public service is in the capacity to harness private and personal interests to public interest causes. Those who will not traffic in personal and private interests (if such interests are themselves within the law) to the point of engaging their support on behalf of causes in which both public and private interests are served are, in terms of moral temperament, unfit for public responsibility.

But there is a necessary moral corollary: a recognition of the morally ambivalent effect of all public policies. There is no public decision whose moral effect can be gauged in terms of what game theorists refer to as a "zero-sum" result: a total victory for the right and a total defeat for the wrong. This ineluctable fact is not only because "right" and "wrong" are incapable of universally accepted definition. It is because an adequate response to any social evil contains the seeds of both predictable and unpredictable pathologies. One can, in the framing of laws or decisions, attempt to anticipate and partly to mitigate the predictable pathologies (although this is rarely possible in any complete sense). But one mark of moral maturity is in the appreciation of the inevitability of untoward and often malignant effects of benign moral choices. An Egyptian once commented that the two most devastating things to have happened to modern Egypt were the Rockefeller Foundation and the Aswan Dam. By enhancing public health, the Rockefeller Foundation had upset the balance of nature with horrendous consequences for the relationship of population to food supplies; by slowing the Nile, the Aswan Dam had promoted the development of enervating parasites in the river. The consequence of the two factors was that more people lived longer in more misery.

The bittersweet character of all public policy needs little further elaboration: welfare policies may mitigate hunger but promote parasitic dependence; vacationing in forests open for public recreation may

[9] *Op. cit.*, p. 222.

destroy fish, wild life, and, through carelessness in the handling of fire, the forests themselves. Unilateral international action may achieve immediate results at the cost of weakening international instruments of conflict resolution. Half a loaf *may* be worse than no loaf at all. It also may be better in the long run but worse in the short run—and vice versa.

Awareness of these dilemmas and paradoxes can immobilize the sensitive policy-maker. That is one of the reasons why both optimism and courage are imperative moral qualities in the public service. At best, however, awareness of moral ambiguity creates a spirit of humility in the decision-maker and a willingness to defer to the views of others through compromise. Humility and a willingness to compromise are priceless attributes in the life-style of the generality of public servants in a free society. For they are the preconditions of those fruitful accommodations which resolve conflict and which allow the new to live tolerably with the old. Humility, however, must not be equated with obsequiousness, nor willingness to compromise with a weak affability. As Harold Nicolson once wrote, "It would be interesting to analyze how many false decisions, how many fatal misunderstandings have arisen from such pleasant qualities as shyness, consideration, affability or ordinary good manners. It would be a mistake . . . to concentrate too exclusively upon those weaknesses of human nature which impede the intelligent conduct of discussion. The difficulties of precise negotiation arise with almost equal frequency from the more amiable qualities of the human heart."[10]

Men and measures, then, are morally ambiguous. Even if this were not a basic truth about the human condition, however, moral judgments in the public service would be made difficult by the shifting sands of context. An awareness of the contextual conditions which affect the arranging of moral priorities is an essential mental attitude for the moral public servant.

The moral virtues of the Boy Scout oath are widely accepted in the United States. But, as Boy Scouts get older, they are faced time and again with the disturbing fact that contexts exist within which it is impossible to be both kind and truthful at the same time. Boy Scouts are trustworthy. But what if they are faced with competing and incompatible trusts (e.g., to guard the flag at the base and to succor a distant wounded companion)? Men should be loyal, but what if loyalties conflict?

To the morally sensitive public servant, the strains of establishing

[10] Quoted by James Reston, in *The New York Times*, April 11, 1957.

a general value framework for conducting the public business is nothing compared to the strains of re-sorting specific values in the light of changing contexts. The dilemmas here are genuine. If value priorities are shifted with every passing wind, the shifter will suffer from his developing reputation as an opportunist. If value priorities are never adjusted, the saints come marching in and viable democratic politics goes marching out. To be consistent enough to deserve ethical respect from revered colleagues and from oneself; to be pliable enough to survive within an organization and to succeed in effectuating moral purposes—this is the dilemma and the glory of the public service.

In general, the higher a person goes on the rungs of power and authority, the more wobbly the ethical ladder. It is not the function of the junior civil servant in a unit of a branch of a bureau to worry about congressional relations—except on specific mandate from above. But a bureau chief, an assistant secretary, under-secretary, or secretary of a department may find himself contextually conditioned to respond frequently to congressional forces whose effect it is to undermine the integrity of the hierarchical arrangements in the executive branch. The heroic proportions of the Presidency become clear when one recognizes that the winds are fiercest and most variable above the timber line. The very fact that the President has fewer moments in the day than there are critical problems to be solved, and that crises often emerge unheralded, means an unevenness in the application of his time and attention to adjusting or influencing the moral niceties of any single issue. Appleby understood this when he wrote, "On many matters he [the President] will appear rather neutral; beyond enumerating items in messages and budgets he can expend his time and energies on only a few things. On as many matters as possible he normally yields for the sake of larger concerns."[11] The crucial word is "yields." Put in another way, if the President had more time and staff assistance he would "yield" to far fewer private and petty claims than he presently supports tacitly or openly.

During the Kennedy administration, the President called together a small group of top legislators, cabinet officers, and executive office staff to advise him on whether he should support the extension of price supports for cotton. His staff reminded him of the bonanza which price supports gave to the biggest and wealthiest cotton farmers. Legislative and cabinet leaders reminded him that a Presidential veto on an important agricultural bill could mean forfeiting key and critical legislative support on subsequent domestic and international matters of

[11] *Op. cit.*, p. 127.

overriding importance to the nation's security and welfare. The President agreed not to veto the bill, but the moral torment was there. According to one witness, he stared at the wall and mumbled to himself, "There is something wrong here. We are giving money to those who don't need it. If I am reelected in 1964, I'm going to turn this government upside down."

President Eisenhower was an honorable chief executive. Yet he publicly lied about the U-2 affair. The context was the crucial determinant.

If the heat in the ethical kitchen grows greater with each level of power, no public servant is immune from some heat—some concern with context. As Appleby has written, "A special favor, in administration even—as by a traffic policeman to a blind person or a cripple—would be regarded as a political good when it appears an act of equity compensating for underprivilege."[12]

There is not a moral vice which cannot be made into a relative good by context. There is not a moral virtue which cannot in peculiar circumstances have patently evil results. The mental attitude which appreciates this perversity can be led, of course, into a wasteland of ethical relativity. But this is by no means either inevitable or in the American culture even probable. Where this attitude tends to lead the mature public servant is toward a deep respect for the inconstant forces which swirl around public offices, and toward a deeper understanding of the reasons why moral men sometimes appear to make unethical public decisions. An old American Indian proverb is relevant: "Do not scoff at your friend until you have walked three miles in his moccasins." Because it is not easy for any man to place himself empathetically in the arena of moral dilemmas faced by another man, charity is a difficult moral virtue to maintain with any constancy. But as we shall review more fully below, charity is an essential moral quality in the public service of a democracy.

The third mental attitude which the public servant of a free society must cultivate is a recognition of the paradoxes of procedures. Justice Frankfurter once wrote, "The history of American freedom is, in no small measure, the history of procedure."[13] Rules, standards, procedures exist, by and large, to promote fairness, openness, depth of analysis, and accountability in the conduct of the public's business. Those who frequently by-pass or short-cut established means are thereby attacking one aspect of that most precious legacy of the past:

---

[12] *Op. cit.*, p. 65.
[13] Felix Frankfurter, *Malinski v. New York*, 324, U.S. 401, 414, 1945.

the rule of law. Official whim is the enemy of a civilized social order. Not only does it sow the seeds of anarchy in organization, it denies to a new idea the tempering which the heat of procedural gauntlets normally provides. John Mill's "market place" is of little utility if an idea is never allowed to enter the town at all.

But, alas, if procedures are the friend of deliberation and order, they are also at times the enemy of progress and dispatch. Furthermore, there are procedures and procedures. There are apt procedures and inept procedures. The only really bitter comments in *Morality and Administration* are reserved for those members of the legal profession who believe that administration should be circumscribed by precise legal norms, and that a series of administrative courts should be the effective arbiters and sanctioners of administrative discretion.[14] And this, of course, is only one aspect of the problem. Juridic procedures aside, both administration and legislation are frequently encumbered by rules and clearances which limit both responsiveness and the accountability they were presumably designed to enhance. The Rules Committee of the House of Representatives is not only the guardian of orderly procedures, it is the graveyard of important social measures. The contract and personnel policies of many agencies—federal, state, and local—have frequently led to what Wallace Sayre has termed "the triumph of technique over purpose." Anyone who has been closely associated with reorganization studies and proposals knows that every shift in organization—in the structural means for accomplishing governmental ends—is pregnant with implications for the ends themselves. Only a two-dimensional mind can possibly entertain seriously the notion that the structural and procedural aspects of government are unrelated to competing philosophies of substantive purpose.

The public servant who cannot recognize the paradoxes of procedures will be trapped by them. For in the case of procedures, he who deviates frequently is subversive; he who never deviates at all is lost; and he who tinkers with procedures without an understanding of substantive consequence is foolish. Of all governmental roles, the administrative role is procedurally the most flexible. But even here procedural flexibility in the public interest is achieved only by the optimistic, the courageous, and the fair.

MORAL QUALITIES

If mental attitudes related to the moral ambiguities, contextual priorities, and procedural paradoxes of public life are necessary prerequisites to ethical behavior on the part of public servants, they are

---

[14] See especially *op. cit.,* Chap. 4.

insufficient to such behavior. Attitudes must be supported by moral qualities—by operating virtues. A list of all relevant virtues would be a long one: patience, honesty, loyalty, cheerfulness, courtesy, humility —where does one begin or stop? One begins beyond the obvious and ends where essentiality ends. In the American context, at least, the need for the virtue of honesty is too obvious to need elaboration. Although Appleby has a chapter on "Venality in Government," he properly dismisses the issue with a single sentence: "Crude wrong doing is not a major, general problem of our government." And he continues with the pregnant remark, "Further moral advance turns upon more complicated and elevated concerns."[15]

The three *essential* moral qualities in the public service are optimism, courage, and fairness tempered by charity.

Optimism is an inadequate term. It connotes euphoria, and public life deals harshly with the euphoric. But optimism is a better word than realism, for the latter dampens the fires of possibility. Optimism, to paraphrase Emerson, is the capacity to settle with some consistency on the "sunnier side of doubt." It is the quality which enables man to face ambiguity and paradox without becoming immobilized. It is essential to purposive as distinct from reactive behavior. Hannah Arendt once commented that the essence of politics was natality not mortality. Politics involves creative responses to the shifting conflicts and the gross discomfitures of mankind. Without optimism on the part of the public servants, the political function cannot be performed. There is no incentive to create policies to better the condition of mankind if the quality of human life is in fact unviable, and if mankind is in any case unworthy of the trouble.

Optimism has not been the religious, philosophical, or literary mood of the twentieth century. But in spite of a series of almost cataclysmic absurdities it has been the prevailing mood of science, education, and politics. It is the mood of the emerging nations; it is the mood of the space technologist; it is the mood of the urban renewer. Government without the leavening of optimistic public servants quickly becomes a cynical game of manipulation, personal aggrandizement, and parasitic security. The ultimate corruption of free government comes not from the hopelessly venal but from the persistently cynical. Institutional decadence has set in when the optimism of leadership becomes a ploy rather than an honest mood and a moral commitment. True optimism is not Mr. Micawber's passive assumption that something will turn up; true optimism is the affirmation of the worth of taking risks. It is not a belief in sure things; it is the capacity to see the possi-

[15] *Op. cit.,* p. 56.

bilities for good in the uncertain, the ambiguous, and the inscrutable.

Organic aging and the disappointments and disaffections of experience often deprive mature individuals of the physical and psychic vitality which in youth is a surrogate for optimism. That is why optimism as a moral virtue—as a life-style—is one of the rare treasures sought by all personnel prospectors whose responsibility it is to mine the common lodes for extraordinary leadership talent. This is true in all organizations; it is especially true in the public service. What else do we mean, when we speak disparagingly of "bureaucratic drones," than that they are those who have entered the gates of Dante's Hell and have "abandoned all hope?"

In the midst of World War II when crises were breaking out at every moment and from every quarter, an ancient White House clerk was caught by a frenetic Presidential aide whistling at his work. The aide asked, "My God, man, don't you know what's going on?" The clerk replied, "Young man, you would be terrified if you knew how little I cared." A sprinkling of such in the public service can be tolerated as droll. If a majority, or even a substantial minority of public servants become jaded, however, especially at leadership levels, an ethical rot settles in, which ultimately destroys the capacity of a government to function effectively in the public interest.

The second essential moral quality needed in the public service is courage. Personal and public life are so shot through with ambiguities and paradoxes that timidity and withdrawal are quite natural and normal responses for those confronted with them. The only three friends of courage in the public service are ambition, a sense of duty, and a recognition that inaction may be quite as painful as action.

Courage in government and politics takes many forms. The late President John F. Kennedy sketched a series of profiles of one type of courage—abiding by principle in an unpopular cause. But most calls upon courage are less insistent and more pervasive. In public administration, for example, courage is needed to ensure that degree of impersonality without which friendship oozes into inequities and special favors. Appleby relates a relevant story about George Washington. Washington told a friend seeking an appointment: "You are welcome to my house; you are welcome to my heart. . . . My personal feelings have nothing to do with the present case. I am not George Washington, but President of the United States. As George Washington, I would do anything in my power for you. As President, I can do nothing."[16] Normally it takes less courage to deal impersonally with

[16] *Op. cit.*, p. 130.

identifiable interest groups than with long-standing associates and colleagues upon whom one has depended over the years for affection and for professional and personal support. This is true in relationship to those inside as well as those outside the organization. Part of the loneliness of authority comes from the fact, again in the words of Paul Appleby, that "to a distinctly uncomfortable degree [the administrator] must make work relationships impersonal."[17] Appleby was quick to see that impersonality invites the danger of arrogance, but he also saw that the courage to be impersonal in complicated organizational performance is generally valuable as far as the affected public is concerned. "Its tendency is to systematize fair dealing and to avoid whimsy and discrimination—in other words to provide a kind of administrative due process."[18]

The need for this kind of courage on a day-to-day basis is probably greater, and more difficult to conjure, in the legislative than in either the executive or the judicial branches of government.

A second area for consistent courage in the public service is to be found in the relationship of general administrators to experts and specialists. It takes quite as much courage to face down minority expert opinion as it does to face down the majority opinion of a clamoring crowd. In some ways it takes more, for relationships with experts are usually intimate in the decisional process, whereas relations with the crowd are often distant and indistinct. Both courage and wisdom are reflected in the words of Sir Winston Churchill: "I knew nothing about science, but I knew something about scientists, and had had much practice as a minister in handling things I did not understand."[19]

Perhaps on no issue of public ethics is Appleby more insistent than on the necessity of experts being kept in their proper place—subordinate to politicians and general administrators. "Perhaps," he wrote, "there is no single problem in public administration of moment equal to the reconciliation of the increasing dependence upon experts with an unending democratic reality."[20] The expert, whether professional, procedural, or programmatic, is essential to the proper functioning of a complex and highly technical social system. But the autonomous or disproportionate power of experts, and of the limited worlds they comprehend, is a constant threat to more general consideration of the public good.

[17] *Op. cit.*, p. 221.
[18] *Op. cit.*, p. 149.
[19] *Life*, February 28, 1949, p. 61.
[20] *Op. cit.*, p. 145.

During World War II, a 25-year-old civil servant in the soap division of O.P.A. found himself, because of the temporary absence of superiors, dealing directly with the president and legal staff of Lever Brothers. After a few minutes of confrontation the president of Lever Brothers turned scornfully to the government employee and asked, "Young man, what do you know about soap?" A strong voice replied, "Sir, I don't know much about soap, but I know a hell of a lot about price control."

This is the courage needed by a Budget Bureau examiner in dealing with the Pentagon; this is the courage needed by an Assistant Secretary of Health, Education, and Welfare in dealing with the Surgeon General; this is the courage needed by a transient mayor in dealing with a career engineer in the public works department; this is the courage needed by a Congressman faced with appraising the "expert" testimony of an important banker in his district.

Perhaps the most essential courage in the public service is the courage to decide. For if it is true that all policies have bittersweet consequences, decisions invariably produce hurt. President Eliot of Harvard once felt constrained to say that the prime requisite of an executive was his willingness to give pain. Much buck-passing in public life is the prudent consequence of the need for multiple clearances in large and complex institutions. But buck-passing which stems from lack of moral courage is the enemy of efficient and responsible government. The inner satisfactions which come from the courage to decide are substantial; but so are the slings and arrows which are invariably let loose by those who are aggrieved by each separate decision. The issues become especially acute in personnel decisions. Courage to fire, to demote, to withhold advancement, or to shift assignments against the wishes of the person involved, is often the courage most needed and the most difficult to raise.

The third and perhaps most essential moral quality needed in the public service is fairness tempered with charity. The courage to be impersonal and disinterested is of no value unless it results in just and charitable actions and attitudes. Government in a free society is the authoritative allocator of values in terms of partly ineffable standards of justice and the public weal. It requires the approximation of moving targets partly camouflaged by the shadows of an unknowable future. The success or failure of policies bravely conceived to meet particular social evils is more frequently obscured than clarified by the passage of time. As R. G. Collingwood once pointed out, "The only thing that a shrewd and critical Greek like Herodotus would say about the divine power that ordains the course of history is that . . . it rejoices in upsetting and disturbing things."[21]

What remains through the disorder and unpredictability of history is the sense on the part of the public and of working colleagues that power for whatever ends was exercised fairly and compassionately. The deepest strain in our ethical heritage is "man's sense of injustice." The prophetic voices of the old Testament repaired time and again to this immemorial standard. "Let Justice roll down like waters . . ." Hesiod, speaking for generations of ancient Greeks, wrote "Fishes and beasts and fowls of the air devour one another. But to men Zeus has given justice. Beside Zeus on his throne Justice has her seat."[22] Justice was the only positive heritage of the Roman World. The establishment of justice follows directly behind the formation of union itself in the Preamble to the American Constitution.

But the moral imperative to be just—to be fair—is a limited virtue without charity. Absolute justice presupposes omniscience and total disinterestedness. Public servants are always faced with making decisions based upon both imperfect information and the inarticulate insinuations of self-interest into the decisional calculus. Charity is the virtue which compensates for inadequate information and for the subtle importunities of self in the making of judgments designed to be fair. Charity is not a soft virtue. To the contrary, it involves the ultimate moral toughness. For its exercise involves the disciplining of self and the sublimation of persistent inner claims for personal recognition, power, and status. It is the principle above principle. In the idiom of the New Testament, it is the losing of self to find self. Its exercise makes of compromise not a sinister barter but a recognition of the dignity of competing claimants. It fortifies the persuasive rather than the coercive arts. It stimulates the visions of the good society without which government becomes a sullen defense of existing patterns of privilege.

The normative systems of politics and organization which Appleby elaborated in his writings are umbilically related to the mental attitudes and moral qualities of the individual moral actor in the public service. They nourish these attitudes and qualities. They condition and promote public morality. But the reverse is also true. Without proper mental attitudes and moral qualities on the part of the public servant,

---

[21] *The Idea of History* (Oxford: Clarendon Press, 1946), p. 22.

[22] Quoted in Edith Hamilton, *The Greek Way* (New York: W. W. Norton, 1930), p. 292.

Appleby's normative systems could neither exist nor be meaningfully approximated.

The intermeshing of the mental attitudes and moral qualities of the individual moral actor with the institutional arrangements elaborated by Paul Appleby produces in effect a working definition of the public interest. Men of good will may disagree on what amalgam of commonly shared interests of the nation's several publics constitutes a *substantive* public interest. What this essay attempts to suggest is that normative, procedural, institutional, attitudinal, and moral standards do exist which preserve and promote a public interest far more fundamental than any set of transient policies can possibly preserve or promote.

Bureaucracy and technology are the pervasive realities of modern civilization. Together they have made possible order, prosperity, and mobility in unprecedented magnitudes; but unfortunately they have demonstrated a perverse tendency to drain from man the blood of his essential humanity. The nobility of any society is especially encapsulated and made manifest to the world in the personal example of its public leaders and public servants. Perhaps, therefore, Appleby's writings about morality and government—no matter how wise and how provocative—were of less importance than the lessons of his example as a public servant. For in selecting the mental attitudes and moral qualities of the moral public servant, I have been guided far more by my memories of Paul Appleby than by my perusal of his writings. Appleby in his public career demonstrated an uncommon understanding of the moral ambiguities, the contextual priorities, and the paradoxes of procedures in ethical governance. Of all men of my acquaintance in public life, he was the most completely endowed in the moral qualities of optimism, courage, and fairness tempered by charity. While his wisdom illuminated everything he observed and experienced, his example shone even more brilliantly than his wisdom.

The Spanish philosopher Unamuno, thinking of Goethe's dying words, "Light, light, more light," declared passionately, "No! warmth, warmth, more warmth, for we die of cold, not of darkness. It is not the night that kills, but the frost."[23]

Without denigrating the richness of his intellectual contributions, Paul Appleby's charity of spirit was perhaps his fundamental contribution to ethics and the public service.

[23] Douglas V. Sheere, "The Golden Rule," in R. M. McIver, ed., *Great Expressions of Human Rights* (New York: Harper & Bros., 1950), p. 55.

· 16 ·

Responsibility in Administration:
An Exploratory Essay

ROWLAND EGGER

Since Democritus in the fifth century B.C. affirmed the reality of atoms, and insisted that all else was merely opinion, and especially since Francis Bacon of Verulam four hundred years ago restated the principles of inductive method, and in so doing hopelessly confused a mere logical technique with truth itself, many men have sought to achieve intellectual impregnability in the denial of reality to anything that is not "objective" fact. In disregard of the evidence readily at hand that there is little significantly quantifiable, measurable, or inductively demonstrable about many of the great "subjective" events which are among the most potent determinants of men's actions, logical positivism has asserted that the only important truths are those objective facts susceptible of inductive proof and empirical demonstration—which, they contend, condition and control all subjective states. In this view, human beings must ultimately reduce themselves to such phenomena as "economic men" inexorably buying in the cheapest market and selling in the dearest, "capitalists" unremittingly accumulating production goods and exploiting labor, "proletarians" endlessly resisting exploitation and awaiting the day when the inevitabilities of history will destroy both capitalism and capitalists, or "psychological types" blindly working out the imperatives of their conditioned reflexes.

At no time in modern history has the primacy of the demonstrable and measurable "objective" fact been less critically accepted in the popular mind than at present. Nor is it without significance that in the very hour of its triumph as an article of popular faith, it has collapsed as a postulate of the sciences the foundations of which were originally constructed on the dogmas of experimental and inductive certainty. I do not know of a single nuclear physicist who would agree with Laplace, for example, that the entire future of the universe could be forecast from the present state and velocity of every material thing in it. Indeed, since Heisenberg demonstrated that it is impossible to determine simultaneously the position and velocity of individual electrons, physics has preferred to speak in terms of probabilities rather than certainties.

The philosophical consequences of this change in the outlook of contemporary scientists are far-reaching. In respect of the fundamental problem of freedom and responsibility Arthur Compton has written:

> Over a considerable part of the history of science it has been thought that the world is a physically determined system, so that the experience of freedom must have little connection with physical events. With the advent of quantum mechanics, some thirty years ago, the thought of physicists in this regard has undergone a significant revolution. It is, I believe, fair to say that modern scientific theory does not dispute the possibility of the type of human freedom that implies human responsibility.
>
> Our scientific knowledge does not, however, give of itself any indication that such freedom exists. That we do in fact shape the world to our desires, just as the fact that we are aware of what is happening, is known only from our first hand experience. These facts are not obtainable through scientific observation, but they are nevertheless consistent with our scientific knowledge of the physical world.[1]

It is within this area of human freedom implying human responsibility, which scientific method cannot demonstrate objectively but which it is, in its newfound reasonableness, willing to admit may exist on the basis of such nonscientific evidence as first-hand experience, that humane knowledge plays its part in man's efforts to cope with his universe. There is a large area of elusive truth, important to all men but especially important to administrators, which it is extremely dangerous to neglect, but in application to which scientific method yields no important consequences or conclusions. In this area, since objective demonstration or experimental finality is impossible, only "operational" consensus can from time to time and for limited periods be achieved. There is very little difference, in terms of relative truth, between operational consensus of this sort and the probability which the physicist expresses as a mathematical equation in describing the nature of light.

Nor, as some psychologists have maintained, is man himself no more than a somewhat excessively elaborated Rube Goldberg production. The self is not, as William James contended, merely the sum of

[1] Arthur Compton, "The Case for Hope," *The Saturday Review*, June 18, 1955, p. 9.

its roles; it is much more significantly that which is aware of what is happening and conscious of itself as having roles. It is this subjective side of selfhood—this pervasive and ineradicable self-awareness—that in the opinion of many modern psychologists invalidates the mechanistic notion of the human personality. The fact that man has self-awareness enables him to choose his response in favor of one stimulus as against another, and in so doing volitionally to break the chain of the conditioned reflex. The more self-awareness he has the less difficulty he encounters in breaking the chain, and the better able he is to use the symbols of abstract thought, to deal with time, and to experience the urges and anxieties which propel him in the direction of independent choices and judgments.

Determinism dies hard. It involves not only the acceptance of responsibility, which is frequently disagreeable, but the confrontation of possibilities which are clearly disquieting. One of the more soporific corollaries of the deterministic view is the notion of the inevitability of progress that seems to have been inherent in at least the popular conception of it. If man is not able to do much about his destiny, the reasoning runs, it is also true that in view of the enormous material advances made by science and technology, he doesn't need to do much about it. What science and technology have done before they can, and will, do again and continue to do *ad infinitum*. Scientific and technological developments have always in the past turned out to be benevolent in their effects, and there is no reason to think that future advances will not redound to the benefit of man's ease, comfort and tranquility. But the collapse of the mechanistic approach to scientific phenomena has shaken rudely the idea of the inevitability of progress in the minds of scientists and philosophers. The development and application of nuclear energy to spectacularly nonbenevolent purposes, moreover, has demonstrated with terrifically sobering effect even to the man in the street that science's "stairway to the stars" runs in both directions. Which way he goes is up to man, and to the values incorporated in the mainly social judgments he makes about how to get there. He is on his own. Science will tell him little more than it has already told him, which is simply that E equals MC^2, and that is precisely where he got into trouble to begin with. As Lord Russell says, "Science can, if rulers so desire, create sentiments which will avert disaster and facilitate cooperation. At present there are powerful rulers who have no such wish. But the possibility exists, and science can be just as potent for good as for evil. It is not science, however, that will determine how science is used. Science, by itself, cannot supply us with an ethic. It can show us how to achieve a given end, and it may show us that some ends cannot be achieved. But among ends that can be achieved our choice must be decided by other than purely scientific considerations."[2]

ADMINISTRATION AND VALUES

Two hundred years ago Dr. Johnson could write, not inaccurately for the times:

How small of all that human hearts endure
That part which kings or law can cause or cure!

Two centuries before that Montaigne finds that he "doubts if he can honestly enough confess with how very mean a sacrifice of his peace of mind and tranquility he has lived more than half his life, whilst his country was in ruins." And the author of A Sentimental Journey enjoyed titillating his sensibilities with the thought that France and England were actually locked in the throes of a nearly mortal combat at the very moment he was posting, unchallenged, unperturbed, and lacking even a passport, down the road from Calais to Paris on his amorous pursuits.

Times have changed. In modern days government has not only the power but sometimes the necessity of influencing and even regulating the lives of private citizens in ways that turn Dr. Johnson's couplet inside out. Even in the best and most tolerant of administrative environments the gentle coerciveness of organized social control presses upon the individual with an intimacy and constancy that Montaigne and Lawrence Sterne would have found unendurable.

Latterly, and in fact for longer than most persons realize, kings and laws and the servants of the kingly and legislative functions at the working level of the public administration have been making value judgments and executing decisions that affect not only the routine transaction of the public business but the very destiny of mankind itself. The role of the public administrator has been pervasive, continuous, and more often than not predominant. The idea of administration, nonetheless, has continued to be relegated to a secondary position in a series of ideological dichotomies—government and administration, politics and administration, law and administration, policy and administration, etc. The dichotomies have actually been more useful in supporting theories of responsible government in an era of continuously expanding administrative activity than in describing the environment of the administrative process. To the extent that they have

[2] Bertrand Russell, "The Science to Save Us From Science," New York Times Magazine, March 19, 1950, p. 33.

encouraged a sense of security amongst the citizenry, and a sense— sometimes a delusion—of power amongst the ordinary politicians, they have served acceptably the needs of the emergent modern State.

These bifurcated pieces of ideological bric-a-brac have introduced an element of mechanistic determinism and at the same time avoided any confrontation of the value problem in the administrative process. If an administrator merely gives effect to constitutional provisions and laws passed by the legislative branch, executes decisions of the judiciary interpretive of the constitution and laws, or carries out policies evolved in the stratospheric echelons of the executive department, the value problem for him is defined out of existence. The legislators may have value problems, the judges may have value problems, and the chief executive or cabinet may have value problems, but the administrator in theory is in the happy position of possessing, so to speak, completely conditioned reflexes, and bearing no real responsibility for the consequences of his actions.

This interpretation of the administrator as a sort of ethical automaton is useful. It is certainly the proper posture for an official confronted with the necessity of appearing before a congressional committee, and few knowledgeable administrators assume any other. For many purposes it is a fiction well worth preserving. It is harmful only when it is believed—when the administrator succumbs to his own protocol. A public servant who is really convinced that his every official action is fully informed by incontrovertible legal sanctions, instructed by clear policy directives, and supported by objectively demonstrable fact is a dangerous person. He requires to be confined in a straitjacket.

For most of the time administration operates on persons and things in ways which constitutions and laws define in no adequate manner, which judicial decisions illuminate most imperfectly, and in which policy provides no explicit directions. Nor do the *quasi* fictions which have been invented to bolster legitimacy by the notion that in acting beyond the bounds of effective legal and political direction the administrator is somehow involved in a continuum of determinations in which the essence of the value problems has at some point been resolved by constitutionally responsible instrumentalities do much more than postpone very temporarily the day of reckoning.

In these circumstances the administrator, who like other rational men feels the need for logic and consistency in his decisions from one day to the next and from one administrative situation to the next, requires some benchmarks for relating the various and frequently conflicting claims of competing values which enter into his official actions. He will not find these benchmarks in the terms of delegated legislation, because all that legislative bodies and the courts have been able to do in protecting the value content of the determinations which they cannot themselves conclude is to describe the methods and procedures to be followed—the procedural due process, but not the substantive values involved—in certain sorts of administrative decisions. Delegated administrative authority, moreover, customarily defines only the level in the administrative hierarchy where the determination is made, not the substantive values of the determination. And in performing one of his most important functions—that of rendering advice to constitutionally responsible instrumentalities of government—the public official is directly involved in the formulation of legislative and executive policy itself. Eventually, the administrator finds his back to the wall, where he must consult his conscience and consider the gods he worships.

The limitations of constitutional and statutory legislation, judicial decisions, and policy directives as comprehensive determinants of administrative action are implicit in the premises. A statute, a judicial opinion, or a statement of policy is an event in time. It normally derives from definite, and often highly specific, circumstances. The ends it seeks to serve are usually technical, at least in their immediate implications. Like administrative decisions and administrative acts, it is the product of large numbers of largely unstated influences and determinants, frequently intuitional. It incorporates the common wisdom of the race in the same fluid and inchoate way that other kinds of intuitional value judgments enunciate the thoughts we live by. The possession of some of the impedimenta of reflective morality—an awareness of some of the organizing ideas around which thought concerning specific ethical issues may be managed—is as necessary to an adequate understanding of law and policy as it is to administrative decision and action. Indeed, the justification for investing time and effort in thought about the ethical aspects of administrative problems is not that it may produce brilliant "revelations" of means for the implementation of incomprehensible law and policy, but that it may reveal the ethical and moral context from which they derive and permit the maintenance of a consistent and perhaps corrective ethical continuum in the administrative process.

In rejecting the traditional dichotomies as oversimplifying the role of the administrator by defining his value problems out of existence, it is important not to swing too far in the opposite direction. Not every administrative situation involves a value problem, and in many administrative situations the value problems are so inconsequential that they can hardly be weighed in the process of coming to a decision. An administrator who wrestles earnestly with all the possible ethical alternatives that present themselves in the course of his life is likely to wind up not only a major administrative bottleneck, but also an extremely harassed man, and perhaps even hopelessly schizophrenic.

When it is said that for certain limited purposes it is possible to differentiate some aspects of administration from the rest of the governmental process—politics, legislation, judicial determination, policy formulation, etc.—what is meant is that some administrative operations derive their immediate values internally from the nature of the process, rather than externally from the purposes of the organization. Certainly, much of what is currently comprehended under the rubric "Organization and Methods" is of this nature, although we are well aware that concern with the policy process is more often than not derived from a desire to change or influence the substantive decisions the process produces. It is important, however, for both practical and philosophical purposes to identify that substantial part of the administrative process that is not dominated by the imperatives of politics, law, policy, and other external values, to protect it from the incursion of irrelevant influences, and to deal with it through the kinds of analysis and evaluation appropriate to operations absorbed into a technological context. To cope successfully with his value problems, the administrator must first establish some limitations on what he is willing to worry about, and make sure that the issues to which he attempts to apply ethical concepts actually call for judgments amongst alternative values. Those that can legitimately and harmlessly be settled by the cost accountants, the time-motion engineers, the sociometricians, and that entire galaxy of intellectual robots animated by the push-buttons of logical positivism had best be left to purely technological evaluation.

It is no easy task merely to isolate the value problems of administrative decisions, to say nothing of analyzing them correctly in the light both of their own alleged imperatives and of what Paul Appleby aptly called the "calculus" of the administrative process. But in a secular society, where administrative values must find their rationale within the precepts of the social system itself, and in a pluralistic society, where few ethical principles are uncontested and few value judgments are unchallenged, there is no refuge in authority and no solace in the confessional. In the American political system, moreover, with its tradition of unlimited legislative investigation and disclosure, it is impossible even to draw the curtain of official anonymity. The administrator can neither live in obscurity nor die in privacy. There is for him no escape from the consequences of his judgments, whatever the fiction of his responsibility.

Administrators have, of course, been confronting value problems and making value judgments for a long time. They have, in the main, solved or failed to solve them by recourse to intuitional judgments— common sense, they are more likely to call it. Common sense is not to be derided. It is a rare and valuable commodity. But it has its limitations. As long as fairly normal administrative problems are being dealt with and there is no necessity for defining terms carefully—which represents the situation in a large number of instances calling for some degree of value judgment—there is usually a considerable amount of consensus about what ought or ought not to be done. But the moment intuitional principles are confronted with unusual or difficult situations the consensus vanishes. Terms which at the outset appeared to be clear and simple are perceived to have contained scores of meanings and covered a multitude of alternatives. When these alternatives are introduced into the statement of a common-sense principle, the so-called common sense is likely to emerge as mere tautology or to lose its self-evident character. Many common-sense axioms, moreover, contradict themselves and each other in any except an extremely limited and literal connotation. If the formulation of higher intuitional principles is attempted in an effort to bring them into harmony and delimit their appropriate applicability, it is either found impossible, or the higher intuitional principle is so complicated that it is no longer self-evident, or the consequences admitted to consideration are so remote that the principle is no longer intuitional. Common sense, in short, is probably good enough for simple, unsubtle, and uncomplicated problems, but it is not likely to provide a satisfactory tool for dealing with difficult, complex, and pluralistic moral issues in which the choice is frequently between good and good.

The Appleby View of Administrative Responsibility

The problem of the administrator in living responsibly is part and parcel of his problem in living ethically. It is true that the institutional context in which he labors, and which in principle defines the limits of his obligations, more often than not fails to furnish the benchmarks of fully responsible choice. But it is no less true that a choice which fails to respond to the institutional context, no matter how fully buttressed by appeals to moral principle or ethical dictates, is always ultimately and often immediately lacking in viability. No administrative philosopher has better understood the interpenetration of responsibility and morality than Paul Appleby, and his preoccupation with morality and administration was in no sense inferior to his interest in administrative responsibililty. In the last book he wrote, *Citizens as Sovereigns,* he summed up in these words:

As Americans mature it is their sovereign responsibility to exact higher types of leadership and to give that leadership better structures in which local egoisms yield more readily to a patriotism which, while deeper than ever, has attained a new breadth. Realization of self-interest can no longer have less than planetary perspective and implementation. But the instruments of the ablest leaders must be basically institutional. Our new professions at the world level will not be in fact reassuring except as we demonstrate that we have learned to conduct our own institutional affairs in sufficiently whole-nation terms.[3]

The ultimate sanction of administrative responsibility, in Appleby's construct, is politics. His commitment to the principle of political control is unequivocal. The immediate sanction of responsibility, however, is administrative hierarchy. What differentiates Appleby's notion of administrative responsibility from the sterile and mechanistic concept of the administrative automaton is his understanding of the potential depth and richness of the policy process in a society dedicated to the achievement of political, social, and economic democracy. Appleby believed in hierarchy, but his hierarchy was not the institutionalization of the pecking order. It was rather the structuring of a network of intelligence and communication which provides a matrix of abundantly diverse and catholic values and influences for the decisions of a pluralistic society. He did not seek simplicity in the processes of an incredibly complicated polity, and he was not really joking at all when in one of the near-puns of which he was fond he assigned a high value on the scale of administrative sophistication to the capacity to "make a mesh out of things." Indeed, he believed firmly that the function of an administrator was to complicate the lives of his political masters at least to the extent of assuring that they did not resolve complex issues on the basis of disingenuously simple criteria.

The central importance of responsibility in administration is a recurrent theme in Appleby's writing and a major premise of his public philosophy. He has directed his attention to the institutionalization of administrative responsibility in several of his books, perhaps in greater depth in his chapters on "Structure, Hierarchy and Co-ordination" and on "Administrative Power" in *Policy and Administration* than elsewhere. In this volume he makes quite explicit the uses of logical and discrete structural arrangements which facilitate and encourage "procedure through proper channels," and of the values contributed by

[3] Paul H. Appleby, *Citizens as Sovereigns* (Syracuse: Syracuse University Press, 1962), p. 200.

various stages in the hierarchy to the decision-making process. He is no enemy of formal organization, nor does his recognition of the behavioral implications of informal organization dilute his conviction that the government normally operates in ways which generally support the institutionalized responsibilities of administrators as they are laid out, for example, in the *Government Organizational Manual*. But he does point out:

> A good deal of circumvention is essential, else all business would be handled by an impossibly difficult number of "steps," all of which are theoretically implicit in any organizational chart. It is circumvention that makes the transaction of business possible, it is the chart that makes the transaction of business responsible. It is the *right of access*—rather than invariable handling—that supports responsibility, and it is the exercise of individual judgment concerning the need of hierarchical associates having the right of access on which the whole business turns. That judgment is quickened by administrative sanctions, competitive prerogatives, and the political environment. Learning comes from burning fingers. That which is likely to make trouble, trouble with associates, competing groups or affected citizens, is that which is "checked" both laterally and perpendicularly before action is taken.[4]

In a governmental system of diffused and interpenetrating power, either lateral or perpendicular checking frequently takes the administrator outside the administrative hierarchy, and injects him into other, and frequently countervailing, power systems. Writing in a broader vein of administrative responsibility, Appleby has observed:

> Administrative power, widely diffused and much more widely influenced and controlled, is just one aspect of governmental power. The power of the government is cooperatively exercised. To a considerable degree it is self-controlled by the interaction of its own parts. But this is so because both the parts and the whole are politically controlled. The problem of power here is less that it may be arbitrary than that it may be unwise. Numbers of participants do not assure wisdom. A free people is free to go wrong. If it remains free, however, it is free to correct its mistakes. . . .
>
> Administrators share with all others in places of special re-

---

[4] Paul H. Appleby, *Policy and Administration* (University, Alabama: University of Alabama Press, 1949), p. 77.

sponsibility the special obligations of leadership. They can, in all innocence, contribute to organizational practices and forms elements which are inimical to popular government. They can help "take things out of politics"—or take themselves too far out of politics. They, like citizens and legislators, are capable of yielding too much to the prestige of military or other experts, too little to the politician who is the central factor in civilian control and popular government. By dealing with the legislature too directly, they may undermine and confuse executive responsibility; by the same tactics they may inadvertently substitute control by members of Congress for control by Congress as a body. By failing to be imaginative about legislative needs, attitudes and prerogatives, they may overburden, and thus degrade, the legislature. Their special duty is in part to help clear the way so that the other parts of government and the other political processes may function well.[5]

An earlier book by Appleby, *Big Democracy*, defines the qualities needed by the men who administer the great government agencies in a way which throws considerable light on his conception of responsibility in administration:

> The qualities include, perhaps first, an ability something like that required for higher mathematics. Trigonometry is no less practical and precise than arithmetic. It comprehends arithmetic but in a way of relating and simplifying the handling of relationships between various arithmetical calculations. What is needed is the ability to handle relationships in their larger and broader terms— the quality of philosophy. This means a capacity to see public policy in tens of thousands of different actions and to relate these actions to each other in terms of public and governmental interest. Efficient "operators" we have in great numbers. They are capable of serving well on the higher levels of government management only if they have this quality of philosophy.
>
> The kind of philosophy is of course important. A philosophy of absolutes and cold logic, a philosophy technical and rigid, would be ruinous. A sound political philosophy must comprehend people's spirits and emotions as well as their reasoned opinions; it must embody the logic of events and sentiments, and not merely the logic of statistics.
>
> The second quality needed by the top executive is "governmental sense," the ingrained disposition to put the public interest

[5] *Ibid.*, pp. 118-19.

first and thus to recognize the great, essential, and pervasive difference that distinguishes public administration from the management of private enterprise.

Related to governmental sense is a third quality of public-relations or political sense. This involves, on the one hand, an appreciation of the necessity for governmental officials and governmental action to be exposed to the citizens and the public affected by them and, on the other, an ability to anticipate probable popular reaction and to make allowance for it. It also includes the capacity to act swiftly in introducing minor administrative adjustments when such action will relieve public irritation and the ability to sense major political shifts in the early stages of their development and gradually to modify the program of the agency accordingly. No matter how elevated they may be, however, administrators can never have the fullness of wisdom. Fortunately, they need not have it. Events and national sentiments will make the bigger and the ultimate decisions. Executives and administrative experts, working together, simply give form to specific programs and mechanisms within the framework of larger national movements. The capacity to sense the coming of these movements is political sense at its highest level.

Ability to be governmental enough to discern the national interest and to insist on programs and procedures so sound that they will be as unyielding rock on which the waves of special interest may break their force in vain; ability to be political enough to seek those concessions which are the needed refinements of the process of making governmental action equitable and smooth; ability to be political enough to read and respond to the messages of public currents; and ability to use administrators who can organize and relate agencies so that they produce organized, integrated action—this is the combination of abilities required for the relatively few top people in the great agencies of government.[6]

Responsibility in administration as Appleby has described it from these three distinct, but thoroughly consistent, points of view obviously goes far beyond statutory authorities, policy directives, and standard operating procedures. It is important for the administrator to have read "the book." It is important for him to square his decisions and actions with the intent of the book. But in a larger sense, and certainly with respect to the vital administrative issues, responsibility takes up where the book leaves off.

[6] Paul H. Appleby, *Big Democracy* (New York: Knopf, 1945), pp. 43-44.

The point at which responsibility takes up is the nexus at which it confronts the notion of the public interest. This issue is, of course, central to the entire body of administrative and political theory. It has been the subject of a voluminous literature, of which Carl Friedrich's collection of essays in *Nomos V*[7] and Glendon Schubert's *The Public Interest*[8] are only the more recent. Paul Appleby never defined his conception of the public interest, probably for the same reason he never philosophized about water or air. He experienced them all constantly at first hand, and the public interest was as real to his conception of his public life as were water and air to the functioning of his physical organism. In his characterization of administration as the eighth political process he revealed his appreciation of the forces and influences which continually define and redefine the public interest in respect of particular issues, but nowhere did he attempt to come to grips with the *Ding an sich*. However, no man who practiced so superbly the administrative arts in the face-to-face society is likely to have been insensitive to the public interest either as a philosophical concept or as a benchmark of responsible administration.

THE PUBLIC INTEREST AS CONCEPT

As one reads and rereads in Friedrich and Schubert—to say nothing of Plato, Aristotle, and John Locke—the briefs of the superlatively brilliant contending counsel in the clash of ideologies concerning the public interest and administrative responsibility, one cannot but be profoundly impressed by the fact that they are all correct, and, to the extent that they pretend to inclusiveness and universality, all equally incorrect. This suggests that the authors are either writing about completely different things, or that their vantage points are so disparate that the things they are writing about appear completely different. Certainly, the public interest means many things to many people. In one context the emphasis is on the word public, and the phrase is assumed to refer to interests of wide or universal appeal as contrasted with interests of limited or special groups in the society. In this view the public interest, one assumes, would be expressed by the general will, and becomes, for all practical purposes, coincident with the general will. Whether an A. F. Bentley or a David Truman would concede the existence of a general will is in the one case impossible, and in the other perhaps impolitic, to discover. But with Bentley's and Truman's

---

[7] Carl J. Friedrich, ed., *Nomos V: The Public Interest* (New York: Atherton Press, 1962).

[8] Glendon Schubert, *The Public Interest* (Glencoe, Ill.: The Free Press, 1960).

rejection of the notion of a consciously held general public interest it is difficult to quarrel. This is not to say that a public interest superior to special interests does not exist, but merely that it does not exist by reason of being commonly held and recognized. Nor would it likely be discovered through a plebiscite.

From another point of view, the public interest may be regarded as the wisest or most foresighted interest. This emphasizes the prudential notion of the action most likely to contribute to the welfare of the maximum number of people, rather than the idea of a recognized interest widely or universally entertained throughout the society. Historically, this view of the public interest has been most frequently invoked in the projection of special interests as having a priority over other special interests by reason of the superior wisdom of their motivation. In its more primitive manifestations it emerges in such form as "What's good for General Motors is good for the country," which Mr. Wilson did not say, but which he could have said without stepping out of character. At the other end of the spectrum, the notion of the public interest as the wisest and most prudent interest is clearly implicit in the thinking of Appleby, Fainsod, Friedrich, Grundstein, and Redford.

In still another context the public interest may be regarded as a moral imperative, and in this interpretation appears ultimately to rest on natural law foundations. Walter Lippmann describes it as "what men would choose if they saw clearly, thought rationally, acted disinterestedly and benevolently." Mortimer Adler goes even further to define the public interest "in its strict meaning as ultimate moral perfection." If there is a categorical imperative for the guidance of public action, derived from theological or other sources, it is obviously in the public interest to pursue this absolute higher ethic. Or if, as some of the "new conservatives" aver, we have a transmitted ethic, rooted in a traditional moral standard which we receive along with our genes and protoplasmic arrangements, this provides the touchstone for the definition of the public interest. In either case, compromise is both unethical and immoral.

Others apparently entertain a wholly contrary view, and regard the public interest as compromise—as the optimum reconciliation of the competing claims of special and private interests. Such is clearly the view of Pendleton Herring, Chester Barnard, Harold Stein, and Avery Leiserson, of Arthur Fisher Bentley and David Truman, and is implicit in the writings of Philip Monypenny and Norton Long. Moreover, the doctrine was explicitly sanctified by the First Hoover Commission. This is not to say that the administrative philosophers who see the public interest as a process of compromise and adjustment embrace a raw and unrestrained doctrine of political Darwinism, or deliver themselves to a mechanistic view of administrative decision-making in which what is is good because it has survived. Pendleton Herring in particular has been at some pains to emphasize the importance of taking care of the unorganized and inchoate interests that may not be effectively represented in the arena of political and administrative combat—of the claims of freedom, of equality, of opportunity—and of making sure that the public interest is not defined solely in terms of those on hand and shouting at the time the issue is joined.

Arthur Holcombe has pointed out that while the public interest is defined by a process of accommodation and compromise, accommodation and compromise do not explain the public interest in its entirety.

> Action in the public interest means an adjustment of the conflicts between special interests in such a way as best to serve the common good of the whole body of people. The public interest is more than a particular special interest which is able to prevail in the adjustment of a conflict with other special interests. It is more than the sum of the special interests which gain recognition in a particular process of adjustment. It is more than the bare fact of an equilibrium among a group of special interests. It is nothing less than such an adjustment of conflicting special interests as can give the people durable confidence in the stability of the state itself.[9]

Is it reasonable to regard the public interest as commonly held value, not in the sense of universally entertained value judgments concerning political and administrative actions but in the sense of a continuing "durable confidence in the stability of the state"?

Is it reasonable to regard the public interest as the wise or superior interest not in the sense of an interest defined as public by a social, political, and administrative elite, but as an interest defined as public by the confluence of informed opinion produced in the formal and informal organization set up or tolerated by societies for their government and administration?

Is it reasonable to regard the public interest as moral imperative, not in the sense of an interest defined by an absolute moral standard, but in the sense of an interest defined by the trust relationship between the government and the governed?

[9] Arthur N. Holcombe, *Our More Perfect Union* (Cambridge: Harvard University Press, 1950), p. 426.

Is it reasonable to regard the public interest as an interest defined as public by the processes of accommodation and compromise in part, but in which accommodation and compromise do not necessarily provide the ultimate standard of the definition?

CULTURE AND THE PUBLIC INTEREST

The idea of the public interest as commonly held value is very much like that of the frictionless machine. Philosophers sometimes call a notion of this sort "an idea in God's mind." Nobody has ever seen a frictionless machine, but the concept of a frictionless machine, as an organizing idea, has been highly useful in formulating thought and experimentation about all sorts of things, including the motor in an automobile. Now this is not Platonism. The reality is not the idea of the frictionless machine in God's mind, or in anybody's else mind. The reality is the motor in the car. But the ideal of the frictionless machine is not less valuable because no one has ever built such a machine, or for that matter that a frictionless machine is a philosophical paradox. And the fact that nobody really expects to achieve perpetual motion, at least at sea level pressure, through the instrumentality of a frictionless machine has not stopped automotive engineers and designers from working on existing principles and processes of propulsion as though a frictionless machine might some day be achieved.

It is possible that if administrative theorists could achieve the same transition in respect of the public interest that engineers have made in respect of the frictionless machine, a great many of the difficulties encountered in the quest for administrative values might be substantially reduced and progress accordingly accelerated. Peter Laslett's recent essay on the face-to-face society provides an interesting beginning in this direction. Laslett makes the point that in thinking about such matters as the public interest we tend to state our criteria altogether in terms of the general territorial society, whereas it is the face-to-face society which is solely capable of directing cooperative action, and in which alone the problem of the discovery of the public interest in respect of specific issues arises. The important ethical characteristic of the face-to-face society is the public trust which it exercises in behalf of the general territorial society. But it is within the face-to-face society that the issue of the public interest must be resolved.

This face-to-face society is not a corporation, nor has it any special corporate consciousness. It is not a social, political, or administrative elite. It is not an Establishment, whatever that newly imported term may signify. Professor Mills to the contrary notwithstanding, it has no vested or *ex officio* membership. It has no communicants who are not expendable, and the rate of turnover, in fact, is fairly high. It is no citadel of undifferentiated power, although there are men of broad and extensive influence who participate in it. It has no special claims to wisdom or omniscience, although there are wise and learned men among its number. Nor is it in any sense a politically representative body, although elected representatives are frequently present in its councils.

The Washington face-to-face society, to take an example, is nothing more nor less than the agglomeration of political executives, civil servants, Representatives, Senators, Justices and judges, people from the military services, financiers, industrialists, labor leaders, lobbyists, socialites, foreign diplomats, and all sorts of other people who are from time to time drawn into its orbit. Its maximum potential membership may perhaps be as large as 2,500, although on a specific issue the active participation is not ordinarily more than two per centum of this number; inactive participation of those with right of access may be substantially higher. It tends to be functionally specialized, in the sense that the leaders in some aspects of its activities are followers—or may not even be consulted—in others. The influence of members varies substantially from one time to another, depending upon the stage in the decision-making process at which an issue of public interest is cast up for critical analysis. The only criterion of membership is a purely pragmatic one: is the putative member normally consulted about decisions in which he wishes to participate?

It is the ethical quality of transactions within this face-to-face society which provides an indication of the way in which value systems influence the processes of administrative decision. What are the special characteristics of this face-to-face relationship that contribute to the discovery and definition of the public interest? The family, of course, is the most intelligible modern example of a face-to-face society, although for the purposes of this analysis it is defective in that it is practically never a political society, nor a territorial society. The Greek city-state is perhaps the best example of a face-to-face society that was at the same time a political and territorial society. But the analogy of the family, if pursued guardedly, has some instructive lessons for the analysis of administrative values.

As Peter Laslett reminds us, the important differentiating characteristic of the family is that its activities are normally carried on by direct oral communication. Husbands and wives and parents and children living as families rarely write each other letters, and practically never prepare memoranda or *aide-mémoire*. Even when they are momentarily separated, they usually communicate by long-distance telephone, because any other means of communication is qualitatively inadequate. Families do not build up dossiers by which the adequacy of procedural due process in reaching a decision may be objectively demonstrated. Families couldn't care less how they get to decisions; the important thing is to understand fully how each member really feels about the matter. This can be discovered only in face-to-face relationships.

Moreover, even when recourse must be had to means of communication other than face-to-face—as when Father is away on a business trip, or Junior goes off to college—the letters and telegrams are comprehensible only in terms of the past conversations that have taken place between the absent member and the rest of the family. If the letters mean anything—and it is notable that they mean less and less, and become more and more cryptic as the separation is attenuated—the meaning is derived from the feeling that the separated members know what each would be saying if the conversation were being carried on face-to-face, and that if they were back together again each would quickly and intuitively know and understand what the feelings of the others were.[10]

The Greek city-state was not a family. Nor was the polis organized on the lines of what the cultural anthropologists are fond of referring to as the extended family pattern. On the other hand, the Greek city-state was much closer in the form and texture of its political and administrative institutions to a family than to any contemporary political society. It was a political society, although in classical Greek one could not say so, because the Greek language had a single word, polis, for society, city, and state. The Greeks could not conceive of a society that was not political. Indeed, the word for private citizens in classical Greek is idiotes, which comes into English as idiots. And the Greeks meant exactly what they said, as Thucydides makes abundantly clear in his report of Pericles' funeral oration.

The Greek city-state functioned effectively as a face-to-face political society for a number of reasons. In the first place, it was always small. Plato, an idealist, fixed his perfect society at a permanent and static membership of 5,040 citizens. Aristotle, an administrative type, set the limit at the number which could be called together by a single herald in normal voice. This meant that the transactions of the city-state could be carried on by the simultaneous mutual confrontation of all the members—in a meeting of the committee of the whole. Its

[10] Peter Laslett, "The Face to Face Society," in Peter Laslett, ed., *Philosophy, Politics and Society* (New York: The Macmillan Company, 1956). See especially pp. 157-59.

area, moreover, was invariably restricted and urban-centered. This smallness and compactness was the peculiar and distinguishing characteristic of the polis which enabled it to function effectively as a face-to-face political society which was at the same time a territorial or general society.

But the efficacy of the city-state as a political society rested upon grounds additional to its size and convenience for face-to-face intercourse. The members of the polis shared a depth and pervasiveness of common history, of common culture, of common understanding, and of common purpose that is all but incomprehensible to moderns. Indeed, no modern, with the possible exception of a few cultural anthropologists, has had the opportunity ever to observe anything like such a society in which all history was shared history, all tradition was shared tradition, all purposes were shared purposes, and virtually all life was shared life, free in its essence from extraneous influences. And even the cultural anthropologists have never encountered a face-to-face society comparable in complexity and grandeur to that which the polis achieved in classical Greece. There is, moreover, nothing in modern society that provides an analogue useful for comprehending the Greek city-state. The contemporary specialization of functions and interests and the pluralization of loyalties, even in territorial societies which are small enough to operate face-to-face, and which partake sufficiently of a common history, culture, and tradition to make face-to-face relationships meaningful, create differences so profound that the easy and complete synaptic contact of the polis is beyond the range even of the imagination.

The polis was small in population and area, and its inhabitants had a community of history, understanding, and purpose which modern students of society are ill-equipped to comprehend, but it had another characteristic which was equally indispensable to its functioning as a face-to-face society. Laslett calls this characteristic the synaptic contact among the individuals in the society. For his word and his definition he invokes a metaphor drawn from neurophysiology:

> Synapse is the term used for the interval, spatial distance, between neurons, and the ease, speed, direction and quality with which a synapse can be "made"—bridged, that is, or traversed—are all of the utmost importance in the study of consciousness. In a face-to-face society like the polis, social synaptic contact, as we may call it, can obviously be made at the maximum ease, speed and continuity, both ways between each unit and in all directions over the whole mass. The analogy breaks down at the point when it is recognized that the individuals within a society can move, whilst

neurons are motionless, but it is, after all, only in a territorial society that such motion is necessary. The polis could be continuously conscious of itself without any individual stirring out of the ordinary area of his everyday business. A territorial society cannot, and though our developed instruments of communication make our situation very different from that in a medieval European monarchy, it is still very distant in the quality of its synapses from the Athens of Plato and Aristotle. For if we press our metaphor to its limit, it is only when individuals are in the presence of each other that the social synapse can be bridged with anything like completeness. Of course, such contact is an important feature of the workings of the political society we live in now. It goes on between rulers and ruled, as well as between the citizens. It even has to be brought about synthetically by broadcasting and television, now politically indispensable. Nevertheless, the broadcast situation is not a fully face-to-face situation, since it does not permit of mutual response and interaction. And it is perfectly obvious that social synaptic contact, partial or complete, natural or synthetic, is not the only and obvious pathway of relationship amongst us, as it was amongst the Greeks.[11]

The face-to-face society of the city-state, moreover, had a great advantage which no modern synthetic face-to-face society has any hope of achieving. It was a generalistic society, in which each man played many roles. Edith Hamilton has perhaps, of all Americans, best been able to think and feel her way back into the spirit of classical Greece. She describes Greek society and contrasts it with our own in these words:

We ourselves belong to an age of specialists, the result, really, of our belonging to an age that loves comfort. It is obvious that one man doing only one thing can work faster, and the reasonable conclusion in a world that wants a great many things, is to arrange to have him do it. Twenty men making each a minute bit of a shoe, turn out far more than twenty times the number of shoes that the cobbler working alone did, and in consequence no one must go barefoot. We have our reward in an ever-increasing multiplication of the things everyone needs but we pay our price in the limit set to the possibilities of development for each individual worker.

In Greece it was just the other way about. The things they needed were by comparison few, but every man had to act in a number of different capacities. An Athenian citizen in his time

[11] *Ibid.*, pp. 165-66.

played many parts. Aeschylus was not only a writer of plays; he was an entire theatrical staff, actor, scenic artist, costumer, designer, mechanician, producer. He was also a soldier who fought in the ranks, and had probably held a civic office; most Athenians did. No doubt if we knew more about his life we should find that he had still other avocations. His brother-dramatist, Sophocles, was a general and a diplomat and a priest as well; a practical man of the theatre too, who made at least one important innovation. There was no artist class in Greece, withdrawn from active life, no literary class, no learned class. Their soldiers and their sailors and their politicians and their men of affairs wrote their poetry and carved their statues and thought out their philosophy. "To sum up"—the speaker is Pericles—"I say that Athens is the school of Greece and that the individual Athenian in his own person seems to have the power of adapting himself to the most varied forms of action with the utmost versatility and grace"—that last word a touch so peculiarly Greek.[12]

The concurrence of these four factors—numerical and spatial limitation, community of history, culture, and tradition, the interchangeability of roles in the society, and the resultant opportunity for full and complete social synaptic contact—produced the intense social and political sensitivity and awareness that chracterized the Greek polis. And nowhere, and at no time in human history, have political interests been more clearly articulated and defined, and the public interest more clearly recognized, than in the face-to-face transactions of the societies of ancient Greece. This is the ideal to which Pindar gives voice when he writes of Corinth:

> There Lawfulness dwells, and her sisters,
> Safe foundation of cities,
> Justice and Peace, who was bred with her,
> Dispensers of wealth to men,
> Golden daughters of wise-counselling Right.[13]

And the fragment of the beginning of a hymn, perhaps by Simonides, reiterates the theme:

> Listen, Fates, who sit nearest of gods to the throne of
> Zeus
> And weave with shuttles of adamant

---

[12] Edith Hamilton, *The Greek Way* (New York: W. W. Norton & Company, 1930), pp. 117-18.

[13] Pindar, Olympian Odes, XIII, 6-8, cited in C. M. Bowra, *The Greek Experience* (New York: World Publishing Co., 1957), p. 73.

Inescapable devices for counsels of every kind beyond
counting,
Aisa, Clotho, and Lachesis,
Fine-armed daughters of Night,
Hearken to our prayers, all-terrible goddesses
Of sky and of earth;
Send us rose-bosomed Lawfulness
And her sisters on glittering thrones,
Right and crowned Peace, and make this city
Forget the misfortunes which lie heavily on her heart.[14]

Aeschylus phrases the aspiration of the Athenians in these words:

Ne'er, I pray, ne'er may that
Root of evil, civil strife,
Rage within her boundaries:
Ne'er may the earth's dust drink of the blood
of her children,
And wroth thereat thirst greedily after revenge.
Blood in requital of blood;
Rather in friendly communion
Gladness be rendered for gladness,
All at one in love and hate.
Therein lies a cure for human ills.[15]

Even the trial of Socrates, imprecise though the indictment may
have been and whatever may be one's views of the judgment, was a
truly classic example of the quest for the public interest. Plato himself
admitted, reluctantly of course, that the proceedings were conducted
with proper moderation, and a majority of the jury felt that the case
against Socrates had been fully established.[16]

THE INDIVIDUAL AND THE GENERAL WILL

The Greeks not only could not conceive of a society which was not
political, but they could not conceive of man being man outside the
polis. Because this special condition of the Greek mind has frequently
not been understood by moderns, they have more often than not failed
to comprehend Aristotle's definition of man as a political animal. They
have regarded it as perhaps a very clever epigram, but nonetheless mere

[14] Fragmenta Chorica Adespota 5 Diehl, cited in Bowra, *op. cit.*, pp. 80-81.
[15] Aeschylus, The Eumenides, 977-87 (G. Thomson), cited in Bowra, *op. cit.*,
p. 81.
[16] *Cf.* John Montgomery, ed., *The State versus Socrates* (Boston: The Beacon
Press, 1954).

description. It is not description. It is definition. It establishes the proximate genus of man as animal, and his essential difference as political. The physis which in the Greek mind ordered the concepts of animal and political in a relationship of which the result was man was a function of the social synaptic contact which existed only in the face-to-face society. For the same reason, of course, Aristotle was defeated by the idea of large-scale political organization. "The creation of order for an infinite number is a task for the divine power which holds together [and reduces to order] the whole of this universe, where beauty [which goes with order] is usually found attending upon number and magnitude."[17]

Aristotle's observation that the creation of order for an organization of large magnitude was a task for divine power appears to be a sort of Delphic utterance but it is nonetheless in retrospect a very perceptive one. For the conditions of the territorial society—the sense of community with others whom one has never seen, the sense of allegiance to a common source of political and social authority, and the sense of oneness within a symbolic brotherhood of political nationalism—partake of an essentially religious psychology. The territorial society, as Locke pointed out, is the product of a supreme act of faith:

> For men being all the workmanship of one omnipotent and infinitely wise Maker—all the servants of one sovereign Master, sent into the world by his order, and about his business—they are his property, whose workmanship they are, made to last during his, not one another's pleasure; and being furnished with like facilities, sharing all in one community of nature, there cannot be supposed any such subordination among us, that may authorize us to destroy one another, as if we were made for one another's uses, as the inferior ranks of creatures are for ours. Every one, as he is bound to preserve himself, and not to quit his station wilfully, so, by the like reason, when his own preservation comes not in competition, ought he, as much as he can, to preserve the rest of mankind, and may not, unless it be to do justice on an offender, take away or impair the life, or what tends to the preservation of the life, the liberty, health, limb, or goods of another.
>
> . . . . .
>
> Political power is that power which every man having in the state of nature has given up into the hands of the society, and therein to the governors whom the society hath set over itself, with

[17] See Ernest Barker, *The Politics of Aristotle* (London: Oxford University Press, 1946), p. 291.

this express or tacit trust, that it shall be employed for their good and the preservation of their property. Now this power, which every man has in the state of nature, and which he parts with to the society in all such cases where the society can secure him, is to use such means for the preserving of his own property as he thinks good and nature allows him, and to punish the breach of the law of nature in others so as (according to the best of his reason) may most conduce to the preservation of himself and the rest of mankind. So that the end and measure of this power, when in every man's hands in the state of nature, being the preservation of all of his society—that is, all mankind in general—it can have no other end or measure, when in the hands of the magistrates, but to preserve the members of that society in their lives, liberties and possessions; and so cannot be an absolute, arbitrary power over their lives and fortunes, which are as much as possible to be preserved, but a power to make laws, and annex such penalties to them, as may tend to the preservation of the whole, by cutting off those parts, and those only, which are so corrupt that they threaten the sound and healthy, without which no severity is lawful. And this power has its original only from compact and agreement, and the mutual consent of those who make up the community.[18]

This is the classic statement of the contract theory, and it brings us into direct confrontation of two completely non-Greek elements. For if the fact of social synaptic contact and interaction is the defining characteristic of the face-to-face society, the individual is equally the defining characteristic of the territorial society. The relationship between the two societies, as Locke makes clear, is a public trust. The Greeks had no use for concepts of either the individual or the public trust, since the terms were incomprehensible in a face-to-face society in which man's existence is without meaning except in relation to the polis. Indeed, one of the profound paradoxes of Greek thought is the primacy which Greek philosophy gives to the notion of liberty and freedom, of which the essence surely must be the dignity and worth of the individual, and its simultaneous failure to develop even the most elementary conceptions of individual psychology. When Plato and Aristotle speculate about the psychology of individuals the result is sheer fantasy. On the other hand, as Edith Hamilton points out:

[18] John Locke, *Second Treatise on Government*, edited by J. W. Gough (New York: Macmillan, 1946), pp. 5 and 87.

What the artist did in his field the statesman did in his. He found the necessary relation between law and freedom. Thucydides makes Pericles say, "We are a free democracy, but we obey the laws, more especially those which protect the oppressed and the unwritten law whose transgression brings shame." Willing obedience to law written and unwritten made the Athenians free, and the clear implication in Pericles' words is that they thought the latter, the unwritten, were the most important. This fact has deep significance for the first self-government in the world. Pericles knew and the audience he was speaking to knew that most of the written laws, as for instance the laws against murder and robbery, were without effect upon the vast majority who had never an impulse to commit the one or the other, but the unwritten laws whose violations bring no court sentence or prison term made a direct claim on every one of them. Obedience to what Professor Whitehead has called the unenforceable, that which no force can compel, the Athenian accepted as the basic condition of freedom for men living together, obedience to kindness and compassion and unselfishness and all the long list of qualities without which life would be intolerable except to a hermit in the desert. The limits to action established by law were a mere nothing compared to the limits established by a man's own free choice.

This conception of what freedom means dawned upon the Greeks. The quality they valued most—the Greek word is *sophrosuné*—cannot be expressed by any single English word. It is oftenest translated by self-control, but it meant more than that. It was the spirit behind the two great Delphic sayings, "Know thyself" and "Nothing in excess." Arrogance, insolent self-assertion, was of all qualities most detested by the Greeks. *Sophrosuné* was the exact opposite. It had its nature, as Aristotle would say, in the excellent and it meant accepting the bounds excellence laid down for human nature, restraining impulses to unrestricted freedom, shunning excess, obeying the inner laws of harmony and proportion. This was the virtue the Greeks esteemed above all others not because they were moderate lovers of the golden mean, but because their spontaneity and ever-changing variety and energy of life had to have the strong control of a disciplined spirit or end in senseless violence.

That was the Greek ideal, and the result was their freedom. The idea that only the man who holds himself within self-chosen limits can be free is one of their greatest legacies to us.

Through *sophrosuné* Greece discovered how men could live together in freedom, and she expressed her discovery by creating the first self-government in the world. An insignificant little town in a small and poverty-poor country made the discovery under the leadership of a single man. It was back in the early sixth century, more than a hundred years before Athens' great day, that a bold and far thinking statesman, Solon, conceived the idea of a completely new kind of state, in which all citizens would have an active share and all would be equal before the law. When he laid the foundations of it in Athens, free government came into the world.[19]

If the Greeks developed highly sophisticated notions of liberty and freedom without giving thought to the psychology of the individuals who exercised the liberty and freedom which, in a very real sense, are Greek inventions, they were equally devoid of any notion of a public trust. Indeed, except for the slaves, there were no elements in Greek society in behalf of whom a trusteeship might be established. And even Solon, who was so meticulous in his respect for the rights of the humblest Athenian citizen, never supposed that a slave or other non-citizen could have any claims upon the polis. In this regard he was no different from the Founding Fathers in Philadelphia twenty-four hundred years later.

This knotty problem of political and administrative theory, the individual, who is both the source and sanction of the territorial society, and the sole *raison d'être* of the face-to-face society, is one that we can neither solve nor ignore. Of his central importance in the entire scheme of things there can be little question. Of his essential nature there is little agreement. He is, and he is important—of that we are sure; but what is he?

Even on the common-sense level, the individual is a collection of paradoxes. He is a unity, but he is a plurality. He is a whole man, but he is also a Presbyterian, a member of the Teamsters' Union, a baseball fan, and an introvert. He is observed to act, and although the fact of action signifies nothing more than the rearrangement of certain physical events in the external world, we assume that he must have a will, which produces the action, and infer that he must have motives, which inform and instruct the will. Sometimes he acts in consistent and even predictable ways, and from this concurrence of events we infer that he has character, and that we can understand and interpret this character in terms of his actions. On the other hand, he is likewise observed to

[19] Edith Hamilton, *The Echo of Greece* (New York: W. W. Norton, 1957), pp. 20-22.

be capable of entertaining apparently an infinite number of separate interests, and of expressing these separate interests through a bewildering variety of organizations. His loyalties to these separate interests and organizations, moreover, are seldom ordered in so systematic a way that they permit the attachment of constant valences by which their relative reaction potential on a particular issue might be discounted. Their compulsiveness, in short, is rarely arranged on any permanent or hierarchical scale. This is the point, of course, at which the common economic determinism of Adam Smith and Karl Marx parts company with reality. Man frequently neither buys in the cheapest market nor sells in the dearest, and economic self-interest fails utterly to provide any viable pattern of predictability for his actions.

If man cannot be categorically described as either one or many—since he is obviously both—the problem arises whether for purposes of explaining his functioning in politics and administration it is possible to differentiate his unitary and pluralistic actions. For there is obviously a very important practical convenience in being able to identify man as man when he is in fact acting as a whole man. Bernard Mayo has suggested that if the notion of an act can be broken down into its constituent elements—he suggests intention and result—it is possible to make a much more accurate prediction of its recurrence than if the act were attempted to be analyzed as a whole. As he points out:

> The intention is more characteristic of the act than is the actual physical result; more important, it is more characteristic of the agent. It implies an element of permanence and reliability, on which we base our forecasts of future events. This is called knowledge of a person's character. In other words, this hypothetical division of an act into intention and result increases our control over our environment. The intention we call the "will," and a series of such intentions exhibits the elements of permanence which enters into individual character.

> It is essential to distinguish "intent" from "motivation." Both terms have their uses, but the dangers of confusing them can be seen, for example, in the shortcomings of the utilitarian political philosophers. By dwelling on "motives" as if this were the only way of referring to the significant element of action, and especially on the motives of pleasure and pain, these philosophers tended to regard the human being as being a bundle of desires and fears— just as later exponents of psychological theories of the state spoke of him as if he were a bundle of complexes. . . . [It] is because it shows him as a unit in action that the term "will" is often useful.

This last point is so important that I think it would hardly be over-stating the case to say that the will "is" this unity. For the unity, from the standpoint of a person's actions, cannot be completely de-scribed in any other terms, and certainly not in physical terms; for a person's actions are not confined to the particular region of physical space occupied by the body.

We have thus arrived at what may be called a pragmatic justification for the use of the term "will" as applied to the indi-vidual. Firstly, it establishes a criterion for judging character and forecasting actions; secondly, it emphasizes the importance of intention as distinct from practical consequences; and thirdly, and most significantly, it represents the individual as a unity.[20]

If there is a pragmatic justification for speaking of the "will" as applied to the individual, what is the situation with respect to the "will" of an entire society, or a "general will"? If the notion has any validity at all, it is possible to derive a concept of the "general will" from pre-cisely the same pragmatic arguments that appear to justify the use of the term "will" in application to individuals. A society is observed to act, we say, when the individuals composing the society conduct them-selves in an identifiably uniform and consistent manner. But like the act of an individual, this signifies no more than the rearrangement of certain physical events in the external world. Just as the integrity of individual action is not to be understood in terms of the totality of the act, so the act of a society cannot be analyzed without resolving it into intention and result. As Mayo points out, this takes us far beyond the familiar dictum that social institutions are to be understood only in terms of their ends or purposes. The ends of society are not the ends of the individual members of the society. Its intention is something quite different from the arithmetical or algebraic sum of the intentions of the individuals of which it is made up. Like the individual, the society cannot be categorically described either as unity or plurality, and only in a pragmatic sense can we think of its actions as falling into one or the other group. Nevertheless, there are facts which may most con-veniently be described as the acts of society rather than the acts of individual members of the society. "The statement that the act of a society is 'really' equivalent to a collection of particular acts of par-ticular members may be logically irrefutable, but it is not of greater value than the statement that the act of an individual is 'really' equiva-lent to a collection of psychological events. If it is permissible, and even

[20] Bernard Mayo, "Is There a Case For the General Will?", in Laslett, *op. cit.*, pp. 93-94.

essential, for certain purposes to regard the individual as a unit in action, it is equally permissible to regard a society as such."[21]

The unity of the individual, which gives rise to the pragmatic justification of the use of the term "will" in analyzing and attempting to predict his actions, and the unity of the state, which sanctions the pragmatic justification of the use of the term "general will," are equally hypothetical. The metaphysical existence of neither can be demonstrated in any objective sense. But the point is that one cannot eat his cake and have it; the same skepticism that leads to the rejection of the unity of the state leads to the rejection of the unity of the individual, and relegates the notion of the individual "will" to the same limbo as that of the "general will."

Those who would like to dispense with the idea of the "general will" but whose philosophical systems require the maintenance of the notion of the unity of the individual will undoubtedly insist that the application of the concept of the "will" to individual and society alike does violence to the well-established distinction between an organism and an organization. Actually, the notion of the general will is entirely compatible with this distinction. There are three senses in which the individual is a unity: materially, the human body is a single piece of matter; biologically, it is a single organism; psychologically the will, as we have seen, unifies the self. It is only in respect of this psychological unity that the concept of the individual will arises. Moreover, as Mayo makes clear, the coincidence between biological and psychological unity is only contingent—schizophrenia is a clear case in point. The distinction between the organism and the organization, between the individual and the society, between the citizen and the state, derives primarily from the fact that while the individual may predominantly be regarded as a unity in material, biological, and psychological senses, society may be regarded as a unity only in the psychological sense. If, as we have seen, there is no necessary identification of will and organism in the individual, there need be no necessary identification of will and organism in the case of society. The fact that societies are organizations rather than organisms entails no inconsistency in the assertion of the pragmatic utility of the concept of a general will while at the same time maintaining the distinction between organisms and organizations.

But, it may be asked, in what consists the manifestation of the general will, and where is the unity of a society to be discovered? If the unity of the individual is to be discovered in his intentions, rather than in the consequences of his actions, it is even more true that the unity of the society resides in its aims, and in the ends which it was established

[21] *Ibid.,* p. 94.

to secure. In small, single-purpose societies the ends are relatively easy to isolate and describe; in large, complex, and pluralistic societies such as the modern state the ends are more difficult to define. Much of the difficulty derives from the differing accounts of the purpose of the society which different individuals offer. This pluralism makes even clearer the central fact that the purpose of a society is something quite different from the sum of the purposes or interests of the individual members.

There is empirical support for the notion of the general will as the unifying and integrating force in a society, in addition to the pragmatic arguments resting on foundations of convenience and utility. This empirical support is derived from the fact that everywhere men are observed to act in ways which seem to indicate their assumption of facts corresponding to the exigencies of a theory of the general will. By whatever name it may be called, they conduct themselves *as though* there were a general will. Bernard Mayo summarizes the empirical argument in these words:

> I can find no explanation for some of the problems of political obligation except by assuming that there are facts answering to the requirements of the general will theory. Are there such facts? Political obligation implies a duty to obey the laws of the state, which are enacted and promulgated by persons. It also implies a duty to obey the executors of the law, such as police and Ministry officials, who are also persons. Yet there is no duty to obey a person with whom I have not entered into a voluntary obligation. My reason for obeying him is not that he is a certain person—I have no duty to him as such—but that he holds a certain office. And this implies, among other things, that I recognize that he will act according to the rules governing the tenure of his office and not in his own personal interest. If it were not known to be possible that a person could act otherwise than in his own immediate interest, there could be no obligation to obey him, and therefore no political obligation.
>
> But if he does not act in his own interest, in whose interest does he act? The answer is immaterial. He acts according to rules, and has his own private interest in doing so. Political obligation arises not because a person in office acts in anyone's interest, but because he acts in accordance with rules which are embodied in a certain structure, and because this structure represents the unity of the state which we have called the general will.[22]

[22] *Ibid.*, p. 96.

Obviously, the general will in the terms of the present argument affords no grounds for assuming that there are universally entertained value judgments concerning political and administrative decisions in respect of the limitation of atomic tests, the amendment of the petroleum depletion allowance provisions of the Internal Revenue Act, or the expansion of the coverage of minimum wage legislation. On the other hand, the general will theory may have a very significant relationship to what was perhaps Paul Appleby's final adjuration to us— that we learn to "conduct our own institutional affairs in sufficiently whole-nation terms."

The following essay consists of selections from the writings of Paul Appleby on the subject of public administration and democracy. In a sense everything Appleby ever wrote related directly or indirectly to the essay's subject; for his enduring concern was to reconcile vigorous administration, which he held necessary to achievement of the goals of society, with democratic government, which he cherished above all things else. The purpose here is to restate his philosophy (though in his own words) at essay length. A few basic themes characterized his thinking and appeared recurrently in his writings; the chief of these are set down here as division heads, under which are arranged a distillate of Appleby's thoughts on the subject.

Paul Appleby wrote five books, two monographs, and about thirty articles. These writings have been combed for comment bearing on the subjects chosen for emphasis here. I have taken the liberty of arranging pertinent passages in accordance with the framework established; but the thoughts, and with the exception of a handful of transitional phrases the words as well, are those of Paul Appleby. In selecting the paragraphs to be included and arranging them in essay form I had the assistance of Malcolm D. Schlusberg, who read Appleby's complete writings and made tentative choices of excerpts and suggestions regarding arrangement. The essay as it stands owes much to his energy and discrimination.

The texts from which quotation is made appear below. Thanks are tendered the publishers for their several permissions to quote. The essay as it stands would not have been possible without their cooperation.

Big Democracy. New York: Alfred A. Knopf. 1945.

Policy and Administration. University, Alabama: University of Alabama Press. 1949.

Morality and Administration in Democratic Government. Baton Rouge: Louisiana State University Press. 1952.

Public Administration for a Welfare State. New Delhi: Asia Publishing House. 1961.

Citizens as Sovereigns. Syracuse: Syracuse University Press. 1962.

"Toward Better Public Administration." *Public Administration Review*, Vol. 7, No. 2 (Spring 1947).

"The Influence of the Political Order." *American Political Science Review*, Vol. 42, No. 2 (April 1948).

R. C. M.

· 17 ·

Public Administration
and Democracy

PAUL H. APPLEBY

Democracy and the Political Process

The public will is flexible and ever subject to change, learning by its own action and by its own experience, so shot through with discretion that it cannot be predicted as though automatic. It is subject to influence by leaders but is capable of discarding leaders. It is energized just as every man is, by trial and error that is its own, capable of highly enlightened self-interest, capable of devoted altruism, prone to error and given to profiting from and correcting its own mistakes. It is not inherently and invariably right; perhaps it is never right except in its own time and terms. It is not inherently the sum total of all the private wills, it is not even the total of all the private wills after canceling out the pluses and minuses of those wills. It is not distilled in a simple, definite, mechanical way, easy to see and easy to weigh in some merely mechanical weighing machine. It is not to be expressed in terms of some near absolute that leaves no questions to be answered; rather, it is eternally inquisitive. It becomes absolute only as a majority will and since there are many possible majorities, it does not uniformly derive from a particular majority and is not something fixed. It is often expressed only as consent and at times as a veto. In many instances it is a thing not developed at all, withheld, even nonexistent.

The public will, then, is a force, largely potential, definite only as majorities form, but always subject to influence of members and leaders. Its capacity to be, more than its being, is the crux of democratic reality. This capacity penetrates the reality of American Government.

The democratic ideology is not anarchic; rather, it is a scheme for the impregnation of government with special popular values which leave open the way to popular determination of other values.

The general theory of democracy, before it is developed into more specific theory of the conduct of its business, calls simply for a state whose people are empowered to make and unmake its government,

333

with freedom of opinion and expression and with equality as citizens. These are the ingredients of the ideal of *political* freedom, but the ideal is only to be realized in the continuing operation of government dedicated to it and at the same time performing its regular and complicated business of governance. The general theory is widely accepted and fairly well understood in its general terms, but there seems to be no adequately comprehensible theory of its application and its relation to the business of governance. The notion of freedom is thinly extended into a vague anarchism in which there is expectation that the governmental discipline will be absent. The notion of democracy is treated in individual rather than in organizationally functional terms, separating the citizen emotionally and intellectually from consistent identification with the popular instrument.

We must remember that there is nothing so fully democratic as the totality of the political processes in a free society. The great distinction between government and other organized undertakings is to be found in the wholly political character of government. Nothing is so representative of the public as the product of the totality of our political processes.

It is the peculiar business of politics working through government to devise responses to popular demands which will gain the consent of citizens generally. Those responses, in the very nature of the process, can hardly ever be fully satisfactory to anybody if they are fairly acceptable to almost everybody. But they can be roughly responsive to the complex of most of the diverse citizen influences. In the long run as they are successively modified in the light of experience and complaint they are so responsive.

Everything having to do with the government and everything the government does is political, for politics is the art and science of government. But in terms of mass, only a small part of politics is partisan. In a sense all issues nominated for public attention are also nominated for party attention. But parties accept only those issues which seem capable of being formulated in ways useful to them in affecting the establishment of a majority consensus. Issues of slightly smaller potential or otherwise manageable are resolved in legislatures along other than distinctly partisan lines. A great many issues of still smaller dimensions are resolved administratively. The administrative level at which they are resolved depends upon the degree of specialized character of a particular issue, the size, location, character and attitude of the public affected. A small public deeply aroused weighs more in political scales than a larger public only mildly dissatisfied. Repetition of complaint and demand is an index of intensity of citizen feeling and a nomination for higher attention. Thus about any matter normally handled at a low level in the administrative hierarchy, a militant citizen group can secure Presidential, Congressional, or public debate consideration. This is the peculiar genius of politics. It is in politics—the interacting of citizen sentiments and political institutions as a whole—that exist the limitations on power of officials, and the power of the people ultimately to require any kind of action, positive or negative, about which they are sufficiently agreed.

Two phrases in the preceding sentence have special significance: "any *kind* of action," and "sufficiently agreed." A numerous people will usually be much more capable of agreeing on a kind of action than on the specific form any action might take. The more agreed they are, the more there is consensus, the easier it is to impose on the government the popular will—actually to control the government. The less agreed they are, the more popular role is to give or to withhold consent. Political processes develop or reveal lack of consensus or consent in the total social context of the moment.

In other words, all of the political processes, and not elections alone, are the means by which in this society [all the] people are continually agreeing on courses of action.

In every case the principal roles of the especially responsible citizens who are officials are: to bring into focus—to resolve and to integrate—these popularly felt needs; to give specific form to responses of the government designed to meet the needs; to inject foresight and concern for factors not readily visible to citizens at large; to try so to organize governmental responses as to secure at least majority consensus or consent. They may make mechanical or automatic responses to popular forces on the one hand, and they may exercise discretion and leadership on the other. The mechanical type of response is itself modified, of course, by the necessity of consciously interpreting public sentiment.

What results from this process of organizational and popular coordination—and it is one way of defining the essence of good administration—is not an arbitrary product but an organized product, an institutional product, a representative product, a political product. It will be a product to which no very great number will much object, one for which no better alternative was clearly available, one that is subject to change and will be changed in the light of experience, in response to popular criticisms. Such should be the products of democratic government.

Politics is the special hallmark of democracy, the prime method of democracy, and democratic government is the peculiar agent of pop-

ular, diversified politics. Politics, politicians, and government are one
and inseparable, and in the large are entitled to respect, and even devotion, while at the same time subjected to our judgment keenly dis-
criminating between better and worse politicians, better and worse
aspects of government, better and worse political structures and functions. We often hear as the counsel of reform, "Let's take it out of
politics, let's put it where the people will not have the *capacity* to
control it." This is carrying the "check and balance" idea to the point
of a blank check and governmental imbalance. This always means that
some group less than the public will have the capacity to control it; that
is not democracy, unless the public consciously elects that course, and
unless the public is left in a position to reassert its capacity for control.
When any function or process is relatively taken out of politics it should
be done reflectively, cautiously, and taken out not so far that it may not
readily be drawn in again for public correction.

Pluralism is both the presupposition and the precipitate of democracy. The government doing many things, not all consistent, is serving a
society doing many things, not all consistent. Cherishing the values of
pluralism, the government cannot but exemplify them to a considerable
degree. Allowing citizens wide areas of choice, sheltering diverse enterprises and interests, giving range to imagination and ingenuity, the
government itself cannot be just one thing or have just one policy. It
must respond to felt needs, but the wisdom which it has in forming its
response, it distills from the totality of the political processes by which
it lives.

DEMOCRACY AND THE ADMINISTRATIVE PROCESS

Freedom, to be meaningful, must be achieved and experienced
socially as well as governmentally. There is no freedom in chaos. There
is no lasting satisfaction for normal persons in isolation. Any kind of
social life requires restraints, just as it poses choices not otherwise
available. Both tyranny and freedom are products of institutions, and
the fundamental problem concerns the form, manner, and spirit of
government institutions. Making civilization possible—maintaining
social order in the face of more and more differentiated preoccupations—is the supreme responsibility of government. Government's
instruments are politics and public administration in the broadest possible meaning of the latter term.

The term "public administration" has very much more content than
is commonly ascribed to it. It is not merely "management" as ordinarily
treated in technical terms, or "administration" as ordinarily treated with
only a slightly broader meaning. It is public leadership of public affairs

directly responsible for executive action. In a democracy, it has to do with such leadership and executive action in terms that respect and contribute to the dignity, the worth, and the potentialities of the citizen.

The democratic, public-administrative process is an important part of the whole process of government. The entire process is one shaped by long years of experience and learning under the tutorial blows of publics and citizens sensitive, critical, and even demanding. It is a process in which techniques unnumbered and often not consciously identified have been developed in harmony with the particular, evolving culture for which this process is both a present expression and an avenue for adjustment and advance. At any given time and in any jurisdiction it approximately embodies the adminstrative-political wisdom effective at that time in that jurisdiction.

It is the means by which government comes alive, and pursues and helps give form and reality to values. Similarly, it gives form and meaning to theory and provides functional materials out of which meaningful theory is created, tested, and modified. The administrative process is the decision-making, action part of the larger process of governance, deriving from it and flowing into it. Administration in this broadest and most proper sense comprises the whole of governmental action, whether the action is "legislative," "executive," or "judicial." To organize for or to stimulate and support organized efforts for getting integrated action that will be acceptable to the public is the job of administration on its highest level.

In a democracy, *everybody's* business quite properly takes precedence over *anybody's* business. This is confusing, because *anybody* knows *anybody's* business and *nobody* can really understand *everybody's* business.

Democratic government gives consideration to anybody, but defers to everybody. The process of giving consideration to anybody and letting the balance fall in favor of everybody is not carried on with mirrors—or with calculating machines. It is carried on through politics and political institutions. It involves heartaches as well as headaches for all who share in governmental responsibility.

Management of the flow of work upward and downward within human hierarchies and between human hierarchies is the art of administration. Management of that process in a political environment within a governmental structure providing for various political processes is the public administration art. It makes distinctly democratic contributions when the political structure and institutions are democratic. Part of the democratic contribution is made visible when controversy flares within the government. The government needs most of the time and finally to find agreement, but preliminary to that it needs also to identify issues, and to serve as an arena within which issues are resolved. It is business that is a product of political vitality.

The administrative hierarchy is an organ receiving messages of popular demands, many of them contradictory. It is an organ responding to such demands, reconciling them, and in the course of response injecting considerations of prudence, perspective, and principle, including regard for other popular demands and aspirations than those expressed in the chorus of the moment. All this is a political process, much of it completed within the area of administration. Administration has this character. Its better performance within this character is the aim of all who study public administration.

As business moves up the hierarchies—first of a bureau, then of a department, and finally of the executive branch—then, it undergoes progressive translation from special-interest and specialized substantive and expert consideration, to more general, more total-governmental, more total public, more completely political consideration. The movement upward for particular business may cease at any level, according to the degree of consensus achieved, according to acceptability, according to popular concern. Any particular business may, when popular concern is sufficient, emerge at the level occupied by political officers. Whenever partisans see in it grist for the mill whose job it is to try to create a majority, it emerges at the partisan-political level. The partisan-political element is the governing rudder—but only that. It derives from the desire to win elections, which is a desire to secure majority support. This, of course, is basic to popular government and in general roughly motivates search for courses of action in the popular interest. Public controversy is simply a moving up of the level of treatment of some particular matter. Anything done within the executive branch can be so moved up if there is sufficient concern about it. Members of Congress generally and members of the opposition party in particular, the press, and interest groups are trying continually to dig out matters for higher attention; they are continually nominating issues as "candidates" for that attention, and citizens vote by reacting or failing to react to these various nominations. Those matters not "elected" are administratively resolved. In their resolution, executive agencies perform a certain representative function, additional to the functions of other representatives of citizen interests.

Public administration is policy-making. It is policy-making on a field where mighty forces contend, forces engendered in and by the society. It is policy-making subject to still other and various policy-makers. Public administration is one of a number of basic political processes by which this people achieves and controls governance. So long as the people vote and have unrestrained the right to complain the whole process of administration is in a sense political on every level. In total it brings to bear the condensed political essence of the entire nation. After insistence on free and regular franchise and the right to complain, nothing is more essential to making and keeping big government democratic than to conceive of governmental power and to develop it as the power of a social and political organism.

It is against a background of some such general, realistic picture of government that administration needs to be considered. Public administration is policy-making. If admission that this is true seems to exalt administration, it must be seen that the emphasis on politics subordinates the administrator, exalts the politicians, and thereby exalts the citizen.

THE CHARACTER OF DEMOCRATIC ADMINISTRATION

Democratic government must be both responsive and responsible. The first need of operating democracy is to achieve response to a public sense of some particular disorder. The second need is to fix and identify officials whom the public may hold accountable for the response as it has been governmentally formulated. The third is the need to differentiate within the ordered unity brought about in response to public need deferring to the pluralistic character of democratic unity. The first is the enduring problem of *e pluribus unum*. The third is the problem of *ad plura unum*. These two are together the problem of responsiveness. The second is the peculiar problem of responsibility.

Administrative decisions tend more and more to be a product of organized consideration in which every relevant factor is brought to bear. The aim is to make them truly representative. They ought to be made to contribute to action. We need to expedite the making of decisions to which a sufficient minority does not sufficiently object. We must develop ways and means of ensuring that discussion will lead to decision. Decisions arrived at through such organized processes, bound to get critical public attention and subject to change as a result of that attention, are not much to be feared.

While the basic, strictly administrative technique supporting responsibility may appear in most respects equally applicable to nonpopular government, it must be remembered that irresponsibility and democracy are not synonymous. Government in democracy must be unified in order to be responsibly democratic, as autocratic government must be unified in order to be autocratic.

Whatever the present state of administration, it seems clear that its development must be built on understanding of hierarchy as the structure of responsibility. Hierarchy characteristically develops institutional judgment and in democratic government also inherently possesses potentialities for the easiest, the most complete, and most flexible processes of appeal and review within human experience in the conduct of complicated action business.

Thus responsibility, not authority, becomes, after politics, the key word in democratic public administration. It is politics that fashions and directs responsibility. It is hierarchy that is the formal structure and instrument of responsibility.

[In addition to being responsive and responsible, democratic administration must also be representative.] A truly representative bureaucracy is in its several parts variously representative of special functions and interests, and highly representative altogether of the public at large. Government cannot properly be merely a fine reflection of private interests. Its machinery must provide for recognition of, and deference to, private interests while reconciling, translating, and sublimating these interests into something resembling the public interest.

Reasonably complete representativeness therefore calls for flexibility in personnel recruitment and assignment, personnel widely drawn, personnel and organizational units representative of diverse functional capacities, and organizations structured and managed to effect coordination oriented to public control.

Requisites for Democratic Administration

Since most governmental actions affect other persons more than they do us as individuals, we all wish governmental action to be what it needs to be with respect to others, while yet, of course, being considerate of us. The truly governmental official in a democracy comes in the course of time to appreciate this. Under the impact of popular demands and lamentations he comes to realize that he must try to operate in a governmental way; that is, through action which is as fair as possible, and as uniform as possible, and which can be taken publicly and publicly explained.

The carrying on of government involves action. No matter how many studies may be required, government in the final analysis is action—organized action. Persons in high positions must have a sense of action. They must have a feeling of the need for decisions to get things done. They must be able to organize resources whether of personnel, material, or information, so that contemplation of objectives will be translated into accomplishment.

So many different functions have to be administered in so many different situations in an advanced society that it is extremely difficult to speak usefully about qualities generally characterizing "good administrators."

Admitting the wide range of variables, some more or less generally requisite qualities may be identified. Out of a dozen such attributes, an effective administrator might usually be expected to have some mixture of an assortment of seven or so. To see all twelve in one person would be to see someone more than a good administrator—a superman, or a man long dead. In actual practice, individual shortcomings can be overcome in large organizations by constituting administrative *teams* with members whose qualities complement each other.

Some qualifications not peculiar to administration must be assumed to begin with. Without basic character, other attributes are insufficient. The good administrator has a high loyalty to his institution, involving a willingness to yield a good deal of himself to its discipline. Aside from the self-interest of income, in public administration there is a special opportunity for a sense of dedication with altruistic and idealistic significance. There are also loyalties to particular programmes, functions, and professions. Sometimes satisfaction of sense of craftsmanship in institutional performance is an important feature of emotional motivation.

After character and motivation more strictly administrative capacities are to be considered:

(1) The most crucial single qualification of this sort is, I think, willingness to assume responsibility. For professional civil servants simple willingness to accept responsibility is probably best; it reflects sober self-confidence that avoids pitfalls of an inflated ambition. Yet this willingness must include courage, a readiness to take risks, a dynamic attitude, not simply an ability to play things safe or to attend to details.

(2) Perhaps the second basic attribute of a good administrator springs naturally from the first. It is demonstrated growing power—a steadily enlarging ability to deal with more problems, more varied problems, and more diverse people.

(3) A good administrator is one with a strong bent toward action. He has discovered the importance of excellence, and will often be highly reflective, but is one with a sense of urgency, one who keeps his eye on deadlines and on his personal responsibility for action; he is one who is likely to feel that his thinking is a by-product of his involvement in action.

(4) A good administrator needs to be, up to a point, a good listener;

beyond this point he needs to be a good initiator of that to which he listens.

(5) A good administrator is one who has been learning how to be unusually effective with people. He is skilled in avoiding personal offense, in seeing how to placate and when to offend, and when to persuade. This means that he can possess quick emotional perceptions.

(6) A kindred point is that a good administrator is one who prefers to have around him the ablest people he can find. He builds his own strength by building the competence of his organization—not by demonstrating how he can tower above incompetents.

(7) It is only a step to the next point. A good administrator uses *his institutional resources,* rather than relying too heavily on himself.

(8) A good administrator is one who aims at effectiveness and avoids using power or authority for their own sake. Using them readily when his responsibility requires, he will usually keep power in reserve, available for the exceptional case. He will prefer to avoid issuing "orders" in favour of ratifying subordinate proposals, or suggesting courses of action.

(9) A good administrator has self-confidence that enables him readily to confess ignorance and personal fault.

(10) The good administrator does not discourage, but positively welcomes, reports of troublesome things lest they reach unmanageable dimensions before he hears of them.

(11) A good administrator is a teamworker. He deals with "subordinates" in a manner showing them the same kind of respect he gives to his superiors.

(12) A good administrator tirelessly pursues means of improving administration of all for which he is responsible. He is hospitable to suggestions for improvement. He is *an initiator in asking new questions about performance* and about seeing new ways to appraise what is going on.

Top-level administrators are generalists. The best ones in government service closely approach the politicians in ability to weigh forces, sentiments and demands. They somehow especially "understand the country," or large parts of it; such understanding, indeed, is the crucial essential to superior public administration. They, better than anyone else, understand the politicians. They understand experts, too.

The functions of top-level administrators are "more political" than the functions of lower-level administrators because they relate to more of the total-governmental area, to more citizens, to more governmental organizations, to more of the political processes. The higher the attainments of public administrators, consequently, the more "generalist" their performances, the more interchangeable they are with respect to assignments, and the more their functions have to do with weighing popular and organized forces. Such functions are not expert but synthesizing.

The ablest [executive] is one who appreciates, utilizes well, develops, and gives general guidance to the operating agency which he heads. The head of any organization has chief responsibility for heightening the morale and increasing the capacities of personnel at all levels before him. When he praises subordinates for the occasional actions he particularly likes, actions of that sort will increase in frequency, whereas if he confines himself to criticizing adversely, his subordinates will become fearful actually of acting, uncertain about how to act, and defensive. Ten measures of praise to one measure of adverse criticism—and the latter so framed as to help and encourage—is a good mixture.

It is always wise for a [top-level administrator] to be slow to make *particular* decisions especially on the basis of information obtained from irresponsible outside sources. All particular decisions should normally be delegated to subordinates, and these subordinates should normally be upheld in their actions. [He] should confine himself to relatively general decisions, and to relatively rare decisions that cannot satisfactorily be made below his level. By and large, the ablest [top-level administrator] will be he who delegates most and who gives most general guidance to the systematic process by which decisions are reached below him. His most fundamental responsibility, indeed, is for the method by which decisions are reached and for the deploying of personnel for the most satisfactory utilization of their abilities. The ability to work on one's proper level is the test of high competence; the tendency of the inadequate is to operate on lower levels than those for which they are in fact responsible.

Ability to be governmental enough to discern the national interest and to insist on programs and procedures so sound that they will be as unyielding rock on which the waves of special interest may break their forces in vain; ability to be political enough to seek those concessions which are the needed refinements of the process of making government action equitable and smooth; ability to be political enough to read and respond to the messages of public currents; and ability to use administrators who can organize and relate agencies so that they produce organized, integrated action—this is the combination of abilities required for the relatively few top people in the great agencies of government.

Morality in the Context of Democratic Administration

Government action has basic moral character when it meets certain crucial requirements, no matter how much it may otherwise fall short of satisfying the ideals or interests of single or factional citizens. These basic requirements include the following: that the action conforms to the processes and symbols thus far developed for the general protection of political freedom as the agent of more general freedom; that it leaves open the way for modification or reversal by public determination; that it is taken within a hierarchy of controls in which responsibility for the action may be readily identified by the public; that it embodies as contributions of leadership the concrete structuring of response to popularly felt needs, and not merely responses to the private or personal needs of leaders. These are general elements of a distinctly democratic morality. Their realization is dependent upon detailed processes and arrangements. The details must provide both system and flexibility, both impersonality and magnanimity, authoritative action but action reviewable and open to scrutiny and simple criticism.

Democratic morality seeks, not the complete elimination of special influence, but its refinement in terms of democratic values. This implies whatever reductions in special privilege seem to be relevant, necessary, and feasible, and the opening of opportunity for the largest realization of the potentialities of citizens generally. It implies the progressive elimination of those prices paid for special influence which in new insight appear venal, wasteful, or discriminatory. It implies making the exercise of power both more responsive and more responsible in whatever respects and degrees seem appropriate and effective in changing time and circumstance. In particular this points to clarifying responsibility of government to the general public and to developing the popular character of the politically effective.

Moral performance begins in individual self-discipline on the part of officials, involving all that is meant by the word "character." But this is not enough. It also requires systematic process which supports individual group judgment enriched by contributions from persons variously equipped and concerned, and differentiations in responsibilities particularly designed to relate these responsibilities to each other and to a whole-public responsibility. The official individually and organizationally must be concerned to go beyond simple honesty to a devoted guardianship of the continuing reality of democracy.

Beyond these requirements are still others—those of citizenship. Self-discipline of citizens with respect to government is too little stressed. For citizens, too, there must be systematic arrangements supporting character in their performance. Also, citizens need to defer more readily to the contributions of citizens differently equipped and situated. They need to strive more often and more consciously to relate their personal concerns to public concerns and to help perfect arrangements supporting these citizen responsibilities.

These ends may be advanced through changing popular and official expectations, through new political institutional arrangements, through new and improved administrative arrangements. At crucial moments and in crucial aspects they will be formulated and organically incorporated in government by enactments of law.

The whole process is a search for more satisfactory government. As a facet of this indicative of political health, it is worth noting that in the United States there is a recognized responsibility for leadership to strive to elevate in the government higher standards than exist generally in organized private society. This is particularly true with respect to the national government. We do all seem readier to suffer mediocrity gladly—or even to insist upon it—among our familiars than among those distant. But it would be reasonable to assume that this higher demand on the national government is associated with the fact that we see the mediocrity around us as the necessary condition of the rank and file, and exact proportionately more of each level of eminence, leadership, and responsibility.

Even so there are governmental loyalty problems, some of them recently emergent, some as old as our democracy, and some as old as philosophy. Of the older ones, our intellectual difficulty turns chiefly on an inclination to make an absolute out of the right of dissent. It is true that loyalty to democracy is a means for determining public values, that disagreement is implicit in democracy, and that disagreement over a long range of different possible opinions is not a test of loyalty. Yet the right of dissent has never covered treason or even some less extreme offenses. The right of free speech, similarly, has never licensed libel or slander, and even the right of franchise is ever subject to legal redefinition. Nor can it be believed that the theory of democracy is so absolute as to deprive future generations of it if only one generation votes so to do. Espousal of an absolute so confining of humanity approaches the absolute zero in absolutes.

LOOKING TOWARD THE FUTURE

Decision-making becomes more and more complicated as civilization advances. It is an art.

Even in science, decision-making is an art, not a science. The choice of a field of inquiry and of ways to pursue it can be well made only as a result of nonscientific learning. In social administration the factors involved in choices veer toward the innumerable and the unidentifiable. Knowledge of these factors can very nearly never be complete, and in any case, knowledge is not at all the same thing as wisdom. Nor is your wisdom or my wisdom equal to social wisdom. In public matters much of the determining stuff of judgment must derive from society itself if we mean what we say when we talk about democracy.

Society can be led, taught, and persuaded, of course. A great deal depends upon leadership. But leadership can exercise discretion on behalf of a people only when it draws a large part of its wisdom from the society, when it is ever and acutely sensitive to the society, and when the society can hold the leadership accountable.

I see public administration professionally and, especially, academically as distinguished by concern with the generality of the conduct of the public business in pursuit of the public interest. If it is to be distinguished it must be profoundly related to the whole content of political and social theory; its practitioners must have not knowledge alone, but the understanding that is wisdom—eminently human, thoroughly earthly, and at the same time highly aspiring.

Believing thus in the importance of public administration, I believe it not only a worthy candidate for university attention, but a candidate we are obliged to admit. This belief is based on the expectation that professional training in public administration will not be concerned with the production of gadgeteers and procedure-hounds, but with administrative statesmen.

Education for the public services must be related to a philosophy about the public service. I would assert that the first essential to superior public performance is an understanding of one's society and its people, and the second is an understanding of politics and government, and the third an understanding of the conduct of affairs in organized institutions. Particular techniques can have their place in a university program if it is a subordinate place in which techniques are related to purposes and philosophy.

Some of these needs might well be restated. There is need in the government and on the campus for a special orientation of all the social sciences toward each other, toward citizenship, and toward public service broadly viewed. There is need for a special orientation of all university training—the natural sciences, law, medicine, engineering, business administration, fine arts, architecture, education—toward the cooperative business of living and working together. There is need for both more general and more intensive study and understanding of organizational service and the psychological and structural relationships between individuals and their organized undertakings. There is need for special orientation toward world collaboration, world functioning. There is need for new understanding, by experts and administrators, of the ways in which expert knowledge can be used to make for better administration.

Efficiency specialists have an important place in government, but no efficiency engineer will ever solve the principal problems of government. Other specialists can make important contributions to the general improvement of government, but those specialists will be social scientists and administrators rather than efficiency engineers.

In the United States we still deal too exclusively with budgeting, personnel administration in limited terms, purchasing, accounting, and the like. We still relate these things inadequately to larger concerns. And we still deal too little with the conduct of the programs which are the essential activities of government. Those other subjects and functions are incidental to program. We deal much too little with the sociological aspects of public administration. We need more sociology in our public administration programs as government moves steadily to more varied welfare concerns. We do not need sociology as much, I think, as sociology and economics need to relate themselves to politics and to administration. We do need, however, more social science content in our programs. And we need to develop better teaching materials dealing with government more realistically.

As in learning so in life: self-sufficiency passes into limbo, and our most compelling necessity is to develop social wisdom proportional to our knowledge; it is to learn all we can about how we may live and work together with an increasing kind of fullness, considerately, effectively, and progressively in keeping with the vast potential of humanity.

The Writings of Paul H. Appleby

A Classified List

BOOKS

Big Democracy. New York: Alfred A. Knopf, 1945. 197 pp.
Policy and Administration. University, Alabama: University of Alabama Press, 1949. 173 pp.
Morality and Administration in Democratic Government. Baton Rouge: Louisiana State University Press, 1952. 261 pp.
Public Administration for a Welfare State. New Delhi: Asia Publishing House, 1961. 105 pp.
Citizens as Sovereigns. Syracuse: Syracuse University Press, 1962. 200 pp.

MONOGRAPHS

Public Administration in India—Report of a Survey. New Delhi: Government of India, Cabinet Secretariat, 1953. 66 pp.
Re-examination of India's Administrative System. New Delhi: Government of India, Cabinet Secretariat, 1956. 59 pp.

ARTICLES

"Organization for Overhead Management, correspondence with Arnold Brecht," *Public Administrative Review*, 2:1 (Winter 1942), pp. 61-66.
"Wartime Relations with Britain," *America's Economic Policy*. London: Hutchinson & Co., 1942.
"Administration in Big Business," *Public Administration Review*, 5:3 (Summer 1945), pp. 252-57.
"Organizing Around the Head of a Large Federal Department," *Public Administration Review*, 6:3 (Summer 1946), pp. 205-12.
"Civilian Control of a Department of National Defense," Walgreen Lecture, University of Chicago (October 24, 1946).
"Bridges For a World Agricultural Community," *Approaches to Group Understanding*. New York & London: Harper & Bros., 1947, pp. 90-99.
"Harold D. Smith—Public Administrator," *Public Administration Review*, 7:2 (Spring 1947), pp. 77-81.
"Toward Better Public Administration," *Public Administration Review*, 7:2 (Spring 1947), pp. 93-99.
"The Influence of the Political Order," *American Political Science Review*, 42:2 (April 1948), pp. 272-83.
"A Reappraisal of Federal Employment as a Career," *Public Administration Review*, 8:2 (Spring 1948), pp. 85-90.
"Who Governs America?" *Social Action*, 14:9 (November 15, 1948), pp. 1-8.

"An American View of the British Experience," *The Public Service and University Education.* Princeton: Princeton University Press, 1949, pp. 180-86.

"For Future Madisons," *Internationalism and Democracy.* Syracuse: Syracuse University Press, 1949.

Review of 6 books on the Administration of Natural Resources, *American Political Science Review,* 43:2 (April 1949), pp. 378-81.

"The Significance of the Hoover Commission Report," *Yale Review,* 39:1 (September 1949), pp. 1-22.

"Political Science, The Next Twenty-Five Years," *American Political Science Review,* 44:4 (December 1950), pp. 904-32.

"Good Administration?" *Public Administration Review,* 11:2 (Spring 1951), p. 102.

"Roosevelt's Third-Term Decision," *American Political Science Review,* 46:3 (September 1952), pp. 754-65.

"Managing Complexity," *The University of Chicago Round Table,* Vol. 796 (July 12, 1953), pp. 11-16.

"The Fragmentation of the BAE," *Journal of Farm Economics,* 36:1 (February 1954), pp. 8-12.

"Bureaucracy and The Future," *The Annals of the American Academy of Political and Social Science,* Vol. 292 (March 1954), pp. 136-51.

"Comparative Public Administration," *Indian Journal of Public Administration,* 1:1 (January-March 1955), pp. 3-7.

"Thinking Big," *Indian Journal of Public Administration,* 1:1 (January-March 1955), pp. 59-60.

"Concerning Ministers," *Indian Journal of Public Administration,* 1:2 (April-June 1955), pp. 89-91.

"History and Precedent vs. Reform," *Indian Journal of Public Administration,* 1:4 (October-December 1955), pp. 303-09.

"Meeting Future Personnel Needs," *Indian Journal of Public Administration,* 2:1 (January-March 1956), pp. 7-11.

"Morale at Subordinate Levels," *Indian Journal of Public Administration,* 3:2 (April-June 1957), pp. 97-98.

"The Role of the Budget Division," *Public Administration Review,* 17:3 (Summer 1957), pp. 156-58.

"Some Thoughts on Decentralized Democracy," *Indian Journal of Public Administration,* 7:4 (October-December 1962), pp. 443-55.

"Making Sense Out of Things in General," *Public Administration Review,* 22:4 (December 1962), pp. 175-82.

Index

Adams, Henry: and "workable systems," 179, 181, 182, 184
Adler, Mortimer: 312
Administrative culture: 39ff., 205–26; early efforts in China, Korea, Southeast Asia, 249
Administrative Management, President's Committee on: 8
Advisory Commission on Intergovernmental Relations: 155ff.
Aerospace Corp.: 64
Africa: effects of colonization, 267
Agency for International Development: 130, 139; advances, 271; reorganization, 269
Agriculture Department: 178, 179; Forest Service, 174; largest research organization, 24; position during Depression, 175; Soil Conservation Service, 176
Alabama, University of: 169
Alliance for Progress: 275
Allport, Floyd: 20; *Theories of Perception and the Concept of Structure*, 20
American Society for Public Administration: Comparative Administration Group (CAG) described, 231; discussed, 231–44 *passim*
American Statistical Association: as adviser, 200
Appleby, Paul H.: career, 2–4, 7, 169, 171, 173ff., 232, 249, 264, 278, 279; interests, 60, 246, 306; personal, 4, 6, 7, 102, 151, 280, 298; philosophy, 5, 10, 14, 17–37, 39, 56, 58, 63, 76–78, 87, 97, 102, 132, 141, 151, 152, 169, 170, 171, 172, 180, 185, 229, 242, 248, 276, 278, 283ff., 307ff., 329, 333–47
Arendt, Hannah: 293
Ashby, Eric, Sir: 59, 60; *Technology and the Academics*, 59
Asia: preparation for development, 266
Atomic Energy Commission: 64, 65
Attorney General (U.S.): 196
Automation: 136

Barnard, Chester I.: 20, 24, 25, 73, 109, 312; "Mind in Everyday Affairs," 25
Bell, David: 186
Bell Telephone Co.: as sample of organizational structure, 22
Ben-Gurion, David: 106
Bentley, Arthur F.: 311, 312
Berle, Adolf: 68, 71, 79
Big Democracy: 7, 87, 177, 180, 309
Boulding, Kenneth E.: 70
Brown, David S.: 200
Brownlow Committee: 129
Bryson, Lyman: 185
Budget Bureau: 2, 34–36, 94, 109, 155, 188, 190; Historical Reports on War Administration, 249
Bundy, McGeorge: 190, 192
Bureaucracy: changing character of, 221; defined, 205; distrust of, 213; fragmentation of, 208; individual in, 224ff.; secrecy in, 222ff.

California: 158
California, University of (Berkeley): Institute of Governmental Studies, 131
Canada: 29
Carnegie Foundation: 233
Census Bureau: 188, 200
Childs, Richard S.: 278
China. *See* Administrative culture
Churchill, Winston, Sir: 295
Citizens as Sovereigns: 8, 306
Civilization: dependent on government, 17
Civil rights: 162
Civil War: 31, 179
Cleveland, Harlan: 21, 45
Collingwood, R. G.: 296
Columbia University: 169
Commerce Department: 189
Commons, John R.: 182, 183
Communication: agency, 113, 122; formal and informal, 33, 114
Compton, Arthur: on science, 300

351